CLASSIC JAZZ

CLASSIC JAZZ

A Personal View of the Music and the Musicians

FLOYD LEVIN

Foreword by
BENNY CARTER

UNIVERSITY OF CALIFORNIA PRESS
Berkeley   Los Angeles   London

Title page illustration: The author and his wife,
Lucille—Emperor and Empress of the 1985 Jazz
Jubilee, Sacramento, California.

Unless otherwise credited, all illustrations are by the
author or are from his collection.

University of California Press
Berkeley and Los Angeles, California

University of California Press, Ltd.
London, England

© 2000 by the Regents of the University of California

Library of Congress Cataloging-in-Publication Data

Levin, Floyd.
    Classic jazz : a personal view of the music and
the musicians / Floyd Levin.
        p.   cm.
    Includes index.
    ISBN 0-520-21360-2 (cloth : alk. paper)
    1. Jazz—History and criticism.   2. Jazz musi-
cians—United States.   I. Title.
    ML3508.L48   2000
    781.65—dc21   00-022554

Manufactured in the United States of America

08   07   06   05   04   03   02   01   00
10 9 8 7 6 5 4 3 2 1

To Lucille, my loving wife and perceptive editor,
who shared these wonderful experiences with me.
Her sincere praises buoyed my efforts, and her
unerring criticisms deftly improved my narration.

CONTENTS

ILLUSTRATIONS

The music called jazz is blessed to have so many devoted friends and fans, none more faithful than Lucille and Floyd Levin. Throughout the years this dynamic duo, a familiar sight at musical events in Los Angeles and elsewhere, have always given their support and encouragement to the performers and promoters.

Somehow, during the years running his own business, Floyd found time to write articles about what he saw and heard. Since his retirement, he has devoted full time to his special interest and increased even further his activities on behalf of our music.

The result is this book, a varied compilation of Floyd's articles over the last forty years. They attest to his wide knowledge, devotion, and intuitive sensitivity to our art form. No one is better qualified to cover this vast material and long span of time. His musical interests are all-encompassing and eclectic, running from the earliest jazz to the present day.

Floyd and Lucille have intimately been involved with the music and the musicians covered in this volume. Their organizational achievements are also multiple. Elsewhere you will read about their work in the founding of jazz societies, the production of jazz events, and the creation of honors to musicians. I am personally indebted to Floyd for creating the Benny Carter Award, presented annually by the American Federation of Jazz Societies.

I first met Floyd and Lucille some fifty years ago and count them among my dearest friends. I am therefore extremely pleased that the

University of California Press is publishing Floyd's *Classic Jazz: A Personal View of the Music and the Musicians.*

This book will join the many other fine volumes covering the development and history of classic jazz and will help to illuminate our genuinely American art form.

Benny Carter
June 1998

For years, when asked, "When are you going to write a book?" my reply has always been, "Never!"

Aware that a book project would require months or perhaps years of preparation, I feared the task would disrupt my ongoing daily activities. They include conducting jazz history interviews; writing album notes; reviewing concerts, festivals, records, and books; corresponding with fans and musicians around the world; and conducting extensive research into the darkened recesses of jazz's origin.

Over the years, my hundreds of essays delineated a personal relationship with the most respected artists in jazz. Several of my articles were highly praised, but they all appeared in publications with limited distribution. I always felt that I would like to assemble a book based on that material if someone was willing to publish it. When approached by the University of California Press to do just that, I gladly accepted.

This volume is compiled from my observations of the music and the gifted musicians who created it during almost half a century of careful listening. It includes my first published piece—a sophomoric review of the great Kid Ory's Creole Jazz Band that was printed in London's *Melody Maker* on February 5, 1949. Ory was a tremendous influence on the course of jazz's development, and, as you will see, he also profoundly influenced my musical perceptions.

Initially, it must be established that this book is not an exercise in jazz history, nor does it follow a strict chronological flow. While segments of historical interest permeate these pages, they reflect the individual perspective of a jazz purist. The key concept here is *classic* jazz. That admittedly narrow perspective is defined below and clearly states the ground rules by which this compilation has been assembled:

> CLASSIC: Of the highest class or rank. Serving as a standard. Something regarded as nearly perfect. An enduring example or model.
> *New Webster's Dictionary of the English Language*

For years, the most obtuse jazz critics have delighted in branding the art form that matured during the first four decades of this century as arcane, archaic, crude, obsolete, and merely a foundation on which "modern" jazz has been constructed. We are subjected to a collage of misguided information patched with unrelated snippets. The image they project is not an accurate reflection of what I call jazz.

Several years ago, for an article called "Jazz Is a Four-Letter Word," my research revealed that few "experts" could agree on a suitable definition of that elusive noun-verb-adjective. Because the basic word means many things to many listeners, the term "classic jazz" will cover an array of related forms, including ragtime, blues, New Orleans, Chicago, Kansas City, Dixieland, traditional, swing, and mainstream.

Also, I have elected not to mention names of those who exercise virtuosity as an end rather than a means. Names appear only to extol jazz heroes whose contributions to the rich heritage of the genre have generated reverence in their listeners' hearts.

A curious literary trend attempts to promulgate the illogical theory that "latest" is synonymous with "best." It is true that all forms of art undergo change. Jazz, too, is an evolving form, and though gradual variations are inevitable, we should never completely forget the music's cornerstones. While technical ability is essential, the vital elements are a sustained beat, combined spontaneous improvisations, and freedom to use imagination, ingenuity, and taste.

True classicism, in every form of art, is always revered and never becomes obsolete. Unlike science, which constantly advances, art only ripens and matures. This principle comes into a sharper focus when we examine other forms of art. Giotto's fourteenth-century Florentine structures have no modern elevators or air conditioning, but can those enduring medieval spires ever be dwarfed by today's monolithic skyscrapers posing as architecture? Despite the development of power tools and laser beams, has sculpture progressed significantly since Michelangelo carved his marble Pietà five hundred years ago?

A treasured art form secures its future by honoring its past. Just as the works of Shakespeare, Dickens, and Steinbeck will always be studied, so will the inspirational music of Jelly Roll Morton, Louis Armstrong, and Duke Ellington remain as influential as Utrillo's paintings, Durer's engravings, or Bernini's fountains. Classic is the word for them all.

Shuffling through a cabinet stuffed with priceless old 78 rpm records can be a thrilling experience. A recent forage amid my treasures unleashed a nostalgic aural avalanche. It carried more than sixty years of musicians' personal statements that will continue to be enjoyed by endless generations—such timeless gems as:

Jelly Roll Morton's brilliant piano solos, "The Pearls" and "Kansas City Stomps" (Gennett, 1922).

"Dippermouth Blues," Joe Oliver's creation of the adored cornet chorus that has become legendary in the annals of classic jazz (Okeh, 1923).

That sparkler from Clarence Williams's Blue Five, "Cake Walking Babies," with youngsters Sidney Bechet and Louis Armstrong tilting until sparks leap from the turntable (Okeh, 1925).

Ellington's memorable "Black and Tan Fantasy"—probably jazz's first and most important tone poem (Brunswick, 1927).

Satchmo's "Potato Head Blues" (Okeh, 1927)—and his masterful "West End Blues" (Vocalion, 1928).

An inspired Jimmie Noone and Earl Hines treading new waters with "I Know That You Know" (Vocalion, 1928).

Almost any of the Art Tatum triumphs—especially "Tiger Rag" (Brunswick, 1932).

The sustaining artistic suavity of Benny Carter's "When Lights Are Low" (Brunswick, 1936).

Coleman Hawkins, like a musical Cezanne, leading us to the frontiers of modern jazz with "Body and Soul" (Bluebird, 1939).

"A Good Man Is Hard to Find," a true jazz epic by the Eddie Condon crowd covering four exciting twelve-inch sides—undoubtedly the best recorded jam session.

We should recall the advancing contributions of second-generation jazzmen such as Muggsy Spanier, Jack Teagarden, Frank Teschemacher, Wild Bill Davison, and Benny Goodman. Influenced by the seminal jazzmen of the '20s, they opened fresh vistas for classic jazz. So, too, did Bessie Smith, Billie Holiday, Mildred Bailey, and Ella Fitzgerald, who elevated the jazz vocal to loftier heights than could ever be attained by today's bevy of scatting shouters.

Equally significant are the third generation of artists propelled by Turk Murphy and Bob Scobey. They polished Lu Watters's San Francisco revival efforts into shining examples for younger musicians to follow. From that formidable mold sprang a fourth generation of jazzmen who, today, are rekindling the embers with their current contributions to the lineage of classic jazz.

Despite the years of denigration, the state of the art prospers from the worldwide proliferation spurred by the pioneer work of Chris Barber in England, Graeme Bell in Australia, Claude Luter and Maxim Saury in France, the Benko Dixieland Band in Hungary, and the Fenix Jazz Band in Argentina, to name but a few. Here in the United States, the music flourishes in all parts of the country thanks to the impetus generated by Gene Mayl's Dixieland Rhythm Kings, the Dukes of Dixieland, Doc Evans's Jazz Band, the Parke Frankenfield All-Stars, Vince Giordano's Nighthawks, the Night Blooming Jazzmen, the South Frisco Jazz Band, and many others.

Please do not think that the adherents of these theories would condemn us to an eternity of hearing "Swanee River" played in ragtime. On the contrary, our music is as viable today as "Dippermouth Blues" and the "Pearls" were more than half a century ago. Bob Wilber, Joe Newman, and Al Grey can be as emotionally moving with that wonderful sixteen-bar chorus of "Mood Indigo" as Barney Bigard, Cootie Williams, and Tricky Sam Nanton were back in 1930. The gusty bravado of Jelly Roll Morton's "Grandpa's Spells" retains its swinging effervescence when updated by Frankfurt's Barrelhouse Jazz Band. Kenny Davern, Ralph Sutton, and Tom Pletcher are as important to today's music as Jimmie Noone, James P. Johnson, and Bix Beiderbecke were six decades ago.

It is gratifying to note that scores of current players are successfully promulgating the sounds of classic jazz in clubs, concerts, festivals, and cruises. A strong light still shines from the music's golden era. That wondrous glow reflects a bright chapter in human achievement that forever altered the history of popular music.

While acknowledging the influence of older masters, today's classic jazzmen are approaching this rich body of music with one ear cocked to the past and the other absorbing gradual modifications designed to acquaint a sophisticated audience with its historical significance. During last year's New Orleans Jazzfest, the two rousing weekends attracted daily crowds exceeding ninety thousand. These patrons paid $16 each to jam the infield of the Fairgrounds, New Orleans' age-old race track. In 1996, the total attendance was 375,000! The figures are mind boggling. The talent budget exceeded a million dollars. Six hundred bands, comprising over seven thousand musicians, appeared on a dozen tented stages. There were scores of famed New Orleans stars on the program, including Pete Fountain, Al Hirt, Ellis Marsalis, Lillian Boutté, Jacques Gauthé, Banu Gibson, the Dukes of Dixieland, and Dr. Michael White. The recent Sacramento Jazz Jubilee featured more than one hundred bands and attracted a quarter of a million fans, a further indication that classic jazz is not obsolete. Scores of similar festivals and jazz parties are attracting large audiences in every part of the country.

I fully expect to be assailed by criticism from misguided fans who might dismiss me as a cantankerous curmudgeon and vehemently disagree with much of what I have to say. They will probably accuse me of living in the past. That might be true. I am happily reveling in the glory of an era that spawned a music that will never die. And there is absolutely nothing wrong with the articulation of the vocal coda, "Ohhhhhhhh Yeaaaaah!—or shouting, "Oh play that thing!" after the traditional "Dippermouth Blues" chorus.

I am not old-fashioned—I am very much a part of the stimulating '90s. However, I must admit that I still enjoy wearing my old trousers with pleats (but I have removed the belts from the backs of all my jackets!) Being fully aware of modern developments in sound reproduction, I have almost decided to abandon my cactus needles and replace my gramophone with a new hi-fi outfit that plays records at 33 ⅓ rpm!

The material that follows is a cross section of articles about classic jazz written over a period of fifty years—from my first published piece, to several that were recently inspired while doing this compilation. Some are exploratory, some are humorous, a few are somber. They are all about classic jazz!

I hope you find the reminiscences interesting and enlightening.

Floyd Levin
July 1998

ACKNOWLEDGMENTS

Thanks to Don Foster. Without his gentle guidance, my musical tastes would have stalled with the sounds from the swing era. Don opened broad vistas that exposed me to the works of Django Reinhardt, Jelly Roll Morton, Coleman Hawkins, and many of the artists mentioned in this book.

Thanks to Richard Roy Miller's generous transcribing expertise, my old manuscripts and faded clippings were transferred to computer disks, from which editing and updating could easily take place.

Thanks to Steven Isoardi, editor of *Central Avenue Sounds*. His encouragement and recommendations made this book possible.

I am frequently asked how I, the owner of a housewares business, began writing about jazz. I am neither a professional musician nor a full-time journalist and thus lack the training one might expect a jazz writer to possess. So how did I break into the field?

The answer begins with an exchange of correspondence between me and the late Sinclair Traill, a noted English jazz journalist who co-edited the regular "Collector's Corner" feature in the London publication *Melody Maker.* At Traill's request, I wrote my initial essay, a piece about Kid Ory's Creole Jazz Band. It appeared in the February 5, 1949, edition of *Melody Maker.* A few months later Traill established his own magazine, *Jazz Journal,* and asked me to submit a monthly column, which I called "The American Jazz Scene." My byline still appears in that fine magazine, currently in its fifty-third year of publication.

As my writing career began to take shape, I benefited from quite a bit of on-the-job training, taking every opportunity to hear jazz performances and educating myself about the music through conversations with the musicians. While listening and learning, I became increasingly aware that much of the information I was getting had significant historical value. Jazz had developed during the lifetimes of the musicians I was fortunate to know. Their tales of triumph and travail constituted fragments of an intricate puzzle; when properly assembled, they created a vivid depiction of jazz history—an important segment of America's cultural development. I felt a strong impulse to share this information and help illuminate an era previously cloaked in the darkness of neglect or indifference.

Before I realized it, I had become a jazz writer. Since this activity offered meager income potential, I kept my day job, running my business for profit and writing for passion. As I traveled around the country, selling aprons, oven mitts, and pot holders, I visited nightclubs and bars, soaking up as much jazz and conversation as I could get. These contacts with jazzmen in various cities added to my knowledge of the music; it also provided the grist from which I put together my monthly "American Jazz Scene" column and feature articles for various magazines. And it helped me build up a reservoir of potential guests for *Jazz on Parade,* the radio program I hosted for many years. *Jazz on Parade* did not reach a very large audience in those early days of FM radio, but it was the first American jazz program broadcast by the BBC in England. My old friend and mentor Sinclair Traill requested transcriptions of the show, and I put together special broadcasts that were aired throughout the United Kingdom.

My small factory office became a storage area for my voluminous jazz files. Each day my attention was divided between business affairs and literary efforts. When I retired from the housewares business several years ago, I had to confess that my resources for the golden years would have been more extensive had I devoted more time to my business and less to jazz journalism.

Yet I have gained immeasurably from the latter and have gleefully continued to pursue it. And without the frequent interruptions of a daily business routine, I can finally do it full-time. My material currently appears in several additional prominent periodicals in the United States, Canada, Europe, and the Far East. The same overfilled file cabinets that once resided at my business address now stand in my home office, and the typewriter table on which I have written hundreds of articles over the years is now occupied by a computer monitor and keyboard. The floor is usually cluttered with photos, clippings, and reference material.

Tread carefully, a jazz writer is at work.

How It Began

It began when I was eight years old; the memory is still very vivid. On a blustery winter afternoon in Chicago's Loop, I watched a man blow a trumpet in a Salvation Army band. The musicians and their small group of listeners were chilled by icy gusts wafting from Lake Michigan.

My mother tugged at my arm and insisted I follow her into the warmth of an adjacent store. I stood inside and looked through the frosty window, my gaze still fixed on the trumpet player. I fell in love with his beautiful shining horn and admired the gracefully twisted brass and those three valves tipped with glistening mother of pearl. My fervent wish was to learn how to play that lovely instrument.

Although my parents approved of my newfound interest in music, they thought that blowing a trumpet would cause my eyes to bulge. So on my next birthday, they surprised me with a xylophone—that's right, a xylophone. It included a series of free lessons. I hated that damned xylophone! My halfhearted attempt to play the thing became a source of family dissension. "Practice" became a dirty word. While friends were happily playing baseball outside, I spent the afternoons resentfully striking strips of wood with little mallets, trying to learn scales and hoping to draw a melodic sound from the wretched instrument.

After I completed the free lessons, the dreadful Deagen xylophone was relegated to the cellar. That was more than half a century ago, and except for a brief stint as a faltering snare drummer in UCLA's ROTC band I have been awaiting the Muse's visit ever since. Should that Greek goddess ever smile at me, I will embrace her, and perhaps this loathsome frustration will vanish.

Since hearing that Salvation Army band, I have watched hundreds of trumpet players and listened carefully to their records. I spent my high school years admiring Bix Beiderbecke's improvisational masterpiece "Singin' the Blues," Bunny Berigan's wonderful "I Can't Get Started," Sonny Dunham's timeless "Memories of You," and Ziggy Elman's unforgettable solo "And the Angels Sing." And then I heard the ultimate—Louis Armstrong's monumental "West End Blues." Had I received that trumpet at the age of eight, I, too, might be able to produce such beautiful sounds. Yes, I have lived with frustration.

That frustration has expanded far beyond the realm of the trumpet. I also covet an ability to blow a clarinet, strum a guitar, tootle a sax, slide a trombone, tickle the ivories, slap a string bass, or beat a drum. (In frequent fantasies, I play them all with grace and beauty.) Only alphorns, bagpipes, kazoos, and accordions have escaped that lust ... so far.

After hearing Red Norvo for the first time, I even came to recognize the xylophone's merit. But I still harbor a secret envy for anyone blowing a trumpet. It matters not whether it is in a symphony orchestra, a brass band, a klezmer band, a mariachi band, or a Dixieland band; the passion is the same.

If I could not play an instrument, at least I could appreciate fine music. By the age of fifteen I was spending quite a bit of time listening to orchestras on the radio and learning the names of their instrumental soloists. George Wettling was the drummer in Artie Shaw's fine band; Johnny Guarnieri played piano, and Billy Butterfield bolstered the brass section. Tommy Dorsey's orchestra included tenor saxophonist Bud Freeman, drummer Dave Tough, and the great trumpet star Bunny Berigan. Bob Crosby's band featured Ray Bauduc, Bob Haggart, Joe Sullivan, Irving Fazola, and several other fine artists. Benny Goodman's famous sidemen included Harry James, Manny Klein, Gene Krupa, and Jess Stacy.

Several orchestras showcased "bands within the band"—Bob Crosby's Bob Cats, Artie Shaw's Gramercy Five, Tommy Dorsey's Clambake Seven, Woody Herman's Woodchoppers, and Benny Goodman's Trio, Quartet, and Sextet. Al Jarvis played records by those bands on his daily program *Make-Believe Ballroom* on KMTR in Los Angeles, and his knowledgeable presentations planted the seeds from which my burgeoning jazz interest grew.

I didn't know it then, but at the time I was growing up, jazz was in the midst of a significant transition. Those swing bands I revered represented a new type of jazz—a milder, more commercial variety. It was the 1940s version of the music that is the subject of this book: classic jazz. Classic (or, as I often refer to it, "traditional") jazz is the authentic music that black musicians conceived in New Orleans, St. Louis, Chicago, and Harlem in the last quarter of the nineteenth century. It evolved out of the same folk traditions that produced gospel music, the delta blues, and other African American sounds. In the 1920s—also known as the Jazz Age—classic jazz broke out of its southern and urban enclaves and entered the broader culture, producing some of America's first pop music stars (including Fats Waller, Billie Holiday, Harry James, Frank Sinatra, and Louis Armstrong).

The Jazz Age ended abruptly in the early 1930s with the rise of swing music. Swing differed from classic jazz in some important respects. Among other things, it was played by big bands with twelve to eighteen musicians, whereas traditional jazz was played by small groups of four to eight musicians. The big bands relied heavily on written arrangements, offering far fewer opportunities for improvisation than the smaller traditional bands. Big-band music was enormously popular—so much so that it literally put traditional jazz out of business. Kid Ory, one of the most successful bandleaders of the 1910s and 1920s, found himself unable to land a paying gig and went into chicken farming. Mutt Carey, a trumpet legend of the Jazz Age, became a Pullman porter.

In 1939, the year I graduated from high school, *Jazzmen,* one of the first comprehensive books on jazz history, was published. It included the early writings of pioneer researchers Charles Edward Smith, Frederic Ramsey, Jr., and Bill Russell. I eagerly absorbed their stories about Bix Beiderbecke, the Austin High School Gang, and the seminal New Orleans musicians who made jazz into a national fad in the 1920s: Buddy Bolden, Freddie Keppard, King Oliver, and Jelly Roll Morton.

Jazzmen whetted my appetite for more knowledge about traditional jazz. I awaited each month's edition of *Down Beat, Billboard,* and *Metronome* magazines and discovered Sidney Bechet, Muggsy Spanier, Jack Teagarden, the Wolverines, and the New Orleans Rhythm Kings. As my awareness of the music's history increased and I delved further into its colorful past, my interest grew to passionate proportions. After reading everything I could find by jazz specialists John Steiner, Stanley Dance, Leonard Feather, Nat Hentoff, Art Hodes, Orrin Keepnews, Marshall Stearns, Dave Dexter, Bill Gottlieb, and John Lucas, I was hooked.

My interest expanded the day I acquired my first phonograph. It consisted of a small felt-lined electric turntable that, when wired to a radio's "hot" tube, played a 78 rpm record through the set's speaker. My friend Marvin Wagner offered me the treasure in exchange for daily transportation to and from UCLA. (Several years later, I discovered that the turntable belonged to Marvin's sister, who was irate when she learned about our transaction.) A neighborhood jukebox operator sold used records for ten cents. Although those were lean financial years, I purchased as many as I could afford. One side was usually badly worn. I began accumulating recordings I heard on Al Jarvis' program. Those treasures are still in my record cabinet.

Regard for the soloists sharpened as my record collection swelled. Eventually, I could identify a clarinetist as Shaw or Goodman, or Barney Bigard, Matty Matlock, or Irving Fazola. Like a distinctive human voice, a drum break by Zutty Singleton, Ray Bauduc, Cozy Cole, or Baby Dodds was immediately recognizable. From a sax section's ensemble sound, I could recognize the orchestras of Jimmy Lunceford, Count Basie, or Duke Ellington.

At about the time I became a devoted jazz fan, traditional jazz began to make a comeback. Lu Watters' Yerba Buena Jazz Band built a sizable following and made some successful recordings. Orson Welles lured Kid Ory out of retirement to appear on a national radio broadcast. Louis Armstrong returned to the small-group format with his All-Stars band. Southern California was a focal point of classic jazz's return to prominence. Many of the old-timers—including Kid Ory, Mutt Carey, Ed Garland, Dink Johnson, even Jelly Roll Morton himself—had moved out West during the 1920s and 1930s. In the 1940s, when traditional jazz found favor again, they began performing at California clubs and theaters.

It almost seems a fantasy, but during that period, scores of elite jazz performers, both swing and traditional, had resident engagements at Los Angeles venues. Red Nichols was featured at Mike Lyman's on Vine Street. Nappy Lamare played regularly at Sardi's on Hollywood Boulevard. Jimmie Noone was down the boulevard at the Streets of Paris, and Kid Ory played across the street at the Jade. Wingy Manone worked at the Waldorf Cellar on Main Street, and Jack Teagarden held forth at the Royal Room. Louis Armstrong appeared nightly at Billy Berg's, Ben Pollack was at the Beverly Cavern, Billie Holiday sang at Tiffany's, and Louis Prima owned his own club, the Jitterbug House, on Vine Street. Nat Cole attracted crowds to the 331 Club, and Albert Nicholas played at the Normandy.

I heard great musicians such as Lionel Hampton, Ben Pollack, Nellie Lutcher, Lorenzo Flennoy, Art Tatum, Marshal Royal, and Teddy Buckner. The famous big bands filled ballroom bandstands at the Palomar, Casino Gardens, Vogue, Plantation, Aragon, Trianon, Cotton Club, Pasadena Civic Auditorium, and Pan Pacific Auditorium.

I listened and I learned. I have been listening and learning ever since.

The Night I Saw a Moose Smile

It's been half a century since I first heard a live Dixieland band, but I recall every detail.

My wife, Lucille, and I had ventured into the Hangover, a small Hollywood bar on Vine Street near Sunset Boulevard. The Hangover's tiny bandstand was barely the size of an average dining room table. Crowded into that bantam space was a well-worn upright piano, a drum set, and Pete Daily's Chicagoans seated shoulder to shoulder—

playing the happiest music I had ever heard. Diminutive Pete Daily sat with his legs crossed and his elbows tucked to his sides as he blew a battered cornet patched together with tape and string. Skippy Anderson's slight frame was dwarfed by the open-front piano. His powerful rhythmic stride shook the brittle placard pinned on the instrument's scarred side; the sign proclaimed: "Keep Cool With Coolidge."

The handsome clarinetist, who wrote the band's arrangements, was Rosy McHargue. I remember the twinkle in his eyes as he executed Larry Shields' intricate clarinet frills on the Original Dixieland Jazz Band tunes he had transcribed for the Chicagoans. Trombonist Warren Smith, a veteran of the Bob Crosby Bob Cats, carefully aimed his slide to avoid hitting glasses on the nearby tables. Joe Rushton's huge bass saxophone, a physical problem on the skimpy bandstand, contributed greatly to the soaring effervescence of the music. Squeezed against the wall behind the horn players, drummer George Defebaugh maintained a steady two-beat cadence and added the anticipated cowbell tag that delighted the listeners.

That fine little band made a deep and lasting impact on me; I felt something happen that altered the course of my life. I will never forget seeing the happy faces, the smiling dancers whirling around the postage stamp–sized floor, and the dusty old stuffed moose head hanging above the Hangover bar. I think the moose was smiling, too!

The evening I have described took place in 1947. I didn't know it then, but traditional jazz was poised to leap back onto the music scene. In 1947 Louis Armstrong and His All-Stars were born. The following year Kid Ory and his Creole Jazz Band would play to a sold-out house at Carnegie Hall, and the inaugural Dixieland Jubilee would draw large crowds in Southern California. Daring independent labels such as Jump and Good Time Jazz were beginning to issue traditional jazz recordings—and finding more than enough customers to purchase them. Traditional jazz's "revival era" was underway—and I was there to enjoy it. I have never stopped doing so.

The passage of time has not dimmed the brilliance of that 1947 evening at the Hangover Club. Even today, fifty years later, a good jazz band playing a fine old Dixieland standard always reminds me of Pete Daily's wonderful little group, which forever influenced my perception of jazz. Like an old photograph, that band provides a vivid link with the past—with a room full of happy listeners; a dusty old moose head smiling from its mount; and a young man and his wife, hearing classic jazz for the very first time.

KID ORY AND
THE REVIVAL ERA

My first published article, which appeared in a 1949 issue of *Melody Maker*, featured the legendary trombonist Kid Ory. How fitting that I should begin with him; for in many ways the story of West Coast jazz originates with this outstanding musical craftsman, who played a key role in a pair of important eras in jazz history separated by two decades. Before World War I, Ory, a giant among New Orleans band-leaders, nurtured a generation of legendary musicians. Many of his sidemen were influential figures in their own right: Joe Oliver, Louis Armstrong, and Mutt Carey all got their start in his band, and greats such as Jelly Roll Morton, Ed Garland, and Johnny Dodds played with him at various times. Ory's trombone can be heard on some of the landmark recordings of the Jazz Age. After World War I he moved to Los Angeles, where he helped cultivate a thriving scene of avid jazz lovers and musicians.

My 1949 *Melody Maker* article appeared during the jazz revival period, in which Ory also played a decisive role. The traditional New Orleans sound had fallen out of fashion at the end of the 1920s, as audiences turned to big-band swing; by the mid-1940s traditional jazz was considered passé. Kid Ory played an important role in its revival. At that time, I wrote, "generations had grown up without hearing real jazz. ... musicians have yielded to more lucrative forms of popular music. Ory has the courage to hold to the traditional style. As a result, his Creole Jazz Band is now the only such group in existence."

Collectors' Corner

Edited by Max Jones and Sinclair Traill

FOR many months past there have been rumours that Kid Ory, the famous New Orleans trombonist, was leaving America for a visit to Europe, but to date nothing concrete has been fixed. That there have been efforts made in the past to get him and his band to this country we know to be true.

Not too many months past one of us tackled the MU on the possibility of their allowing Ory a permit. The idea was to feature the band with the film "New Orleans," but, although at one time things looked promising, negotiations fell through.

At the present time there is another plan to get the Kid Ory Band to Europe, and, with this in mind, we think the following piece from Floyd Levin, of Los Angeles, will be of interest to our readers. Floyd claims that Charles Delaunay is arranging for Ory concerts in France, Belgium, Switzerland and other countries. So you might hear Ory yet.

ORY'S CREOLE JAZZ BAND
By Floyd Levin

ONE night last year the Kid Ory Creole Jazz Band was playing a concert at the American Legion Hall in Pasadena. Having never seen a *real* New Orleans jazz band, it was with mixed feelings that my wife and I entered the hall.

As a record collector, I had gone through the various phases of "likes." I naturally began with swing music—Shaw, Goodman, Lunceford, etc.—and, as my tastes changed, my record collection grew (some 3,000 discs now grace my shelves). Gradually I advanced to small-band music—Condon, Hawkins, etc.

I finally reached the point where I found that unless the music had a definite New Orleans sound I could not enjoy it completely. Those Goodman discs, which had previously thrilled me, seemed to lack some indefinable quality. However, a Jelly Roll, an Oliver or a Hot Five disc could always interest me. It was then I realised that I had succumbed to the inevitable.

When I read about Ory's appearance I knew that I must see, in person, this man who had done so much to create New Orleans jazz. My wife Lucille (who had followed me through the various musical phases) had not yet "arrived" at my latest phase. She dutifully accompanied me to see the Ory band. Her pessimism was apparent.

We thought the concert was to begin at 8.30, so we arrived at 8.15. We then learned that the music was scheduled to begin at 9. We seated ourselves in the front row and awaited the arrival of the musicians. After a short wait, a small, stocky fellow came down the aisle. He carried two heavy cases which he piled on to the stage. He removed his coat and tossed his battered hat on the piano. His bald head shone as the footlights played upon him. This lone musician proceeded laboriously to unpack the first case.

I then realised he was the drummer and, consulting the programme notes, learned that he was Minor Hall. When I spoke to him during intermission he informed me that his friends call him "Ram." Ram Hall worked with pliers, wrenches and screwdrivers, and soon most of his equipment was set up. It was a very warm night, and, as Ram worked, the perspiration rolled off his smooth head. Several more fans had arrived, and Hall remarked:

"I wish I had taken up the fiddle. I have to put in a night's work before we play a note."

THE MUSICIANS

By this time another character had appeared on the stage—Ed Garland, the diminutive bass player. His instrument towered over his head—also bald. I found it difficult to understand how such a small man could play so large an instrument.

Three more musicians entered. Buster Wilson seated himself at the piano. After a few moments he began to finger the keys softly. The trumpet and clarinet soon made themselves heard.

At this point, an impressive-looking man appeared on the stage, preceded by a long cigar. He removed a guitar from its case and took his place next to Garland. This was Bud Scott, the great guitarist who had played with King Oliver, Jimmy Noone's Apex Club Orchestra, and Jelly Roll Morton's Red Hot Peppers.

Ram Hall had replaced his coat by the time Ory entered. The hall was now filled, and a tremendous ovation was extended to the slim, greying trombonist. They were ready to play. Bud Scott had thrust his cigar into a pocket; Joe Darensbourg held his clarinet poised before his lips; Andrew Blakeney nervously fingered the valves of his trumpet; Ram Hall, surrounded by his drums, grinned expansively; Kid Ory tapped the beat and they began. . . .

THE PROGRAMME

The first number was "At The Jazz Band Ball." The pulsating rhythm shook the room. I realised that Garland was creating the strongest beat I had ever heard from a bass. He seemed a combination of Pops Foster and Wellman Braud. Blakeney played the melodic lead with driving force. His full tone was strongly accentuated by Ory's magnificent glissandos. Darensbourg's low-register clarinet wove a beautiful pattern between the two brass instruments. The rhythm section was the strongest I have ever heard. This was the real jazz!

At the completion of the first number the room was filled with shouts of requests. After several moments the uproar subsided, and the band went into "Basin Street Blues." In this slower tempo I was even more impressed by the true New Orleans spirit that was evident. Joe's wonderful clarinet seemed inspired. He seemed to combine Dodds' fine tone with the vibrant feeling of the great Noone. Blakeney, swaying from side to side, was playing with his eyes closed.

When the number was completed the crowd again roared their approval—"South," "Eh La Bas," "Muskrat Ramble." Ory smilingly waited for silence. He then tapped out the rhythm and the band began "Eh La Bas." Much to the delight of the audience, Ory sang his original lyrics in Creole. He speaks and sings in a soft, warm voice. His vocal attempts are sharply contrasted by his full-tone, brazen horn work. He had the fans enthralled.

Thus for four hours I listened to this fine group of musicians. About half way through the concert I became aware that much of the shouting was coming from my previously reticent wife. She had completely succumbed to the charm of New Orleans jazz.

THE FUTURE

The Kid, at 59, is playing better than ever before. Despite his fame, Ory is a wonderful fellow. He is quiet, unassuming and a little shy. Above all, he loves to play. I know that I will always cherish the memories of seeing this great band in action. I sincerely believe that the Kid Ory Creole Jazz Band is the greatest New Orleans band of all time.

The American public has been subjected to poor commercial music for such a long time that generations have grown up without hearing real jazz. Most other "jazz" musicians have yielded to the more lucrative forms of popular music. Ory has had the courage to hold to the traditional style. As a result, this band is now the *only* such band in existence.

Shortly I plan to bring the band to Europe for a tour through the Continental countries. European audiences have never had the privilege of seeing a real New Orleans jazz band. I feel confident that they will extend acclaim far greater than any of these men have received in their native land. Ory is looking forward to meeting his European fans, and I am certain that they are equally anxious to see and hear this fine jazzman and his wonderful Creole Band.

Floyd Levin's first article, originally printed in Melody Maker, *February 5, 1949.*

It was my privilege to know Kid Ory and all the members of his band. They were not only great musicians but also great people. My recollections follow in this chapter.

Kid Ory

Edward "Kid" Ory was born on Christmas Day 1886 at Woodland Plantation, near La Place, Louisiana (about thirty miles from New Orleans). When he was eight years old he started his first band with a group of youngsters, all of them playing handmade string instruments. Within a few years Ory had surfaced in New Orleans, playing string bass and leading his own jazz band. By 1914 he had switched to trombone, and his Brown Skin Babies were the highest-rated band in the Crescent City. The Babies featured the legendary Joe Oliver on cornet; when Oliver left for Chicago, young Louis Armstrong took his place.

"We worked every night at Pete Lala's 25 Club in the 'district,'" Ory said as a guest on my radio program many years ago. "My band included Joe Oliver on cornet, Johnny Dodds, clarinet, Emile Bigard, violin, Lorenzo Staultz, guitar, Ed Garland, bass, and Henry Martin on drums. We played softly ... we didn't have to play loud to produce good ragtime music. It's the feeling that makes it swing. The bands would come to Lala's when they got off work. We'd have jam sessions that started at 4 A.M. and continued until dawn."

When crowds exceeded the capacity of Lala's cabaret on Iberville Street, Ory moved the band to Co-operator's Hall, where frequent police raids impeded attendance. He learned that Pete Lala, who had "connections," was resentful of the change and arranged the harassment that continued wherever Ory moved the operation. The trombonist decided to leave New Orleans.

Turning down an offer to join Oliver in Chicago, Ory moved to California in 1919 and established his Creole Jazz Band, the first resident New Orleans band on the West Coast. He sent for Mutt Carey and opened at the Cadillac Cafe on Central Avenue with clarinetist Wade Whaley, pianist Manuel Manetta, and drummer Alfred Williams—all from New Orleans. The Cadillac job lasted almost a year.

Ory left Los Angeles during the 1920s and headed back east, playing for some of his former sidemen. His trombone supplemented Louis Armstrong's Hot Five and Hot Seven in Chicago; he later worked with King Oliver's Dixie Syncopators, Jelly Roll Morton's Red Hot Peppers, and the New Orleans Wanderers (Armstrong's Hot Five with George Mitchell on trumpet instead of Louis). Important recordings by those leading groups vividly document Kid Ory's tremendous contribution to the Jazz Age. After several triumphant years with these great bands in Chicago and New York, Ory returned to Los Angeles in 1929 and resumed leadership of his Creole Jazz Band until 1933.

By then the swing craze had dampened the public's interest in small-band jazz, forcing Ory into semi-retirement. He set his instrument aside for ten years and raised chickens for a living. Then, in April 1943, Rudi Blesh and Bill Colburn staged a landmark New Orleans jazz concert at the Geary Theater in San Francisco. The event, featuring Bunk Johnson and a band Kid Ory assembled for the occasion, reputedly marked the first time New Orleans jazz was presented on a concert stage. These were the initial rumblings of the New Orleans jazz revival—and of Ory's return to the jazz scene.

A year later, Orson Welles decided to feature an authentic New Orleans jazz band on his popular CBS radio show *Mercury Theater.* He asked Marili Morden of the Jazz Man Record Shop to locate a band for a one-night appearance, and Morden called Ory, who assembled a cadre of old New Orleans colleagues. The lineup included Mutt Carey on trumpet, Buster Wilson on piano, Bud Scott on guitar, Ed Garland on bass, Zutty Singleton on drums, and clarinetist Jimmie Noone, who had been working at a Hollywood club with a quartet.

The Mercury Theater All-Stars debuted on Welles' show on March 15, 1944, and were enthusiastically received by jazz fans throughout the country. Yielding to overwhelming audience response, the band appeared on the program each week for the next three months. The sixth program, on April 19, included Welles' touching eulogy for Jimmie Noone, who had died the previous evening. The band's soul-searching "Blues for Jimmie" touched the hearts of listeners throughout the country. Wade Whaley sadly replaced Noone that night. Barney Bigard, who earlier had encouraged Ory to resume his playing career, handled the clarinet for the balance of the programs.

After the Welles broadcasts, another radio series, sponsored by Standard Oil Company, brought the sounds of Ory's New Orleans jazz to a nationwide audience. The music was acknowledged by critics as "the highest point of intelligence that jazz has reached on radio."

Encouraged by the success of these programs, Marili Morden and her husband, Nesuhi Ertegun, launched the Crescent Record Company, issuing the first recordings by Kid Ory as a leader since his his-

Kid Ory's Creole Jazz Band, as it appeared on CBS Radio's Mercury Theater, hosted by Orson Welles, on March 15, 1944. From left, Ed Garland, Buster Wilson, Jimmie Noone, Mutt Carey, Zutty Singleton, Kid Ory, and Bud Scott. The woman at back left is Marili Ertegun, who helped arrange the appearance.

toric Sunshine/Nordskog releases twenty-three years earlier. During the initial Crescent date, the band recorded "Blues for Jimmie" in tribute to their recently departed friend. *Time* (February 3, 1945) said the Crescent recordings "are probably as close as anything ever put on wax to the spirit of old Storyville, New Orleans' gaudy bawdyhouse district." When the recordings were later reissued in LP format, Ertegun, in the album notes, referred to them as "among the most significant jazz records ever made."

Another Ory recording date, produced by Dr. William Exner (a dentist from Seattle, Washington), took place in February 1945 at C.P. McGregor Studios in Hollywood. For the first time, we heard the pure fidelity of the band on Exner's newly introduced vinyl surface. Collectors clamored for a copy of "Dippermouth Blues," highlighted by Papa Mutt's poignant solo. Sessions for Decca and Columbia followed, both held in Los Angeles. In each case, the sounds leaping from those grooves represented the pure essence of New Orleans jazz.

Ory's late-'40s work renewed interest in traditional jazz and attracted a growing number of musicians to the style. In Northern California, Lu Watters' Yerba Buena Jazz Band was emulating the dual cornet format of King Oliver's Creole Jazz Band. Independent records soon appeared by Graeme Bell's fine Australian jazz band, Claude Luter's orchestra in Paris, and Humphrey Lyttelton's English band. The jazz revival also developed in New York City, where Bunk Johnson built a following at Stuyvesant Casino and young Bob Wilber gained attention with a band of New Orleans veterans that included Sidney Bechet and Pops Foster. The big town was ready for the Ory men. Early in 1948, producer John Schenck invited Kid Ory to New York for a Carnegie Hall concert. The band had traveled very little, and this was its first opportunity to perform in the East. The concert was a triumph. The Ory band, at the crest of its popularity, continued leading the surging revival spirit that still prevails.

Kid Ory died in 1973, but his influence has endured. Trombonist Roger Jamieson, who featured Ory sidemen in his band for several years, still responds to the command in his mentor's song title, "Do What Ory Say!" In England, Geoff Cole, without copying, manages to capture effectively the true New Orleans spirit that propelled Kid Ory to his lofty position. A visit to the New Malden Jazz Club's Monday evening sessions at the Brewster Pub in Surrey will confirm Geoff's expertise. Another English trombonist, Mike Owen, now lives in New Orleans, where he sustains Ory's image and sound.

Kid Ory's Legendary 1921 Nordskog/Sunshine Recordings

On November 13, 1949, at the height of the New Orleans jazz revival, London's *Melody Maker* reviewed some old recordings that had just been reissued on a private collector's label. "The band generates fine swing," wrote the reviewer, Sinclair Traill. "These sides have lost little over the years and remain fine historic examples of genuine New Orleans Jazz."

The band with the "fine swing" was Kid Ory's Creole Jazz Band, and the recordings in question were the first ever made by a black New Orleans jazz band. They had originally appeared in 1921—before King Oliver's landmark Creole Jazz Band releases, before Jelly Roll Morton's famed piano solos, and several years prior to Louis Armstrong's Hot Five classics on Okeh. By 1949 the Ory records were long

The 1921 Kid Ory recordings bore the imprint of two competing record companies: Reb and Johnny Spikes' Sunshine label was pasted over the black and gold label of Nordskog Recording Company.

forgotten, and the circumstances surrounding their production and release were shrouded in mystery. Their age alone made these recordings historically significant; the story behind them only added to the drama.

The first unusual thing about the fabled Ory recordings is that they were made in Southern California, which in 1921 was a provincial outland separated by several thousand miles from the music centers of the country. Even more startling, these historic discs bore the insignias of two competing record companies: the black and orange Sunshine label, owned by the legendary Spikes brothers; and, hidden underneath, the black Nordskog label, imprinted in gold with the slogan, "Established in 1921—First on The Pacific Coast." Through conversations held over a period of forty years with the participants in that pivotal recording session, I have pieced together much of the puzzle. Yet so many details remain in dispute that the true genesis of these seminal jazz recordings may never be known for certain. Appropriately, much of what we do know came from an interview with Benjamin "Reb" Spikes, a principal protagonist in this drama, and from the personal files of Arne A. Nordskog, the founder of the recording firm that bore his name.

In 1951, *Jazz Journal* published an interview I conducted with Reb Spikes, who owned the Sunshine label with his brother, Johnny. The two had entered the music business during the 1910s in Muskogee, Oklahoma, where they operated an open-air playhouse, the Pastime

Theater, that featured traveling jazz bands and blues singers. In 1918 the brothers moved to Los Angeles, and the following year they opened the Spikes Brothers Music Store, which soon became the center of the city's black music scene. Eventually the brothers became involved in every facet of the entertainment business. Their Dreamland Cafe on Fourth Street was a mecca for local musicians. When the Spikes brothers opened their Watts Amusement Park in May 1921, they sent for Jelly Roll Morton, who became the musical director and star performer. Morton engaged Kid Ory, the thirty-one-year-old trombonist, to appear at the Wayside Cafe with his Creole Jazz Band. Already successful as retailers and club owners, the brothers decided to venture into record production. Reb Spikes told me in 1951:

> Back in those days, our store was the only place in Los Angeles where recordings by black artists could be purchased. As a result, we did a huge record business. The early blues recordings were quite risqué for that time. Wealthy Hollywood people would drive up in long limousines and send their chauffeurs in to ask for "dirty records." When the local distributor received a shipment of Mamie Smith or Ma Rainey records, we'd take the entire lot ... a few hours later, they'd all be gone. We were selling as many as a hundred copies a day of Alberta Hunter's Black Swan recording of "Someday Sweetheart," a song Johnny and I had recently written.
>
> We decided to make our own records to sell in the store. We asked Kid Ory, who was working with his band in Oakland at the Creole Cafe, to come back to Los Angeles to play on the recordings. We wanted him to accompany two local blues singers, Roberta Dudley and Ruth Lee, recording some of our tunes we had just published. Ory complained that his band would not be heard enough, so we suggested he do a few instrumentals, including "Society Blues," and his own tune, "Ory's Creole Trombone."

The sessions took place at the new Nordskog facility in Santa Monica, just a few blocks from the Pacific Ocean. The first recording studio on the West Coast, it was the brainchild of Arne Andrae Nordskog, a pioneer of Los Angeles' classical music scene. Nordskog, the son of Norwegian settlers, began as a singer in his native Iowa and joined the Seattle Grand Opera Company in 1914. Two years later he became the leading tenor with the Knickerbocker Light Opera Company in Los Angeles. In 1921, at the age of thirty-six, he became general manager of the recently opened Hollywood Bowl.

Nordskog launched his recording studio later that year. Initially, his goal was to preserve the sounds of the classical artists he introduced to Hollywood Bowl audiences. The earliest Nordskog releases featured tenor Charles Harrison, soprano Margaret Messer Norris, and pianist

Charles Wakefield Cadman. On one recording, Nordskog sang "Because." The first recordings by the famed black tenor Roland Hayes soon appeared on the label.

The studio used recording equipment designed and built by Nordskog's father-in-law, Frank Lockwood, who had no previous recording experience. He constructed large wooden horns that transmitted the sound to a vibrating needle. As Lockwood turned the mechanism by hand, the needle cut grooves into a thick rotating wax disk. The wax underwent two electroplating operations that produced the nickel stamper from which the records were pressed—also by hand. The stamping operation was launched shortly after the Kid Ory records were produced. Nordskog owned six hydraulic presses that could turn out a million records a year; no statistics exist to confirm the quantity actually pressed.

The sessions were scheduled for June 1921. "Nordskog had some recording equipment out in Santa Monica," Reb Spikes said in 1951, "and we arranged for him to cut the masters for us. Ory's band was assembled in a small room, and they played into conical shaped boxes. There was one for each horn; the piano, bass, and drums shared a box. Mutt Carey's cornet recorded the strongest—he was probably closest to the wooden horns."

Jelly Roll Morton's brother-in-law, Oliver "Dink" Johnson, played clarinet on the Nordskog session, using an instrument borrowed from the Spikes Brothers Music Store. "Wade Whaley was Ory's regular clarinetist," Johnson recalled in 1950. "He and Buddy Petit came to Los Angeles from New Orleans in 1911, and Whaley also stayed here. Something prevented him from making the recording in Santa Monica, so Ory asked him to substitute." One of the songs recorded that day by Roberta Dudley was Dink Johnson's "Krooked Blues," composed in collaboration with the Spikes Brothers, who published the tune. It was recorded the following year by King Oliver's Creole Jazz Band.

Bassist Ed "Montudie" Garland, for many years the sole survivor of the original Ory band, also played on the sessions. He came to California in 1921, touring with King Oliver; when Oliver left Los Angeles, Garland stayed to join Ory, resuming a relationship that had begun a decade earlier at Pete Lala's 25 Club in New Orleans. "They didn't know how to record the bass in those days," Garland later said of the 1921 sessions. "There wasn't room for me near one of those large recording horns. Ben Borders' drums were too loud, and you can't hear the bass."

Nordskog was the first record-pressing plant on the West Coast. Under
Nordskog's recording system, a vibrating needle cut grooves into a hand-
turned wax master disk.

Ory himself always seemed reluctant to reminisce about the famed recording sessions. He did once describe, with embarrassment, a prank played on him that day. "This was my first recording," he said, "and I didn't know what I was supposed to wear. Montudie Garland told me that tuxedos were in order, so I was the *only* one who showed up in a tux and a stiff shirt. We were all very nervous, I remember. No one seemed to notice the full dress."

Ory and his sidemen recorded at least seven songs on that historic day; the titles included "When You're Alone Blues," "Krooked Blues," "Ory's Creole Trombone," "Society Blues," "That Sweet Something Dear," "Maybe Some Day," and "Froggie Moore." The full lineup was: Kid Ory, trombone; Dink Johnson, clarinet; Mutt Carey, trumpet; Ed Garland, bass; Freddy Washington, piano; and Ben Borders, drums. There may have been additional recordings made, but some of the masters apparently were lost soon after the session. Reb Spikes explained:

> There were no processing or pressing plants on the coast at that time. We had the records made back east by the Standard Music Roll Company, which operated Arto Pressing Company in Orange, New Jersey. They went out of business the following year. We lost several masters going through the hot desert. The heat melted the wax and they had to be discarded. One of the masters that melted was "Froggie Moore," a tune by Jelly we were planning to publish. We almost lost "Ory's Creole Trombone." The wax did crack — you can hear the click on every pressing.

Ed Garland confirmed the loss of masters in the desert heat, including one for a blues he had written for the Ory band. The tune never appeared on a record; Garland was unable to recall the title.

After the surviving masters were delivered to Arto and pressed into wax, Spikes told me, more trouble arose:

> For some reason, Nordskog put his label on our records. He called Ory's Sunshine Orchestra "The Seven Pods of Pepper." He had no business doing this — they were our property. We contracted for five thousand pressings that should have had our Sunshine label. We had to paste our label over the Nordskog label. They had to be oversize to cover it and almost overlapped the last grooves.
>
> All of the records were sold in our store except a small amount we shipped to Chicago — we had placed an ad in a Chicago paper and received a few mail orders — but every copy passed over the counter of our shop. When the five thousand were gone, we did not order any more.

Most collectors who have found copies of those rare records are aware of the double labeling. The black and orange Sunshine label, emblazoned with a glowing sunset behind a California mission, has usually eroded over time, exposing portions of the black Nordskog logo beneath it. In many cases the entire Sunshine label has disappeared, and only the original Nordskog nameplate exists. These rarities are still eagerly sought by collectors. Their original retail price was seventy-five cents; mail-order auctions have attracted bids in excess of $500.

Eight years after my interview with "Reb" Spikes appeared in the December 1951 edition of *Jazz Journal,* London-based *Jazz Monthly* published a comprehensive article about Arne Nordskog in its May 1959 issue. The authors, John Bentley and Ralph W. Miller, presented a version of the Nordskog/Sunshine debacle entirely different from the one given by Reb Spikes. According to Bentley and Miller, both highly respected historians:

> The Spikes Brothers, who had a music store in the Negro district on Central Avenue in Los Angeles, arranged for Kid Ory's band to make the recordings at the Nordskog Laboratories in Santa Monica. They were released under the Nordskog label to merchants throughout the world, with the Spikes Brothers ordering a great number for sale in their own store, where they sold like hot cakes to the Negro trade.
>
> When Spikes failed to pay for the Nordskog records they had received, Nordskog filed suit in Superior Court in Los Angeles and obtained judgment, which was only paid in part.
>
> Kid Ory, also having a grievance, broke with the Spikes Brothers and obtained a quantity of the recordings and pasted his own label, "Sunshine Records," over the Nordskog label and called them "Kid Ory's Sunshine Orchestra."

The suggestion that Kid Ory pasted his "own" Sunshine label on the records seems implausible, since the Sunshine label bears the bold imprint: "MANUF. BY SPIKES BROTHERS PHONOGRAPH RECORD CO. INC. LOS ANGELES." The suggestion of a lawsuit also must be called into question, as city court files contain no record of a Nordskog suit or judgment.

While examining Arne Nordskog's voluminous files, I came across a personal memo to John Bentley dated November 22, 1958—about five months before the publication of the *Jazz Monthly* article. Apparently this memo served as Bentley and Miller's primary source; it narrated the events exactly as the authors did in their article.

Another memo in Nordskog's files confirmed Spikes' recollection that Arto Pressing Company pressed the records. The memo states:

"When Arto went into bankruptcy in 1923, it had in its possession eighty sets of Nordskog Records' masters, mothers, and stampers. A claim was filed in the sum of $20,000 for the loss of those sets." Apparently Arto's assets did not justify payment of the claim, so Nordskog received no compensation for the loss. And what a loss for jazz fans and historians! One can only speculate on the material those eighty masters contained. Did they include the original blues Ed Garland wrote for the session? Or the missing "Froggie Moore"?

Here is another tantalizing possibility: perhaps the lost recordings included masters from a rumored King Oliver–Jelly Roll Morton session. Morton had engaged the Oliver band to appear at the Spikes' Wayside Park Cafe in 1921, and when the pianist, Lil Hardin, had to return to Chicago, Morton filled in for her. In one of my conversations with Johnny Spikes, he spoke about a recording by Oliver's band, with Morton on piano, that might have been made in Santa Monica. I could never authenticate this information, but it is not far-fetched to speculate that, if the session did take place, the masters ended up in Arto's hands.

There is a further revelation in the 1958 Nordskog memo: Apparently Arto and Nordskog agreed in 1921 to exchange material for release on each other's labels. At the time Arto was issuing records by the blues singer Lucille Hagamin, and it soon launched the recording career of the Original Memphis Five (Phil Napoleon, Miff Mole, Jimmy Lytell, Frank Signorelli, and Jack Roth). The memo indicates that Arto also had many "trade secret" recordings by bands "consisting of first chair musicians in prominent New York orchestras under contract with Victor and other leading recording companies ... who made the records being released by Arto and Nordskog."

Arto had access to all of the West Coast material. Might the company have surreptitiously released some of the Ory material on its own label? Is it possible that Arto issued recordings from the rumored Morton-Oliver session, using pseudonyms to avoid payment to the participants? It appears unlikely that this occurred, since no such recordings have surfaced to date, but the possibility exists.

We do know that Nordskog included the Ory band's 1921 recordings in its November 1922 catalog. The sheet lists the Ruth Lee and Roberta Dudley titles as: "Vocal—Spikes Orchestra" (the actual Nordskog record labels merely state: "Orchestral Acc."). "Ory's Creole Trombone" and "Society Blues" are credited to the Seven Pods of Pepper Orchestra. The 1922 catalog also lists Eva Tanguay (the "I

Don't Care Girl"), Herb Wiedoeft's Famous Orchestra, the Hollywood Syncopators, the Big Bear Melody Boys, the Catalina Social Seven Orchestra, and Abe Lyman's Ambassador Orchestra. (Brian Rust's discography *Jazz Records 1887—1942*, contains no Lyman listings before 1923.) A search of the Nordskog files failed to reveal the personnel of these California groups.

The modest Nordskog catalog could not have consumed the pressing capacity of a million records per year, as the company's files boasted. Is it possible that Nordskog pressed and released some of the "trade secret" recordings from the Arto masters under a different label? There is some evidence to suggest as much. M. B. Armstrong Music Co. in Oklahoma City submitted a purchase order to Nordskog on October 31, 1922, for fifty copies of "Teddy Bear Blues"—which does not appear in the catalog.

After the appearance of my 1951 interview with Reb Spikes, I had an opportunity to speak with Robert Arne Nordskog, son of the pioneering record producer. Although he was a very young boy at the time of his father's brief foray into the recording industry, Robert Nordskog clearly remembered the period. He spoke glowingly of his father's varied career and many accomplishments and said that my *Jazz Journal* story about the Spikes brothers had left him very disturbed. He did not know about Reb Spikes' assertion that the Ory records should have been issued on the Sunshine label. Vehemently defending his father's integrity, Nordskog told me: "This could have occurred during the period when the Nordskog records were still being processed in the East. I know by 1922 my father had extended himself financially—probably from his heavy investment in the pressing equipment. He soon went into bankruptcy."

Robert Nordskog theorized that the New Jersey pressing plant was responsible for the mislabeling. They might have pressed the copies, he suggested, to sell as payment for a Nordskog debt. Since the Arto Pressing Company and Nordskog both ceased operations the following year, the full explanation might never be known.

For decades, the very obscure Nordskog and Sunshine records were almost forgotten. Eventually, collectors learned about those rare aural documents—the first recordings of black New Orleans jazz. They have long pondered the perplexing mystery of the dual labeling. The confusion was compounded in 1951 when Nordskog reissued the Kid Ory and Eva Tanguay records on a replica of the original label. Making matters even worse, Kid Ory reportedly sold an original Sunshine

The Nordskog Recording Company production facility in Santa Monica, California, where Kid Ory's Creole Jazz Band recorded seven sides in June 1921. The building is still standing.

record to Paradox Industries for $90. "Ory's Creole Trombone" and "Society Blues" soon appeared on the Paradox label, apparently dubbed from Ory's copy. About six years later, the same pairing was issued by Hip, a Hollywood label that appeared when 45 rpm records first came into popularity. This tangle of competing releases may forever obscure the thread of historical truth.

Thankfully, some concrete pieces of the past remain. The old Nordskog building, site of the historic tapings, still stands in its original location; the decorative urns have been removed from the parapets, but the structure is otherwise unchanged. It is presently occupied by a shoe repair shop and a veterinarian's clinic. Until recently the original Nordskog recording equipment, some old wax masters, metal discs, and many rare pressings were still in the possession of Robert Nordskog, who displayed them in a small private museum he maintained in one of his industrial buildings in a Los Angeles suburb. The attractive exhibit housed original Nordskog contracts, stock certificates, publicity photos, and much more. After Robert Nordskog's death in 1992, these items were placed in storage. When I advised the Smithsonian Institute in Washington, D.C., about these treasures, it eagerly accepted the material, which now occupies a prominent position in its archive.

Thanks to the foresight of the Spikes brothers, the technical prowess of Arne Nordskog, and the musicianship of Kid Ory's band (whose members are profiled in the following pages), the earliest sounds of pure New Orleans jazz have been preserved. This recording effort will always rank among the most memorable achievements in the history of classic jazz.

Papa Mutt Carey

During the thirty-six years he blew his horn, Mutt Carey always seemed to be overshadowed by more flamboyant colleagues who enjoyed wider acclaim. He was the last of the truly great original New Orleans trumpet players, a member of a select club that included Buddy Bolden, Freddie Keppard, Manuel Perez, Bunk Johnson, and Joe Oliver. Yet, except for a few brief articles written half a century ago, his rightful place in jazz history has been sadly neglected. This oversight is especially appalling in view of his many accomplishments.

Mutt was among the first musicians to introduce jazz to audiences in the North and on the West Coast. He participated in the first recordings and the first radio broadcasts of authentic black New Orleans jazz in the early 1920s. Three decades later, during the revival era, trumpet players throughout the world tried to emulate his elusive sound. Carey favored muted tones; he and Joe Oliver introduced what he called "freak" sounds. Those subtle shadings distinguished Mutt Carey's individual style, coloring his work in a soft glow of muted pastels. The heat was there, but it boiled gently beneath the surface. When he occasionally played without the mute, his open tones were strong and harmonically interesting.

In 1973—twenty-five years after his death—Carey's influence was still being felt. That year Marvin Hamlisch used a 1902 Scott Joplin rag called "The Entertainer" in the soundtrack for *The Sting*. Hamlisch based his arrangement for the piece on Mutt Carey's 1947 recording of "The Entertainer" for Century Records. When Hamlisch's soundtrack record was released by MCA, it achieved gold record status. In large part, then, the great popularity of ragtime music today is traceable to Mutt Carey's 1947 Century recordings.

Thomas Carey was born in Hahnville, Louisiana, in 1891. He was the youngest of seventeen children, many of whom were musicians. As a teenager in New Orleans, he listened to Buddy Bolden playing in a city park and admired the Olympia Orchestra, led by another young cornetist, Freddie Keppard. Encouraged by his brother Jack, young Thomas abandoned his ambition to become a fireman. He began playing the cornet in 1912 and was soon working in his brother's Crescent Band and in the venerable Imperial Orchestra, replacing Manuel Perez. Carey joined Kid Ory's band in 1914, beginning a lengthy association that continued until 1947.

Carey briefly left Ory's band in 1917 to tour with Billy Mack's vaudeville troupe, leading a four-piece ensemble that included Johnny Dodds on clarinet and pianist Steve Lewis. The tour ended in Chicago, where Carey replaced Joe Oliver at the Dreamland Ballroom. After that engagement he returned to New Orleans and rejoined Ory. Over the years, Carey also led his own dance orchestra and organized brass bands for parades. Ed Garland recalled: "He was a powerful hornman. I remember a big parade when Mutt was playing in the Tuxedo Brass Band. Joe Oliver and I were playing in the Onward Band, and we were ahead of the Tuxedos. Joe could hear that powerful Carey horn behind us, and he dropped out of the band, tossed his cornet in a trash can, walked into a pawn shop, and bought another horn! Joe improved a lot. He copied some of Mutt's tricks and became 'King' in New Orleans much later."

Kid Ory moved to Los Angeles and sent for Mutt to join him in the fall of 1919. Their first job was at the Cadillac Cafe on Central Avenue. Patrons, unaccustomed to hearing the pure New Orleans sounds, were astounded by the range, tonal clarity, and sheer swing of Mutt's playing. He soon became the most popular member of the band. Reb Spikes later told me: "Mutt, who was actually the leader of that band, called the tunes and set the tempos. When we hired them to play at our Wayside Park Cafe at Leek's Lake in Watts, we billed the band as Ory's Creole Orchestra—the tune 'Ory's Creole Trombone' was so popular that we used it as a drawing card. But Mutt led the band." Wayside Park's advertisements always included the phrase: "Till Mut [sic] plays 'Farewell.'"

In 1925, when Ory moved to Chicago (where he played on the landmark recordings by Louis Armstrong and his Hot Five and the King Oliver Dixie Syncopators), Carey took over the Creole Orchestra. He kept the band busy at parties, country clubs, taxi dance halls, and local clubs, including Frank Sebastian's Cotton Club in Culver City. L. Z. Cooper played piano, Minor Hall was the drummer, and Les Hite played reeds. Carey's big band, the Jeffersonians, worked regularly in Hollywood, providing atmospheric music on silent film sets. During the Depression years, when the music business dwindled, Carey worked as a railroad Pullman porter.

I accompanied Bill Russell, the prodigious historian of New Orleans jazz, when he came to Los Angeles to interview Carey just a few months before the trumpet player's death in 1948. Mutt had recently left the Kid Ory band after a relationship that lasted more than thirty years. During the interview, I sat with Russell and Carey on the sofa in his modest southwest Los Angeles home. Speaking softly, with a warm Southern drawl, he was enthusiastic about the success of his recent Century Records releases (including "The Entertainer"), the small role he played in the film *New Orleans,* and his new band. The group, Mutt Carey's New Orleans Stompers, was soon to appear at Don Foster's Jazz Band Ball series at Pasadena's American Legion Hall.

Discussing his work with Ory's band, he told Russell:

> We always played waltzes, rumbas, tangos, Ellington tunes, anything requested. We played a lot of popular songs, current hits—even hillbilly numbers. On most of our jazz dates, the producers just wanted the old Dixieland standards. Last year, we worked in San Francisco at the Green Room, in the basement of the old CIO Union building. The people who came there came to dance—and we played dance music, popular tunes of the day, like we used to play in New Orleans years ago. We mixed a few jazz standards into the program. We were a big hit.

For reasons he never explained, Mutt left the Ory band after the 1947 Green Room date. Recordings of the dates are available on *Kid Ory at the Green Room,* Vols. I and II (American Music, AMCD-42, 43).

On May 14, 1948, the New Orleans Stompers made a very successful debut. The band featured pianist Buster Wilson from Ory's Creole Jazz Band and Bill Perkins playing a twin-necked guitar. Mutt's beautiful tones filled the American Legion Hall. With his melodic, rhythmic punch and exhilarating swing, he swept the band along in his wake. The group was very well received. Unfortunately, this was the Stompers' only engagement. Though another booking and a recording session were scheduled in San Francisco, they never took place. Mutt, just fifty-seven years old, died suddenly on September 3, 1949.

Mutt Carey's New Orleans Stompers debuted at the Los Angeles American Legion Hall in May 1948. Carey stands second from right, flanked by trombonist Leon White, drummer Everett Walsh, guitarist Bill Perkins, pianist Buster Wilson, clarinetist Arcima Taylor, and an unidentified bassist. Photo by William Painter.

Sadly, death took him just as his career was hitting its stride. By 1951 the country's best-selling jazz records featured Papa Mutt in his prime, leading those brisk ensembles with the Kid Ory band. The May 1951 issue of *Record Changer* magazine listed the winners of its all-time all-star readers' poll. Kid Ory, logically, was rated number one in the trombone category. Two of Ory's sidemen, bassist Ed Garland and guitarist Bud Scott, came in second on their respective instruments. But in the trumpet division, Mutt Carey—probably the most influential New Orleans trumpet player at the time—came in twelfth!

Mutt, a very unassuming man, preferred to stay in the background, and as a result he received little individual acclaim. Except for those brief moments in a New York studio when he led his all-star band and his short reign just before his death at the helm of the New Orleans Stompers, he always remained a sideman. Fortunately, Carey's recordings preserve his trumpet in pristine lucidity. He played with extraordinary finesse—a sustained tone, a silent moment, or a counterphrase. Mutt never dominated, instead creating subtle gaps for the other horns to create smooth, improvised ensembles.

Papa Mutt Carey has never been fully appreciated. I hope that, as succeeding generations of fans become aware of his achievements, his talents will finally receive the full recognition they deserve. I enjoyed the hours I spent with the great New Orleans jazzman, and I will never forget him.

Buster Wilson

In mid-October 1949, I borrowed a Webcor tape recorder and spent a memorable afternoon at the Central Avenue apartment of Buster Wilson. Schooled at Jelly Roll Morton's elbow, the fine pianist compiled an impressive resume during the 1920s, playing with Mutt Carey, Lionel Hampton, Les Hite, and other jazz greats. During the revival era of the 1940s, he was an indispensable member of Kid Ory's rhythm section. Only one thing was missing from Wilson's long list of accomplishments—he had never recorded any piano solos.

I knew some people in the record business and thought I might be able to help Wilson land a recording contract. That autumn afternoon we taped several numbers to use as demos for my record-industry contacts. Buster was in good spirits and played very well. He was pleased with the sample recordings and looked forward to a formal record date that might soon occur.

It never came; Wilson unexpectedly died on October 23, 1949, no more than ten days after our taping session.

Few publications reported his death; today his name stirs only a modest response in most well-informed jazz circles. Except for some discographical references and scattered archival footnotes, there are few printed references to the musician who played such an active role in the jazz saga. Wilson, whose graceful, tapered fingers produced an especially relaxed keyboard style, deserves far more recognition.

I met Buster Wilson in the late 1940s, when he was playing with Kid Ory's Creole Jazz Band in Los Angeles. Though he was not from New Orleans, his thorough familiarity with the Crescent City idiom made him a perfect fit for the band. Lucille and I spent many wonderful evenings seated next to the piano at the old Beverly Cavern listening to Wilson's subtle touch while Andrew Blakeney, Joe Darensbourg,

*Buster Wilson played with Leon Herriford, Jimmie Noone,
Paul Howard, and Les Hite before joining Kid Ory's
Creole Jazz Band in 1945.*

and Kid Ory occupied the spotlight. The pianist delicately elaborated
on the resounding beat established by Bud Scott's guitar, Ed Garland's
string bass, and Minor Hall's drums. He played a minimum of notes
with no lavish display of technique, but his lilting stride propelled the
great little band, and his eyes twinkled as he smiled at the fans enjoying his music. His solos reflected a lifelong admiration of Jelly Roll
Morton. Few fans are aware that Wilson arranged many of Kid Ory's
popular numbers.

Buster Wilson was born in Atlanta, Georgia, on August 18, 1897;
his family moved to California when he was six. He began studying
music in grammar school with Bessie Burke, the first black teacher in
the Los Angeles public schools, and continued with several years of
classical training at the Wilkins Academy of Music. He first took an interest in jazz after hearing Freddie Keppard's Creole Orchestra, one of
the first New Orleans bands to play in Los Angeles. A few years later

he heard Jelly Roll Morton at the Spikes brothers' Wayside Park Cafe in Watts. Morton generously coached the young pianist. When King Oliver's Creole Jazz Band played Wayside Park in 1921, Oliver's pianist, Lil Hardin, had to return to Chicago. Jelly Roll Morton filled in for her, and he often turned the piano bench over to young Buster Wilson during the engagement.

He played with Dink Johnson's Five Hounds of Jazz at the Harmony Inn on Twelfth Street and with the Ebony Idols Orchestra at clubs and dance halls on Central Avenue. He also alternated at the posh Vernon Country Club with pianist Sonny Clay. In 1923 he began working at the 15th and Main Ballroom with the Sunnyland Jazz Orchestra, a cooperative group led by alto saxophonist Charlie Lawrence, one of the few jazz musicians born in Los Angeles. The band included Jesse Smith on tenor saxophone, Ashford Hardie on trombone, James Porter on trumpet, Howard Patrick on banjo, Clarence Williams on bass, and Ben Borders on drums. Wilson served as pianist, musical director, and spokesman for the group. Though the Sunnyland Jazz Orchestra was one of Los Angeles' premiere musical attractions in the mid-1920s, the historical record contains few references to the group. Apparently they never made any recordings.

During a conversation with Papa Mutt Carey many years ago, I learned that Buster Wilson played with Carey's Liberty Syncopators in 1927 at the Liberty Dance Hall, a taxi dance spot on East Third Street. By 1929 Buster was leading his own band, the Hot Six, at the Apex Night Club on Central Avenue. He soon joined Leon Herriford's orchestra, which featured Andrew Blakeney and young Lionel Hampton, at Frank Sebastian's Cotton Club in Culver City. During the 1930s he appeared with bands led by Jimmie Noone, Curtis Mosby, Paul Howard, and Les Hite.

In 1945 Buster began an extended engagement with Kid Ory's band at the Jade Palace on Hollywood Boulevard. He was very affable and responded warmly to his fans. Eventually he and I became close friends, often visiting between sets at the Beverly Cavern. Buster always enjoyed reminiscing about the 1920s, but his sights were still set on the future. It is a shame he died so suddenly, with so many performances—and, perhaps, recording sessions—still left to play.

The little demo tape we made just before his death failed to generate the response I had hoped it would. Though some A&R men agreed that the music was quite good, they all felt that it was not commercial enough to sell. The tapes gathered dust for more than forty years, but the public finally did get the chance to hear those Buster Wilson piano solos. Thanks to the tenacious research and dedication of producer Barry Martyn, the music on my brittle old tape recording from October 1949 was released, along with some other fine examples of Buster's work, on an American Music compact disc titled *Buster Wilson 1947–49* (AMCD-89). Released in 1996, the CD is the fulfillment of Buster's ardent wish and a living testament to the artistry of this fine musician.

Andrew Blakeney

Praise him with the sound of the trumpet.
                              150th Psalm, Verse 3

It would be impossible *not* to praise the sound of Andrew Blakeney's trumpet. He was a true gentleman of jazz.

I have a clear image of him crowded against the corner of the old Beverly Cavern in Los Angeles. He always rocked gently as he played, his battered mute on the floor beside him. I often spoke to Andy about the deplorable condition of that old aluminum cup mute. Dented and bent, it bore the scars of many long years of service; the cork collar had hardened, and the metal plunger disappeared long before. But Blakeney wouldn't hear of giving it up. "This is my good luck mute," he'd say. "It was given to me years ago by Louis Armstrong."

I would counter that a musician of his stature should not use such a disreputable item and offered to buy him a new one in exchange for the time-worn mute. He respectfully declined my offer but promised to make me a gift of the old warhorse if he ever replaced it—or if he died.

Blakeney was born in Quitman, Mississippi, on June 10, 1898; his grandparents were former slaves. When he was eighteen years old, he moved to Chicago and eventually became an important member of the city's flourishing jazz scene. Remembering those early years, Blakeney told me: "During the days I worked in a meat packing plant, and I studied music at night. My teacher was Erskine Tate's grandfather, William Jackson, a classical musician. Several of us youngsters formed a little band. George Orendorf and Shirley Clay were in that group. Later George came to Los Angeles and played with Paul Howard's Quality Serenaders and the Les Hite band. Shirley became the lead trumpet player in Claude Hopkins' orchestra. Lionel Hampton was playing with us when he was only fifteen years old."

Blakeney got his first big opportunity in the mid-'20s, when Joe Oliver hired him to play at the new Plantation Club in Chicago, replacing Tommy Ladnier. "Oliver had a wonderful rhythm section," Blakeney recalled. "Paul Barbarin sat up there with the biggest set of drums I had ever seen. Bert Cobb was on tuba, Bud Scott played guitar and banjo, and Barney Bigard played clarinet and tenor sax. When I moved to Los Angeles later, I played with Bud in Leon Herriford's orchestra at the Lincoln Theater on Central Avenue—that was in the '30s."

After his stint with Oliver, Blakeney landed various jobs in Chicago, playing with Jimmy Archey, Snag Jones, and Charles Cook. In 1926 he accepted an offer to move to Los Angeles. One of his first jobs there was with Les Hite and Lionel Hampton in a small band led by violinist Johnny Mitchell. "Hampton was just coming into his own," Blakeney said. "Lionel played with us until he joined Paul Howard's Quality Serenaders. I think we worked in a Mexican taxi dance hall. I also played with Tin Can Henry's band at Frank Sebastian's Little Club. We did several jobs in the old silent pictures. I guess it was around 1934, Leon Herriford hired me to play at the Cotton Club. Lionel Hampton and Paul Howard were also in that orchestra. That's when I met Buster Wilson, who later played piano with us in Ory's band."

Except a few years before and during World War II, when he led his Brown Cats of Rhythm in Honolulu, Blakeney made his home in Southern California. After the war he joined Horace Henderson's big band in Los Angeles, playing in the trumpet section with Jake Porter and George Orendorf. When Papa Mutt Carey left Kid Ory's band, Blakeney was selected to take his place.

I first saw Blakeney in 1949, playing with Kid Ory's Creole Jazz Band. In my first published article in *Melody Maker*, I wrote:

> He played the melodic lead with a driving force. His full tone was strongly accentuated by Ory's magnificent glissandos. ... swaying from side to side, soulfully playing with his eyes closed, Andy seemed oblivious of the audience. His powerful playing keeps the band rocking.
>
> Fame has somehow escaped Andrew Blakeney. After hearing him perform, it is difficult to think of any musician—past or present—who can equal Blakeney's efforts on the lead horn. I predict that, in time, his name will occupy a revered position in the minds of traditional jazz lovers.

Unfortunately, my prophecy has not yet come true. Blakeney's accomplishments remain underappreciated, despite a long career that saw him playing well into his eighties. During the latter part of his ca-reer, when he traveled extensively with Barry Martyn's Legends of Jazz, fans in many parts of the world became aware of his talent. After a performance in London in 1975, critic Eric Townley reported: "The trumpet playing of Andrew Blakeney at 77 was most astonishing. Pos-sessing lip and lungs that might be envied by someone half his age, he played excellent trumpet with power, precision, beautiful time, and perfect technique."

Early in 1984, Blakeney called and said, "Floyd, I have decided to put up my horn. I am not able to play as well as I could, and I do not want to perform unless I can give my best. I am through playing." My protestations were shunted aside. I was unable to convince him that his fans would appreciate the opportunity to continue hearing him—and they would probably not notice any slight reduction of his powers.

For a year, Blakeney's trumpet was silent. But in 1985, when I was honored as Emperor at the Sacramento Dixieland Jubilee, I was sur-prised to see Andy in the opening parade playing with the Resurrection Marching Band, a group assembled by the Southern California Hot Jazz Society. The band marched past the reviewing stand as I was proudly accepting the regal scepter presented to me by the outgoing Emperor, Bob Crosby. As Andy strutted by, he winked at me. When I questioned him later about his surprise appearance, he said, "I just had to participate in that celebration. I wanted to be a part of this honor you have received."

On February 10, 1989, I conducted a lengthy interview with Blake-ney for Tulane University's Jazz Archive. The one hundred pages of transcribed text cover a broad range of jazz's history. The interview was published in England in *New Orleans Music* in the April and June 1990 issues.

Blakeney died on February 12, 1992, just a few months before his ninety-fourth birthday. After I delivered the eulogy at his funeral, Andy's wife, Ruth, remembered his promise to me: she gave me that battered old mute he had used so many years ago at the Beverly Cavern. I proudly display it in my home alongside many other jazz treasures.

Ram Hall

Over a period of nearly forty years, Minor "Ram" Hall provided the buoyant beat that propelled Kid Ory's Creole Jazz Band. His modest drum kit included only a minimum of accessories—a snare drum, tom-tom, bass drum, and cymbals—yet in his hands they produced a gentle pulse or a driving beat depending on the material involved. One of the last of the outstanding New Orleans jazzmen who migrated to Chicago in the early '20s, he continually demonstrated the correct way to play drums in a New Orleans jazz band. Never obtrusive, continually supplementing the arrangements, Ram always simmered beneath the surface. He created an irresistible momentum without intruding on the band's unified sound. When the Ory band was really swinging, it was the subtle drumming of Ram Hall that made it happen.

Hall was born in 1897 in Sellies, a small town near New Orleans. In 1916, after some brief drum lessons from his brother Alfred "Tubby" Hall, he got his first New Orleans job with Ory at Pete Lala's club in old Storyville. He replaced Henry Martin, who (he later told me) was his inspiration, the best rhythm drummer he ever heard. Recalling the Ory band, he told Orrin Keepnews in the January 1949 issue of *Record Changer* magazine: "That was one of the best bands in New Orleans. We played in parades and dances and advertised those dances using a wagon with a couple of horses, a couple of mules, and we drove around with Ory sitting in back playing on the tailgate."

I was able to learn more about Ram's background between sets at the Beverly Cavern in Los Angeles, where he liked to reminisce while puffing on his fat cigar:

> In about 1917 my brother got a job in Chicago playing with Sidney Bechet, and soon my family moved there. When the army took Tubby, I replaced him at the DeLuxe Cafe. That was where I met Ed Garland; he was playing bass. A young girl, Lil Hardin, was the pianist, and Lawrence Duhé played clarinet and led the band.
>
> Mutt Carey joined us briefly, but when he went back to New Orleans, Joe Oliver took over and renamed the group King Oliver's New Orleans Jazz Band. We traveled to California in 1921 to play at the Pergola Dancing Pavilion in San Francisco and at Leek's Lake in Los Angeles with Jelly Roll Morton. Ed Garland stayed there, but I returned to Chicago to join a band led by Jimmie Noone. Baby Dodds took my place in Oliver's band.

Hall left Noone's band when he received a call from Mutt Carey to work in a group he was forming in Los Angeles. For several years, Carey's Jeffersonians, with Hall and clarinetist Joe Darensbourg, worked in saloons, taxi dances, and night clubs, eventually landing a featured gig at Frank Sebastian's Cotton Club in Culver City.

Minor "Ram" Hall played drums for Kid Ory from 1916 until 1956. Photo by Don Johnson.

The first time I heard Ram Hall, he was playing in the Punch Bowl, a lunchtime gathering place for factory workers at Douglas Aircraft Company during World War II. He had recently been discharged from the army and was working in a production control booth at the Santa Monica plant. A few years later, I recognized him as Kid Ory's smiling drummer at the Jade Palace in Hollywood. He would remain with the Ory band for the rest of his career.

Very little has been written about Hall; his name occurs briefly in a few reference books, usually to mention his work with Ory. A dedicated baseball fan, he could quote the batting averages of almost every player in the National and American Leagues. Hall was also an accomplished Creole cook. Much to the annoyance of the Beverly Cavern's irascible Chinese chef, he often brought a pot of his specialty, red beans and rice with sausage, to serve the band between sets. From personal experience, I can confirm his culinary skills.

In 1956, Ram fell ill during a European tour with Ory. When his illness required hospitalization, he was admitted as a welfare case at the Sawtelle Veterans Hospital. Hall died of cancer in 1959. He was only sixty-two years old.

During his staid military funeral, I stood with a few of Ram's friends watching the somber army drill team discharge a loud rifle salute. Twenty-one salvos reverberated across the vast West Los Angeles cemetery. They seemed to echo the cadence of Ram Hall's expressive bass drum.

His pearlized snare drum, a pair of sticks, and a small brass cymbal are among the treasures that I will eventually donate to the New Orleans Jazz Museum. I will always remember Ram Hall—his bald pate, his sly grin, and his flirtatious behavior when a comely fan caught his eye. And he never missed a beat.

Dink Johnson

Dink Johnson, one of the first New Orleans musicians to migrate to California, played drums with Freddie Keppard in the celebrated Original Creole Orchestra. Born on October 18, 1892, Dink had appeared as a drummer and occasional pianist in the sporting houses in his native Biloxi, Mississippi, before leaving for Las Vegas in 1913. His older brother, string bassist Bill Johnson, had been playing in the Los Angeles area since about 1908. Guitarist Norwood Williams and violinist Jimmy Palao arrived shortly after Dink; cornetist Freddie Keppard, ace reed player George Baquet, and trombonist Eddie Vincent soon followed. In 1914 they organized the Original Creole Orchestra, or Creole Band, as they often were called. Together they toured the vaudeville circuit, introducing New Orleans music to the rest of the country long before the Original Dixieland Jazz Band moved north.

Although he played drums with Keppard and Jelly Roll Morton (Dink's brother-in-law) in Los Angeles, Johnson also built a reputation as a barrelhouse piano player. Much of this reputation was based on several exuberant recordings he made in 1945 for Bill Russell's American Music label.

During the summer of 1950 I learned that Johnson was living quietly in Santa Barbara, California. My wife, Lucille, and I traveled up the coast from Los Angeles one Sunday afternoon to see if we could find him. We located his address in the telephone directory. The small house was easy to find, but no response came when I knocked on the door. A neighbor watering his lawn next door volunteered that Dink spent his afternoons in the back room of a nearby barber shop. We found him there chatting with the barber. When he learned that we had driven from Los Angeles to hear him play, he said, "My piano needs repair, but I would be happy to play for you at a bar around the corner. They have a good piano." We promptly accepted the offer. As we left the shop, he casually told the barber, "The great Dink Johnson has out-of-town visitors who are anxious to hear me play." The barber did not seem impressed.

Johnson made the same boastful announcement to the bartender and a few patrons at the tavern. After pausing at the bar to ask for a few beers (and graciously allowing me to pay for them), Dink led us into a dimly lit back room. With a pretentious flourish, he tossed back the tablecloth that covered the piano keyboard. He sat down, confidently tested the keys with a few lavish runs, turned to us, and asked, "What would you good people like to hear?" My immediate reply was: "The Pearls." He responded by playing "Kansas City Stomps." After romping zestfully through Jelly Roll Morton's composition, he concluded with the phrase: "Mr. Johnson is signing off."

His questioning glance indicated that another request was in order, so Lucille asked for "Maple Leaf Rag." Dink raised one eyebrow and launched into a most beautiful performance of "Grace and Beauty," displaying more that a little of both. Our pianist said he was thirsty again, so I replenished his supply of beer. We sat in the dingy back room enjoying this private concert for more than two hours. Every tune concluded with the "signing off" coda. Johnson continued to solicit requests—and continued to ignore them. We asked for "Fidgety Feet," "Indian Rag," "Sister Kate," and "Jelly Roll Blues"; he played "Cannon Ball Blues," "High Society," "Take Your Time," and "Melancholy." We didn't mind. Johnson performed each tune with lightly textured stride figures. The fifty-seven-year-old musician obviously had been practicing. His mind was alert and his fingers were agile. After the vocal coda on "Melancholy," Dink loosened the top button of his shirt and said, "A fella sure gets dry playing all this jazz!" I stepped into the adjacent bar and returned with two more beers.

Duly refreshed, Johnson announced, "Now I'm gonna play my cuttin' tune, 'The Pigeon Walk.'" Blazing through the flamboyant piece, he struck a strong chord that pleased him. He repeated it with a broad grin and remarked, "That's a chord I dug in Siberia—me and Joe Stalin were havin' a ball one night. ... Man, this is sure fine beer!"

Even with an audience of just two people, Johnson showed himself to be the consummate entertainer. Lucille and I couldn't have enjoyed ourselves more. As we left the tavern, I asked Dink if he would appear at a Southern California Hot Jazz Society session. He seemed delighted with the invitation and agreed to attend. We drove him back to his home, and he asked us to stay for dinner and try his famous red beans and rice. We declined but arranged a date for his forthcoming jazz club appearance.

About a month later, Dink came to Los Angeles as planned. We met him at the Greyhound station. Looking very dapper with a felt hat set at a jaunty angle, he very formally addressed me as "Mr. Levin." He entertained our club members in a small room at the Echo Park Recreation Center. After introducing him, I asked Dink to play "The Pigeon Walk," his "cuttin' tune." True to form, Dink nodded obligingly, then played "Stomp de Lowdown." Apparently this was his first public performance in several years, and he enjoyed the attention and the enthusiastic response to his happy-sounding jazz. Despite my admonitions, he continued to call me "Mr. Levin" throughout the evening.

After the very successful session, we went to the 400 Club, where Kid Ory's band was waiting. Dink sat in with them and played "Make Me a Pallet on the Floor." Those of us in attendance will never forget this dramatic reunion of three jazzmen who had played together in New Orleans' Storyville forty years earlier—Dink Johnson, Kid Ory, and Ed Garland. During the intermission, he and Garland remained on the stand playing duets for about half an hour—mostly blues.

Unfortunately, well-meaning fans plied Dink with too much bourbon, and the evening ended abruptly. I had intended to ask him a few questions about New Orleans jazz around the turn of the century, but he fell asleep in the back seat as we drove him to the bus station. His hat was slightly rumpled and pushed to the back of his head when I helped him onto the bus. Abandoning his "Mr. Levin" formality, he said "Goodbye, Daddy-o"—and kissed Lucille on the cheek!

That was the last time I saw Dink Johnson. When he died a few years later in Portland, Oregon, he was sixty-two years old.

Bud Scott

I had already become a very efficient guitarist. In fact,
I was known as the best, until I met Bud Scott, one of
the famous guitarists of this country. When I found out
that he was dividing with me my popularity, I decided
to quit playing guitar and try the piano.

Jelly Roll Morton, Library of Congress Interviews

I was fortunate to have known each member of Kid Ory's Creole Jazz
Band, but my relationship with guitarist Bud Scott was probably the
warmest—and, regretfully, the shortest. His death in 1949 occurred
less than a year after we met. He was only fifty-nine years old.

Bud's intimate musical associates were the famous names in classic
jazz, and he helped shape the course of the music during its formative
years. Despite his tremendous influence, his name seldom appeared in
print. But he had a richer musical background than most jazzmen. He
was respected and revered by his colleagues, and he played to perfection the role of the band's rhythm man.

Arthur "Bud" Scott, Jr., was born in New Orleans in 1890. His first
job, at the age of fourteen, was with John Robichaux, the most active
dance band leader in New Orleans history. "Robichaux was quite a
promoter," he recalled. "We were hired for picnics, lawn parties, house
parties, and dances. Later the band worked regularly at the Lyric Theater."

By 1911 Bud was playing guitar in Freddie Keppard's Olympia Orchestra. I was surprised when he told me he never played a banjo in
New Orleans. "Except for novelty effects, the guitar was always used,"
he said. "I did not own a banjo until I went north. The bands played in
larger rooms and the banjo could be heard better."

He left New Orleans in 1912, traveling with a large variety show. A
few months later, after the revue's New York booking, he remained in
the big city, where more opportunities for work and study existed. Bud
joined the Clef Club, a musical society for black artists such as Marion
Anderson, Roland Hayes, and Paul Robeson. When the 125-piece Clef
Club Orchestra, conducted by James Reese Europe, played the historic
"Concert of Negro Music" at Carnegie Hall on May 2, 1912, Bud
Scott was in the string section. He was twenty-two years old.

"That was the first time jazz was heard in that sedate hall—although we called it 'ragtime' then," he proudly said. "We received a

Kid Ory (center, on trombone), 1947, flanked by two stalwarts of his Creole Jazz Band: guitarist Bud Scott and trumpet player Mutt Carey.

standing ovation from the first racially mixed audience ever permitted in Carnegie Hall."

The successful concert altered established views about the ability of black musicians. Clef Club members found first-class employment, opening doors previously closed to black artists in New York City.

Bud often talked about seeing the Original Dixieland Jazz Band in New York at Reisenweber's Restaurant, an enormous cabaret complex on Columbus Circle. "There was music, dining and dancing on several floors," he recalled. "I remember seeing Jimmy Durante playing piano there with a small band, and Ben Selvin led a dance orchestra on one level. The Original Dixieland Jazz Band was in the largest room. They packed the place every night. I knew most of them as young white kids in New Orleans trying to copy our music."

Bud refuted ODJB's claim of having made the initial jazz recordings in 1917. He recalled playing on numerous Victor recordings with James Reese Europe's Society Orchestra in 1913. "It was about a year after the Carnegie Hall concert—with a much smaller band," he said. "I remember we did some ragtime numbers." I later found some of those old Victors in a Salvation Army Store and gave them to Bud, who said he had not heard them previously.

He continued working with Europe at a nightclub operated by the popular dance team of Vernon and Irene Castle. The distinguished clientele included the Astors and the Vanderbilts—"and one night the millionaire 'Diamond Jim' Brady came in and tried to tango with Irene Castle!" When Europe's Society Orchestra left in 1917 to accompany the Castles' first national tour, Bud remained in New York to study music theory with Walter Damrosch; he later graduated from the Peabody School of Music.

Bud moved to Chicago in 1923, replacing Bill Johnson in King Oliver's Creole Jazz Band. Shortly after his arrival he recorded "Dippermouth Blues" with Oliver, adding his memorable vocal break: "Oh! Play that thing!" He also recorded with Johnny Dodds, Jimmy Blythe, Erskine Tate, and Jelly Roll Morton's Red Hot Peppers.

"I was the first one to use a guitar in a modern dance orchestra, led by Dave Payton at Chicago's Cafe de Paris," Bud said. "The star of the show, Ethel Waters, wanted me to leave the band and become her accompanist. I declined because I had accepted a job with Jimmie Noone and Earl Hines at the Apex Club. While I worked at the Apex, I was doubling in the pit band at the Regal Theater—the music business in Chicago was very good during the '20s."

In 1929, Bud followed the ongoing migration of New Orleans musicians to California. "I joined Mutt Carey's band playing in clubs around Los Angeles," he told me during a radio broadcast interview. "From 1930 until 1944, I played every conceivable sort of date to make a living. I played solos, worked in vaudeville shows, film and radio studios, and the pit orchestra at the Lincoln Theater. I formed a trio and played in some of the best Hollywood spots including the Florentine Gardens."

When the New Orleans revival heated in the mid-'40s, Bud Scott and the Kid Ory band led the way. Except for Ory, he was the oldest in the group. He was also the most musically literate, with a very substantial background. Fans were not aware that Bud wrote the majority of the band's arrangements. Because of his exceptional ability, he earned the nickname "The Master."

As the rhythm guitarist and occasional vocalist, he was not as dominant a presence as the band's more exuberant performers. His rigorous beat, however, was testimony to his musical talent. Bud continued to confirm composer-critic Will Marion Cook's appraisal of him years before as "one of the greatest rhythm men of all times."

Bud had a severe stroke in September 1948, shortly after the death of his friend Mutt Carey, and was forced to return from San Francisco, where the Ory band was playing at the time. During his illness I visited him frequently and sat at the bedside in his modest southeast Los Angeles home. It seemed strange to see him without his ever-present cigar. Occasionally he would ask me to hand him his guitar—"my box," as he called it. Bud's wife, Alice, and I were the only audience for these private concerts. He always played "Sweet Lorraine," which he felt was "the best recording I ever made—with Jimmie Noone's Apex Club Orchestra in 1928." Another of Bud's bedside songs was "Beale Street Blues," a number he recorded with Jelly Roll Morton's Red Hot Peppers. Each time he played it, he said, "I guess this tune has been recorded a hundred times, but I still think Jelly's version was the best—and probably one of the first."

A group of Bud Scott's friends planned a benefit concert to help pay his medical expenses. I was in charge of inviting the participants. On January 23, 1949, the small Cricket Club on Washington Boulevard was crowded with fans and musicians honoring their esteemed friend. The program featured Pete Daily's Chicagoans, the Firehouse Five Plus Two, Ted Vesley's band, Albert Nicholas, Eddie Miller, Zutty Singleton, Errol Garner, Nappy Lamare, Nellie Lutcher, Danny Barker, Blue Lu Barker, and T-Bone Walker. Bebop king Dizzy Gillespie sat in with Vesley's Dixieland band and the Firehouse Five Plus Two. Benny Carter played solo piano. We charged $1.20 admission.

The highlight of the afternoon was a set by Kid Ory's Creole Jazz Band, with Ralph Peters taking over for the ailing Bud Scott. They concluded with "Blues for Jimmie," in honor of Jimmie Noone's widow in the audience. Alice Scott was presented with $400, the profits of the benefit.

A few months later, when Bud died, T. Gibson, Theatrical Editor of the *Los Angeles Sentinel,* in his front-page obituary, wrote: "There's a tear in the heart of Los Angeles. Arthur 'Bud' Scott, a great jazz musician, died Saturday morning, July 2, the result of a stroke."

Kid Ory wept during prayers at Bud Scott's Masonic funeral. So did I. It was a great privilege to know this scholarly man.

Joe Darensbourg

Joe Darensbourg was the youngest member of the Kid Ory Creole Jazz Band. Unlike the rest of Ory's sidemen, who stayed with him for many years, Darensbourg moved around, playing with many of the great bandleaders of the day.

Born in Baton Rouge in 1906, Darensbourg took piano and violin lessons at an early age, then switched to alto saxophone and, finally, clarinet. He perfected his skills on this instrument through study with the legendary Crescent City clarinetist Alphonse Picou, whose stirring chorus on "High Society" is still the main proving ground for aspiring clarinetists. In 1924 Joe played with Buddy Petit, Sam Morgan, Papa Celestin, and Paul Barbarin in New Orleans; later he traveled with bands in carnivals, medicine shows, and the Al G. Barnes Circus. He played with New Orleans brass bands, in midwestern clubs and road-houses operated by gangsters, and with Jelly Roll Morton in East St. Louis. He appeared on authentic Mississippi riverboats and later on ocean liners and the sternwheeler *Mark Twain* at Disneyland.

After moving to Los Angeles in 1945 he worked with Ory, Teddy Buckner, Joe Liggins, Redd Fox, Pete Daily, and the Firehouse Five Plus Two. He appeared with Gene Mayl's Rhythm Kings in Dayton, Ohio, in 1953 and led his own band (the Dixie Flyers) from 1956 through 1961. That year he joined the Louis Armstrong All-Stars, and in 1973 he began touring with the Legends of Jazz.

Darensbourg joined Kid Ory's Creole Jazz Band in 1945 and re-mained with the trombonist until 1953. As the clown of the band, he delighted in singing risqué numbers and telling jokes and tall tales. He used to don a turban fashioned from one of his wife's bras, drape a tablecloth over his shoulders, roll up his pants legs, and sing "I'm the Sheik of Araby" while standing on a chair.

Darensbourg possessed a distinctive playing style, characterized by the "slap tongue" technique. "Few clarinetists can do the slap-tongue thing," he once told me. "It's like spitting something off the end of your tongue. You have to create a suction between the tongue and reed to create that 'slap' sound." He was also a talented composer; his "Lou-easy-an-i-a" has been recorded by scores of bands in the United States and Europe. He also wrote "Sacramento Jubilee," named for the annual Dixieland event in Northern California. (In 1980 the Jubilee honored Joe and his wife, Helen, as Emperor and Empress of the festi-val.) Another Darensbourg tune, "Monkey Snoots and Dumplings," though not as well known, remains a potential hit novelty number. Darensbourg's recording of "Yellow Dog Blues" with his own group, the Dixie Flyers, was a national hit in 1957; it sold over a million copies and received *Down Beat* magazine's Record of the Year Award. And his 1951 recording of "Sweet Georgia Brown" with Brother

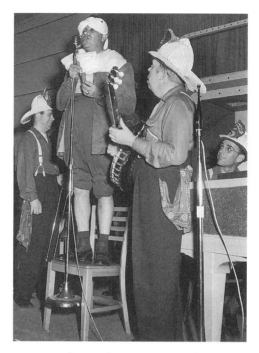

Joe Darensbourg, the youngest member of Kid Ory's Creole Jazz Band, was famous for his rendition of "The Sheik of Araby." He appears here as a guest of Firehouse Five Plus 2.

Bones (Freeman Davis) became the signature song for basketball's famed Harlem Globetrotters and sold millions of copies worldwide.

Perhaps the most famous recording on which he played was "Hello, Dolly!" recorded in 1964 with Louis Armstrong's All-Stars. "It was just something the record company gave us in the studio," he told me. "We left town immediately after the session and never played the tune again. Several months later, we were working in Puerto Rico and people began requesting 'Hello, Dolly!' We didn't know the record had come out—and it was a hit! None of us could remember the tune. Louis called Joe Glaser's office and they sent us a copy. I remember we played it the first time on New Year's Eve in 1965—and at every performance after that."

Like many Louisianans, Joe was a masterful Creole chef. He zealously guarded his culinary trade secrets, especially his private recipe for red beans and rice—the therapeutic New Orleans equivalent of Jewish chicken soup. But Joe lowered his guard one evening in the Beverly Cavern kitchen as the Ory band rested between sets. After a few drinks, he disclosed some of his proprietary cooking tactics, forcing me to swear I would never reveal them. The clarinetist first looked around carefully to be certain that Kid Ory, another skilled Creole cook, was not listening; then he whispered: "Always cook the rice with a tight cover and place a towel between the lid and the pot to keep the moisture inside. Cook the beans slowly for several hours until each one bursts. That gets the poop out."

After keeping my promise of confidentiality for almost half a century, I think the time has finally come to share this valuable information. But please do not tell anyone where you read it.

Joe was also a great storyteller and used to insist that his exaggerated, often ribald narratives were true. One of his fantasies involved a certain "Rooster" Jenkins and his trained chicken, Sonny Boy, who "sang" a duet on the vaudeville circuit. "One day Sonny Boy got out of his cage while 'Rooster' was eating in a Chinese restaurant," Joe explained. "The Chinese chef killed the bird and made a batch of chicken chow mein. The police arrested 'Rooster' for attempted murder when he attacked the chef with a cleaver." After telling one of his outrageous fables, Joe would always solemnly raise his right hand and say, "Honest, Floyd, this really happened!" (Those bizarre stories could fill a book—and they do. Many of them appear in *Jazz Odyssey: The Autobiography of Joe Darensbourg*, edited by Peter Vacher.)

Darensbourg played with the Legends of Jazz from 1973 until 1975, and he liked to tell his "Belgium king" story at each concert. "When the king of Belgium heard my slap tongue version of 'Sweet Georgia Brown,'" the tale went, "he offered me one of those old brick Belgium castles—one brick at a time!" If the crowd did not laugh loudly enough, he would mutter, "A little humor there"—to which my wife, Lucille, his stooge in the audience, always added, "*Very* little!" Then Joe would play his signature song. Fans became very familiar with the "Belgium king" yarn—and his slap tongue exercise on "Sweet Georgia Brown."

In 1985 he was hospitalized by a stroke, and I went to visit him at Valley Hospital Medical Center. As I entered his room, he said, "You just missed him, Floyd. Pops was here—he just left. We had a very nice visit." Joe was hallucinating and thought Louis Armstrong, who had died fourteen years earlier, had come to see him. On a later visit he was rational and asked me to ensure that his friend Barry Martyn in New Orleans eventually receive his extensive collection of memorabilia. Joe died within a few days, on May 24, 1985. He was seventy-nine.

Several years later, after Joe's wife died, I fulfilled his final wish and packed up his mementos for Barry Martyn. Sorting through cartons of photos, awards, sheet music, and correspondence, I came across a gag gift he had received from the Jazz Forum, a Los Angeles organization. In 1983 the Forum had honored Darensbourg as Jazz Man of the Year. Included in the special tribute was a proclamation from the mayor of Baton Rouge, Louisiana, declaring July 17, 1983, "Joe Darensbourg Day in Baton Rouge." As part of the tribute, the clarinetist was presented with an elaborately wrapped package. It contained a very heavy brick glistening with gold paint and glitter—from the king of Belgium?

I must confess, I kept the brick.

Ed "Montudie" Garland

(There are several reasons why this is the longest profile of the Kid Ory band members. Ed Garland's career spanned eight decades; he had the sharpest memory and great communicative skills. I spent more time with him and had many opportunities to gather details of his experiences covering most of jazz's history. F. L.)

The place: New Orleans, Louisiana. The year: 1904. Local leaders are still flush with civic pride over the brand-new electric lights Thomas Edison has installed on Basin Street. Affluent residents are planning a trip up the Mississippi River to the St. Louis World's Fair, honoring the hundredth anniversary of the Louisiana Purchase.

It is a hot summer evening, and a large crowd is dancing in Kenna's Hall—more popularly known as "Funky Butt" Hall—on Perdido Street. On a small bandstand at the far end of the steamy hall is an ensemble led by cornetist Buddy Bolden, the first "king" of a strange new music gaining popularity in New Orleans. Next to him stands Willie Cornish, playing the valve trombone; he uses an empty whisky bottle as a mute. The clarinetist is Frank Lewis; Brock Mumford is the guitarist. The band features two drummers, Jamie Philips and John Vigne. There is no piano—that will come later. Bolden and his sidemen are playing "2:19 Blues," very softly and at a slow tempo. The shuffling sound of the dancers' feet can be heard above the music as the undulating couples rock and sway sensuously.

On the stage, behind the string bass, stands nineteen-year-old Ed Garland. Though he doesn't know it, he is on the threshold of a remarkable musical career. For almost eighty years he will participate in

Ed "Montudie" Garland, Kid Ory's longtime bassist.

every segment of jazz history. He will bridge the gap between Buddy Bolden and Wynton Marsalis; his journey will take him from Funky Butt Hall to Carnegie Hall. Garland will become one of the first New Orleans musicians to move north and bring jazz into America's cultural mainstream. Later he will help found a West Coast jazz colony, joining fellow New Orleanians Kid Ory, Mutt Carey, and Jelly Roll Morton. He will play a significant role in classic jazz's revival era during the 1940s and 1950s. He will thrill fans at home and abroad, remaining on the stage until his very last days. All of this lies ahead for the nineteen-year-old gent thumping out the bass line on "2:19 Blues."

Edward "Montudie" Garland was ninety-five years old at the time of his death in 1980. He helped bring about one of the most exciting artistic flourishings since the Renaissance, one that began in New Orleans before 1900 and eventually excited the entire world. Jazz has become our nation's musical legacy; and Ed Garland was a witness at the creation. Any assessment of his life must necessarily document the entire history of jazz.

Perhaps you have wondered about the nickname, "Montudie," or "Tudie" for short. New Orleans musicians have a penchant for bestowing nicknames on their colleagues—"Kid," "Bud," "Ram," "Mutt," "Cornbread," "Few Clothes," and so on. To this day, the membership directory of the New Orleans Musician's Union lists nicknames for many of its members. Kid Ory's band saddled the bassist with the nickname "Montudie" in the mid-'20s because of his always-dapper appearance. The name was "borrowed" from a Mr. Montudie, a very stylish patron of a Los Angeles cafe where the band played. The original Montudie faded into oblivion, but his namesake sustained his reputation by always being the best-dressed musician on the stand.

Garland was born on January 9, 1885, in New Orleans. His mother, Dora Bynum, came to the city from Arkansas and married Walter Garland shortly after he had moved from West Virginia in 1879. Ed was the youngest of three children. His sister, Irene, died when she was very young; his older brother, Johnny, was a violin maker and gave lessons on the instrument for many years. When he died in 1952, he left two violins to Ed Garland. Those instruments are now in the New Orleans Historical Society archives.

"My first bass was handmade," Tudie told me. "I attached a stick to a hole in a milk can and ran a string to the top. That's where the term 'gut bucket' came from. Ory made a banjo out of a cigar box, and we played together in front of saloons for tips. When I was about eleven years old, I remember hearing Alphonse Picou's seven-piece band at the Independence Hall. I was too young to enter, but I heard them from a side window."

By the age of thirteen, Garland had joined the Onward Brass Band as a parade drummer. He played alongside the legendary Black Benny, reputed to be the strongest bass drummer in the city. (Benny was a "bad" man and spent much time in jail, but he would often be released to play in important parades; once, it is said, Benny shot a heckling bystander during a parade down Canal Street.) Tudie press-rolled and snared through the New Orleans streets in Frankie Duson's Eagle Band alongside Sidney Bechet and Bunk Johnson, and he played the bass drum in Manuel Perez's Imperial Band and Buddy Petit's Security Brass Band.

> I don't remember how many brass bands we had in those days. There must have been hundreds—black and white. I can think of so many—there was the Excelsior, Diamond Stone, Old Columbus, Reliance, and many more. Charlie Dablayes had a brass band. So did Frank Welsh, George McCul-

lum, Frankie Duson—there were a gang of bands. Oh yes, I remember the Jefferson City Buzzards and Johnny Fischer's Brass Band.

Mardi Gras was an important time for the street bands. We'd have a parade every day for a week before Carnival, usually five or six parades on the final day, with maybe a dozen bands in each parade—a couple hundred musicians playing. We'd start at Calliope Street and St. Charles and march up to Canal, down Royal to Orleans to Beauregarde Square—it used to be called Congo Square, where the slaves danced on Sunday afternoons.

There was always an excuse for a parade in New Orleans. We marched for elections, national holidays, church holidays, Andrew Jackson's birthday. And funerals—those funerals were something! We usually started at Geddis and Moss Funeral Home, where we would be hired by the club that the deceased brother belonged to. It was like burial insurance. He paid dues all his life, and when he died, a brass band would be hired to put him away. My snare drum was muffled as we walked to the cemetery playing a dirge like "Nearer My God to Thee" or "Flee as a Bird." The ceremony at the grave was very brief. Then we'd strut from the cemetery. I'd flip on my snare, and we'd cut out on "Didn't He Ramble?" or "High Society." The kids'd march behind us—that was the "second line." They carried cold beer in case the musicians got thirsty—and they usually did.

Montudie often warmly recalled young Louis Armstrong, who as a child used to follow the brass bands through the streets. "He could hardly walk when he started chasing after us. I knew him as a baby. He lived with his mother in the Fourth Ward on Liberty Street. The city tore that house down—they should have kept it as a memorial. Louis used to sing on the streets for nickels and dimes before he started with that horn—I'm talking about when he was nine and ten years old!"

Many of New Orleans' pianists worked in Storyville, the infamous forty-block district named after alderman Sidney Story, who in 1896 had convinced the city to set aside part of the French Quarter for legalized prostitution. Bounded by North Basin, Robertson, St. Louis, and Iberville Streets, Storyville included clusters of brothels, saloons, gambling joints, dope dens, barrelhouses, and cabarets. From 8 P.M. until the wee hours of the morning, jazz bands provided the music so important to the high life of the district.

Ed Garland vividly remembered many of the Storyville spots where he had performed "for about $2.50 per night, plus tips." He spoke of Hilma Burt's sporting house, where Jelly Roll Morton used to entertain; of Tom Anderson's Cafe, where Garland worked with a trio the year after Morton left New Orleans; and of Billy Phillips' 101 Ranch, in the heart of the district, where he played with Joe Oliver.

The 101 Ranch was across the street from the Tuxedo Dance Hall. One night [in 1913] the owner, Billy Phillips, walked across to the Tuxedo Dance Hall to hear Papa Celestin and was killed in a fight. Shortly after, the manager of the Tuxedo was also killed in a shooting, and the place was closed as a result. Storyville quieted down; the police kept a close eye on things, and customers stayed away. During this slow period, Freddie Keppard fired his bass, guitar, and violin [players] and hired Buddy Christian to play piano with him. As far as I know, this was the first time a piano was used in a jazz band.

Things gradually picked up. The man who took over the 101 Ranch wanted to change things, so he made the name the *102* Ranch and hired a bunch of young white musicians like Henry Regas, Eddie Edwards, Nick LaRocca, and Yellow Nunez. Later they went to Chicago and became very famous as the Original Dixieland Jazz Band.

I played at Pete Lala's 25 Club on Iberville with Freddie Keppard in 1906 and again four years later in Kid Ory's Brown Skin Babies. Ory's band included Joe Oliver on cornet, Johnny Dodds on clarinet, Emile Bigard on violin, Lorenzo Staultz on guitar, and, I think, Henry Martin played drums. I worked in another place on Iberville—it was a tent and freezing cold in the winter. I can't remember the name.

In those days, we played tunes like "Careless Love," "Idaho Rag," "Make Me a Pallet on the Floor," and "Oh, Jack Carey," which was named after Mutt Carey's brother, who played trombone. Later it was called "Tiger Rag." Folks think Nick LaRocca wrote it, but we were playin' the tune in New Orleans when he was still wearin' short pants. Mostly, I'd use a bow when we played—sometimes I'd slap the strings. I think Bill Johnson, who traveled with Keppard, plucked the bass first when a drunk broke his bow one night. I still like the sound of a bowed bass, but few musicians do this now.

When we played the blues, I'd give the rhythm a bouncing low-down beat. I guess that's how the term "low-down blues" started. This was sort of "barrelhouse" music. There were lots of barrelhouses in the district. Folks'd go there after the cabarets had closed so they could continue drinking. Usually there was no music, but sometimes they'd hire a second-rate pianist who'd play all night for tips and all the beer he could drink. Barrels of beer were lined up on both sides of the room. A large glass cost five cents. You'd better keep it filled or you'd be kicked out. The customers could drink all night—they usually did, until they ran out of nickels or fell down drunk. These were really low dives.

While Storyville played an important role in the New Orleans music scene, jazz was a vital part of Negro life in every section of town. Bands played on trucks to advertise dances, prize fights, even commercial products such as soap, coffee, beer, and cigars. Frequent street parades used organized brass bands that strutted in the hot sun through the Vieux Carré. Garland enjoyed reminiscing about the orchestras he played with at Spanish Fort and Milneberg on Lake Pontchartrain. There was music at picnics in New Basin Canal, Bucktown, and West End on Sundays. He spoke of dances in the country at sugar plantations.

> We'd always be playing for parties. At the slightest occasion, they'd buy a keg of beer, cook a gang of crawfish, hire three or four of us to play, and have a big party for their friends. And there were lots of private social and political clubs that hired us on weekends. We played for the Bulls, the District Carnival Club, Buzzards, Mysterious Babies—I can't remember them all.
>
> I recall riding on the back of a wagon to play a party one night. I didn't notice, but my bass was standing against the side of the wagon and it got hooked on a low tree and we drove off and left it hanging there. When we arrived at the party, I noticed the bass was missing and we had to ride back looking for it. Sure 'nuf, we found it hanging there in a tree. From then on, I always laid the bass down in the wagon.

Garland, one of the last living links with the primal jazz of the legendary Buddy Bolden, gave a surprising appraisal of the legendary cornetist's style. Most accounts describe a fiercely penetrating tone that could be heard miles away, but Garland said: "He usually blew softly to draw the dancers nearer. Occasionally, he would stroll among them playing into young ladies' ears—the gals loved it."

Indeed, Bolden's manner with women made quite an impression on young Ed Garland. "The girls were always around him. He'd have two or three with him at all times. One would carry his coat, another his horn. When he played dances, they would crowd around him, handing him coins. He never went home alone. One night at Longshoreman's Hall, some of their boyfriends got angry and a fight started—almost a riot. Buddy jumped out the back window."

Montudie previously played with Bolden at Rice's Cafe on Custom House Street. He remembered this as "a very tough part of town. They'd get drunk in there and set off fireworks in the toilets. They finally burned the place down." Unfortunately, Buddy Bolden's time was very short; he was admitted to the East Louisiana Mental Hospital in 1907, when he was only thirty-eight years old, and never was released. His death in 1931 was not mentioned in the local press.

It has long been rumored that Buddy Bolden recorded several early cylinder records with his band in 1906. Collectors are still searching for them. Although Ed Garland remembered the sonorous tone of Bolden's horn, he was unable to provide any information regarding those elusive cylinders.

Ed Garland was among the first musicians to take New Orleans music northward. In 1912 he boarded an Illinois Central train with a group of musicians to tour the Midwest, accompanying vaudeville performer Mabel Elaine. His band included trombonist Roy Palmer, guitarist Louis Keppard, Lawrence Duhé on clarinet, Herb Lindsay on violin, and Sugar Johnny Smith on trumpet. This advance guard spearheaded a movement that eventually saw Crescent City jazz invade Chicago, New York, Los Angeles, and eventually the entire world. New Orleans had lost Ed Garland for sixty years; he would not return until 1971.

The vaudeville tour lasted two years. "We probably could have continued," Garland muttered, "but I got tired of seeing Mabel jump out of a cotton bale every night. She was a white girl wearing blackface makeup. We traveled with a riverboat backdrop—it was supposed to be 'The Good Ship Lady Lee'—the audiences loved it." After scuttling the "Lady Lee," Garland kept the band together and stayed on the vaudeville circuit arranged by the Theatre Owners Booking Association (TOBA)—better known as "Tough on Black Asses" because of its rigorous tours. During this period, Jim Crow conditions made it difficult for black artists to appear in most theaters, so a special circuit had to be arranged.

After several years on the road, Ed Garland and his band settled in Chicago, playing in various Southside spots. They went to Milwaukee for the summer of 1917, appearing at Schlitz's Palm Gardens, then returned to Chicago and opened at the DeLuxe Cafe with Freddie Keppard on trumpet and Ram Hall playing drums. He lost that job at the DeLuxe to the Tennessee Ten, who were traveling with Florence Mills.

One day a young girl pianist came to Garland's attention demonstrating sheet music in a State Street dime store. Her name was Lil Hardin.

"When I first heard Lil, she was playing classical music," Garland told me. "I knew she would fit in our band because of her great timing and a perfect ear. She was a terrific artist. Later she worked with Sheldon Brooks in a Broadway review. I think she was also in Eubie Blake's *Shuffle Along.*

Reflecting on the Chicago scene, Garland said, "The Lambs Club hired one of the first white bands from New Orleans. They were there when I got to Chicago. It was a fine group led by Tom Brown. He played good trombone—tried to copy Ory. Larry Shields was playing clarinet with Brown. He had a thin tone, but his execution was brilliant—I think he had classical training. He joined the Original Dix-ieland Jazz Band a few years later and became very famous."

Just as jazz was catching on elsewhere in the country, it was hitting hard times in New Orleans. Storyville was closed by the U.S. Navy in November 1917 after four sailors died there in a brawl. With the red light turned off, jazzmen moved northward to search for work. Many of them followed Ed Garland to Chicago, which quickly replaced New Orleans as the nation's jazz center. The new arrivals found lucrative jobs in the underworld clubs that sprung up after passage of the un-popular Volstead Act, which launched the Prohibition era in 1919. The Windy City's thriving cabaret scene lured patrons with the promise of illegal booze and the exotic sounds of New Orleans. As a result, jazz, still bearing the stigma of sin from its Storyville roots, now became as-sociated with the hoodlums and bootleggers of Chicago's Southside.

Prohibition provided the backdrop for Joe Oliver's move to Chicago, one of the important events in the saga of jazz. And Ed Gar-land was very much involved in the historic event.

> When Mutt Carey, who replaced Freddie Keppard, left my band, I sent for Joe, who was still in New Orleans and had become quite popular. He was now known as "King" Oliver. I met his train when he arrived in Chicago and found a hotel for him to stay until he got settled. Honoré Dutrey, who had played with me in the Excelsior [Brass] Band in New Orleans, was just released from a Navy band in Chicago, so he became our trombone man. Johnny Dodds left a road show at the Monogram Theatre and joined us. We had Minor [Ram] Hall on drums, and Lil Hardin and myself. We didn't use much music. We had a few lead sheets from a music store on Dearborn Street where Lil used to work. Joe'd tear off the titles so visiting musicians didn't know what we were playing. The band was billed as "King Oliver's New Orleans Jazz Band."
>
> For awhile, we played two jobs a night. We'd work at the DeLuxe Cafe until closing at 1 A.M., then move to the Pekin Cabaret on State Street and play until 6 A.M. The Pekin was the scene of several gangland shootings, and we were told to always keep playing regardless of any turmoil that may take place.

Oliver and Garland's band became a Chicago favorite. As its fame spread, the band received some out-of-town offers. They took to the road in 1921 and headed West to play a date arranged by Kid Ory, who had moved to California in 1919 following the Creole Band's pio-neering venture to the West Coast. On June 12, 1921, Garland played his first California gig, appearing with the Oliver band at the Pergola

Dancing Pavilion at 949 Market Street in San Francisco. After a successful engagement at the five-cents-a-dance hall, they headed to Southern California, playing at the Spikes brothers' Wayside Park Cafe in Watts. Jelly Roll Morton replaced Lil Hardin, who returned to Chicago following the Pergola job, and Kid Ory replaced Dutrey on trombone for the Watts engagement. Tudie, Ory, and Oliver were together again, a dozen years after they first shared the stage at Pete Lala's 25 Club in Storyville. Oliver soon returned to Chicago, but Garland remained in Los Angeles with Kid Ory. The association would last most of his professional life.

There was a great deal of musical activity in Southern California in the early 1920s. The burgeoning motion picture industry hired many local bands to provide background music to set the mood for the actors. Occasionally the musicians were seen on the screen, but usually they played off-camera, creating an atmosphere to accompany the action. Ed Garland's music was heard on many Charlie Chaplin sets long before sound was added to the movies.

While much of his work was with Kid Ory, Garland recalled many other jobs in the '20s. He played with saxophonist Paul Howard in Jelly Roll Morton's band at Leek's Lake near Los Angeles. Morton later brought his group into the Cadillac Cafe at Fifth and Central to appear with the famed entertainer Ada "Bricktop" Smith for a six-week engagement. Early in 1922, Garland took a small band to San Francisco, playing on the notorious Barbary Coast for a year. He rejoined Ory at the Wilshire Country Club in 1923 and followed him to the Midnight Frolics at Ninth and Spring for the balance of 1923 and most of 1924.

In 1925 Garland helped found the One-Eleven Syncopators Orchestra, which played at the One-Eleven Dance Hall at Third and Main. The lineup included Garland on bass, Everett Walsh on drums, Joe Parker on banjo, Mack Straw on trombone, Russell Masengale on cornet, Adam "Slocum" Mitchell and Theo Bonner on saxophone, and Fred Washington on piano. The One-Eleven was a seedy dime-a-dance joint catering to sailors. Paul Howard told me that a ten-cent dance with a "beautiful hostess" lasted only a few minutes—the arrangements were reduced to sixteen or thirty-two bars.

With the onset of the Depression in the 1930s, the Los Angeles music scene slowed to a near halt. Most of the cabarets were forced to close. The few that remained attempted to survive by hiring larger, mostly white bands that were embracing the newly evolved swing music. Ed Garland found the once-fertile fields almost barren of opportunity. Throughout the country, interest in the music symbolic of the carefree '20s rapidly diminished. Most old-style jazz musicians were forced to seek other work. Kid Ory retired to a chicken farm in 1933; Garland managed to survive by playing occasional engagements and private parties staged by members of the still-affluent Hollywood film colony. But the music scene was abysmal for practitioners of traditional New Orleans music and would remain that way for a decade.

During the waning years of the Depression, a revival movement cast a very dim ray of hope on this otherwise gloomy period for traditional New Orleans music. It began in Northern California, spearheaded by a group of young musicians led by Lu Watters. San Franciscans began streaming into the Dawn Club to hear the Yerba Buena Jazz Band recreate the music made popular by King Oliver's Creole Jazz Band almost twenty years earlier. The Ory band reunited for a major concert in San Francisco, played on a series of radio broadcasts, and made some new recordings for the Crescent Record Company label. Throughout the country, young musicians heard Ory's broadcasts and recordings and began emulating this style. New Orleans jazz enjoyed a resurgence in New York City. Bunk Johnson had been attracting fans for three years at Stuyvesant Casino, and young Bob Wilber was gaining attention with a band of New Orleans veterans, including Sidney Bechet and Pops Foster. The big town was ready for the Ory men.

Early in 1948, New York impresario John Schenck engaged the Ory band to play a concert in Carnegie Hall. On Friday evening, April 30, 1948, Ed Garland made his debut on that fabled stage. As he looked over Ory's shoulder at the filled auditorium, he remembered the countless steamy evenings he and Ory had played together so long ago in New Orleans. The music they pioneered was now featured at the nation's most celebrated concert hall, where the world's greatest artists had performed. Tudie's terse comment: "It was a good feeling."

The band played the next evening in Boston's Orchestra Hall. When the reviews appeared in New York and Boston papers, Ed Garland received a major share of the plaudits. The music critic for the *New York Times* said, "The stirring rhythmic sounds from Edward Garland's bass propelled the beat to a near frenzy. The 63-year-old bassist is truly a dynamic performer." The band returned to California elated with the tremendous ovations they received.

For the next seven years, Ed Garland and Kid Ory performed together at various Southern California locations, including the Rendezvous Ballroom in Santa Monica, Ace Cain's on Western Avenue, and the Beverly Cavern at Beverly and Ardmore. It was a thrill to hear Garland, then at the peak of his powers, sparking the best rhythm section that ever supported a Dixieland band. Minor "Ram" Hall seldom took drum solos, but his firm beat provided a sublime pulse that was buoyant and steady. Pianist Buster Wilson's long, slim fingers moved gracefully across the keys, filling any hollow spots, and Bud Scott's metronomic guitar added a resilient crispness and tremendous drive to the beat. Montudie was truly amazing as he stood on the riser next to Ram, his melodic rhythms providing a rock-solid foundation for every tune.

In 1954 the band was playing a San Francisco engagement at the Club Hangover, famous for its mural-decorated bandstand. There, after working together amicably for more than forty years, Garland and Ory had a misunderstanding that flared into a bitter dispute. It culminated with a rousing punch from the diminutive Garland that sent Ory sprawling amid the glasses and bottles on the bar below the stage. The two old friends did not speak to each other for almost seventeen years.

Earl "Fatha" Hines, whose band followed Ory's into the Hangover, asked Tudie to join his group, and Garland handled the bass chores for him for the next two years. In 1957 he briefly joined Turk Murphy's San Francisco Jazz Band before returning to Los Angeles, where he lived for the balance of his life.

In the fall of 1958, Tudie briefly returned to his musical roots to play the snare drum in a brass-band sequence for the Universal Pictures film *Imitation of Life.* Publicity stills depict Garland strutting in his band uniform, flanked by trumpeters Andrew Blakeney, Teddy Buckner, and George Orendorf. When he saw this photo in my collection, he remarked, "This is how I must have looked going down Claiborne Street with the Onward Band when I was thirteen years old."

In April 1971, Garland finally made it back to those childhood streets. He had decided to visit his birthplace again, after an absence of sixty years, to take part in the Fourth Annual New Orleans Jazz and Heritage Festival. Aware that few of his contemporaries would be alive and none of the familiar landmarks remained, he made the trip with mixed feelings. Over the years, his sight had gradually failed, and he was almost blind.

I sat next to Montudie during the four-hour flight to New Orleans. After an enthusiastic airport greeting by members of the New Orleans Jazz Club, he settled into the Olivier House. We took him to dinner at

Felix's Oyster House. Later, strolling down Iberville Street, he exclaimed, "This is about where Pete Lala's place was!" Still energetic despite the long flight, Tudie insisted on visiting Preservation Hall. Three musicians occupied the stage when we entered: Kid Sheik on trumpet, Albert Burbank on clarinet, and Louis Nelson on trombone. Although these venerable musicians were New Orleans fixtures with full careers behind them, Tudie had never met them; when he left town back in 1912, Nelson and Burbank were only ten years old, and Kid Sheik was only eight. Garland sat in with the band, sending an electric charge through the audience. After a lapse of six decades he was back in New Orleans, playing his string bass just a few blocks away from the old Funky Butt Hall. The cycle was completed—a jazz pioneer had come home at last.

Throughout the week-long festival, Tudie played with young European musicians in various spots around the city. They were overjoyed to perform with a man who had played such an important role in launching the art form they knew so well. One late jam session at Bonaparte's Retreat, across Decatur Street from the famous French Market, lasted until 6 A.M.—and Tudie was still going strong.

When festival producer George Wein learned that Garland was in town, he hired the veteran bassist to play the closing event at the Municipal Auditorium. The final concert featured Kid Ory, who was also returning to New Orleans for the first time since his departure in 1919. Although Ory was younger than Garland, it was evident when he stepped off the plane that the years had not treated him kindly. He was a very sick man. I watched the two aged jazzmen embrace at the pre-concert rehearsal. This was their first meeting since that bitter conflict in San Francisco seventeen years before.

Ory's final performance was very pathetic. He sang a few numbers, but there was no gusto in his almost inaudible horn. He died in 1973, two years after this brief reunion with Ed Garland.

Tudie attended Ory's funeral at Holy Cross Cemetery in Los Angeles. There was a small tear in the old man's eye when the Southern California Hot Jazz Society Marching Band played Ory's "Muskrat Ramble." After Teddy Buckner's muted "Closer Walk With Thee," my fellow pallbearers and I carried the trombonist's casket to the waiting grave. As we walked to our cars after the brief services, I looked back and noticed Ed Garland standing at the grave site. He slowly bent over, picked up a gardenia, and said a silent farewell to his old friend. Tudie was now the last survivor of the Storyville jazz scene, one of the few people alive who could still remember the sound of Buddy Bolden's horn rising above the crowd at the Longshoreman's Hall. He was eighty-eight years old; but there was still a lot of music left in him.

Later that year Barry Martyn, an English drummer who had met Montudie four years earlier at a tribute concert, decided to assemble his dream band for a local concert. The band included trombonist Louis Nelson from New Orleans; Alton Purnell, whose piano sparked the Bunk Johnson and George Lewis bands; Andrew Blakeney on trumpet; and Joe Darensbourg on clarinet. Naturally, Martyn asked Garland to play bass. At an age when most men would be content to bask in the warm memories of a long career, Garland enthusiastically accepted the invitation to join this newly formed band, named quite accurately The Legends of Jazz.

With Blakeney, Darensbourg, and Garland, the Legends reunited almost half of the former Kid Ory Creole Jazz Band, which had introduced the living sounds of New Orleans to so many listeners during the jazz revival of the 1940s. Martyn added guitarist Nappy Lamare, pianist Lloyd Glenn, the famed clarinetist Barney Bigard, and an authentic New Orleans brass band to the lineup, and he asked me to be his partner and the master of ceremonies. When trombonist Trummy Young accepted my invitation to appear, we knew we had a potentially successfully venture in work.

On Saturday evening, September 8, 1973, "A Night in New Orleans" played to a capacity audience in Los Angeles' Wilshire Ebell Theatre. The Legends were a smash success in their debut, and Ed Garland upstaged the rest of the band with his antics. The little old man behind the string bass won the hearts of the audience. The concert was such a success that Martyn and I proposed a cross-country tour for these musical senior citizens. Most of Garland's friends felt he was too frail to travel, but Tudie rose to the occasion as we barnstormed across the country. When I introduced him at Cami Hall in New York City, the crowd gave him a standing ovation. We were just across the street from Carnegie Hall, and Montudie recalled the triumphant appearance he'd made there with Kid Ory twenty-five years earlier. The Legends recorded their first album on that 1973 tour.

"A Night in New Orleans" became an annual affair for the next seven years, as The Legends of Jazz continued to gain fans. In 1974 they completed another U.S. tour, recorded their second album with guest clarinetist Barney Bigard, appeared at the New Orleans Jazz and Heritage Festival, and made their European debut. Jazz fans around the world welcomed the opportunity to meet Ed Garland. When fans asked for his autograph, he obligingly complied with a very slow and deliberate hand. While the rest of the band waited patiently, he would scrawl, "Ed 'Tudie' Garland, Bass" on record covers, programs, and, once in Germany, on the blouse of a buxom *fraulein*. To facilitate Garland's many requests for autographs, I had a rubber stamp of his signature made.

Garland might have met his many European fans a quarter of a century earlier. Back in 1949, I had completed arrangements with Charles Delauney in Paris to bring Kid Ory's Creole Jazz Band to Europe. Dates were booked in France, Switzerland, Belgium, and Italy, and we sought several additional venues in England to offset the air fares. Shortly before our departure, though, the English musician's union refused to authorize the appearance of an American band, and the tour had to be cancelled.

We celebrated Ed Garland's ninetieth birthday on the bandstand at the Inn of the Golden West in Odessa, Texas, as the Legends of Jazz began their third cross-country tour. The tour ended in New England, and from there we flew to Manchester, England, for a series of one-night stands in Barry Martyn's homeland (where the musician's union had long since lifted its ban on U.S. performers). After touring the continent for several weeks, the Legends appeared as the featured artists at the Breda Jazz Festival in the Netherlands. When I emceed the opening concert, broadcast throughout the country, four hundred thousand Dutch listeners heard Tudie play his famous bowed solo on "Blues for Jimmie."

After the Breda appearance, we headed to Antwerp to launch the first international production of "A Night in New Orleans." Besides the Legends of Jazz, the show featured Barney Bigard, Nappy Lamare, Wingy Manone, the Louisiana Shakers Band, the New Orleans Society Orchestra, and the Eagle Brass Band. We played in Antwerp, London, Berlin, Vienna, Gratz, and Gent. Despite near-blindness and hearing difficulties, Garland weathered the arduous travel quite well. After the final concert of the tour, we all retired about midnight in preparation for an early departure the following morning. Garland was in the room next to mine at the Terminus Hotel. I was awakened by a shuffling sound. It was 3 A.M. when I looked into Tudie's room. He was sitting on the bed next to his packed suitcase, fully dressed and wearing his heavy leather coat and hat. "Why are you awake so early?" I asked. He muttered, "Isn't it 7 A.M.? Where is everyone? We'll miss our flight."

Actually, he almost did miss that return flight to the United States. A group of well-intentioned Belgian fans volunteered to transport the musicians and their gear to the Brussels airport, approximately sixty miles away. The young man driving Garland was not familiar with the road and got lost. They arrived at the airport only minutes before the flight's scheduled departure.

Now in his nineties, Ed Garland continued to travel with the Legends of Jazz throughout the United States, Canada, and Europe. He made his final concert appearance on September 27, 1977, in Hanover, Germany, and had to be hospitalized for a week before returning to Los Angeles. A few days after coming home, Tudie entered Cedars-Sinai Medical Center. In a final display of Southern vanity, he deducted several years from his correct age for the hospital records. He spent a week in the hospital avidly watching the World Series from his bed and muttering about the Los Angeles Dodgers' poor performance.

We all feared Ed Garland was about to die. But he completely recovered and soon was twirling his bass at local jazz events. He no longer could travel with the Legends of Jazz, but he appeared with them whenever they worked in the Los Angeles area. Tudie enjoyed three more years of relative good health. When he died on January 22, 1980, the final chapter of a saga that had begun ninety-four years earlier was complete. Ed Garland, the last survivor of Kid Ory's Creole Jazz Band, finally joined Mutt, Buster, Bud, Ram, and Kid. The joyous sounds of that great little band will always remain vivid to those who heard it. We will never forget Ory's dynamic rhythm section or the slight, energetic bass player who propelled it.

It rained the day we buried Ed Garland. Several hundred friends assembled in Forest Lawn's Church of the Recessional in Glendale, California, to say a final goodbye to the seminal bassist. His instrument stood proudly amid the array of flowers next to the casket.

As we entered the chapel, an organist was playing "Way Down Yonder in New Orleans." Turk Murphy and his band flew down from San Francisco to play for their departed colleague. Pat Yankee, standing beside the open casket, sang "Lonesome Road," and Murphy's band played "1919 March." Gordon Mitchell led the Southern California Hot Jazz Society's Resurrection Brass Band in a version of Ed Garland's favorite hymn, "Amazing Grace." In my eulogy, I emphasized that the services were more a tribute to a man's life than a mourning for his death.

A few months later, before boarding a plane for New Orleans to attend the 1980 Jazz and Heritage Festival, I personally carried Tudie's bass into the plane's luggage compartment. Following the instructions in his will, I delivered the instrument to the New Orleans Jazz Museum. It is now on permanent display in the foyer.

Teddy Buckner

Teddy Buckner joined Kid Ory's Creole Jazz Band at the Beverly Cavern in Los Angeles on July 16, 1949. He replaced Andrew Blakeney, a particular favorite of mine, so I was initially disappointed to learn about the change. My disappointment evaporated the moment Buckner blew his first note. His Armstrong-influenced tones, tinged with melodic integrity and stunning technical prowess, filled the little club with warmth and vitality. Those same attributes were integral to Teddy's personality. During the years he worked with Ory, he rose to prominence and became a favorite of jazz fans the world over. Our friendship gradually mellowed into a warm relationship, but I always remained a dedicated fan.

Teddy Buckner was born in Sherman, Texas, in 1909; his family moved to Los Angeles when he was eight years old. After he admired a young cornet player in a marching band, his mother promptly bought Teddy a silver horn and arranged for music lessons. "It took a lot of practice after school instead of playing ball," he said, "but I was determined to play music." He began his professional career in Los Angeles at the tender age of fifteen, working a succession of jobs. During the 1920s and 1930s he played with bands led by Speed Webb, Sonny Clay, Edythe Turnham, Lorenzo Flennoy, Les Hite, Lionel Hampton, and Benny Carter.

"I was twenty-seven years old when Lionel Hampton hired me to play with him at the after-hours Paradise Club in 1936," Buckner recalled. "One night Benny Goodman, Gene Krupa, and Teddy Wilson came in after their gig at the Palomar Ballroom. They all sat in, and we had the greatest jam session until 4 A.M. When Goodman hired Lionel, he [Hampton] turned the band over to me. I stayed at the Paradise Club until I joined Benny Carter."

In 1954, after five years with Kid Ory, Buckner formed a great little band of his own, Teddy Buckner and His Dixieland All-Stars. It soon ranked among the most successful Dixieland groups in the country and played a vital role in the Los Angeles jazz scene for many years. With few changes of personnel, the group played extended engagements at the 400 Club and the New Orleans Hotel in Los Angeles, followed by four years at the Huddle in West Covina and sixteen years at Disneyland's New Orleans Square. Buckner's recordings with members of Louis Armstrong's All-Stars, triumphant tours in Europe, and wonderful 1959 French record sessions with Sidney Bechet added to his fame. He was featured in many Hollywood films (both onscreen and on the soundtrack), including *Pennies from Heaven* with Bing Crosby, *Pete Kelly's Blues, Hush, Hush, Sweet Charlotte,* and *St. Louis Blues.*

Buckner was always pleased when told he sounded like his idol, Louis Armstrong. Their physical resemblance was also striking, and he often was hired as a screen stand-in for Armstrong. In 1970, when I produced "Hello Louis!" to celebrate Satchmo's seventieth birthday, I chose Buckner to play Armstrong in the Hot Five segment of the chronological program.

His first number was "West End Blues," considered by many to be Louis' finest recording and one of the greatest of all jazz records. Teddy always masterfully met the technical challenge of the elaborate trumpet introduction that has astonished and intimidated several generations of musicians. But with his idol watching from the wings, Teddy could not deliver his usually flawless performance of the difficult cadenza. Perhaps because of Armstrong's presence, or possibly because he had taken several gulps of gin to bolster his confidence, he faltered on the opening flurry of descending notes and never gained the momentum necessary to forge the harmonic tones that swirled upward to establish the monumental richness of the remarkable solo. Visibly shaken, Teddy completed the set without his usual verve. He left the stage with a tear in his eye. As he passed me, he muttered, "I'm sorry, Floyd. I'm terribly sorry." He shrugged off my attempt to console him and sadly walked away.

Teddy remained active for another twenty years, but he never forgave himself for that embarrassing blunder during his most important appearance. He continued to accept requests for "West End Blues," but with each performance I am sure he remembered those agonizing moments on the Shrine Auditorium stage.

A dedicated family man, Buckner was happily married for more than sixty years to his dedicated wife, Minnie. They had three sons, eight grandchildren, and four great-grandchildren. The two often entertained us in the modest home they occupied for forty-six years. The walls of the small rooms were decorated with photographs and plaques documenting Teddy's successful career.

Buckner died on September 22, 1994, at the age of eighty-five, after a long illness. I shall always treasure the warm friendship we shared.

(2)

A PERSONAL VIEW
OF THE MUSIC

In today's world of compact discs and 'round-the-clock radio, it is hard to imagine a world without recorded music. Yet that is the type of world from which jazz came forth. By the time recorded music began to emerge, right after World War I, jazz was already thirty years old. Those early recordings were hit-or-miss affairs, with poor technology and scanty documentation—musicians often received no credit for their performances or were forced by contractual strictures to use pseudonyms. In many cases, pressings were so meager that all the copies have long since vanished.

Piecing together the origins of great jazz recordings, hit songs, and important performances can be frustrating, and it may hinge on luck as much as on dogged research. As often as not the essential facts have never been written down and reside only within the memory of the participants—and those who participated in jazz's formative period are fast disappearing. Yet it is vital to record these stories, so that we and our descendants can reconstruct the world out of which American popular music emerged.

Exploring jazz's colorful history can be a very revealing experience. The cumulative result of the years I spent probing behind the scenes creates an extended personal view of the music. Some of the episodes covered in this chapter shaped our culture for years to come; others represent snapshots of an evolving art form, capturing the flavor of a bygone era.

A 1919 advertisement for Jim Europe's 369th Infantry Jazz Band.

Lieutenant Jim Europe's Hellfighters— The 369th Infantry Jazz Band

James Reese Europe could hardly have been more aptly named. As the leader of the 369th Infantry Jazz Band, also known as the "Hellfighters," he introduced the sounds of American ragtime to Europeans during World War I. Although his career was very brief, he profoundly influenced the course of popular music, not just in the United States but throughout the world. Yet his name probably would not arouse much of a response among most jazz fans.

Just a few weeks after returning from the war, Europe and his Hell-fighters recorded eleven tunes for the Pathé Freres Phonograph Company of Brooklyn. The list contained such interesting titles as "Moaning Trombones," "Jazz Baby," "Russian Rag," and "On Patrol in No Man's Land." He made the first recorded versions of several tunes that still appear in the repertoires of today's Dixieland bands—"Darktown Strutters' Ball," "Ja Da," and three W. C. Handy classics—"St. Louis Blues," "Memphis Blues," and "Hesitating Blues." "St. Louis Blues" would not be recorded again until 1921, when the Original Dixieland Jazz Band helped establish the song as a hit. Handy himself recorded it the following year.

Europe was already a well-established musician by the time World War I made him famous. In 1910 he had organized the Clef Club, a musical society for black artists in New York City. Two years later his 150-piece Clef Club Orchestra became one of the first jazz bands to perform in staid Carnegie Hall. For the first time, the Carnegie suspended its rules regarding segregated seating, and the bastion of high art reverberated with the sounds of "Down Home Rag" and "That Teasin' Rag." The concert's success added prestige to the Clef Club and altered the musical life of New York City. The club, which functioned as both a booking agency and trade union for black performers, soon secured many prominent engagements and opened a world of new opportunities for its members. Bud Scott told me that, within twenty-four hours after the Carnegie event, he received an offer to record several Joplin rags with a white banjo band.

The following year Europe formed his Society Orchestra, which began entertaining wealthy New Yorkers at posh venues such as Delmonico's and the Hotel Astor. (Noble Sissle, who with his songwriting partner Eubie Blake would later achieve worldwide fame, was a member of the Society Orchestra.) Advertisements referred to Europe as the "Paderewski of Syncopation." The orchestra's initial jazz recordings, the first by a black band, appeared on the Victor label in 1913, four years ahead of the Original Dixieland Jazz Band's initial releases and eight years before Kid Ory's historic California recording session. These early Victor records helped sustain the ragtime era.

The innovative Europe liked to experiment with syncopation, creative reed voicings, and muted brass. His use of saxophones brought a new measure of respectability to that instrument, until then regarded as a novelty device. His compositions, arrangements, and orchestral direction reflected the ragtime style popular at the time and fostered the dance frenzy nurtured by the Jazz Age. In 1913 he became musical director for the successful dance team of Vernon and Irene Castle. His "Castle Walk" helped them introduce the fox-trot and establish the style of ballroom dancing that has continued for generations.

When the United States entered World War I, Sissle and Europe enlisted in the army together and organized a regimental band. The group accompanied the acclaimed 369th Infantry Regiment, the first American unit to arrive in France. The brave black unit, including the band, earned the nickname "Hellfighters" for its participation in several vital military campaigns.

By the end of the war, the 369th Infantry Jazz Band ranked among the greatest bands in the world. Its personnel, as identified in Brian Rust's *Jazz Records 1887—1942*, included Noble Sissle on violin, Herb Flemming on trombone, and Russell Smith on trumpet. Flemming, only nineteen at the time, went on to have a long, distinguished career, performing with Earl Hines, Fats Waller, Benny Carter, Duke Ellington, Louis Armstrong, and Tommy Dorsey. Russell Smith became one of the outstanding lead trumpet players in the big-band era two decades later.

After the war, Europe proudly led his Hellfighters band in the nation's first parade of returning World War heroes. More than a million fans, watching the victorious march up New York's Fifth Avenue in mid-February 1919, gathered along the parade route to salute the heroes of the famed 369th Infantry as they strutted from Madison Square to Harlem.

Europe and Sissle had written "On Patrol in No Man's Land" during their tenure overseas, and it quickly became a favorite among U.S. veterans. Pathé leaped at the opportunity to capitalize on its popularity as the doughboys returned to the United States. It was easily the most successful of the eleven recordings the 369th Infantry Jazz Band made for Pathé in March 1919. Based on the success of "On Patrol in No Man's Land," James Europe's band scheduled an extensive tour of the country. Advertisements proclaimed: "65 BATTLING MUSICIANS DIRECT FROM THE FIGHTING FRONTS IN FRANCE — THE BAND THAT SET ALL FRANCE JAZZ MAD!"

Ironically, after surviving the deadliest war in world history to that point, Europe failed to live through the Hellfighters' national tour. A member of the drum section, irate at Europe for what he considered poor treatment, murdered him on May 10, 1919. The funeral march took place in New York, the first public memorial service held for a black person in the city's history. The somber procession followed part of the same route the 369th had marched in its victory parade just three months earlier. Lieutenant Europe was buried with full military honors at Arlington Cemetery in Washington, D.C.

Noble Sissle, assisted by Eubie Blake, assumed leadership of the 369th Infantry Jazz Band, which completed its scheduled bookings. The tour culminated with a very successful engagement at the prestigious Palace Theater in New York City. Later, the two leaders took a smaller group on the road for a lengthy vaudeville junket, launching their productive partnership.

At the time of his death, James Reese Europe was only thirty-nine years old and at the forefront of the emerging jazz movement. We can only speculate about what further contributions he might have made had he lived another few decades. He was on the threshold of a brilliant career and might have become one of the most important figures in the world of popular music. His death came less than two months after the Hellfighters' historic recordings for Pathé. In its promotional catalog, the record company proclaimed that Europe was "the world's greatest exponent of syncopation. You hear every moan of the trombones, every roar of the saxaphones [sic], every shrill note of the clarinets. The swing of the rhythm, and the fascination of the Jazzing makes you want to dance! You can't sit still!"

Prophetically, the back page of the Pathé catalog predicted: "Jim Europe's jazz will live forever!" And so it has; Memphis Archives, a record company dedicated to preserving America's rich musical heritage, recently released a carefully remastered compact disc of the rare Pathé recordings.

"I Wish I Could Shimmy Like My Sister Kate"—The First Recorded Hit of the Jazz Age

All the boys in my neighborhood,
knew she could shimmy and it's understood. . . .

Jim Europe's hit "On Patrol in No Man's Land" captured the concerns of America's wartime generation. By contrast, "I Wish I Could Shimmy Like My Sister Kate," the first jazz hit of the 1920s, reflected the carefree attitudes of a victorious, prosperous nation.

The song romanticized a ragtime dance craze popularized by Gilda Gray. The "shimmy" involved frantic, sensuous gyrations of the hips and shoulders, personifying the madcap exuberance and permissive morals of the Jazz Age. It inspired several additional songs, including "Shimmee Town" (featured in the Ziegfeld Follies of 1919), "Shim-Me-King's Blues" (recorded by Mamie Smith in 1921), and the New Orleans Rhythm Kings' "Shim-Me-Sha-Wabble" (1923).

"I Wish I Could Shimmy Like My Sister Kate" was by far the most prominent of the "shimmy" songs. It was recorded more than two dozen times during the 1920s, by such stars as Earl Hines, Bessie Smith, Clarence Williams, Joe Oliver, Ray Miller, and Coleman Hawkins. A generation later, during the late '40s and early '50s, the enduring tune became a mainstay in performances of Kid Ory's Creole Jazz Band at the Beverly Cavern in Los Angeles. As he introduced the song, Ory frequently implied that the tune, with different lyrics, had been written many years before by Louis Armstrong in New Orleans. I often asked Ory to sing Armstrong's original version. He steadfastly refused, claiming that the words were "too dirty."

During a radio interview with Ory in 1950, I asked him about the true origin of "Sister Kate." He told me that when Armstrong joined his New Orleans band back in 1918, the young cornetist gave him a copy of his original composition titled "Keep Off Katie's Head." Ory thought the title might have referred to Kate Townsend, a Basin Street madam who had been brutally murdered before the turn of the century. In Ory's recollection of events, Armstrong sold the tune for $50 to Clarence Williams, who was then managing Pete Lala's Cafe in Storyville, and the song, with revised title and lyrics, was published by the Williams and Piron Publishing Company. Words and music were credited to Williams' partner, Armand J. Piron. These facts were later supported by drummer Zutty Singleton, who remembered hearing Piron's orchestra play the number at the Grunewald Hotel in New Orleans.

The first recording of "I Wish I Could Shimmy Like My Sister Kate" was made by a very young Bessie Smith. The singer, then unknown, used the song on an audition record for the Okeh Phonograph Company in January 1921. The pianist on the recording was none other than Clarence Williams, who also organized the session. The record was never issued, however.

Despite this false start, dozens of recordings of "Sister Kate" soon appeared. The Original Memphis Five, an early Dixieland quintet, made the first commercial recording of "Sister Kate" on June 14,

Original sheet music for "I Wish I Could Shimmy Like
My Sister Kate." Courtesy of Harold Jacobs' Collection.

1922. This early release on the Paramount label and its subsidiary, Puritan, credited the composition to Clarence Williams. Sheet music for
"Sister Kate" soon appeared, with the Original Memphis Five's picture
on the cover and the boastful caption: "Kings of Dance Music. PIO-
NEER EXPLOITERS OF THIS NUMBER." A very popular New York group,
the Original Memphis Five was led by trumpeter Phil Napoleon and
featured influential trombonist Miff Mole. During the next few
months they recorded the tune for four different labels using pseudonyms such as Ladd's Black Aces and the Cotton Pickers to appeal to
Negro record buyers.

   In November 1922, Clarence Williams accompanied his wife, singer
Eva Taylor, on an Okeh recording of "Sister Kate." A few years later
he again attempted to record the song with Bessie Smith, this time for

Columbia, but as before, he could not obtain a usable version. Undaunted, Williams recorded the tune again in 1928, this time for QRS, featuring Joe "King" Oliver on cornet. Scores of additional recordings by diverse groups appeared in the United States, France, and England. Although "I Wish I Could Shimmy Like My Sister Kate" remained a standard among traditional jazz bands throughout the world, Louis Armstrong never received any compensation beyond the $50 for which he sold the song back in the teens. Nor did he get recognition as the original composer of the tune.

Recently, while writing liner notes for a CD release, I listened to a 1959 Kid Ory concert recorded in Copenhagen, Denmark. The program included "I Wish I Could Shimmy Like My Sister Kate"—and, to my amazement, Ory sang Armstrong's original "dirty" words. Apparently, he felt the Danish audience was sophisticated enough to hear them. The unexpurgated lyrics, transcribed from Kid Ory's vocal at that 1959 performance, went like this:

> Why don't you get off Katie's head?
> Why don't you keep out [of] Katie's bed?
> It's a shame to say this very day,
> She's like a little child at play.
> It's a shame how you're lyin' on her head.
> I thought sure you would kill her dead.
> Why don't you be nice, boy—and take my advice,
> Keep off Katie's head, I mean—get out [of] Katie's bed.

This may be the first time Satchmo's "shocking" words have appeared in print.

A PARTIAL DISCOGRAPHY OF "I WISH I COULD SHIMMY LIKE MY SISTER KATE" DURING THE '20S AND '30S

Alabama Jug Band '34—(with Willie "The Lion" Smith)—Decca 7001

Red Allen-Coleman Hawkins '33—Brunswick—(rejected)

California Ramblers '22—(Adrian Rollini)—Vocalion 14436

Bill Coleman (Paris) '38—Swing 214

*Cotton Pickers '22—Brunswick 2338

Jan Garber '28—Columbia 4935

Georgians '22—Columbia A3775

*Pseudonym for Original Memphis Five

Goofus Five '27—(Adrian Rollini)—Okeh 40767

Joe Haymes '36—Vocalion 3307

Earl Hines '29—(with Hines' vocal)—Victor 22683

Edgar Jackson (London) '32—Decca F-3307

*Jazzbo's Carolina Serenaders '22—Cameo 269

Anna Jones '23—(acc. by Fats Waller)—Paramount 12052

*Ladd's Black Aces '22—Gennett 4938

Viola McCoy with California Ramblers '27—Cameo (rejected)

Ray Miller '27—Brunswick 3829

New Orleans Feetwarmers '38—(Sidney Bechet-Carnegie Hall)—
  Vanguard VRS8523

Original Capitol Orchestra (Middlesex, Eng.) '23—Zonophone
  2355

Original Memphis Five '22—Paramount 020825, Puritan 11161

Charles Pierce, '28—Paramount 12640

Savoy Havana Band (London) '23—Columbia 3276

Boyd Senter '28—(Dorsey Bros., Eddie Lang, etc.)—Okeh 41018

Abe Small Melody Boys '23—Strong 10002

Bessie Smith '21—Okeh (rejected)

Bessie Smith '25—Columbia (rejected)

Southern Five '22—Melody 1410

*Southland Five '22—Columbia (rejected)

Muggsy Spanier '39—Bluebird B10506

Mary Straine—(Fletcher Henderson)—Black Swan 14115

Eva Taylor '22—(acc. Clarence Williams)—Okeh 4740

University Six '26—(Adrian Rollini)—Harmony 414H

Varsity Eight '27—Cameo 1280

Virginians (Paul Whiteman Group) '22—Victor 18965

Whoopee Makers '28—Columbia 14367-D

Clarence Williams '28—(Joe Oliver)—QRS R-7044

*Leona Williams' Dixie Band '22—Columbia A3713

*Pseudonym for Original Memphis Five

The World Premiere
of "Rhapsody in Blue"

Violinist Kurt Dieterle had a long and successful career as a musician, but one concert stands out above all the others he performed: As a member of the Paul Whiteman Orchestra, he helped introduce George Gershwin's "Rhapsody in Blue" to the world. The composition that came to symbolize the Jazz Age debuted on February 12, 1924, at the Aeolian Concert Hall in New York City. Nobody knew it at the time, but this performance would emancipate jazz from its "low" status and mark its arrival as a legitimate cultural form.

Whiteman had commissioned Gershwin, then just twenty-six years old, to write a serious piece illustrating how the jazz configurations that were rapidly becoming part of popular music could be employed in a concert setting. The composer responded with "Rhapsody in Blue"—the first, and probably the most significant, example of symphonic jazz ever written. Gershwin himself was the featured piano soloist at the premiere, advertised as "A Concert Performance in Jazz." (The concert's title on the program booklet was: "An Experiment in Modern Music.")

Dieterle was hired for that single event but remained with Whiteman for eleven years. He came to the job with an extensive classical background. "At the age of eleven," he later explained, "I had two scholarships offered to me in Cincinnati—at the conservatory and at the university. Both heads of the violin departments wanted me to come and live with them so they could supervise my playing, but my father thought I was too young to be away from home." Eventually, his father allowed him to join the famed Rooney's Boys of Chicago, a group of talented youngsters who played concerts in thirty-three states. He made his debut at Carnegie Hall at age seventeen, playing a Tchaikovsky concerto conducted by Christian Kriens. Dieterle was twenty-five years old at the time of the "Rhapsody" performance.

> When I joined Paul, he controlled eleven bands in New York and seventeen on the road. It was my job to enlarge the string section. The orchestra originally had only one permanent violinist. Whiteman played some violin occasionally, and there was also an accordion player who doubled. We expanded the section to six violins, two violas, and two cellos. These were all classically trained musicians—skilled players accustomed to sight-reading difficult scores.
>
> I remember, at the very first rehearsals, the brass—Henry Busse and the different players—they were such big shots. They'd come in with derby

hats, raccoon coats, and those floppy shoes, but when they had to play "Rhapsody in Blue" they didn't do so well. So those of us with a classical background had a big laugh.

Ferde Grofé was there. He had been arranging for Whiteman for some time—"Japanese Sandman," "Limehouse Blues," things like that. He did the orchestration of "Rhapsody in Blue" for twenty-three musicians. Gershwin wanted to eliminate the slow main theme that you always recognize—"*da ... da ... da ... daaaaa.*" He felt it impeded the rhapsody's momentum. Ferdé said, "No, George—that's your best theme." He was responsible for keeping that important strain in the "Rhapsody."

Contrary to popular belief, this was not the first time jazz was heard in a classical setting. Three months before the Whiteman concert, singer Eva Gauthier had included jazz-oriented songs by Irving Berlin, Jerome Kern, and Gershwin (her accompanist) in a recital. And more than a decade before that, Jim Europe directed a ragtime program at Carnegie Hall. However, neither of those events had the impact that the "Rhapsody in Blue" concert would have.

In his autobiography, Paul Whiteman described the scene before the concert:

> Fifteen minutes before the concert was to begin ... I put an overcoat over my concert clothes and slipped around to the entrance of Aeolian Hall. It was snowing, men and women were fighting to get into the door, pulling and mauling each other as they sometimes do at a baseball game, or a prize fight, or in the subway. I wondered if I had come to the right entrance. And when I saw Victor Herbert going in, I knew it was the right entrance. The next day, the ticket people said they could have sold out the house ten times over!

The Aeolian Hall program began with "Livery Stable Blues," a tune introduced seven years earlier by the Original Dixieland Jazz Band on a Victor Talking Machine Record. The twenty-three numbers that followed illustrated the advances of popular music since "Yes We Have No Bananas!" Whiteman conducted recent works by Jerome Kern, Rudolph Friml, and Victor Herbert, as well as "Limehouse Blues," "Alexander's Ragtime Band," and "Mama Loves Papa." Gershwin's "Rhapsody" appeared immediately before the closing number, "Pomp and Circumstance," a march by Sir Edward Elgar.

Dieterle clearly remembered the hushed response as clarinetist Ross Gorman began "Rhapsody in Blue" with an electrifying trill. It melted into a soaring upward slur and established the mood that continues to enchant audiences whenever the composition is performed. "George had written an ascending scale," Dieterle recalled, "and it was ex-

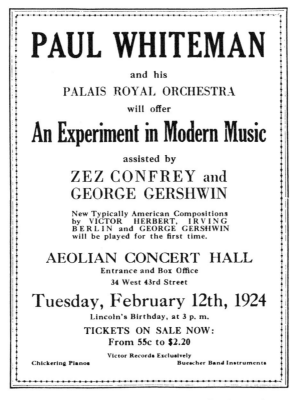

Program for the 1924 world premiere of "Rhapsody in Blue."

tremely difficult. So Ross, who could make incredibly odd sounds with his instrument, started experimenting. Finally, he just made a whooping slide up the scale right to the top. George loved it, and that's the way it's been played ever since."

Among the prominent composers and performers attending that afternoon were Mischa Elman, Jascha Heifitz, Leopold Stokowski, Igor Stravinsky, John Philip Sousa, Fritz Kreisler, and Sergei Rachmaninoff. Perhaps they came out of curiosity, but they stayed—and cheered. Jazz, the child of brothels and barrelhouses, had matured into a serious art—and a major force in American culture.

During his eleven years with Whiteman, Dieterle played alongside such jazz greats as Bix Beiderbecke, Frank Trumbauer, Arthur Rank, Steve Brown, Jack Teagarden, and the Dorseys. The Whiteman Orchestra made more than two hundred records over that period. Dieterle played on the orchestra's 1924 acoustic recording of "Rhapsody in Blue" with Gershwin and again when it was re-recorded electronically in 1927. (Nathaniel Shilkret led the orchestra when Whiteman left the studio in a dispute over the starting time.) Other memorable recordings followed:

> Paul hired Bing Crosby and Harry Rinker in 1926. The collegiate singing team from Gonzaga University in Spokane, Washington, was not too impressive—especially Bing. When they added pianist-singer Harry Barris to the act, they called themselves the "Rhythm Boys," and their fortunes took an upswing. Crosby became a nationally known vocalist after we recorded "Mississippi Mud."
>
> One of our biggest hits was "When Day Is Done." Paul had just returned from Vienna. He brought back a tune that he liked very much. It was called "Madonna, You Are Prettier Than the Sunshine." Buddy De-Sylva wrote English lyrics and changed the title. During one of our recording dates, in about 1926, Paul decided to include the European tune. We had no arrangement, so we made one up on the spot. [Arranger Bill] Challis said, "Let's make a cadenza here ... but do a string chorus first ... , then let [Henry] Busse do his thing." He played a softly muted trumpet chorus—and that's the way "When Day is Done" was recorded.
>
> When we went to Hollywood in 1929 to do the film *King of Jazz,* Harry Barris' sister, Mildred Bailey, joined us. I think she was the first girl singer with a major dance orchestra. During the next few years she became one of the most famous vocalists in the country. Mildred left the orchestra to marry xylophonist Red Norvo.
>
> Paul was very generous with his musicians. I was making $175 a week in 1928. That was a lot of money in those days. And remember, he had a payroll of about thirty-five people—including a valet.

Dieterle left the orchestra in 1935 when Whiteman accepted an offer to appear in "Jumbo," a giant attraction at the New York Hippodrome. The violinist joined André Kostelanetz and became very active in network radio, playing on *The Kraft Music Hall, The Telephone Hour, The Arthur Godfrey Show, The Jack Benny Show,* and *Gene Autry's Melody Ranch.* (Dieterle played on Autry's hit recording of "Rudolph, the Red-Nosed Reindeer.") Studio work for films, radio programs, and television shows sustained him for the next several decades.

In 1984, to celebrate the sixtieth anniversary of the "Rhapsody" concert, Maurice Peress conducted the exact program at Town Hall, just across Forty-third Street from the original site of Aeolian Hall. Dieterle, then eighty-five years old, was the only living member of the original orchestra—and, as in 1924, he occupied the first violin chair. Ivan Davis played Gershwin's piano part in "Rhapsody in Blue."

*Paul Whiteman listening to his concertmaster,
Kurt Dieterle, playing his newly discovered
instrument, the "Violiphone."*

Dieterle maintained a busy schedule well into his nineties. His activities included weekly recording sessions for television's *L.A. Law* and occasional commercial recording dates. At least two mornings a week, he played golf at the Wilshire Country Club. He valued the memories from his long and successful career, none more so than the "Rhapsody in Blue" premiere.

> The Aeolian Hall concert changed everything—including my way of life. I had been hoping to become a concert violinist, but from that day I was a bandman all the way—I was in demand. Some of the highbrows back then thought this [jazz] would be just a passing phase—that it would soon be forgotten. How wrong they were! I was lucky to be there—and I will always be grateful for it.
>
> It was a unique experience, especially for a classical musician, to be closely associated with several of the Jazz Age's most important participants. Bix [Beiderbecke] was very intelligent. He had a great sense of humor. What a wonderful sound he got from his cornet. His improvisations were beautiful—but, as you know, he drank too much. Our arranger, Bill Challis, transcribed several of his solos for Charles Margulis, who played

next to him in the trumpet section. When Bix was unable to handle his solo, he would nod to Charles, who played the chorus intended for Bix.

Dieterle was ninety-two when I interviewed him; he died in November 1994 at the age of ninety-five. A few years later, on February 12, I happened to be editing my transcript of the interview for the Smithsonian Oral History Archives when I heard the sounds of "Rhapsody in Blue" coming from my desk radio. A local station was playing pianist Oscar Levant's recording of the Gershwin composition to commemorate the anniversary of the Aeolian Hall concert—the day the world heard a jazz masterpiece for the first time. Kurt Dieterle would have been proud.

"Relaxin' at the Touro"— Memories of Muggsy Spanier

Several years ago, while in New Orleans attending the annual Jazz and Heritage Festival, I visited the Touro Infirmary, made famous by cornetist Muggsy Spanier's hit song "Relaxin' at the Touro." The record appeared in 1939, shortly after the musician recovered from a medical emergency that nearly cost him his life. Spanier, thirty-one at the time, had been rushed to the emergency room suffering from high fever, a perforated gastric ulcer, and advanced peritonitis. He was playing cornet in the Ben Pollack Orchestra at the Blue Room of the Roosevelt Hotel (now the Fairmont). The Touro house staff summoned a young surgeon, Dr. Alton Ochsner, who stabilized all vital signs and performed three life-saving surgeries. The grateful Spanier wrote "Relaxin' at the Touro" while convalescing in his hospital bed.

After his recovery, Spanier formed his own eight-piece group, the Ragtime Band. The group made sixteen popular recordings for Bluebird Records, helping to revive New Orleans jazz in the '40s. These recordings, which have since been reissued numerous times, are still cherished by collectors throughout the world. "Relaxin' at the Touro" was the Ragtime Band's biggest hit, selling more than a million copies and assuring Muggsy Spanier a permanent place in jazz history.

Spanier got his nickname at age fourteen for his devotion to New York Giants manager John "Muggsy" McGraw. He was a master with the plunger mute given to him by his idol, King Oliver, during the early '20s. "When I was a kid in Chicago, I used to stand on an apple crate

*Trumpeter Muggsy Spanier (left) with the
author, 1965. Photo by Darnell Howard.*

in the alley behind the Lincoln Gardens to hear Joe Oliver's Creole Jazz
Band," he later recalled. One of only a handful of truly original cornetists, Spanier had a soulful, straightforward, immediately identifiable
style. He could be quick-tempered and irascible, traits that surfaced in
a 1950 altercation with jazz critic Leonard Feather. Spanier confronted
the writer outside a Chicago nightclub to complain about a caustic review. After a vehement exchange, the diminutive cornetist floored his
antagonist with a lightning-quick punch. At a recording session the following day, Spanier recorded an instrumental tune he titled "Feather
Brain." It became a permanent part of his repertoire; when he introduced it, Spanier always slyly dedicated it to Leonard Feather.

    After his close brush with death in 1939, Muggsy Spanier enjoyed
two decades of relatively good health. But when age began to catch up
with him in the 1960s, he again turned to the doctor who had saved
his life at the Touro: Alton Ochsner. "Whenever Muggsy had a medical

problem, he liked to streak back to New Orleans to get fixed," wrote
Bob Morris in a 1990 issue of *Second Line.*

> He showed up at Ochsner's Foundation Hospital in January 1965 after
> shortness of breath (actuated by acute pulmonary congestion) cut short a
> lucrative tour.
>   The Ochsner team tested his heart and lungs. Readers of the daily paper
> were startled to see a photo of Muggsy blowing a cornet while lying on his
> back in the hospital. He was using just one hand because a long thin tube
> had been run through a vein in his left arm all the way to his heart. As
> Muggsy blew his horn, doctors, watching an X-ray screen, observed the ef-
> fect on his heart action.

According to *Time,* Spanier played strains of "St. Louis Blues" and
"When the Saints Go Marching In" while the catheter was in his heart.
The final diagnosis: Spanier was advised to wait six months before
blowing his horn again. But the very next day, upon learning that a
New Orleans funeral parade was scheduled, the cornetist rapidly
dressed, grabbed his horn, and took a taxi downtown to join the On-
ward Brass Band. The crisp sound of his horn echoed through the
French Quarter.

    Ochsner's trailblazing technology led to innovative procedures that
now routinely save the lives of heart patients throughout the world.
Spanier was grateful for the outstanding medical treatment he received.
After the much-publicized heart test, he wrote a thank-you song for his
surgeon, titled "Oh! Dr. Ochsner!" He also used his musical talents to
support various medical causes. "Shortly after I returned to Sausalito
[his California home] following that heart experiment," he told me
some years later, "the Louisiana Heart Association had a fund-raising
event in New Orleans. They arranged a telephone hookup with a head-
set, and I played at home into the phone with the Crawford-Ferguson
Night Owls, who were in the Royal Orleans Ballroom. It worked out
very well."

    After his heart problems in the mid-'60s, Spanier made sporadic ap-
pearances and took on a few students, but his performing days were
over. He never truly regained his health, and on February 12, 1967, at
the age of sixty-one, he died in his sleep.

Established in 1852, the Touro Infirmary is the oldest private hospital
in New Orleans. This medical landmark had a humble beginning, with
an initial staff of four doctors. They worked in a riverfront house donated by Judah Touro, a son of a rabbi, who came to New Orleans at

the beginning of the nineteenth century. Now located in uptown New Orleans, the modern facility has hundreds of staff doctors and thousands of employees.

I arrived on a Saturday afternoon, intending to photograph a plaque in the lobby commemorating Muggsy Spanier's famous 1939 stay. No plaque was in evidence, and the Touro office staff was out for the weekend. An attendant suggested I contact executive secretary Rochelle James after the weekend. I phoned her the following Monday to request a photo of the plaque. She explained, quite emphatically, that there is no such marker. Tourists have been looking for the item for years, she told me, but it never existed. She faxed me a sheet prepared by the hospital's marketing department that explained the misunderstanding. It read: "Muggsy's tune ['Relaxin' at the Touro'] turned the Infirmary into a tourist attraction. When the LP reissue of Muggsy's *Great Sixteen* appeared in the mid-1950s [RCA Victor LPM-1295], notes on the album cover said, 'The original record is still at Touro, where you can see it imbedded in the lobby wall.' Jazz enthusiasts who came to see it were sadly disappointed."

A month later, I received a letter from Catherine C. Kahn, archivist of the Touro Infirmary. She wrote:

> There actually is a plaque on the walls of the Touro honoring Muggsy. It reads: "In This Room In 1939 The Late Jazz Great Francis J. 'Muggsy' Spanier Convalesced And Wrote 'Relaxin' at the Touro.'" This plaque is located on the seventh floor in an elevator lobby, as the actual room no longer exists. What has caused the confusion is a story that was published on the back of a record album which said a gold record of "Relaxin' at the Touro" was imbedded in the main lobby wall. This is not true.

I found the plaque on my next visit to New Orleans; it was there on the Touro Infirmary's seventh floor, right next to the service elevator. The special marker honors the memory of a legendary musician.

A fine English band honors that memory in a different way: by giving life to Spanier's music. The group, Muggsy Remembered, is led by cornetist Alan Gresty and clarinetist Brian White. Gresty has faithfully mastered Spanier's torrid cup mute style, and the band ably re-creates those wonderful Bluebird recordings in British music halls and at jazz music festivals in the United States.

Shortly after Muggsy died, Ruth Spanier asked me to help her dispose of a large cabinet of music that included the arrangements used by her husband's Ragtime Band. There were no written cornet parts— Muggsy never learned to read music! I kept the papers in my basement for several years before Ruth donated the material to the Institute of Jazz Studies in Rutgers, New Jersey, where they now repose.

If you visit New Orleans, be sure to look for the Touro Infirmary. Take the elevator to the seventh floor to see the "missing" plaque near the service elevator. If you listen carefully, you might hear the spectral tone of a softly muted cornet.

It is a privilege to have known Muggsy. He was a frail little man but a giant of jazz.

Spud Murphy

When I was in high school, *Down Beat* and *Metronome* magazines (which I read religiously) used to carry regular advertisements for stock jazz-band arrangements published by the Robbins Music Corporation. They cost seventy-five cents per song and included individual instrumental parts to accommodate small or large groups. I remember those ads well, particularly the distinctive name of the arranger: Spud Murphy.

Throughout the swing era, Murphy's brilliant arrangements brought fame and prosperity to any number of prominent bandleaders. He was well known among his peers and highly respected by generations of musicians. Robbins Music and Leo Feist, Inc., published more than three hundred of Murphy's stock arrangements in the 1930s and '40s. Though out of print for years, they are still being played by orchestras throughout the world—an impressive testimony to Murphy's writing skills.

Murphy was born in Berlin, Germany, in 1908 and reared in Utah. "I really didn't have any musical training," he said in a 1992 interview. "When I was eight years old, I wanted to play in the local boys' band, but they didn't want to bother with me. I kept annoying them until, finally, the bandleader handed me an old 'peck' horn, an E-flat alto—a beat-up thing. I taught myself how to play it so I could get in the band." (Incidentally, the bandleader was Professor E. W. Nichols, father of famed jazz star Red Nichols.) When queried about the source of his nickname, he said, "I'm asked that all the time. It seems that nobody knows, but everybody should. In Ireland they call potatoes 'Murphys,' and where I come from they call them 'Spuds,' so it's just double-talk."

Murphy began his professional career in 1925 as half of a two-piece "orchestra" working for tips in a Mexican border town. His first big-time job was playing saxophone in Jimmy Joy's orchestra in the mid-'20s. "I heard the band on a local radio show," he recalled. "It was called, 'Jimmy's Joys'—his name was Jim Maloney. MCA [Music Corp. of America] began booking them and insisted on having a leader's name—so it became Jimmy Joy and his Orchestra. I played saxophone and wrote some of my first arrangements with that band."

Soon hired by Jan Garber as a saxophonist-arranger, Murphy found himself playing next to the legendary clarinetist Frank Teschemacher. As his arranging skills became known, Murphy moved through the ranks of swing-era orchestras playing in the reed sections and writing their arrangements. In 1932 he assembled a band for Mal Hallett that included Jack Jenny and Jack Teagarden on trombones, Toots Mondello on alto sax, pianist Frankie Carle, and Gene Krupa on drums. After a year with Hallett, he decided to strike out on his own and headed for New York to establish a career as a freelance arranger. To keep track of his progress, he listed his writings in a ledgerbook. The first entry, dated October 12, 1933, read: "Arrived in New York, broke. My intentions are to see if I can make a living for my family and myself while arranging music. Tried the same thing last year and failed. Well, here goes!"

Murphy filled page after page in his ledgerbook; when he got to 585 arrangements, he stopped keeping track. "I figured I had made it by then and decided not to continue the entries," he shrugged. Among the arrangements he listed were several that became hit recordings for such well-known bandleaders as Isham Jones, Joe Haymes, Vincent Lopez, Buddy Rogers, Ozzie Nelson, and Freddy Martin. He wrote more than a hundred sets of charts for Benny Goodman and seventy-four for Glen Gray's Casa Loma Orchestra. Fletcher Henderson, who was himself writing for Goodman, commissioned Murphy to arrange several numbers for the Henderson orchestra. When Hal Kemp, leader of a top-ranked "sweet" band, decided to restyle his format in 1940, he engaged Spud to write a new set of band arrangements stressing the elements of swing. He sadly recalled, "The day I reported for work, Kemp died as a result of an automobile accident."

Asked how he could write without formal piano training, Murphy laughed and said: "Arrangers are born, not made. You either are one or you aren't. I knew the instruments. I could play flute, oboe, bassoon, saxophone, trumpet, and valve trombone. I played 'arranger's piano'—I plunked a few notes." His successful formula for the Robbins Music stocks? "I had no set method in arranging. I interpreted each tune as I felt it. A good 'stock' has to be melodic enough to please the song's publisher, rhythmic enough to please the average band, and simple enough so that any group can read it at sight."

In addition to arranging, Murphy led his own moderately successful orchestra in the late '30s. He arranged and recorded Ray Noble's "Cherokee" before the composer's own version was issued—and three months before Charlie Barnet made the song into a smash hit. The band also recorded Murphy's arrangement of "Quaker City Jazz" a year and a half before it was committed to wax by bandleader Jan Savitt, who wrote the tune and used it as a theme. The CD *An Anthology of Big Band Swing 1930–1955* (Decca GRD-2-629) includes Murphy's 1938 orchestra playing his progressive arrangement of David Rose's "Transcontinental." In his definitive book *The Big Bands* (Macmillan Company, 1967), George Simon succinctly describes Murphy's band as "an avant-garde outfit which fascinated the musicians who heard it, but failed to attract any appreciable segment of the paying public."

Of all his accomplishments, Murphy took most pride in his Equal Interval System, a course of instruction he developed for advanced music students. "The course is a system of horizontal composition based on equal intervals—an original method of creating and developing a new world of sound," he noted in 1992. "It is contained in a dozen large volumes—four hundred and some pages in one volume alone. I teach two days a week in my home. I have for the last forty years. I don't have many graduates because I don't have too many students, and it's a long course. It takes about five years to go through it. But all of my graduates are working—every one is doing fine." Among those who completed the difficult program are Irving Ashby, Walter Bishop, Jr., Buddy Collette, Abe Most, Tommy Mancini, Gerald Wiggins, and Oscar Peterson.

In 1990 the Los Angeles Jazz Society presented Murphy with its Jazz Educator Award for his outstanding contribution to the professional music community. He has received many accolades over the years but, like any great teacher, takes more pride in the achievements of his students than in the honors accorded himself.

"If a teacher has one outstanding student out of a hundred," he said, "he or she can be considered a successful educator. I can proudly say that all of my students have been outstanding—most of them are millionaires."

That is quite a proud achievement—especially for a man who never took a lesson in his life.

A Memorable Jack Teagarden Record Date

The Jump Record Company was among the few independent firms treading the unprofitable waters of pure jazz during the 1940s. Despite appeals from collectors, the major record companies steadfastly refused to reissue the wealth of classic jazz material held in their vaults, and newly recorded jazz material was almost impossible to find. In 1944, producers Clive Acker and Ed Kocher attempted to fill the void, investing their savings to establish the Jump label. Their aspiration: to provide frustrated fans all over the world with new recordings by noted jazz artists. Eventually other independent record companies joined Jump, and traditional jazz finally blossomed into full resurgence in the early 1950s. But that comeback might never have happened without the courage and foresight of Acker and Kocher. Those old Jump 78s, now rare collector's items, are cherished by those of us who still have the original issues.

In February 1950, Clive Acker invited me to attend a Jump recording session featuring Charlie LaVere's Chicago Loopers, with guest artist Jack Teagarden. Writing in *Jazz Journal*, Steve Voce said: "Teagarden is probably the most gigantic of all the giants of jazz—an acknowledged leader on his instrument and an inventor of great brilliance and technical accomplishment." At the time of the session, Teagarden was in town to play an engagement with Louis Armstrong, who was appearing with his All-Stars at the Bal Tabarin in nearby Gardena. Acker and Kocher were fortunate and very pleased to have the famed trombonist join the roster of jazz greats who had previously appeared on their innovative label.

The session took place at Radio Recorders, a small Hollywood studio on Santa Monica Boulevard. When I arrived, Kocher and Acker were seated with an engineer in a tiny control booth, looking through a glass panel. I stood next to photographer Ed O'Shaughnessy and waited quietly for the session to start. The four-man front line occupied the center of the room. Clarinetist Matty Matlock and tenor saxophonist Jack Chaney (who had come to California a dozen years earlier to join the Ben Pollack band) were seated at a single microphone.

Jack Teagarden during a February 1950 recording date for Jump Records. Photo by Ed O'Shaugnessey.

Facing them, and standing on the other side of the mike, were cornetist Rico Vallese, making his recording debut, and the great Jack Teagarden. The members of the rhythm section, seated with their backs facing the control booth window, included Nick Fatool at the drums, Country Washburne (a veteran of Ted Weems' orchestra) on bass and tuba, and George Van Eps on guitar.

The leader, pianist Charlie LaVere, had helped launch the Jump series six years earlier; this was his fourth recording session with his Chicago Loopers, Jump's best-selling group. Acker credited the band's success to LaVere, whose career spanned a good segment of jazz history. He had previously recorded with Jack Teagarden in 1933, and he now kept busy accompanying Bing Crosby and Dick Haynes in Los Angeles film and radio studios. Matlock and Fatool participated on twelve Chicago Looper recordings.

After a quick mike check, the engineer indicated he was ready. Teagarden loosened his tie (emblazoned with a large "T") and awaited La-Vere's nodding downbeat. The session began. For the next several hours, I witnessed one of jazz's most memorable sessions. They recorded "It's All in Your Mind," "A Monday Date," "Lover," and "Love Lies." The latter two recordings are now acknowledged as jazz classics.

Teagarden set the rapid tempo for "Lover." His carefully molded phrases and technical control transformed the popular 1933 waltz into an exuberant four-beat extravaganza. Except for Matty Matlock's impeccable clarinet solo on the bridge of the last chorus, "Lover" was a Teagarden showcase. He deftly explored the descending chromatics of Richard Rodgers' popular composition. The final eight bars, prodded by Fatool's appropriate punctuations and Teagarden's searing tailgate break, left us breathless. After a brief silence and a click from O'Shaughnessy's Speed Graphic, the band burst into applause. I glanced through the control booth window and saw a broad grin on Clive Acker's face. I am sure that grin reappeared whenever Clive replayed "Lover," the masterpiece we watched Jack Teagarden create that afternoon in 1950.

"Love Lies," presented in a jewel-like ballad arrangement, featured an equally masterful performance by "Big T." I stood at his elbow, relishing his casual inventiveness and melodic phrasing. After the session, I asked him about the beautiful tune. He said, "I heard that number for the first time back in Texas in 1921. I have no idea who wrote it— or if has ever been recorded before."

The true genesis of "Love Lies" remains an enigma. At various times, songwriting credit has erroneously been assigned to Terry Shand, Earl Hines, and others. Pianist Ralph Sutton, one of few musicians to include the lovely melody in his repertoire, did some research and learned that the music was originally published in Los Angeles in 1923 by Dean Rogers, with lyrics attributed to Harry Kerr. Later, Sutton found a piece of sheet music published in London in 1928 by the Lawrence Wright Music Company, which attributed words and music to Carl Kellard. The verse in that version of "Love Lies" differed from the one Charlie LaVere arranged for the Jump date. This fact seems to justify the theory of Stephen LaVere, Charlie's son, who feels his father rewrote the verse the afternoon of the recording session. But what of Jack Teagarden's recollection of hearing the song in 1921? Perhaps one day jazz scholars will unearth the exact origin of the arcane tune.

With assistance from collectors around the world, I have since accumulated a ream of contradictory material about the roots of "Love Lies." I discovered, among other things, that the title appears on sev-

eral different songs. Frank Sinatra recorded an unrelated number
called "Love Lies" with Tommy Dorsey's orchestra in the 1940s. Years
later, the title appeared on another tune recorded by heavy-metal rock
star Jon Bon Jovi.

Whatever its true heritage, this lovely version of "Love Lies" may be
the definitive Jack Teagarden recording of all time. It stands tall amid
the hundreds of wonderful records he made during a long career.
Ralph Sutton, who learned the song from Teagarden years ago, continues to play it for audiences throughout the world. Trombonist Bob
Havens, an avowed Teagarden disciple, frequently duplicates the challenging Jump Record versions of "Love Lies" and "Lover" as sincere
tributes to his mentor.

Many years later, Acker marveled at the professionalism displayed
by jazz musicians of that era. "Think about making records without
rehearsals," he said. "Often the musicians had not met or never had
played together. There were no written arrangements—just a few notations conceived on the spot. Perhaps they would run through an introduction or an ending. Otherwise it was, 'Let's go! Let's see how it
sounds!' And it usually sounded great on the first take. Charlie made it
happen—he made it fun, not a chore."

Driving home from that unforgettable session, I heard "Lover" over
and over in my mind. Impressions of the wonderful experience occupied my thoughts. Although fifty years have passed, I can still conjure
the sound of Jack Teagarden's eloquent horn, often graced with brilliant clusters of sixteenth notes—dramatic proof that the lip trills can
be quicker than the slide. And I can still hear Rico Vallese's distinctive
cornet playing; the four tunes played during the session were the only
recordings he ever made. I will never forget Vallese's warm legato chorus gently following Jack's vocal on Charlie LaVere's theme, "It's All in
Your Mind."

I also remember Country Washburne's four-bar tuba quotes, fram-
ing "A Monday Date" like a pair of burnished brass bookends, as well
as Matty Matlock's fine clarinet and George Van Eps' formidable
seven-string guitar flurries. I certainly remember the tasty drumming
by Nick Fatool, who, now in retirement, remains my favorite small-
band drummer.

Few jazz masters have achieved the stature of Jack Teagarden, considered by most critics to be the finest of all jazz trombonists. He died
more than thirty years ago, yet most of today's trombonists, perhaps

unwittingly, continue to reflect his brilliant playing. Teagarden's influence still ripples through our jazz.

Nick Fatool and I are the only survivors of that memorable recording date in February 1950. Photographer Ed O'Shaughnessy died in September 1999.

The Duke Ellington Sacred Music Concert—New Orleans, 1970

On a humid Sunday afternoon in New Orleans in 1970, Lucille and I followed a steady stream of jazz lovers down St. Ann Street toward the Municipal Auditorium. Entering the large building, we were refreshed by cool air and cheered by the anticipation of hearing the culminating event of the 1970 New Orleans Jazz and Heritage Festival: Duke Ellington's famed Sacred Music Concert. This was its first performance in the city that gave birth to jazz. The liturgical masterpiece had premiered five years earlier in Grace Cathedral, San Francisco.

Ellington introduced the program with his usual charm and warm sincerity. Standing mid-stage, flanked by the full orchestra, a thirty-five member choir, and five vocal soloists, he said very softly: "During this program, you will hear a variety of musical statements without words. If the phrase has six tones, I think you should know it symbolizes the first six syllables in the Bible, 'In the beginning, God.' It's our theme—we say it many ways." Then the music began, and the audience, reverently silent at first, became deeply engrossed in the sounds that filled the auditorium. Before the afternoon was over, we were clapping our hands and stamping our feet.

In "Praise God," Harry Carney led the way with stirring choruses of fiery Hebraic chants. He utilized the full range of his baritone sax, and his beautifully controlled tones injected a majestic quality to the number. The sound of Carney's horn reminded us of his important contribution to this orchestra for more than forty-five years. "Supreme Being" featured the Concert Choir of New Orleans, conducted by twenty-two-year-old Ellington protégé Roscoe Gill, Jr. Cootie Williams, playing the role of Shepherd of the Night Flock, coupled an unsmiling visage with growling trumpet sounds.

When he introduced "Heaven," Duke avowed, "Heaven to be—is the ultimate decree!" The lovely soprano voice of Devonne Gardner blended with the pure gliding tones of Johnny Hodges' alto sax to create silky curtains of sound. Introducing the following number, Ellington said solemnly: "This next portion is about a word. It's a very large word—a gigantic word—but it's actually a small word. This word is used a lot—sometimes it's overused. The word is 'freedom.'" The hand-clapping spiritual that emerged was a three-part musical conversation, with Hodges, tenor saxophonist Paul Gonsalves, and the choir exchanging gospel truths. Before the reprise, a somber Ellington paid tribute to colleague Billy Strayhorn, who had recently died. "Billy lived by four basic freedoms," he said. "Freedom from hate—unconditionally. Freedom from self-pity. Freedom from the fear of doing something that might possibly help someone else more than him—and freedom from the kind of pride that could make a man feel he was better than his brother."

Ellington introduced "Meditation" as "a selection by our piano player." The Duke's meditative and sensitive solo was tastefully accompanied by Joe Benjamin's resonant bowed bass. Seated at the keyboard, surrounded by a stage full of musicians and singers, Ellington became completely engulfed in the music. His relaxed and thoughtful harmonies, seemingly created at that moment, cast a spell over the attentive audience. When the delicate piece ended, several seconds of silence preceded the clamorous applause.

As a sharp contrast, "Fire and Brimstone Sermonette" transported us on a wild ride through a maze of melodic intersections. Ellington described them as "tremendous, insidious crossings where all sorts of temptations are ready to trap the unwary traveler. The pavement is slippery; the going is rough; people are dressed like friends. So continue down that straight and narrow highway—down at the end—where all ends end: 'Just Before the Beginning.'" Our guide on this perilous journey was articulate drummer Rufus Jones, whose furious solo was unexpected but appropriate to the musical text. Jones' explosive technique made a definitive statement. With sheer power and tenacity, he seemed to blast through those dark intersections Ellington so eloquently described—and triumphantly entered the brighter world beyond.

Evoking earlier vocals by Adelaide Hall, the willowy Patricia Hoy came to the microphone for "Wordless Melody," described by Ellington as "our attempt to capture the essence of that original nonconformist, Jesus Christ." "Don't Go Down on Your Knees to Pray Until You Have Forgiven Everyone" featured a rousing liaison between the orchestra and the choir, which merged to form a celestial background for Tony Watkins' vocal. This was Ellington's purposeful prayer of forgiveness for the sins of humanity.

The exciting finale, "Praise God and Dance," drew its lyrics from the 150th Psalm. Sung by Nancie Lund, it featured several instrumental soloists and a group of grotesquely painted bodies dancing down the aisles. The writhing forms, scantily clad in shimmering bits of thin fabric, fluttered and vibrated in time with the spirited music. The orchestra abruptly ended a wailing riff—and the choir shouted: "In the beginning—God!"

The entire audience rose to its feet, shouting approval. The applause continued while each soloist was introduced. When Ellington returned for a final bow, the old auditorium quivered with applause and joy. The triumphal work brought down the curtain on the 1970 New Orleans Jazz and Heritage Festival.

It also, sadly, brought down the curtain on the career of the great Johnny Hodges. We soon learned that we had witnessed the saxophone master's final appearance; he died, suddenly and unexpectedly, during a dental procedure the following week (presumably of a heart attack) at the age of sixty-four. The stellar saxophonist had not played a major role in the Sacred Music Concert; I remember seeing him seated majestically in the reed section, seemingly bored, his arms folded against his golden Selmer horn. The warm tones emerging from that beautiful instrument had thrilled millions of fans since he joined Ellington back in 1928.

My many memories of the world-famous alto saxophonist include a little incident that occurred on a flight from Los Angeles to New Orleans. By coincidence, the entire Ellington orchestra was on board. Duke sat in first class, and the band members were scattered among the tourist seats. Hodges, seated across the aisle from us, furtively entered the forward section and returned with a bottle of champagne and a handful of glasses. With a broad grin, he walked through our cabin dispensing the wine. After repeated trips to the first-class section, he purloined enough champagne to serve us all. Our flight to New Orleans was brightened by Hodges' humorous antics.

Unlike some of Duke's serious efforts, the Sacred Music Concert retained a hearty jazz flavor and a strong imprint of Ellingtonia. Directing one of his most impressive works, he led us through a series of emotional experiences, revealing his personal form of worship. Here, at last, was a golden altar at which a resolute agnostic could reverently kneel. This was a sincere expression of Duke Ellington's faith in music: "In the beginning, God."

Dick Hyman's Historic Direct-to-CD Recording Session

Through the years, the evolution of jazz has paralleled the advance of recording technology. From their early years, each benefited from the other. Each successive generation of jazz musicians encountered a new generation of recording technologies. Together, they progressed from cylinder records through 78 and 45 rpm discs, long-playing records, hi-fi, stereo, reel-to-reel and cassette tape, and digitally recorded compact discs.

It was my privilege to be present at one of the breakthrough recording sessions along this evolutionary journey: the unprecedented direct-to-CD production of *Dick Hyman Plays Duke Ellington,* issued by Reference Recordings (RR-50DCD). The music was originally performed in a house in West Los Angeles on March 24 and 25, 1991. The live renditions were digitally encoded and stored in a computer; seventeen months later, the digitized data were used to activate a reproducing piano, and those sounds were transmitted via satellite directly to the CD pressing plant.

Dick Hyman was the ideal musician for this project. He has long been hailed by his peers as the most versatile and brilliant pianist on the jazz scene. A decade ago, Leonard Feather wrote in the *Los Angeles Times:* "He can outswing any man in any house, in any style from ragtime and stride to the School of What's Happening Now."

I drove Dick Hyman from his hotel to inventor Wayne Stahnke's home studio for the sessions. A specially equipped C-7SE Yamaha grand piano occupied a large portion of Stahnke's living room. Three heavy cables like giant umbilical cords joined the instrument to a locked metal "black box" nearby labeled "STAHNKE'S REPRODUCING PIANO." Here, in admittedly oversimplified form, is a description of the highly technical procedure:

As Hyman played, a set of optical sensors below the piano's keyboard would carefully analyze the slightest movements, scanning every key eight hundred times a second. Additional sensors were positioned to assess the speed at which the piano's hammers encountered the strings, and the instrument's pedal action was similarly measured and the tiniest variation monitored. These delicate sensors would capture Hyman's performance in full detail, picking up every emotion and subtle touch. Noise from outside—traffic, birds chirping, children at play—would not affect the encoding process. The music would flow directly from Hyman's finger tips into Wayne Stahnke's mysterious black box for digital encoding. After meticulous editing and sequencing, the data would be transferred to a computer's floppy disc. Eventually, the data would activate a reproducing piano in a studio environment, and those sounds would be transmitted directly to the CD masters.

Stahnke's innovations represent the latest achievement in a 250-year process. Mechanical musical devices—music boxes, carousel organs, and gigantic mechanical "orchestras"—date to the eighteenth century. These automated music-makers eventually gave rise to the pneumatically operated player piano, which provided home and public entertainment during the nineteenth and early twentieth centuries. At the time, these instruments represented the epitome of automatic musical reproduction; however, their technical limitations resulted in a bland tonality, never capturing the nuances of a live performance. In 1905, German inventor Edwin Welte developed the first system for re-creating touch and dynamics; by the early 1920s, piano rolls could produce a range of over one hundred levels of dynamics.

Stahnke's system encodes more than a thousand. It also measures the pedals' positions in gradations from 1 to 256—not merely on or off.

THE ENCODING

Stahnke's intricate technology rendered many of the customary engineering complexities obsolete. Hyman was free from the distractions and stresses found under normal studio conditions. There were no tapes, no intimidating microphones, and no tedious sound checks; the pianist could relax and concentrate on his playing. Hyman casually occupied the piano bench, and Stahnke sat at a nearby computer. I was the only other person present.

During the previous evenings, Hyman had appeared at a local club, fine-tuning his Ellington program before live audiences. He was relaxed and ready for the session, but the keyboard felt cold to him. Before beginning, he carefully warmed the piano keys with a hair dryer.

I listened as he played several extraordinary Ellington compositions. Not pleased with the initial efforts, Dick repeated each number, recording as many as six takes. When he was at last satisfied with a performance, he would rise from the piano bench and listen to the "playback." At a command from Stahnke's computer, the piano instantly replayed the different versions. After selecting the best take, Dick, grinning with approval, would return to the piano and continue the program.

Hyman had selected a group of songs representing several periods in Ellington's long career. They included: "Doin' the Voom Voom," probably never before recorded as a piano solo; "Jubilee Stomp," one of many Ellington themes based on the harmonization of "Tiger Rag"; and the beautifully titled "On a Turquoise Cloud," an ethereal composition known for Kay Davis' soaring wordless vocal and the memorable trombone chorus by Lawrence Brown. A hint of a waltz tempo added to the romanticism of "Prelude to a Kiss."

After lunch, Hyman decorated "Day Dream," Billy Strayhorn's beautiful collaboration with the Duke, with gorgeous filigree runs. Following a flawless first take, Dick muttered, "Not bad. Not bad at all. I better do it again." He put a sensuous, undulating bass introduction on his delicate portrayal of "Echoes of Harlem," then admitted: "I never played it before." I enjoyed the partly atonal rendering of "The Clothed Woman," which Hyman had transcribed note-for-note from the Ellington recording. The humorous "Tonk" and expressive "Drop Me Off in Harlem" wrapped up the session.

Pausing only for brief lunch breaks, Hyman and Stahnke completed the encoding procedure over three productive days. Hyman's masterful conceptions of Duke Ellington's gems now resided somewhere in Stahnke's black box.

THE RECORDING

The actual recording of this superb program took place on Sunday, August 25, 1992—seventeen months after Hyman's performances entered Stahnke's black box. The site was the auditorium of the fifty-year-old Santa Ana High School, about forty miles away from Stankhe's cottage in West Los Angeles. It was selected for its legendary acoustic qualities. Dick Hyman was there in spirit only.

A nine-foot Bosendorfer 275SE concert grand piano arrived from Indiana just in time for this eventful recording. A piano technician stood by in case adjustments might be necessary. This unique $170,000 instrument, designed by Stahnke and handcrafted in Vienna, is the most sensitive automatic piano in the world, engineered to recreate any performance in exact detail, with every nuance of sound and sensitivity.

An IBM computer transmitted digital information into the piano's "brain," and the keys responded exactly as they had when Hyman played at the sessions in Stahnke's living room. As the sounds emerged, their waveforms were transformed into a digital bi-stream and carried via a thin wire through a complex control panel to a truck parked outside. A large microwave saucer on the vehicle's roof beamed the signal directly to a mastering machine at Disctronics Manufacturing's plant several miles away. Each of the resulting limited-edition CDs represented a "first generation" recording of the fourteen Ellington tunes Dick Hyman had played in Wayne Stahnke's studio more than a year earlier.

Although there is a popular conception that digital recordings do not vary from copy to copy, many serious audiophiles are convinced that digits are often transposed or altered during production. Reference Recordings' unprecedented procedure eliminated all copying and manipulation of the original material, ensuring a pure reproduction of the virgin sound.

While a relaxed, casual ambience reigned during the encoding process, the actual recording session was laden with tension. The auditorium's backstage area was a cluttered maze of wires and cables connecting control panels, monitors, and various electronic devices. Keith Johnson, Reference Recordings' chief engineer, was at the helm; he had designed all the elaborate technical conduits between the piano and the disc mastering machine. Another engineer, "Pflash" Pflaumer, was standing by. Producer J. Tamblyn "Tam" Henderson, president of Reference Recordings, carefully assessed every detail. Jim Turner was also there to represent Bosendorfer Pianos of Vienna. Stahnke stood silently off to one side, a mere spectator at this final phase of the complicated cycle he began months earlier.

There were several delays before the recording began, as the sensitive microphones kept detecting mysterious sounds. These were eventually traced to a ticking school clock and a noisy toilet. The stage manager cushioned the clock and locked the toilet. The glistening piano stood alone on the dark stage, facing an empty auditorium. Its keys were shrouded with a heavily padded blanket to muffle the slightest sound of key movement. The piano lid was fully raised, and micro-phones stood on overhead stands. No one was permitted on stage dur-ing the recording process. and complete silence was necessary back-stage, as the microphones could pick up sounds on the other side of the curtain. The mastering plant technicians called to say they were ready, and the launching countdown began: "Five … four … three … two … one."

At the final count, Tam Henderson touched a few computer keys, and the strains of "Jubilee Stomp" filled the room. The sound was crisp and bright. It was hard to believe that Dick Hyman was not there.

The engineers carefully watched the monitors to make sure that the computer was accurately activating the piano's keys and all dial set-tings were correct. They seemed relaxed as the music continued. Tune after tune emerged from the huge piano, and the broad beam on Tam Henderson's face reflected his rapture.

Suddenly, the phone rang. It was the mastering plant—a major glitch had occurred. Johnson halted the computer, and the piano be-came silent. The problem was diagnosed as a "time code drift," a flaw that would cause an error during playback. We had to start all over. The producer's rapturous expression faded.

After another countdown, "Jubilee Stomp" again flowed from the piano on the adjacent stage. We listened to each number with mount-ing tension, dreading another call from the mastering plant that might necessitate yet another replay of the entire program. The tunes we heard previously rolled by again without interruption; then the rest of the program played out. Finally, after sixty-one minutes, the piano stopped. The room remained silent momentarily; then the phone rang. It was the mastering plant, calling with the happy news that the process was successfully completed.

An audible sigh broke the silence, followed by a loud burst of ap-plause. The broad smile returned to Henderson's face. The historic recording was finally completed.

A PERSONAL VIEW
OF THE MUSICIANS

It has been my privilege and good fortune to know many outstanding jazz musicians personally. Some of them began their careers when jazz was in its infancy and helped to create the genre. Others came later, during the heyday of the Jazz Age, when the New Orleans sound captivated audiences throughout the nation and the world. And still others reached their prime in the revival years, when traditional jazz reclaimed its place as the nation's original indigenous music. It has been a joy for me to listen to all of these great artists—not only to their music but also to their stories. They lived an important part of American history, and their memories of long-forgotten people and places bring that history to life. Here are their stories.

Benny Carter

While the adjectives "towering" and "monumental" are often used excessively to praise a prominent personality, they very accurately describe Benny Carter.

His contributions over the years profoundly influenced the development of jazz as an internationally recognized art form. His strong leadership—from the '20s through the '90s—has penetrated eight decades of jazz history. Several generations of jazzmen have been influenced by Carter's exemplary life and his great artistic skills.

Benny Carter (center) flanked by fellow Esquire Jazz Award winners (left to right) Woody Herman, Benny Goodman, Barney Bigard, and radio personality Al Jarvis.

Benny generously added prestige to worthy efforts by endowing them with his personal support. In 1970 he accepted the titular chairmanship of the Louis Armstrong Statue Fund and contributed his services to the successful "Hello Louis!" production that launched the fund. By generously lending his name, he helped the statue of Louis Armstrong become a reality, and eventually a park in New Orleans was established as a home for the large bronze figure (see Chapter 8). After he authorized the American Federation of Jazz Societies to use his sculpted image for its annual Benny Carter Award, the activities of that national service organization achieved worldwide attention.

In 1995 Carter was presented with a star on Hollywood's Walk of Fame and a Grammy for the best solo instrumental from his CD *Elegy in Blue*. In 1993 he received the Duke Award from the American Society of Composers, Authors and Publishers (ASCAP). He also has received honorary doctorates from Rutgers and Harvard, and acclamations from organizations throughout the world.

I am extremely proud that Benny, a friend for many years, has written the foreword to this book.

James P. Johnson

To commemorate their golden wedding anniversary in 1949, my grandparents rented a large banquet room in the old Hollywood Athletic Club. They arranged a catered dinner, invited friends and relatives, and decided to hire a band to make this a truly gala occasion. They enlisted my help in finding the musicians, and I asked clarinetist Albert Nicholas if he would get a small group together for the party. Delighted to help, he contacted bassist Leonard Bibbs, pianist Gideon Honoré, and a young guitar player by the name of Louis Gonzales (the uncredited guitarist featured on Dink Johnson's 1945 recordings for William Russell's American Music label).

We asked the musicians to arrive about 8:30 P.M., shortly after the dinner. At the scheduled time, Nicholas asked to see me in the lobby. He held a clarinet case in one hand and extended the other hand in a resolute gesture of despair. "I'm sorry, Floyd, but I've let you down," he blurted. "Gideon had another job, and I had to grab a substitute piano player." As I contemplated the situation briefly, Nick said, "Shake hands with James P. Johnson."

James P. Johnson, the world's greatest stride pianist? Playing at my family's private party? I was overjoyed. Nick explained that Jimmy had just arrived in town, had nothing scheduled for the evening, and would enjoy playing for our party. I knew Nick and James P. were old friends. They had played many jobs together in New York City and were featured on Rudi Blesh's radio program, *This Is Jazz,* with Danny Barker, Pops Foster, Baby Dodds, Wild Bill Davison, and Jimmy Archey.

Shaking hands with James P. Johnson was an unforgettable experience. His huge fist was soft and warm, and it thrilled me to hold the powerful right hand that had produced so much delightful music. A very large man, he possessed a massive face dominated by a great lower lip that protruded sharply and glowed pink against his black features. Many would view him as ugly, but he looked beautiful to me as he waddled into the ballroom to find the piano.

The large instrument was dwarfed by Johnson's bulky frame. He seemed satisfied and settled into position, sitting with his left leg beneath the piano, his body at right angles to the keyboard. From this position he could see the audience and seemed to enjoy watching the happy crowd as they danced. I was the only person in attendance who was aware of our pianist's identity. And no one else knew that our clar-

The legendary James P. Johnson (at piano) performs at author's grandparents'
anniversary party, 1949. From left: guitarist Louis Gonzales, bassist Leonard
Bibbs, Johnson, the author, and clarinetist Albert Nicholas.

inetist was the legendary Albert Nicholas, student of Lorenzo Tio, who
had played with Joe Oliver and Jelly Roll Morton. They enjoyed
Nick's elegant runs and glorious Creole tone and danced to the piano's
strong beat without realizing how fabled was the strong left hand providing that wonderful cadence. But they danced, they applauded, and
they told me "my" band was great! "Lots of pep!" an aunt exclaimed.
    Midway through the second set, Nicholas introduced his pianist and
asked Jimmy to play a medley of original compositions. As Johnson
romped through several famous numbers, the guests gradually realized
they were witnessing something very special. His demonstration of
technical prowess on "Carolina Shout" brought thunderous applause;
"Snowy Morning Blues," played with impeccable taste, gave me a
thrill (his old Columbia recording of the latter tune had always been
one of my favorites); his swinging version of "Porter's Love Song"
struck a responsive chord; and his "Charleston" received a wild ovation. Johnson concluded his solo interlude with "I Can't Give You
Anything But Love," and when my aunts and uncles clamored for

more, he obligingly encored with "Runnin' Wild." Happy listeners who had never heard of James P. Johnson surrounded the piano. They recognized the tunes and shouted their praises.

This extraordinary evening occurred almost fifty years ago, but I remember it in every detail. The American Federation of Musicians contract for the event is still in my files. Scale for the band was $64, including $6 federal tax. Albert Nicholas' leader's fee was $19. Bibbs, Gonzales, and James P. Johnson each received $13.

Johnson's stellar career stretched back to the 1910s. His 1921 Okeh recording "Keep Off the Grass"/"Carolina Shout" still warrants serious listening, as do his remarkable duets with Bessie Smith. Johnson composed many of the blues numbers that Smith turned into hits; his piano buoyed her expressive voice and established the mournful mood. Their 1927 recording of "Back Water Blues" shows them at their best. He was musical director and arranger for Smith's 1929 film *St. Louis Blues* and appeared briefly during a cabaret sequence. (The famous comedian Johnny Lee played an imbibing bartender in the movie. "I sipped real liquor during the film," he said. "I was drunk by the time the scene was finished." Lee later played a comedy role in the film *Stormy Weather,* was the voice of Br'er Rabbit in Disney's *Song of the South,* and starred as lawyer Algonquin J. Calhoun on the early television series of *Amos 'n' Andy.*)

That anniversary party at the Hollywood Athletic Club gave rise to a warm friendship. During Johnson's stay in Los Angeles, I spent many interesting hours listening to him recount the experiences that had shaped his life. He often visited our home and played with our young son. The great musician moved into our hearts. It was easy to love James P. Johnson.

In a way, he was an extremely bitter man—bitter with the awareness that the world had passed him by. Then fifty-eight years old, Johnson. knew his talent was recognized by only a few jazz fans; as a black musician in an unenlightened white man's world, he had never received great public acclaim. He had watched less talented composers gain riches and fame, while many of his own fine tunes had been sold for a few dollars to greedy publishers who, he said, considered them "coon songs." Johnson stoically accepted this situation and maintained a moderately comfortable life with an adoring wife, Lillie Mae, on Long Island. He was proud of the large pipe organ installed in his house, despite neighbors' complaints that the instrument's vibrations shook the pictures from their walls.

Johnson came to Los Angeles to supervise the rehearsals of a musical he had recently co-written with Flournoy E. Miller of the early vaudeville team of Miller and Lyles. *Sugar Hill,* which opened at the Las Palmas Theatre in July 1949, adroitly merged Miller's libretto and lyrics with several new James P. Johnson melodies. Their remarkable score included "You Can't Lose a Broken Heart," "My Sweet Hunk of Trash," "Peace, Sister, Peace," and the rousing "Chivaree." Columbia Records issued a cast album, and several songs were recorded by Nat Cole, Louis Armstrong, and Billie Holiday.

During the several weeks the show was in rehearsal, I took every opportunity to spend time with this great man. He lived in a beautiful West Los Angeles home rented from one of the Mills Brothers (who were then on tour). The large, tastefully furnished house had a fine concert grand piano on which Johnson often entertained me and my wife, Lucille. Once, when I brought a tape recorder to interview him for my radio program, he delighted me by playing several tunes. His hands were still swift and his mind very agile. I recently unearthed those brittle old tapes and again enjoyed his private performances of "Old Fashioned Love" and "Just Before Daybreak." When asked the name of an unfamiliar up-tempo number, he responded: "Just a rag, Floyd." I never knew if that was the title or a description. Of another composition, he said: "About thirty-five years ago, when I played in a hole in the wall, it was originally called 'Over the Bars' but later became famous as 'Steeplechase Rag.'" That was Johnson's first recorded effort, in 1917.

Occasionally I brought Fats Waller's name into our conversations. Waller, James P.'s pupil, always exhibited a strong Johnson influence in his piano playing. He had died five years earlier, and his mentor found it difficult to speak about him. Once he murmured, "I loved Fats like a son. I tried to teach him everything I knew about music. He went on and expanded his skill and became one of the world's greatest entertainers. We were close friends for twenty-five years. He was a great person." Tears appeared in Jimmy's eyes.

As a record collector, I asked Johnson to help me identify many of the uncredited artists who played on early recordings. For example, I thought King Oliver played the cornet accompaniment on Eva Taylor's 1929 Victor recording of "You Don't Understand." Johnson played piano on the tune (his style is easily recognizable), and he vividly recalled the recording session. The cornetist, he said, was not King Oliver but Ed Anderson.

Johnson also disputed my theory that jazz was born in New Orleans. The Harlem pianist told me he played jazz long before any of the early Crescent City bands traveled north. Jimmy recalled hearing jazz in Kansas City, St. Louis, and Baltimore before he ever heard of Jelly Roll Morton, and he had been influenced by musical styles emerging from places like Charleston and Memphis back in 1912. He remembered the great ragtime pianists from the Midwest who introduced a new wave of rhythms that influenced much of our popular music. The great Duke Ellington, a follower of James P. Johnson's style, had spent his formative years in Washington, D.C., without the influence of New Orleans music.

If a true birthplace of jazz must be identified, I think Jimmy would claim Harlem for that honor. New Orleans pianists were showcased in brothels and barrelhouses, but Harlem's keyboard masters played at "house-rent" parties. "To advertise a rent party," Johnson said, "we'd tie a rag to a broom handle and stick it out the window. A crowd would soon gather—sometimes a hundred in a small apartment. They paid twenty-five or fifty cents, drink beer and eat hog maws, 'chitlins,' and fried chicken. That helped pay the rent." Johnson reminisced about the great house-rent pianists who conducted "cuttin'" contests and displayed their skills to establish themselves as "champions." Those Harlem stride players created an exciting brand of music, blending ragtime with the blues to produce a rhythmic pattern that kept toes tapping during the harsh Depression. His favorite "chitterling pianists" were Fats Waller, Willie "The Lion" Smith, Stephen "The Beetle" Henderson, and Raymond "Lippy" Boyd. "I cut them all, Floyd," Johnson immodestly stated.

Johnson was greatly inspired by Luckey Roberts. Early Johnson Aeolian piano rolls clearly reflect Roberts' romping influence, which Johnson developed fully as his technique matured. Those swift left-hand patterns were influenced by a Harlem bordello musician known as Abba Labba (Richard McLean).

Sugar Hill was Jimmy's final contribution to the world of music. Despite complimentary local reviews, the show never made it to Broadway. Shortly after the Los Angeles opening, Johnson returned to New York. He soon suffered a massive stroke and remained an invalid until he died a few years later.

Yes, I remember James P. Johnson. I remember hearing him play his beautiful concerto and excerpts from two complete symphonies. I remember his stories about Bessie Smith and Clarence Williams. The colorful vaudeville tales, when he was billed as "The Outstanding Exponent of Ragtime Piano," would interest any serious student of jazz history.

Brun Campbell and Scott Joplin

Ragtime is a form of music characterized by a syncopated melody superimposed on a strongly accented accompaniment. The world will be a better place with the resurgence of this happy music.

                                        Brun Campbell

Brun Campbell was among the last living connections with the ragtime era and its most prominent figure, the legendary Scott Joplin. Known as "The Original Ragtime Kid" around the end of the nineteenth century, Campbell had studied with Joplin and became part of the ragtime scene in St. Louis, the genre's epicenter. He quit professional music in 1908 and came to California in 1928, where, following his father's trade, he earned a living as a barber. But he tirelessly championed the music he loved and helped preserve it as a living art form well into the twentieth century.

Campbell looked upon ragtime as America's first pop music. It initially attracted a youthful audience rebelling against the mono-rhythmic waltzes of the Victorian age. By the turn of the century it had spread throughout the nation. Printed sheet music reached every small-town piano player and every theater pit orchestra. For two decades the nation whistled, sang, danced, and strutted to these wild new rhythms. "In 1908, the year I retired from music, the rag craze had reached the peak of its frenzy," Campbell told me. "Adeline Shepherd's 'Pickles and Peppers' was so popular, it became a best-selling campaign tune for William Jennings Bryan in one of his unsuccessful bids for the presidency."

I met Campbell in the early '50s. He was the intermission performer at Santa Monica's Rendezvous Ballroom, where Kid Ory's Creole Jazz Band was featured. The young listeners, probably hearing pure ragtime piano for the first time, crowded around him, enchanted by these "new" sounds. Ory introduced us, and Campbell promptly invited me to his barber shop in Venice. The shop served as a meeting place for local ragtime enthusiasts, who enjoyed hearing Campbell's endless tales

Brun Campbell at age 16, 1900.

about the old St. Louis scene. A customer was seated in the barber chair when I entered; I thumbed through a worn copy of *National Geographic* while Campbell completed his task. Then he hung the "closed" sign on the door, pulled the shade, poured a Coke, and invited me to relax with him.

Sanford Brunson "Brun" Campbell was born March 26, 1884; he told me his birthplace was Washington, Kansas (his death certificate lists it as Oberlin, Kansas). The first rag he could remember having heard was a two-step called "Mississippi Rag," written in 1897 by Chicago bandleader William Krell. Another early favorite was Tom Turpin's "Harlem Rag," the first ragtime piece published by a Negro composer. "His full name was Tom Million Turpin," Campbell said, recalling the pianist's lightning-fast St. Louis style. "He operated several gambling houses, dance halls, cafes, and sporting houses in St. Louis' bawdy district. His death in 1922 coincided with the end of an era that saw the birth and development of ragtime music."

Campbell remembered all the prominent St. Louis ragtime masters who played along Market, Chestnut, and Eighteenth Streets and could still rattle off their names. Our conversation was generously sprinkled with tales about Arthur Marshall, Otis Saunders, Sam Patterson, Charley Johnson, and Euday Bowman. He had particular praise for Louis Chauvin, a young student of Turpin's who became one of ragtime's greatest pianists. While Chauvin achieved fame primarily as a performer, Campbell thought Turpin probably incorporated several of Chauvin's ideas in his compositions. Louis Chauvin's name appears with Scott Joplin's on "Heliotrope Rag," an indication of Joplin's appreciation for the young pianist's ideas.

Campbell held Scott Joplin in the very highest regard. He still had vivid memories of the famed composer, whom he met in about 1900. Campbell learned to play Joplin's tunes from original manuscripts and proudly noted that he was the composer's only white pupil.

> I ran away from home when I was fifteen—to see the world. I got as far as Oklahoma City. There, in a music store, I saw an early copy of "Maple Leaf Rag," written by Scott Joplin. When I played the rag in the store, I fell in love with the sound.
>
> I was told that Joplin lived in Sedalia, Missouri, about three hundred miles away. I hitchhiked to Sedalia and found him playing in a small barroom. After hearing me play, he agreed to be my teacher. I learned his "Maple Leaf Rag" and "Original Rags," and I learned his syncopation, "ragged time," that is traceable to Civil War cakewalks and work songs.
>
> Joplin was thirty-two years old, and fame had not yet come his way. He was a very black Negro, about five feet seven inches tall, solidly built, a neat dresser, musically very serious—and an excellent sight reader. I never forgot the way he played "Maple Leaf Rag"—I still play it exactly like he did.

Campbell considered his mentor the creator of a serious musical form that later became the foundation of traditional American jazz. Joplin, who was born in Texas in 1868, wrote "The Original Rags" in 1897 while attending the George R. Smith School of Music in Sedalia, which attracted many young black musicians from the Midwest. He eventually published about seventy compositions, of which "Maple Leaf Rag" will always stand as his monumental achievement. He also wrote a ballet, "Ragtime Dance," and two syncopated operas, "A Guest of Honor" and "Treemonisha."

Joplin was extremely enthusiastic about "Treemonisha," which filled 230 pages of sheet music in the piano version published in 1911, but he could not interest producers in financing the huge project. In 1915, at his own expense, he presented a single performance at the Lincoln Theater in Harlem, hoping to secure backers. The opera was presented without scenery or an orchestra; Joplin personally played the entire score. The reviews were not favorable, and the show closed after the initial performance. Joplin never recovered from this great disappointment. His depression deepened and accelerated a chronic illness, and he died in Manhattan State Hospital on April 1, 1917, at the age of forty-nine.

"When he died," Campbell said, "those few who realized his greatness bowed their heads in sorrow. This was the passing of the king of all ragtime writers, the man who gave America a genuine native music. His music was the finest. In my opinion, it deserves the same acclaim given to the old classical masters. Joplin was a pioneer who carved his music from the pulse of a new nation. He followed the guideposts of classical traditions. Joplin's creation, despite its turbulent path, may eventually eclipse even the undying prominence of the old masters he revered."

Campbell donated his impressive Scott Joplin collection of sheet music, letters, and materials collected during the ragtime era to Fisk University, a traditionally black college. He continued sending profits from his writings and recordings to Mrs. Scott Joplin.

He was disturbed by various hybrid forms of ragtime achieving commercial popularity. Pop tunes employing "rag" in their titles contained few, if any, of the basic ragtime ingredients; Tin Pan Alley publishers had rushed into the movement with popularized versions that greatly diluted the original sound, and Campbell felt they distorted the "grace and beauty" of pure ragtime. "They completely missed the point," he said disdainfully. In his opinion, the only legitimate descendent of ragtime was jazz: "The purest forms of ragtime found their way to New Orleans to later appear in the music of Tony Jackson, Jelly Roll Morton, and Clarence Williams. Kansas City jazz took its inspiration from the same roots, and the aura of Sedalia is evident in the works of Bennie Moten, Julia Lee, and Pete Johnson."

Campbell believed that Jelly Roll Morton was influenced by Joplin. For example, he claimed that in 1906 Morton sent his "King Porter Stomp" to Joplin, who augmented and arranged the piece. "In 1927," he added, "ten years after Joplin died, Jelly Roll was a boarder at Mrs. Joplin's apartment house in New York City. According to her, while living there he thoroughly studied her husband's compositions, no doubt incorporating Joplin's ideas in his own numbers."

Campbell also heard Joplin's influence in the work of such New York musicians as Luckey Roberts, Willie "The Lion" Smith, Jack The Bear, and James P. Johnson and in the styles of Chicagoans such as Pine Top Smith, Meade Lux Lewis, and Albert Ammons.

By the time I met Campbell, ragtime had long faded from the popular music scene. Audiences considered it "corny," merely barroom tinklings in Westerns. Obsessed with popularizing this music and his personal hero, Scott Joplin, Campbell wrote several articles on his favorite subject for *Jazz Journal* and *Record Changer*. The July 1949 issue of *Jazz Journal* included his "From Rags to Ragtime and Riches," one of the earliest published biographies of Scott Joplin. He also wrote a barrage of letters to music publishers, record firms, radio stations, and film producers urging them to make pure ragtime accessible to the public. His dream was to see Hollywood make a film about Joplin's career. (In 1976, twenty-four years after Campbell's death, Billy Dee Williams starred in *Scott Joplin,* with Eubie Blake playing a featured role.)

Campbell made his most important contribution toward a ragtime revival as a performer. In the mid and late 1940s he recorded several solos with technical assistance from Ray Avery and Cecil Charles Spiller. They initially were issued in 78 rpm format on the Brun label—blank on one side. ("If they want to hear two tunes, let them buy two records," the pianist liked to say.) Long-playing versions of the recordings appeared on Paul Affeldt's small Euphonic label. Then in his late sixties, Campbell recorded "Maple Leaf Rag" and "Sunflower Slow Drag," performing them exactly as Joplin had taught him half a century earlier. Gradually, audiences embraced the genre. Wally Rose, pianist with Lu Watters' Yerba Buena Jazz Band (and one of Campbell's students), set the pace in 1942 with a landmark recording of "Black and White Rag," and Pee Wee Hunt's Dixieland version of Euday Bowman's "12th Street Rag" ranked among the best-selling records of the 1940s.

Spurred by brilliant young players, interest in ragtime slowly increased. In the '50s, hiding behind pseudonyms, several notable pianists brought undistorted rags into the commercial spotlight. They were Joe "Fingers" Carr (Lou Busch), "Crazy Otto" (Johnny Maddox), and "Knuckles" O'Toole (Dick Hyman). Soon Max Morath, merging scholarship and entertainment, presented a deeper understanding and appreciation of turn-of-the-century American music.

They All Played Ragtime, by Rudi Blesh and Harriet Janis, was published in 1950, adding legitimacy to an almost forgotten music. Campbell acknowledged the talents of several young players, including Armand Hug in New Orleans ("one of the greatest in this generation"), Don Ewell, Johnny Wittwer, Knocky Parker, Marvin Ash, Ralph Sutton, and Burt Bales.

In his zeal to expound the joys of Joplin's work, Campbell helped orchestrate the resurgence of this happy music. Fan clubs and newsletters proliferated; *Rag Times,* the Los Angeles Maple Leaf Club's publication edited by Dick Zimmerman, continues to lead the way after thirty years. In 1973, when Marvin Hamlisch utilized Joplin's music for the soundtrack in *The Sting,* ragtime's popularity got a substantial boost. Ragtime festivals are now regular occurrences in the United States and Europe and feature an ever-increasing roster of artists and composers.

In his definitive appraisal of Campbell in the January 1988 issue of *Mississippi Rag,* Paul Affeldt said, "Brun was important because he focused public interest on ragtime. It was a wonderful experience to have known a man of such dedication and excellence."

Rex Stewart's Memories of Jelly Roll Morton

Jelly Roll Morton [Ferdinand Lemott] was one of the most controversial, flamboyant jazz artists that I have ever met.

I recall he chose the nom de plume "Morton" to protect his family from disgrace if he was identified as a whorehouse "professor."

During his multi-faceted career, he was a composer, gambler, philosopher, and, last but not least, a "lover boy"—which accounts for his nickname, "Jelly Roll." In the circles in which Morton was a self-styled king,

when the gentry spoke of "Jelly Roll," they were not
referring to cake!

> Rex Stewart, in his autobiography, *Boy*
> *Meets Horn* (edited by Claire P. Gordon,
> University of Michigan Press, 1991)

William "Rex" Stewart was born February 22, 1907. He gained fame
as a jazz cornetist during his successful years with the Fletcher Henderson and Duke Ellington orchestras. After leaving the Duke in 1945,
Stewart achieved additional acclaim by writing about jazz. In his autobiography he told a number of revealing stories about Jelly Roll Morton, many of which convey facets of the great man's philosophies
about life, art, and music. The following impressions have been transcribed from Stewart's handwritten notes, generously given to me by
his editor, Claire P. Gordon. He wrote them shortly before he died in
1967.

"THE IMAGE," BY REX STEWART

Music is a luxury and, as such, requires a considerable amount of applied
imagination to communicate with an audience and to be salable to the
public.

People have a great love and desire for music; but, with the exception
of the most remote regions, there is a plethora of music of all kinds
around these days. So it becomes incumbent upon the individual to create
some form of *image* that will set him apart from the mass of competition.

The idea of communicating one's artistry, by a projecting definite image
or style, is an age-old concept dating back to the days of the troubadours
and the meistersingers. During the Roaring Twenties, many piano players
transfixed the nearest listeners with a hypnotic eye. This was the fashion of
the day, and, at the time, no one knew that the "stare" was a means of trying to communicate and thereby create an image.

Imagery was of paramount importance in the history of jazz. The old-
timers, like Jelly Roll Morton, were aware of the necessity to be different in
order to stand out in a crowd. In those bygone days of the piano-playing
"hustlers," one had to come up with something spectacular.

In Jelly Roll Morton's case, it was diamonds. Among the "professors"
(as piano players were labeled in that era), Morton exemplified everything
that I had been told about the glamorous piano players of the bordellos,
where they reigned supreme.

Jelly Roll's career spanned several generations. From Storyville in New Orleans, he started his upward climb to achieving respectability as an innovator and creator of jazz (although he did not invent the music, as he claimed).

He still clung to the older concept and to his image, which at the time I met him was "flash, diamond-studded flash!" He was a real eye-popping bon vivant of that age—always immaculately attired.

Morton was a rather tall, well-built, apricot-colored person with features that reminded me of a Spanish grandee who had become a bit jaded with life. His eyes were most fascinating as they darted from face to face, emphasizing his sometimes disputatious monologues.

Morton was a fixture at the Rhythm Club in New York during the late '30s. He was either playing cards or, most likely, playing pool. Whatever he played, he usually was the winner. Bill "Bojangles" Robinson virtually supported Jelly trying to beat him playing pool.

When he held court, his spiel would be delivered from his customary soapbox on the S.E. corner of 132nd Street and Seventh Avenue in New York's Harlem.

Jelly Roll would be resplendent in a tailor-made suit, and diamonds sparkled from his belt buckle and his shirt front. He was never seen without the big stickpin he wore in his cravat—it glowed like a star on his chest—and a big diamond on his pinkie finger. The picture would be completed by the smaller diamond that glistened in his gold tooth.

He evidently was a lonely person, because if the weather was good you could count on him being on that Harlem corner. He always had an audience of five or ten musicians who held on to every word the master uttered. Youngsters like Jimmy Harrison, Chick Webb, and Benny Carter, among others, were spellbound by his tales and the pronouncements the great man would make.

I remember his three standard topics very well: women, baseball, and how the musicians were ruining his music—the music he had personally invented.

On reflection, Morton, with the passage of years, has become a virtual Nostradamus of jazz, at least in my mind. Many of his predictions, which we laughed at, later came true.

Outside of dwelling on how great he was personally, one of his favorite lectures was:

"You bunch of hard-headed kids, ya got no sense running around copying each other. That will get you no place. Ya gotta be different. Try something new. What the hell are you afraid of? The worse that can happen to ya is you'll wind up digging ditches, and most of you will be digging ditches anyway!

"You will have to learn how to protect yourself. Here you sit on your do-nothing can, feeling high and mighty because you can blow a horn, beat a drum, or plunk on a piano. Why, you are nothing! All of you are just a bunch of dumb-ass mules, because most of you that can play, can't read music. If you can read music, you are so satisfied thinking that you are better than anyone else that you can't play!

"Look at me. I can not only read, but I invented jazz, doggone it! I owned jazz until the white man started stealing it from me. But I found out how to protect myself. How many of you are gonna listen to me and learn?

"In twenty or thirty years there's gonna be so many phonograph machines playing music there ain't nobody gonna need you for nothin'. They got a union, you say? Sure, they got a union—but they don't want you! Of course, eventually they will take you in and let you beg for jobs that you always had before they had a union. Remember that, boy!

"Remember, I'm telling you that in the early days of ragtime, we black ones played the parties, the cotillions. New Orleans, New York, Chicago, it was all the same. If it was a good-paying job, and they wanted good entertainment with their music, they called us. Of course, that was before the damn unions.

"Oh yes. There will come a day for the union. First they will stand you in the corner with your own little union. Then they will get so hungry for power, they will pull you all together into one union. But you will still stand together waiting for crumbs from the bosses' tables. Live long enough, and you will see.

"Another thing you will see, if the booze and the women don't get you first, is you ain't gonna have a place to play. I see more and more 'Patties' hanging around Harlem. They bring their horns; line up at the bars with you, buy you a sandwich—and as soon as they get to know you, they say, 'Let's go jam!' Go right ahead, you dumb SOBs. Go ahead and teach them your music so they can set up their phonograph machines, and then your children can someday read how you used to create and play music."

I'll never forget another impromptu lecture by Jelly Roll Morton when he hauled the publishers over the coals—that evening he was really on fire. I was on my way to Big John's, a bar on Seventh Avenue, when I noticed a bigger than usual crowd on the corner. So I stopped to listen. Jelly was frothing at the mouth, saying:

"They just ain't no damn good—none of them! I'll tell you, and you just better listen! All you young studs, and you old ones too, better learn these three rules: Write your music out. Send it to Washington to be copyrighted. And then hire a lawyer to see that you get a fair deal.

"I'm Jelly Roll Morton, and it's me telling you that none of those music publishers are worth the powder to blow them to hell! They make you promises—then they steal your stuff. You wind up begging them for a handout while they lollygag around in their big cars and yachts. Ya better wake up, ya stupid knuckleheads!

"A Negro has to be ten times as smart to get an even break in this business. Watch and see if some of those *peolas* [whites] don't come up with some so-called new kind of music. That's to get in the act, 'cause I ain't never heard none of them that was able to play my kind of music yet—except a couple of piano plunkers way out West."

There again, Jelly was right. Almost so. The evolution came from his own people—more so than from the *peolas*.

Well, from where I sit surveying the scene, it appears that Jelly Roll was right. Despite the awareness that this is undoubtedly hindsight, still, I have the pleasure of remembering, "He told me so."

Further, in these days of reappraisal, it occurs to me that we might examine the truths that Jelly spoke about because they exist in far greater proportions than even he dreamed of.

My position here is not to advocate specifically any examination into the inequities of the Negro in jazz. It is merely a plea for some form of assistance for American jazz regardless of who writes or performs it, so that a significant American contribution to the arts may live and flourish—not continue to dry up and perish.

Paralleling the significant decline in jazz is the loss of tradition and the legends of this American art form. It seems to me that the musicians and the public blithely follow the pied pipers of commercialism with faint regard for the music's background or the people who made it possible.

Nor do the masses understand the cultures and psychological impact this music has made on the world. It is unfortunate that our educators, for the most part, when they are enlightened enough to admit its existence, continue to cast a leering, smirking eye on the subject.

We can thank New Orleans for Jelly Roll Morton. He is a legend who enriched our culture and the lives of everyone who knew him.

Long live the memory of Jelly Roll Morton.

Anita Gonzales and the Untold Story
of Jelly Roll Morton's Last Years

These cold details appear in bold black type on California Death Certificate No. 9682:

Full Name:	Ferdinand Morton
Date of Death:	July 10, 1941
Place of Death:	Los Angeles, Calif.
Cause of Death:	Cardiac decomposition
Birthplace:	New Orleans, Louisiana
Birthdate:	September 20, 1889
Occupation:	Musician
Business:	Victor Company
Father's Name:	Edward Morton
Mother's Maiden Name:	Louise Monette
Wife:	Anita Morton
Informant:	Anita Morton

Such are the bare facts of the life of Ferdinand Joseph Lamothe—better known as Jelly Roll Morton, one of the most towering figures in the history of American popular music. This flawed document doesn't even hint at Morton's lasting contributions to our nation's culture—the hundreds of songs he composed, the piano style he pioneered, the many musicians he inspired. The certificate does contain a couple of noteworthy errors: Morton's actual birthdate was October 20, 1890, and his father's name was Edward J. Lamothe (Edward Morton was his stepfather).

The last name on the document often goes unrecognized, but it carries considerable weight. Anita Gonzales inspired at least two of Morton's compositions: "Sweet Anita Mine" and a subtle tango called "Mama 'Nita." The sister of pioneering clarinetist-drummer-pianist Oliver "Dink" Johnson, she was a beautiful Creole woman whose relationship with Morton dated back many years—probably to the very beginning of the twentieth century, before his departure from New Orleans. Gonzales also played an influential role in the jazzman's life in California after World War I, a thinly documented period of his career. She was with Morton in his last days and was one of the last people to see him alive. Though she is listed as the pianist's wife, researchers have never found conclusive proof they were actually married.

Most jazz fans are familiar with the story of Morton's triumphant emergence from Storyville's brothel parlors. He achieved great prominence and wealth as leader of the famous Red Hot Peppers, probably the most thrilling recording group in the history of New Orleans music. Never known for his modesty, Morton walked around with a stash of $1,000 bills, carried diamonds in every pocket, and proudly claimed (with considerable justification) that he personally invented jazz. His business card pompously announced:

> JELLY ROLL MORTON — ORIGINATOR OF JAZZ AND STOMPS
> VICTOR'S NO. 1 RECORDING ARTIST
> WORLD'S GREATEST HOT TUNE WRITER

During the 1920s Morton achieved unprecedented success and notoriety, but his rapid rise was followed by an equally rapid downfall. By 1930, the Jazz Age was nearing its end. Victor did not renew Morton's recording contract, and bookings for his Red Hot Peppers slowed, then stopped completely. Jazzmen struggled to compete for the few entertainment dollars available in the Depression, and by 1934 Morton was down to his last diamond, a half-carat gem imbedded in his front tooth.

That year he endured the embarrassment of playing on an inferior Wingy Manone recording date for Columbia; his uninspired piano solo is heard briefly on the tune, "Never Had No Lovin'." Wingy neglected to mention Morton's name as he happily introduced such unlikely sidemen as Artie Shaw, Bud Freeman, and John Kirby. Columbia wisely chose not to issue the records until twenty years later, when they appeared on the company's Special Edition collector's series.

The burgeoning swing craze put a final coda to Morton's golden era, and small groups such as his Red Hot Peppers seemed dated to younger listeners. Ironically, they acclaimed the popular swing versions of Jelly's tunes and riffs beings recorded by most of the popular bands.

"F. Morton" appeared in tiny print beneath the song titles on millions of records, but the public paid no attention to the composer credits. Morton never received proper compensation for his huge-selling compositions; a disagreement with his publishers and ASCAP limited his royalties.

Morton knew he had helped create the big-band sound, but he never received due credit. Desperate, bitter, and in failing health, he resurfaced briefly in 1938, playing for a few faithful followers at the

Jungle Inn, a seedy club over a hamburger stand in Washington, D.C. His historic Library of Congress recordings led to a final Victor date in 1939, which brought a brief flurry of renewed recognition, and the General Record Company timidly released several Morton piano solos and some band numbers; but poor marketing, coupled with public apathy, severely limited the success of these offerings.

In 1940, with music still surging through his productive mind, Morton decided to move to Los Angeles, hoping to regain his health and rejuvenate his career. In *Mister Jelly Roll: The Fortunes of Jelly Roll Morton, New Orleans Creole and "Inventor of Jazz,"* Alan Lomax described the pianist's cross-country journey. Morton made the trip in his battered Lincoln, towing his Cadillac behind on a chain. Forced to abandon the Lincoln in an Idaho snowdrift, he continued in the Cadillac, which was loaded with clothes and a scrapbook filled with faded mementos. He also brought with him a dozen new big-band arrangements that he planned to record with fellow New Orleans expatriates Kid Ory, Mutt Carey, Bud Scott, Ram Hall, and Ed Garland.

After Morton arrived in Los Angeles, Garland assembled this illustrious group and rented the Elks Hall on Central Avenue for rehearsals, but the pianist's physical condition had seriously deteriorated. He valiantly attended the sessions but had his former pupil, Buster Wilson, stand in for him at the piano. But if Morton's body was failing, his musical mind was as sharp as ever. "Jelly's arrangements were very interesting," Ed Garland told me. "He knew that the popular swing bands were playing his songs. Benny Goodman's record of 'King Porter Stomp' and Hampton's 'Shoe Shiners Drag' were heard daily on the radio. He wanted to show those bands how his music should be played."

Unfortunately, the recording date never took place; Morton died on July 10, 1941. The golden era of our music heard the last of Jelly's creativity—and the world hardly noticed.

An ironic twist of fate denied an opportunity for me to own the arrangements Morton wrote for his anticipated record date. His handwritten scores remained in Buster Wilson's front room for almost a decade. They were in a large trunk draped with a silk shawl on which stood a tarnished brass lamp. Buster promised to sort through the trunk "one day" and offered to give me those old manuscripts.

I repeatedly reminded him of his offer, but he never managed to open the trunk. After Buster's death, I informed his widow, Carmelita, of his promise. I discreetly called her several times, but she seemed reluctant to let me have the arrangements. The phone eventually was disconnected. Carmelita moved. She apparently left the city, and I was unable to contact her again.

With that I gave up all hope of ever locating these historic scores, and they remained lost for decades. They finally resurfaced in the 1990s, as reported by Phil Pastras in *Dead Man Blues*. The thirteen-piece big-band arrangements were found among the huge catalogue of material left by Bill Russell to the Historic New Orleans Collection. An orchestra assembled by Don Vappie performed four of these compositions at the 1998 New Orleans Jazz and Heritage Festival.

Two witnesses to the event, musician Jacques Gauthé and writer Barry McRae, both praised Morton's apparent mastery of the big-band idiom, and both commented on the "modernism" of one particular piece, "Gan-Jam." McRae compared it to the work of Charles Mingus, Gauthé to that of Stan Kenton.

The private recording of the event verifies that the piece is indeed very modern in conception. Morton recorded two of the pieces— "Mister Joe" and "We Are Elks"—in earlier forms, and they contain no great surprises. "Oh! Baby," by contrast, sounds like a contemporary (circa 1940) swing arrangement, and the great surprise, "Gan-Jam," looks forward at least ten years in its bold use of dissonance and eastern modal scales.

The style of the group Vappie assembled is New Orleans Revival; one wonders how much more modern the arrangements might sound if played by a more contemporary group.

It is regrettable that Jelly Roll Morton's last days were such sad ones. He spent them trying to pull himself out of obscurity and reclaim his rightful position as one of the nation's most important and accomplished musicians. The man who claimed to have invented jazz simply faded away.

When they buried Jelly Roll Morton in Calvary Cemetery in east Los Angeles, the diamond was missing from his front tooth. Pallbearers included Kid Ory, Mutt Carey, and Ed Garland. David Stuart of the Jazz Man Record Shop was the only white man attending the Catholic funeral. A story in *Down Beat* magazine reported that Duke Ellington and Jimmy Lunceford, the two most prominent black bandleaders of the day, were noticeably absent from the burial services. Ellington was appearing at the Mayan Theater in his production "Jump for Joy," and Lunceford and his band were booked at the Casa Mañana in nearby Culver City.

Jelly's grave—Number 4, Lot 347, Section N—lay on a gently slop-ing grass-covered hill. It remained unmarked and unattended, and the music world seemed to forget the genius buried there. Nine years later, tall weeds had overgrown the grave, and the surrounding area was badly neglected. Apparently, perpetual care fees had not been paid.

Early in 1950, members of the Southern California Hot Jazz Society decided to raise the funds for a marble identification plaque and per-petual care. We reserved the Maynard Theater on Washington Boule-vard for a September 30, 1950, benefit concert, then set about lining up performers. Blues singer Monette Moore, a contemporary of Bessie Smith's, volunteered to appear. Albert Nicholas, Zutty Singleton, and Joe Sullivan joined the bill. Young Johnny Lucas, original trumpet player in the Firehouse Five Plus Two, also offered his services. To as-sure a full program worthy of the sixty-cent admission price, we also invited Conrad Janis' Tailgate Jazz Band, winners of *Record Changer* magazine's amateur band contest in 1949.

Bob Kirstein and I—SCHJS vice president and president, respec-tively—both hosted weekly radio shows on a small FM station, and we took advantage of our air time to advertise the event. Ticket sales were slow at first, but by mid-September we knew there would be a full house.

That's when Anita Gonzales appeared on the scene.

The radio station manager received a phone call from a woman identifying herself as Jelly Roll Morton's wife. Why, she demanded to know, was his station publicizing an event to raise money for her hus-band's gravestone? She sounded irate and insisted the activity be halted immediately.

Kirstein and I apprehensively returned Anita's call. She emphatically informed us she would not allow the Jazz Society to buy the marker. In fact, she intended to purchase the plaque herself and would not con-done a charitable effort that would embarrass the memory of her de-parted husband. To placate her, we asked if we could meet her in per-son. We hoped to persuade her that our project was a sincere tribute from Morton's fans and in no way could be construed as "charity." We resisted the temptation to ask why she had waited ten years to make the purchase—and why the grave was not properly maintained.

Gonzales invited us to visit her the following day at the Topanga Beach Auto Court, a small motel she operated on Pacific Coast High-way in nearby Malibu Beach. She greeted us with a friendly smile and introduced us to her husband, J. F. Ford. Despite the acrimonious tone of her telephone conversation, she seemed genuinely pleased to see us. A large, pretty woman, she spoke in warm tones with an accent reflecting her New Orleans heritage. A portable record player and several albums stood on a bookcase near the door; I wondered if the stack included any of Morton's rare old records. A large theatrical blowup of a nearly nude girl hung on one wall. Noticing my interest, Gonzales said: "That's my daughter. Her name is Aleene. She's a striptease dancer at the Follies Theater."

"I'm fixing a batch of fried chicken," she continued. "Would you please stay and have some? I'm famous for my fried chicken." She brought us each a plate of steaming fried chicken and a cold bottle of beer. As we munched the delicious food, she reminisced about her years with the great Jelly Roll Morton:

> I used to sing, you know. Not really as a professional—but I had a good voice and knew all of the old songs. I pleaded with Jelly to let me sing with his band, but he never would. He was very old-fashioned. He didn't want me to work. When I ran a hotel years ago—in 1918, I think—he made me hire people to clean and rent the rooms. He refused to allow me to do any of the work.
>
> We were sweethearts years ago back in New Orleans. My brother, Dink Johnson, reintroduced us here in L.A. before the first World War. Dink was playing drums with Freddie Keppard and the Creole Band at the Orpheum Theater. He lives in Santa Barbara now, but I seldom see him.
>
> Jelly and I traveled a lot in those days. We went up the coast to Oregon for several months—even into Canada. Everywhere we went, people loved his music. Did you know he wrote a tune for me? I used to have many of Jelly's records, but most of them were broken over the years. He made a record here in Los Angeles long ago, but I don't know if it ever came out. Jelly did a lot of recording after he left to go back east. He sent many of them, but they usually arrived cracked.

I hesitated to interrupt her recollections but finally generated the courage to broach the subject of Morton's grave. I reminded her that the SCHJS concert was only about a week away and said that, because we had publicized the event as a fundraiser for the marker, we felt obligated to spend the money for that purpose. Gonzales' mood changed, and she became quite adamant. "I cannot allow strangers to buy the stone for my beloved. Tomorrow I plan to visit the cemetery and purchase the plaque. I'll have it no other way." From the tone of her voice, it seemed evident she was determined to halt the project we had worked so hard to complete. "I realize you are trying to do something good," she added, "but Jelly would never forgive me if I allowed this to happen."

Bob Kirstein suggested perhaps the SCHJS could give her the proceeds from our show. If she used those funds to make her purchase, we would have fulfilled our objective. She refused. We told her that all the tickets were sold, and it was not possible to cancel the benefit. The patrons and the musicians expected all profits to go toward the purchase of Jelly's grave marker. Gonzales shook her head and said, "I'm buying the plaque tomorrow."

She eventually agreed to a let us put a second identification on the grave; that way, we could satisfy our commitment to spend the money on a Morton marker. But the next day, Calvary Cemetery informed me that it permitted just one identification per grave. So we were back to square one.

With the concert date now so close, it was too late for a cancellation; we had no choice but to continue as planned. Kirstein had invited Gonzales to appear on his next broadcast, and we hoped he might be able to change her mind and gain her support.

The radio interview, interspersed with Morton's records, went quite well. "You know," Gonzales remarked after listening to Morton's "New Orleans Joys," "he had a special touch that was unique. Somehow, when Jelly played, he got a different sound from the piano— maybe it was because he loved the music so much." After a long pause she said, "The world has forgotten him, but I always remembered what he accomplished. Without Jelly, we'd still be doing the waltz. He mixed all music together—rags, symphony, marches. That's how jazz started, and Jelly did it. Someday, he'll get the credit."

Gonzales spoke emotionally of Morton's decline and death. "He expired in my arms," she sobbed. "I cared for him ... nursed him during a terrible illness. He came back to me when he knew his time was short. I was the only woman he ever loved."

Recalling the last time Morton played in Los Angeles, Gonzales said:

> When he arrived the last time, he was too sick to play. He kept thinking he would get well enough to take some of the jobs he was offered. He never could take any of them.
>
> I think the last time he actually played in L.A. was back around 1936. Jelly came here with a colored burlesque show called "Brown Skin Models," and they played at the Burbank Theater on Main Street, down on Skid Row. The girls didn't strip. They did a lot of motionless posing behind a sheer curtain. It was quite risqué at the time. Peg Leg Bates was the headliner; Jelly's name was not advertised. He only played in the pit and never soloed. What a waste! But those were the Depression years, and Jelly was glad to have the work.

Jelly Roll Morton (third from left) in 1921, Cadillac Cafe, Los Angeles. The famous entertainer Ada "Bricktop" Smith is at Jelly's left.

This is probably the first reference to Morton's participation in "Brown Skin Models," a seedy touring company of black artists who played second-rate burlesque theaters in the 1930s. My great-uncle, the late Jack Rothschild, co-produced the show with his partner, Irvin C. Miller (brother of Flournoy Miller, a member of the Miller and Lyles vaudeville team of the 1920s). As a high school student, I saw the show during its various stops in Los Angeles. On one trip, Uncle Jack booked the Models for a week at the Million Dollar Theater. Knowing of my budding interest in jazz, he invited me to hear the new piano player in the show—Jelly Roll Morton. At the time, however, I was more interested in Benny Goodman, Artie Shaw, and Tommy Dorsey. So, to my everlasting dismay, I did not take advantage of the opportunity to see—and, probably, to meet—the great Jelly Roll Morton.

After Kirstein's radio program concluded, Gonzales reached into her purse and handed me a gift. It was an envelope containing a brittle sepia photograph of Morton. "That was taken before 1914," she told me. "I am sure of the date because the picture is of Jelly in blackface with Rosa, his partner in a vaudeville act he left in 1914." On the back

Ferd & Rosa to Dear Godmother Laura Hunter

Chicago

Jelly Roll Morton (at right) with his vaudeville partner, Rosa.

of the old photo, written in Morton's bold hand, were the words: "Ferd and Rosa to Dear Godmother Laura Hunter. Chicago."

We had made arrangements to take Gonzales to Mike Lyman's, where Kid Ory was appearing with his Creole Jazz Band. As we were leaving the studio, she suggested that we take her car, which was parked at the curb. "How would you like to drive Jelly's Cadillac?" she asked, handing me the keys. It was a beautiful 1938 sedan, long and black with maroon leather seats—the same car Morton drove during his move to Los Angeles ten years earlier. I eagerly slid behind the wheel, started the motor, and headed down Sunset Boulevard. Driving Jelly Roll Morton's car was one of my greatest thrills. The trip to Lyman's was very short, and I hated for it to end.

During a break between sets, Ory's band came to our table. Naturally, the subject of Jelly Roll Morton dominated our conversation. "He was a very tough man to work for," recalled Ory, who played on many of Morton's Red Hot Pepper recordings. "He knew exactly what he wanted and would not permit any variation from his arrangements. They were tough to play—the tempos were difficult, lots of key changes. But he was always right; the records sounded great."

Throughout the discussion, Ram Hall looked very perplexed. Later he called me aside and said, "That's not Mrs. Morton! I used to go to her house in New York for gumbo—but that's not the same woman! Who is she?" Kid Ory repeated Hall's observation: "I never saw that woman before in my life. I knew Jelly's wife very well. Why did you bring her here and introduce her as Mrs. Morton?"

Apparently, Ory and Hall were referring to Mabel Bertrand, a former dancer at the Plantation Cafe in Chicago who lived with Morton from 1927 until his 1940 move to California. Morton immortalized this woman with a brilliant Victor recording titled "Fussy Mabel," and Ory and Hall must have thought she was his wife.

From the data on Morton's death certificate, Anita was with him when he died in Los Angeles a decade earlier. Why did Ory and his band not remember seeing her during those last rehearsals of Morton's big band arrangements? This is a question that will probably never be answered.

We left the club and drove back to the radio station. On the way, I made a final plea for permission to place a marker at Morton's gravesite. "I ordered the plaque yesterday," she snapped. "And it will be placed on the grave next week." Her decision was final. The evening ended with her dismal announcement; she left us at the station and sped off in Jelly's old car. That was the last time we saw Anita Gonzales.

It was too late to cancel our benefit concert, so we held it as scheduled. The event was a great success; a capacity audience enjoyed an evening of outstanding music, and we raised several hundred dollars. SCHJS treasurer Bill Miskell quietly deposited the proceeds in a bank

Jelly Roll Morton's grave.

account titled, "The Jelly Roll Morton Fund." It remained untouched, gathering interest for many years. In 1966 we were saddened by the death of Johnny St. Cyr, who played banjo on many of Morton's Red Hot Pepper recordings. St. Cyr had moved to Los Angeles in 1955, made many friends among the jazz fraternity, and eventually became president of SCHJS. We decided to use the sixteen-year-old Jelly Roll Morton Fund to purchase Johnny St. Cyr's tombstone. Out of respect for Flora St. Cyr, Johnny's widow, this benevolent act was never publicized; it is revealed here for the first time.

Anita Gonzales followed through on her promise to purchase a headstone for her husband's grave. Bob Kirstein and I went to see it a few days after the Maynard Theater concert. As we climbed the slight knoll toward the grave, we noticed the neatly trimmed grass and a fresh bouquet in a bronze urn. A handsome plaque gleamed brilliantly in the afternoon sun. Carved into the black marble were the words: "Ferdinand Morton—Jelly Roll—1890–1941." We placed a large garland of flowers next to the new marker. The gold letters on the bright red ribbon read, "MR. JELLY ROLL." We took several photos and left the cemetery, comforted with the knowledge that the extraordinary musician's grave was finally suitably marked.

I learned later that Anita Gonzales died April 24, 1952, about a year and a half after our encounter. Her death certificate indicates that she, like Morton, is buried in Calvary Cemetery.

Jelly Roll Morton's influence on the world of jazz is still strongly felt. Maybe he did not personally invent jazz, as he claimed, but his great and everlasting contributions to the art form cannot be disputed. With the possible exception of Louis Armstrong, Jelly Roll Morton was the most creative figure in the history of New Orleans jazz.

Johnny Guarnieri

We will never forget his boyish face, the ever-present pipe, and the beaming grin as he eagerly discussed his favorite subjects—music and baseball. He could quote a handful of major league statistics as accurately as his deft description of Art Tatum's grace notes.

It was during the first week of 1985 when the startling news of Johnny Guarnieri's sudden death swept through the jazz community. The gifted pianist had lived almost sixty-eight years, and most of them were crammed with illustrious achievements that could, and probably will, fill volumes.

He made hundreds of fine records, played on thousands of radio broadcasts, and was featured with several popular bands. Yet, surprisingly, he never achieved the prominence his talents deserved. When the full impact of twentieth-century music is definitively assessed, Johnny Guarnieri will have attained an exalted position among those who made important contributions to the history of jazz.

He was born in New York City on March 23, 1917. He was a descendant of an Italian family of violin makers who came the United States around the turn of the century. They were so poor they had to burn some violins for warmth during their first winter in New York City.

He drew from a variety of musical experiences, including his formidable contribution to the swing era in bands led by Jimmy Dorsey, Benny Goodman, Artie Shaw, and Raymond Scott. Guarnieri was always willing and anxious to share his vast knowledge with anyone who would listen.

For almost ten years, Southern Californians had the opportunity to hear Guarnieri at the Tail o' the Cock in Studio City. He presided nightly at the restaurant's piano bar. Sadly, he was just a fixture in the minds of most patrons; they would dash through the cocktail lounge to

*Pianist Johnny Guarnieri was a fixture at Tail o' the
Cock in Los Angeles.*

the adjacent dining room, oblivious to the extraordinary pianist they
passed.

The left side of the faceboard on Guarnieri's piano was deeply
gouged with fingernail scars, the residue of thousands of chords. Those
scars truly expressed the exuberance of stride piano, a style in which
Guarnieri excelled. During his pounding rendition of "Hand Full of
Keys," his left hand, darting down the keyboard, was a blaze of incredibly accurate motion. He liked to employ unusual time signatures
and often shifted keys in midstream as he romped through a number.
These flashes of technique never detracted from the structure of the
composition; they did, however, engrave each number with a buoyant
originality. Guarnieri possessed an impeccable sense of timing. The
deft bass figures of his pile-driving left hand provided seamless foundations for the agile melodies he constructed with his nimble right hand.
One would swear that a third hand was being overdubbed by an invisi-
ble engineer.

Guarnieri did not have the large hands one would think necessary
to achieve his James P. Johnson–like stride; he often would press his

outstretched palm against a woman's to show that her fingers were longer. Retaining his grip on her fingers with his right hand, he would then launch a fervent southpaw version of "My Funny Valentine."

An evening of Guarnieri music would provide an object lesson in jazz tempos. He often began with a twelve-minute romp through "Stealin' Apples," doubling the tempo with each successive chorus until he had attained a bulletlike pace. His lighter-than-air "Take Me Out to the Ball Game" would merge into a 5/4 treatment of "Maple Leaf Rag." The set might conclude with a dozen choruses of "I'm Just Wild About Harry," each played in a different key.

Guarnieri's favorite pianists included Luckey Roberts, James P. Johnson, Fats Waller, and Art Tatum, and his interpretations of their tunes bore the stamp of genius. Without mimicking, he became an extension of each artist; his warmth and compassion revealed a keen insight into the hearts and minds of his heroes. Few musicians can accomplish this subtle feat as adroitly as Guarnieri did.

He was equally impressive on a simple melodic piece such as "Mood Indigo." Once, after playing a lovely ballad, Guarnieri leaned over from the piano and told me, "I love playing simply. When I worked in New York on Fifty-Second Street years ago, I rotated with Art Tatum and Eddie Heywood. Tatum was the greatest. During his sets, the sparks flew as he outdid himself with each number. Pianists in the club were amazed. He'd conclude his set with blazing fury. Then Heywood would come on with something very simple—just a basic one-line figure in the bass—a quiet moment that would bring the house down. It was perfect."

Countless musicians have spent their entire careers at a level of expertise from which they have never progressed—but not Johnny Guarnieri. His endless quest for excellence propelled him to hone his impressive talents to ever-sharper proportions. He was also a fine teacher, always willing and anxious to share his vast knowledge with anyone who would listen. He heaped encouragement and instruction upon a group of thriving new generation of jazzmen (he called them "my boys") that included Norvin Armstrong, Ted Ziedses des Plantes, and Jim Turner. To repay Johnny for a decade of inspiration, some of "his boys" financed several recording sessions on a tiny independent label, Taz-Jazz.

Guarnieri left a golden legacy of more than six hundred great compositions. "The Great Fred Harding Circus Shout" is a thrilling tour de force of dynamic phrasing so difficult to execute properly that few pi-

anists even attempt it. His unique "The Lion Is Alive in Five" extends a
5/4 salute to the memory of another Guarnieri favorite, Willie "The
Lion" Smith. "Turner Shout" was written for Jim Turner, who recorded it a few years ago on the Euphonic label. He matured under
Johnny's guidance and is now included among the most promising pianists of our day.

Lucille and I frequently took Eubie Blake to the Tail o' the Cock.
From his piano bench in the lounge, Johnny could see the front door.
As we entered, he would immediately switch to a romping stride version of "I'm Just Wild About Harry." Eubie greatly admired Johnny's
playing; in a 1976 letter, he said:

> Dear Floyd and Lucille,
>
> Please give my regards to Johnny G.?—I can never call his name—let alone
> spell it! He is the greatest pianist I've ever heard—next to "One Leg"
> Willie—and I've heard all of them since 1902. But Johnny's my favorite.

To the last days of his life, Johnny was always striving for improve-
ment. "Give me two more years," he told me, "and I'll be as fast and
accurate as anybody ever was. *Anybody.*"

He died before those two years were over, in January 1985—but we
all knew he had already achieved his goal.

I'm Just Wild About Eubie— Memories of Eubie Blake

The 1969 New Orleans Jazz and Heritage Festival featured one of the
best collections of musical talent ever assembled. It starred Count Basie
and His Orchestra (whose members included Buck Clayton, Dicky
Wells, Buddy Tate, and Earl Warren). The six-day festival also included
performances by Benny Carter, Roy Eldridge, Bobby Hackett, Clark
Terry, Zoot Sims, Milt Hinton, Jacki Byard, Alan Dawson, and Bob
Green. New Orleans bands led by Jim Robinson, Sharkey Bonano,
Pete Fountain, Al Hirt, Louis Cottrell, and Johnny Wiggs also appeared. Barry Martyn brought his group of young jazzmen from En-
gland, and Papa Bue's Viking Jazz Band came from Denmark. Dizzy
Gillespie, Roland Kirk, Gerry Mulligan, Paul Desmond, Eddie Miller,
Willie "The Lion" Smith, Zutty Singleton, Harry Shields, Tony Parenti,
and Sarah Vaughan rounded out the roster of jazz giants.

Amid this mind-boggling array of talent, the festival's most impressive segment may have been a twelve-minute interval by a frail, eighty-six-year-old pianist. He needed assistance entering the stage when producer Willis Conover announced his name. As the applause mounted, his halting gait became a vigorous stride, until at last the little man was scampering toward the piano bench with his hands clasped over his head like a prize fighter. The next few moments were sheer magic. The pianist played with power and joy, juxtaposing an intricate right-hand melody against an electrifying left-handed "oom-pah" bass to create an intense ragtime syncopation.

That was my introduction to James Hubert "Eubie" Blake. In my festival review for *Jazz Journal,* I wrote:

> An 86-year-old charmer, Eubie Blake, recalled an era when ragtime was the vogue. After shocking his southern audience with a few irreverent bars of "Marching Through Georgia," the composer-pianist exchanged some ad-lib remarks with Willis Conover before striding into his "Charleston Rag."
>
> He paid tribute to his contemporary C. Luckey Roberts with the latter's "Spanish Venus," followed by a most stirring ragtime version of Sousa's "Stars and Stripes Forever." The Blake-Razaf classic "Memories of You" received an ovation from the appreciative audience responding warmly to Eubie Blake's youthful ebullience.

After the concert, I noticed the pianist standing alone in a quiet corridor backstage. I complimented him on his excellent performance and requested permission to take his picture. He graciously agreed and posed with bassist Milt Hinton, who approached at that moment. When I offered to send him a copy of the picture, he scoffed and quipped: "You guys have been takin' my pictures for seventy years—and I've never seen one of them!"

I promised to send the photo and asked for his address. He opened a small silver case and handed me a business card engraved with the words:

EUBIE BLAKE
PIANIST-ARRANGER.
COMPOSER OF SHUFFLE ALONG
I'M JUST WILD ABOUT HARRY
LOU LESLIE'S BLACKBIRDS

That was three decades ago. The card, with my scrawled notation "SEND PIC," is still in my Eubie Blake file.

Within a week, I sent him the photo. In a few days, I received the first of many handwritten letters he sent to me over the years. His at-

Composer Eubie Blake (right) with the author.
Photo by Lucille Levin.

tractive letterhead, emblazoned with the ASCAP insignia, listed, on the
left margin, names of his Broadway shows and titles of his song hits.
He wrote:

Hello there, friend,

Then, switching to red ink, he added,

And I do mean friend.
Like Geo. M. Cohan used to say —

Then, alternating ink colors on each line, he continued:

My Mother thanks you [green ink]
My Father thanks you [blue ink]
My Sister thanks you [red ink]
My Marion (my wife) thanks you [black ink]
And I thank you! [blue ink]

Sincerely, Your friend

Eubie Blake

P.S. I love the picture with Milt Hinton. I'll have it blown up and hang it in
my gallery of great artists.

In 1995, when his image appeared on a thirty-two-cent stamp, my
photo of Eubie and Milt Hinton was printed on the first-day-of-issue
cachet, mailed during the annual jazz festival at Monterey, California.

Blake was born in 1883 in Baltimore, Maryland; his parents were
both freed slaves. He began playing the piano at age four, getting his
first lessons on a battered old parlor upright. His mother disapproved

of all secular music, but Eubie loved ragtime. He was sixteen years old when he wrote "Sounds of Africa" (later titled "Charleston Rag") in 1899—the same year Scott Joplin's "Maple Leaf Rag" was published. "I didn't *write* 'Charleston Rag' then," he said. "I *composed* it. I learned to write about fifteen years later."

Eubie regretted that ragtime's early association with saloons and houses of prostitution earned it a reputation as "trashy" music. "We're the only race that threw away its heritage because we were brainwashed by white people who couldn't play it," he once told me. "They said ragtime was 'low down'—and it wasn't art. You will notice I never use the vulgar word 'jazz'—I always say 'ragtime.' By the time I was nineteen, with my long fingers, I could span an octave and a half. My mother always told me to keep my hands in my pockets—she was afraid people would imagine I was a pickpocket because of my long fingers. But I could play tenths easily."

Around the turn of the century, "Little Hubie" began sneaking out of the house every night to play piano at a bordello in Baltimore's tenderloin district. "I didn't dare tell my parents about the job," he said. "I was still a teenager—but I made more money in one night than my father made in a week working as a stevedore on the Baltimore docks. My mother took in washing to earn a few dollars. I hid my earnings under the linoleum in the parlor. Finally, when the pile got too high, I showed them the money. It was several hundred dollars. They no longer insisted I only play religious music."

In 1919 Blake was touring the country with Jim Europe's 369th Infantry Jazz Band when the bandleader was tragically murdered. Noble Sissle assumed leadership of the band for the remaining bookings, and he and Blake hit the vaudeville circuit when the tour ended. They billed themselves as the Dixie Duo, with Sissle singing and Blake at the piano. It was the beginning of a long, very successful partnership.

"Right from the start," Eubie emphasized, "we refused to appear in 'blackface'—and no funny shoes and overalls. We came out in beautiful tuxedos, spoke proper grammar—none of that 'dees' and 'dem' stuff. Ours was the first Negro class act." Assiduously avoiding the stereotypes that hampered black performers, they remained a class act throughout their careers.

In 1921, Sissle and Blake joined another black team, Miller and Lyles, in *Shuffle Along,* the first all-black Broadway show in more than a decade. It introduced "I'm Just Wild About Harry" and twenty additional Sissle-Blake tunes. The "showgirls," including Adelaide Hall,

Josephine Baker, Freddie Washington, and Florence Mills, received $30 a week. The show ran for 504 performances and spawned three *Shuffle Along* road companies, which broke color barriers in theaters all across the country.

Al Jolson's 1927 film *The Jazz Singer* is usually identified as the first American motion picture to include sound; the first talking movie actually appeared four years earlier. It was advertised as a "De Forest Phonofilm—it actually talks and reproduces music without use of a phonograph." Sissle and Blake were the only black performers in the stellar vaudeville cast, which also included Weber and Fields, Eddie Cantor, and Phil Baker. The film premiered at the Rivoli Theater in New York City in April 1923, making Sissle and Blake the first black performers to appear in a "talkie." Blake made several more film appearances over the years. His last was in *Scott Joplin,* starring Billy Dee Williams, in 1976—fifty-three years after his screen debut.

"Memories of You," Eubie Blake's most successful ballad, written in collaboration with lyricist Andy Razaf, was in the Broadway show *Lew Leslie's Black Birds of 1930.* Eubie was always generous in his praise for the Casa Loma Orchestra's trumpet star, Sonny Dunham, who championed "Memories of You" as a jazz tune in the late '30s. Benny Goodman's recording a few years later firmly established the tune as a standard.

During the 1930s, Blake collaborated with Noble Sissle for several New York and London shows. He toured as musical director for USO productions during World War II. After the war he joined the faculty of New York University and toured as a lecturer and ragtime artist. In the 1960s he resumed recording, and in 1972 he established a publishing company. In 1970 he received the Presidential Medal of Freedom.

Eubie lived on Stuyvesant Avenue in a three-story brownstone house, the family home of his second wife, Marion. (If Marion was not in the room, he slyly remarked, "When I got the chicken, I also got the coop!") Memories of a long career filled every corner of the house. From the entry door, a long narrow stairway led up to their central living area. Hanging on both sides were framed tributes (including the Presidential Medal of Freedom) and honorary doctorates from Brooklyn College, Dartmouth, Rutgers, the University of Maryland, and the New England Conservatory. There were also medals, citations, and photos—including hundreds of autographed pictures of musicians, four U.S. presidents, and members of European royalty. This was his gallery. The small upstairs living room, dominated by a baby grand piano, was cluttered with pictures, records, and sheet music. He told me he practiced there three hours each day.

Although he lived to see his one hundredth birthday, Blake's daily diet violated every nutritional guideline. His favorite meal consisted of half a dozen doughnuts and a bottle of 7-Up. "If I knew I'd live this long, I'd have taken better care of myself," he once told me. "People think I'm always drunk, because I stagger a lot. I don't drink anything; it's my arthritis." Blake did smoke, prolifically—two packs of cigarettes a day. "When I was a child," he explained, "my mother always gave me a penny to buy candy on the way to school. I noticed the bigger kids bought cigarettes instead. I began smoking when I was six years old—and never stopped."

Blake always seemed happiest on the stage. In the '70s and '80s, when his popularity was at its peak, it seemed he would continue forever. Although he resisted air travel until he was ninety, Eubie was a busy bicoastal entertainer. He said, "I've never been on a plane and never expect to unless I'm handcuffed to a sheriff." He would arrive in Los Angeles by train to make guest appearances on talk shows hosted by Merv Griffin, Johnny Carson, and Mike Douglas. During those occasions, he usually visited our home, relaxing on a recliner, smoking a cigarette, and talking about musicians who had long been forgotten, including many who lived and died around the turn of the century. When I asked him about "One-Leg" Willie, a pianist he'd once mentioned in a letter, Blake said:

> His name was Willie Joseph. His mother worked for some rich white people who recognized his talent and sent him to the Boston Conservatory. He was the first Negro to graduate as a classical pianist. He lost a leg in a skating accident in 1900. In those days, Negros weren't supposed to read music. We pretended we couldn't read and people would marvel at the way we could play show music and rags—they thought by ear. The only arrangement I ever copied was Willie's "Stars and Stripes Forever"—I still play it.

In December 1979, the Huntington Hartford Theater in Hollywood hosted the West Coast premiere of Blake's Broadway show, *Eubie!* Lucille and I sat with Eubie and Marion in the front row. The gleam of a pinpoint spotlight hung like a halo over Eubie's bald head during the entire first act. After the final curtain calls, an on-stage ceremony honoring him featured surprise appearances from members of the show's New York cast, including Maurice and Gregory Hines. The after-show reception glittered with Hollywood stars, musicians, and fans.

A few months later, Adelaide Hall, who had been living in London for forty years, made a rare appearance in New York City at Michael's Pub. We were the Blakes' dinner guests at the dazzling opening night and shared Eubie and Adelaide's reunion. Still youthful and attractive at seventy-six, Hall reprised the momentous 1927 wordless vocal on Ellington's "Creole Love Call," confirming the still-regal splendor of her voice. Then she introduced Blake, who climbed on the stage to accompany her on "Memories of You." Seated at our table between sets, the singer reminisced fondly with the eminent composer who had launched her career in 1923.

Blake often said he would never retire. "I'll keep performing until, one day while I'm on stage, the man upstairs says: 'Nine, ten, you're out!' "

A distinguished cast came together to celebrate Blake's one-hundredth birthday on February 7, 1983, with an incredible two-hour concert. Adelaide Hall came from London to sing a medley of tunes from *Shuffle Along,* and pianists Dick Hyman, Dick Zimmerman, John Arpin, Max Morath, Billy Taylor, Terry Waldo, and Bobby Short added their talents to the show. The stellar rhythm section featured Howard Alden on banjo and guitar, Milt Hinton on bass, and Ron Traxler on drums.

Blake, stricken with pneumonia, was unable to attend the hundredth-birthday concert; he watched a special closed-circuit broadcast of the event. The huge bouquet of yellow roses next to his bed was a gift sent by his friend, comedian Bill Cosby.

It was five days after his one hundredth birthday when, as he predicted, the man upstairs said: "Nine, ten, you're out!" At the time Eubie took the final count, he was the only one left who could authentically talk about and play the music from the ragtime era. He was there at the beginning.

The Maryland Historical Society and the Baltimore Cultural Arts Program received his huge collection of memorabilia, documenting the pianist's journey from bawdy houses to concert stages. The Eubie Blake National Museum and Cultural Center, also located in Baltimore, features several large displays and a bronze head of Eubie by noted sculptor Dr. William Douglas Hartley, a gift Lucille and I presented to the museum in 1988.

Eubie Blake's life and work spanned a considerable portion of our nation's musical history. He began in medicine and minstrel shows, made cylinder recordings and piano rolls, and became a major force in the development of the American musical theater. His songs will continue to be a source of joy to music lovers.

Eubie Blake enriched the lives of countless friends and fans. I am fortunate to have been a member of both groups.

Jess Stacy

Jess Stacy appeared on my *Jazz on Parade* radio program on February 6, 1950. Born August 11, 1904, in Bird's Point, Missouri (which lies on the Mississippi about halfway between Memphis and St. Louis), he got his start playing on riverboats with jazzmen such as Bix Beiderbecke, Louis Armstrong, and Fate Marable. He became part of Chicago's flourishing jazz scene in the mid-1920s and spent the swing era in popular big bands led by Benny Goodman, Bob Crosby, Tommy Dorsey, and others. Stacy dropped out of sight in the early 1950s, but in the 1970s he made a brief, unexpected comeback.

By then we were neighbors, and I used to visit the aging pianist frequently. During one of our afternoons together, he said, "Years ago, I thought about writing my autobiography—about my days on the riverboats, Chicago in the '20s, and so on. I started it once, but, I guess I forgot about it." He gave me a wrinkled carbon copy of a handwritten manuscript he authored in 1946, perhaps as the first chapter of his intended autobiography. Published here for the first time, the document is steeped in the atmosphere of early jazz.

"RAMBLIN'," BY JESS STACY

When I was the kid, I worked in Clark's Music Store in Cape Girardeau, Missouri. At night, after everyone had gone, I used to put one of those new-fangled flat records on our modern megaphone-type "His Master's Voice" phonograph and sweep the store to the beat of the latest jazz band recordings. Clark's was unquestionably the best-swept music store in the country at that time.

There was a big event three times a year at Cape Girardeau when the SS *Capitol* steamed into town to play a Mississippi River excursion. What excitement! They used to advertise the coming of the *Capitol* just the way they advertise jazz concerts and one-night stands these days. On the evening of the excursion we would go down to the levee early to listen to a wonderful jazz band playing up on the deck. They attracted customers that bought tickets and went up the gangway for an evening's sailing.

Like all young boys, my mother made me take piano lessons, and I was beginning to try to sound like those riverboat bands. It was my burning ambition to get a job on the *Capitol,* but the players in those bands were such important musicians, it seemed that I would never make it.

I distinctly remember one night I went down to the levee, and up on the deck of the *Capitol* there was a new trumpet player, Louis Armstrong. It was Fate Marable's band, and in addition to Louis it featured two young brothers who played clarinet and drums—Johnny and Baby Dodds. The band played "Skeleton Jangle," "Tiger Rag," and the popular ballad "Whispering"—yes, the same "Whispering" that Dizzy Gillespie is playing today. But the most exciting of all was their version of "Railroad Man," one of tunes that accompanied my nightly sweeping chores at Clark's Music Store.

Louis was young and green—in his late teens. He hadn't even seen St. Louis yet. He was on his way up the river for the first time. You can't imagine such energy, such musical fireworks Louis Armstrong played on that boat. The instrumentation of the band was piano, clarinet, drums, two trumpets, trombone, and, I think, a couple saxophones. Most of their material consisted of head arrangements, but occasionally they would fake around simple old-time dance orchestrations. Certainly there was no music written for that band. Who could write anything better than they could play naturally?

The next time the steamer *Capitol* tied up at Cape Girardeau was early on a fall evening. I ran down to see the boat because I knew that the famous jazz band called Tony Catalano's Iowans from Davenport was on board. Jimmy Cannon was the clarinetist, and Lyle Sexton played trombone. But when I got there, the band was silent, and Tony Catalano was looking for a piano player. Somebody pointed me out. He said, "Kid, get some long pants and come back here right away, you've got a job for tonight only."

After that, I did get a regular job on the steamer *Majestic* for a while and soon joined Catalano's band on the *Capitol.* When we docked in Davenport, everybody knew Bix Beiderbecke, and all the cornet players in the bands around there used to imitate him before he was hardly known up in Chicago.

I remember one night Bix came on board in Davenport, his home town. At that time he was about nineteen years old and had just recorded "Riverboat Shuffle" with the Wolverines. Jimmy Cannon and Lyle Sexton greeted him by singing his chorus on that record. Bix picked up Tony's cornet—he had his own mouthpiece—sat in and played "Eccentric" and "Skeleton Jangle" with us. He used the first valve most of the time and did the work of the other two valves with that wonderful lip. Of course, he knocked everybody stiff. And then, when he finished, he took over my bench at the piano, played "Give Me a June Night," "Baby Blue Eyes," and "Clarinet Marmalade," and assassinated everyone all over again.

I didn't see Bix after that for about three years, the night he joined Paul Whiteman. I remember he didn't have a tuxedo; he had to borrow Jimmy McPartland's. His battered silver cornet was green with corrosion, and Bix carried it wrapped in a paper bag. I think he was still in his 20s when he died just a few years later.

More than two decades later, when he appeared on my radio show, Stacy was still performing Beiderbecke's songs (he played "In a Mist" during the broadcast). When he named Beiderbecke and Louis Armstrong—both trumpeters—as two of the musicians who influenced him most, I remarked that it was unusual for a musician to be so heavily influenced by someone playing a different instrument. "I've been accused of playing a trumpet-style piano," Stacy quipped.

Asked to reminisce about the Chicago jazz scene of the 1920s, he said: "King Oliver was playing at the Plantation at 35th and Calumet. Directly across the street, Louis Armstrong had a band at the Sunset Cafe. And upstairs, at a little supper club called the Nest, Jimmie Noone had a small group. I played out at the Midway Garden Ballroom. Some of my buddies were Muggsy Spanier and Frank Teschemacher—they were in the band. ... We'd go over and listen to King Oliver, then try to play the same tunes as best we could." He spoke glowingly about Frank Teschemacher, whom he met in Chicago. "My buddy, Tesch, was way ahead of his time," he said. "He patterned his phrasing on Bix Beiderbecke's cornet style and greatly influenced Benny Goodman."

Stacy himself contributed to Goodman's sound. His beautifully improvised short segment on "Sing, Sing, Sing," recorded with Goodman during a 1938 concert at Carnegie Hall, ranks among the most celebrated of jazz piano solos. The brilliant two-minute statement has an ecstatic quality, building slowly in graceful spirals. His other recordings, with such stars as Eddie Condon, Ziggy Elman, and Lionel Hampton, gave Stacy quite a following; he won *Down Beat*'s 1940 poll as best pianist.

By the time of his appearance on my show, Stacy had moved to Los Angeles and was playing at a little place called the Radar Room, tossing off riffs with Albert Nicholas, Johnny Lucas, Archie Rosati, and other friends. The Radar Room was among scores of locations where he played during more than a decade in the Los Angeles area. I have a stack of postcards announcing his various engagements. During that period, he maintained an extensive mailing list and diligently addressed an announcement whenever he moved to another club. Most of the venues were dismal piano bars where the customers were more concerned with conversation (or the blonde on the next stool) than the music. Occasionally Jess would have a few appreciative fans listening to him, but usually his music was merely a background for imbibing, and his audiences were seldom attentive.

"You know," he used to say, "the public likes to hear things that look challenging. No matter how good it is, if it doesn't look hard, they pay no attention. You can play a simple riff, and if you beat your brains out and make it look difficult, they'll think it's wonderful and yell for more."

One evening in North Hollywood, Jess was working at the piano bar in Leon's Steak House (he called it the "Snake Pit.") The piano needing tuning, the drunks were noisier than usual, and an unsteady matron, requesting "Beer Barrel Polka" for the third time, spilled beer in his lap. That did it. Stacy stopped playing in the middle of a tune. He resolutely closed his piano, reached for his coat, stalked out of the club, and never returned—not even to pick up his paycheck. His bitterness was so intense, he refused to touch his piano for many years and firmly announced his profound hatred for the "@#%&*%" music business."

After more than a decade of self-imposed isolation, Stacy returned to live performing with an appearance in "A Night in New Orleans," the concert series I co-produced with Barry Martyn. It took many months to convince him that there was still a large group of fans anxious to hear him play. After much cajoling, he reluctantly agreed to play. On September 20, 1975, we featured Stacy in "A Night in New Orleans" at the Wilshire Ebell Theatre in Los Angeles. He shared piano duties with Ralph Sutton; the two were appropriately billed as "The Keyboard Giants." Stacy claimed he was extremely nervous, but he played with his usual verve and was rewarded by a standing ovation from an enthusiastic audience.

Buoyed by this success, Stacy briefly resumed his career. He traveled to New York and recorded his second album for Hank O'Neal's

Chiaroscuro label, and he contributed to the soundtrack of the Paramount film *The Great Gatsby.* But his comeback was short-lived; he made only a few appearances and, after the late 1970s, again withdrew from the musical scene. He spent the remainder of his life living quietly in his Laurel Canyon home with his wife, Pat.

On New Year's Eve 1994, during his final days at the Good Samaritan Hospital in Los Angeles, Jess turned to his wife and said: "Teschemacher! Teschemacher!" Was he delirious? Or was he thinking about rejoining his old buddy? Jess died the next evening, on January 1, 1995.

Dedicated jazz historians have carefully researched Jess Stacy's long career, and the following books are currently available: *Oh, Jess! A Jazz Life,* by Keith Keller (Mayan Music Corporation, 1989), and *Jess Stacy, the Quiet Man of Jazz,* by Derek Coller (Jazzology Press, 1997).

Milt Hinton

Bass is the base—the bottom—the support. We hold
the thing up—like Atlas of the music world.
> Milt Hinton, addressing the world's
> greatest bassists at the International Society
> of Bassists Convention, Los Angeles, 1988

During the last six decades, Milt Hinton's career has been inextricably woven into every segment of jazz history—as a musician, producer, author, historian, teacher, and photographer.

Milt Hinton rose to fame playing string bass in Cab Calloway's orchestra from 1936 to 1951. He has since appeared with Duke Ellington, Count Basie, Benny Goodman, Louis Armstrong, and many other major jazz artists. Hinton's bass can be heard on hundreds of recordings spanning a broad range of styles. Bassists around the world agree that "The Judge" (as Hinton was fondly nicknamed) elevated the bass from back-of-the-bandstand anonymity to a featured role in modern jazz orchestras. He took the bass into previously uncharted territory.

With the steady beat of a fine watch, Hinton was always the mainspring of the rhythm section. Exercising a violin-like agility on his cumbersome instrument, he delved deeply within a tune to expose the roots from which its rhythmic and melodic impulses emerged. Hinton was always in full control, effortlessly establishing propulsive base lines to support the efforts of his sidemen; as a soloist, he enhanced each performance with individuality and charm.

Hinton was born in Vicksburg, Mississippi, on June 23, 1910. He often spoke about his grandmother, who had been a slave on a Vicksburg plantation.

In 1917 his family moved to Chicago, where Hinton studied violin and played in the high school orchestra. "We never played any jazz," he said. "This was symphony stuff. The music was written out—there was no ad-libbing whatsoever."

As a teenager, Hinton delivered newspapers in the Chicago Loop. "I started my route in the early morning," he told me. "I was impressed with the well-dressed musicians I saw as they were leaving their jobs. This was the first time I had seen black men in tuxedos. I knew then that I would become a professional musician."

After switching to tuba, he got his first job in 1929 while still a senior in high school. When the string bass gradually replaced the tuba, he took bass lessons from Dmitri Shmulkovsky of the Chicago Civic Opera Orchestra.

During the 1930s, Hinton worked in the Chicago area with Eddie South, Tiny Parham, Jabbo Smith, and Erskine Tate. After fifteen years with Cab Calloway, he settled in New York and soon was one of the city's most sought-after bassists. He became a member of the Count Basie Orchestra, traveled with the Louis Armstrong All-Stars, and accompanied Bing Crosby on several overseas tours. He recorded with hundreds of artists, including Frank Sinatra, Percy Faith, Barbra Streisand, Lena Horne, Sarah Vaughan, Ella Fitzgerald, and Quincy Jones. Because of his almost daily recording schedule, he kept a bass stored in a Manhattan loft to avoid having to carry the cumbersome instrument on the subway.

By the 1970s he was featured in jazz festivals around the world. He taught and conducted workshops at Hunter College in New York City and lectured at universities throughout the country. Invariably, Hinton was the senior member of the band when he performed, yet his youthful enthusiasm encouraged and inspired his younger colleagues. His heavy schedule included frequent performances until illness sidelined him in the 1990s. Exuding indefatigable energy, with his beloved Mona always at his side, Hinton hopped and skipped around the planet at a pace that would exhaust a performer half his age. He was a familiar sight at the world's airports—pushing his large bass ahead of him and dragging his heavy amplifier on a cart. Several times, when I offered assistance, he refused, saying: "I'll have to handle this load when no one is available to help, so I might as well do it now."

In addition to achieving greatness on stage, Hinton is an acknowledged master at jazz photography. His books *Bass Line: The Stories and Photographs of Milt Hinton* (Temple University Press) and *Overtime, The Jazz Photographs of Milt Hinton* (Pomegranate Art Books) are widely acclaimed by photographers and jazz fans alike. In 1993 he became the first recipient of the Jazz Photographers Association's Milt Hinton Award for Excellence in Jazz Photography. The beautiful bronze plaque was conceived by JPA member Bill Wishner and sculpted by noted artist Jim Casey. It was my privilege to present Hinton with the award. In his acceptance speech, he said, "I will spend the rest of my life trying to live up to this honor."

Hinton's home is filled with tributes and citations presented to him for his musical achievements. The prestigious JPA award was the first recognition he received for his second artistic love, photography.

Hinton was the guest of honor at the 1993 Los Angeles Classic Jazz Festival. The program included the West Coast premier of his very unique composition, "The Judge Meets the Section," a jazz etude for string bass. Hinton had premiered the composition at his elaborate eightieth birthday celebration, held three years earlier at Town Hall in New York City; the L.A. festival marked its second performance. Hinton, seated in the center of the stage, was flanked by a dozen renowned colleagues. Only once before had so many esteemed bassists been assembled on one stage. This was the setting when they played "The Judge Meets the Section":

Bob Haggart		David Stone
Herb Mickman		Ira Westley
Greg Cohen	Milt "The Judge" Hinton	Bob Finch
Morty Corb		Isla Eckinger
Paul Gormley		Jennifer York
John Leitham		Roger Krum

As the rich resonance of thirteen bowed basses filled the ballroom, a large screen displayed images of Milt Hinton at various periods in his long career, as well as many of his renowned photographs. The audio/visual presentation showcased his two loves—the string bass and the camera. Milt played his bass from 1929 on and created important photographic remembrances of his peers beginning in 1935.

Every musician will agree that time holds a band together and contributes the syncopated pulsation that makes it swing. Milt's famous signature tune was, appropriately, "Old Man Time." He played and sang it at every performance. During the last few years, as he sped past the eighty mark, the tune took on a sentimental air and caused tears to appear in many eyes.

> Old Man Time, he's so mean,
> He's the meanest man you've ever seen
> He gave me youth, then he took it away,
> He took my curly hair, and turned it gray
>
> He made me rich—made me poor
> Oh, he's mean that's for sure!
> All my dreams and all my schemes
> Don't mean a thing!
>
> He gave me beauty, charm and grace
> Then put wrinkles in my face
> That's Old Man, Old Man Time
>
> Some people call him arthritis
> And others say bursitis
> But no matter what his name
> His game is still the same
> To make me forget what I went to the store for
> Or what it was I used to chase those girls for
> That's Old Man, Old Man Time
>
> > "Old Man Time" by Cliff Friend/
> > Jack Reynolds (EMI Miller Catalog, Inc.
> > 1961); closing chorus lyrics by Milt Hinton

While he epitomized the phrase "musician's musician," Milt Hinton attracted friends from throughout the jazz community: players, technicians, producers, promoters, and—especially—listeners. They all share an abiding admiration for the great jazzman. The key word here is "love." Hinton radiated a sincere love for his friends, and they returned his warm affection.

Spiegle Willcox

Trombonist Spiegle Willcox was the sole surviving member of the 1925 Jean Goldkette Orchestra, where he played alongside Jimmy Dorsey, Frank Trumbauer, Joe Venuti, and Bix Beiderbecke.

In 1995 I visited him at his home in upstate New York. My mission was to interview the nonagenarian for the Smithsonian Institution's Jazz Oral History Program. His home was not visible from the narrow back road; a rural postal box on an unmarked lane was the only indi-

Spiegle Willcox receives the 1995 American Federation
of Jazz Societies' Benny Carter Award from AFJS
director Floyd Levin. Photo by Norman Vickers.

cation of its presence. The long private route wound through a rustic
grove, passed a pair of trout lakes, and crossed a little bridge leading to
the house. In the winter, Willcox drove a small truck with a plow at-
tachment down the snow-covered road every morning to retrieve his
mail.

A few days earlier, during the Jersey Jazzfest at Stephens College in
Hoboken, New Jersey, I had presented Spiegle with the American Federation of Jazz Societies' Benny Carter Award. The bronze figure was
proudly displayed on his mantle when we arrived at his house. Our
conversations were recorded in a large family room overlooking his
private lake—where he often caught a fresh trout for his morning
breakfast. During our two day-long sessions, he told me about many
incidents that highlighted his long career.

Willcox was born on May 2, 1903; his real name is Newell Lynn
Willcox. "I don't remember when or why I got the nickname
'Spiegle,'" he told me, "but it's easier to remember than 'Newell.'"
When he was nineteen years old, he went to New York with an eight-
piece band from Cornell University. They were hired to appear as Paul
Whiteman's Collegians. "We played at a very swanky nightclub called
the Rendezvous—a lot of celebrities came in. I remember seeing Will
Rogers and William S. Hart. The boss's girlfriend was Gilda Gray, the
famous shimmy dancer in the Ziegfeld Follies. We made a few Victor

recordings. Our pay was a hundred dollars a week—quite a sum in those days."

When Tommy Dorsey left the California Ramblers in 1925, Spiegle replaced him for a few weeks before joining Jean Goldkette's Orchestra at the Graystone Ballroom in Detroit. "We had no microphones in those days," Willcox recalled. "We played our solos into megaphones." (He still had the large conical contraption and later demonstrated how his horn sounded when he blew into the early "amplifier.") Goldkette had four orchestras operating under his name and also employed the Orange Blossom Band and McKinney's Cotton Pickers. "Our group was conducted by Russ Morgan," said Willcox. "Bill Challis became our arranger. Goldkette seldom appeared; he handled the band's business. Once, during a week's engagement in a Detroit theater, he played piano on 'Rhapsody in Blue.' "

For the next two years Willcox was in the "big time," playing on radio broadcasts and at parties and college dances. The band continued its engagement at the Graystone, rehearsing in the basement of the building:

> Russ Morgan conducted in public, but Fuzzy Farrar, our lead trumpet player, handled the rehearsals. He put the brass, reeds and rhythm players in different rooms to rehearse their sections separately before bringing it all together. We worked on each tune for several days until it was perfect.
>
> Bix Beiderbecke and Frank Trumbauer joined the band in the spring of 1926. Bix was down to earth and a very nice guy—very modest, almost shy. The audiences were not particularly aware of him, but the musicians in the other bands recognized his skills. I knew he was a great player and also knew the band was very good—but I never dreamed we would be legends half a century later.
>
> Steve Brown [the band's bass player] had been with the New Orleans Rhythm Kings—did a lot of nice bow work and was an expert with the slap bass technique.
>
> With our new Challis arrangements of "Blue Room" and "On the Alamo," plus Trumbauer's "Clarinet Marmalade" and "Singin' the Blues," the band became very successful. We were a big hit on our New England tour during the fall. Bix played the best horn of his whole career—and when Itzy Riskin needed a break, Bix took over on piano.

Spiegle married his hometown sweetheart, Helen Gunsaules, in 1925. A couple of years later, when he took a few days off to return home to be with Helen for the birth of their son Newell, Jr., he asked Tommy Dorsey to take his place in the Graystone Ballroom band. "Bix, Don Murray, and some of the Goldkette players were checking the horses running at a Chicago racetrack that day," Willcox remembered, "and they noticed an entry named 'Helen's Babe.' It was a long shot, but they each put in a few bucks and bet on the horse to win. It did! They made a couple of hundred dollars."

Shortly thereafter, Willcox left the Goldkette band and returned to upstate New York, where he entered the family coal business. He continued playing in the Ithaca-Syracuse area and kept a band busy on weekends for many years. Several large posters advertising "Spiegle Willcox and His Orchestra" adorn the walls of his home, along with framed vintage photos of the young trombonist playing in the Cortland YMCA Band, Paul Whiteman's Collegians, and the Goldkette Orchestra.

In 1975, forty-eight years after he left the Goldkette band, Willcox returned to New York to participate with former Goldkette players in a Carnegie Hall tribute to Bix Beiderbecke. He was invited to another Bix tribute during the Newport Jazz Festival that year and soon found himself back on the road with his old colleague, Joe Venuti. After that, Willcox's career surged ahead at full steam.

He was featured at the Palm Springs Jazz Festival in 1989 with C-Melody saxophonist Rosy McHargue and Harry Gold, the English bandleader and bass saxophonist. I enjoyed conducting a symposium with the three musicians, all in their late eighties. They played together and fielded questions from the audience. Willcox's daughter Cynthia was beaming in the front row, holding her father's battered horn case on her lap. That afternoon was a joyous exercise in jazz history I will never forget!

In 1995 Spiegle was the featured artist at a jazz festival in Yuba City, California. He grinned when he said: "At ninety-two, I was their first choice as poster boy—at the Prune Festival!"

While in his mid-nineties, Willcox travelled frequently to jazz festivals in the United States and Europe. He always had a broad smile, retained a youthful alertness, and enjoyed reminiscing. Jazz fans throughout the world considered him a friend. So did I.

Spiegle died August 26, 1999.

Eddie Miller

The history of jazz has been brightened by scores of great musicians. Their contributions, individually and collectively, have endowed the

music with a bountiful legacy from which future generations of fans
and musicians will always draw inspiration. Among those in the Pan-
theon of Jazz Greats, just a few—perhaps only one or two on each instrument—are ranked as true titans.

These towering "Giants" have shaped the paths jazzmen will continually follow in whatever direction this music might ramble. Tenor
saxophonist Eddie Miller will forever be included in this select group.

Eddie lived near us in Studio City. He and Edna were teenage sweethearts when they were married in New Orleans more than sixty years
before. We often met them walking side by side at the neighborhood
Hughes Market. Edna selected the groceries and Eddie pushed the
shopping cart. Although on stage he seemed taller, he was actually a
very short man. We were always amused to see the acknowledged jazz
giant completely dwarfed by his huge load of groceries.

Eddie established clear guidelines for the way a tenor saxophone
should be played in a Dixieland band. He skillfully added warmth and
depth to the ensembles by spinning graceful musical webs between
trombone, trumpet, and clarinet.

His beautifully developed solos, logical extensions of a tune's roots,
bloomed with majestic splendor. This magic, continuing over the years,
appears on hundreds of classic jazz recordings that include his easily
identifiable sound. Regretfully, his golden Selmer horn has been silent
for almost a decade.

It has been sixty years since I heard my first Dixieland record—and
it was an Eddie Miller recording! It was a joyous, relaxed Bob Crosby
Bob Cats' version of "'Till We Meet Again" played by Jack the Bell
Boy during his all-night radio program in Los Angeles. I was extremely
moved by the thirty-two-bar saxophone solo—and bought the record
the next day!

The beautiful 78 rpm blue label Decca (No. 2825) with bright gold
printing cost thirty-five cents, a formidable amount in those lean years.
The fine print identified the tenor sax player as Eddie Miller. He was in
good company: Billy Butterfield was on trumpet, Matty Matlock played
clarinet, Warren Smith was the trombonist, Joe Sullivan majestically
handled the piano keys, Nappy Lamare was strumming his guitar, Bob
Haggart played string bass, and Ray Bauduc was the drummer.

This was 1939—the peak of the big band era, and Bob Crosby's orchestra was riding the crest of the musical wave. They enjoyed the choic-
est bookings and received nationwide radio exposure. My high school
homework was frequently interrupted by their nightly "remotes."

I can still hear the saccharine-voiced announcer purr his introduction to the Crosby broadcasts "from the beautiful Casino Ballroom at romantic Catalina Island overlooking the harbor lights of Avalon Bay and the blue Pacific." I listened attentively to my bedside radio anxiously awaiting the Bob Cats, the small group that usually spotlighted Eddie's saxophone.

Eddie Miller (Edward Raymond Muller) was born in New Orleans on June 23, 1911. His earliest musical activity was with a local youth band. "I was just starting out, fourteen years old—taking alto sax lessons," he told me several years ago. "I heard about this newsboys' band—everyone in New Orleans had a band in those days. I wasn't very interested in selling papers, but I got a job at the *New Orleans Item* so I could join their band."

Two years later, he was a professional musician. At seventeen he was playing with the eminent New Orleans Owls at the Hotel Grunewald on Canal Street. After a few years in the Crescent City's "big time," Miller yielded to the lure of New York City. He was immediately recognized as an upcoming talent and played his alto saxophone with several prominent Gotham bands.

In 1930, at the age of nineteen, Eddie was hired to play tenor sax in the very successful Ben Pollock Orchestra at the Park Central Hotel. The Pollock band included Eddie's fellow New Orleanians Nappy Lamare and Ray Bauduc, and future associates Matty Matlock and Gil Rodin.

When Pollock's band broke up in 1934, Miller, Rodin, Lamare, Matlock, and Bauduc formed the nucleus of a co-op group. They hired Bing Crosby's young brother, Bob, the handsome vocalist with the Dorsey Brothers' Orchestra, to front the band.

Until interrupted by World War II, the great band showcased near-forgotten Dixieland standards dressed in brilliant arrangements by Deane Kincaide and Matty Matlock. Amid the surfeit of fine "swing" bands, this was the only group sustaining the earlier sounds of New Orleans during the big band era.

Eddie Miller's contribution to the Crosby band's success was immeasurable. Their Decca records, now rare collectors' items, preserve his best efforts. Eddie's clarinet can be heard on the timeless "South Rampart Street Parade" and "Dog Town Blues." On "Slow Mood," a Miller original, his landmark solo vividly displays the tenor sax skill that attracted worldwide acclaim.

Most of the instrumentalists at Dixieland jazz festivals around the world have never witnessed live performances by the original Bob

Crosby orchestra; however, its strong influence on younger players is still very apparent. Many tunes they play, and the manner in which they play them, are based on Bob Crosby recordings. Often, this motivation has led succeeding generations of musicians to trace the earlier roots of the music that also inspired the Bob Cats half a century ago.

Eddie Miller's horn enhanced hundreds of records during his long career. None are more memorable than the 1949 Jump Record sessions, when he eloquently shared the mood with pianist Stan Wrightsman and the guitar master George Van Eps.

Duke Ellington's beautiful composition "Sophisticated Lady" was always a Miller favorite. Probably his most impassioned version is on an extraordinary recording with a fine Italian guitarist, Lino Patruno, and the Milan College Jazz Society.

I recently replayed my treasured copy of "'Till We Meet Again." The passing years have not dimmed the brilliant sounds that introduced me to Eddie Miller's music. That singular experience eventually led to a rewarding lifetime quest for knowledge about jazz and the men who play it. I often thought I should thank him.

We are fortunate to have seen and heard Eddie for years. He frequently appeared with his own band, periodic reunions of the Bob Crosby Orchestra, with Pete Fountain's band, the World's Greatest Jazz Band, Abe Most's groups, the Lawson-Haggart Jazz Band, and at Bob Taber's Poor Angel Jazz Parties.

The last time I spoke to him was during the 1987 Los Angeles Classic Jazz Festival. He was seated on his horn case near the bandstand awaiting his next set. As I approached, he greeted me with the familiar beaming smile accentuating his flushed cheeks and boyish face. Only the lines around his eyes betrayed his seventy-six years. Eddie's soft voice retained a trace of his New Orleans drawl. We spoke briefly, and I took his picture.

Unfortunately, I overlooked this last opportunity to thank him for the years of musical pleasure he had given to me—and to the world. Two years later, when the Los Angeles Classic Jazz Festival was dedicated to his lifetime achievements, he was too ill to attend.

Eddie Miller died April 1, 1991.

Morty Corb

In 1947, after leading a big band for many years, Louis Armstrong decided to return to the small-band format of his New Orleans roots. He assembled a formidable group of musicians: Jack Teagarden on trombone, Barney Bigard on clarinet, Dick Cary on piano, Sid Catlett at the drums, and Velma Middleton on vocals. And the bass player for this seminal ensemble was Morty Corb.

Since his arrival in Los Angeles in 1946, Corb had established a stellar reputation; his mastery of the string bass brought him offers in every phase of the music business. He was in constant demand for club dates, concerts, recordings, radio and television programs, and films. When Armstrong's manager, Joe Glaser, phoned from New York and asked Corb if he would be interested in joining the new group Armstrong was assembling, the popular bassist jumped at the chance.

Louis Armstrong's All-Stars opened in Los Angeles at Billy Berg's Vine Street club on August 13, 1947. They were an immediate hit, playing to packed houses and garnering rave reviews. But when Armstrong decided to take the band on a world tour, Corb balked.

"My biggest compliment was when Louis said, 'I like your playing. I would like you to go to Europe with me,' " Corb told me in a 1988 interview. "I declined—partly because I do not like to fly, but also because I was just starting to get roots in the studios, and that was what I wanted to do." Arvell Shaw took over on bass for the All-Stars.

Corb was born in San Antonio, Texas, on April 10, 1917, and learned to play the ukulele at the age of six. Without any formal training, he graduated to the guitar and soon came under the influence of blues recordings by the legendary guitarist Jimmy Rodgers. While still in high school he heard radio broadcasts by the Light Crust Doughboys, a jazz-oriented Texas group that included Knocky Parker on piano. He fell in love with the sound of the string bass in the band and persuaded his father to buy him a bass for $60.

As a youngster, he listened to most of the Texas bands, including groups led by Troy Floyd, Alphonse Trent, Don Albert, Boots and his Buddies, Terry Shand, and Peck Kelly. He played his first professional job at seventeen, earning $3 a night with a San Antonio dance band led by John Fielder.

In 1939 he joined an Arkansas traveling band led by Carl "Deacon" Moore, earning $47.50 a week. After four weeks of one-night stands, he joined Dusty Rhodes' band for a hotel engagement in Kansas City, Missouri. "I was ready to go back to San Antonio when the Rhodes band folded," Corb told me in 1988, "but I received a wire from Joe Reichman [then known as the 'Pagliacci of the Piano'] asking me to join his band as a guitarist. The salary was about three times what I had been getting, plus extras."

Corb made his first recordings with Reichman, and his travels with the band took him to Los Angeles for the first time. "On our night off, I visited many of the clubs in L.A.," he told me. "I heard Nat Cole at the 331 Club; Art Tatum was at the Streets of Paris. The town was loaded with jazz."

After serving in World War II, Corb returned to Los Angeles for good and began his studio career, working at radio station KLAC. His career soared considerably after his successful 1947 engagement with Louis Armstrong. Before long he was recording almost every day. The hundreds of artists with whom he recorded included Ella Fitzgerald, Pearl Bailey, Nat Cole, Judy Garland, Pete Fountain, Jess Stacy, Stan Kenton, Jack Teagarden, Kid Ory, and scores of others. He played bass on the entire Time-Life series of recordings. In addition, Corb appeared in films with Red Nichols, Peggy Lee, Gene Krupa, Woody Herman, Benny Carter, Ray Anthony, and Les Brown. He played nightclub and concerts dates throughout the Los Angeles area with Abe Most, Al Hirt, Kay Starr, Jimmy Durante, Ray Conniff, Helen O'Connell, Connie Haines, Eddie Fisher, Errol Garner, and Walter Gross.

When he died on January 13, 1996, at age seventy-nine, hundreds of colleagues and fans turned out for the memorial service. The musical program at his funeral included the cheerful jazz he played for six decades—songs like "Easy to Remember," "Frankie and Johnny," and his personal favorite, "You'd Be So Easy to Love." Joyous applause filled the crowded chapel after each number.

Several of his friends participated. Each expressed an individual memory tinged with humor and love. Collectively, their sincere comments created a vivid perception of the man whose life they celebrated. During an extremely moving moment, Dave Caughren, a friend for fifty years, played a tape recording of Corb singing an original tune at a recent job.

As a final touch of class, his bronze casket was majestically transported to the nearby mausoleum in a glistening forty-five-year-old Rolls Royce hearse. While the pallbearers slid his casket into its marble niche, a tall palm, framed in an adjacent glass portal, swayed vigorously in the wind, as if to wave farewell. We all returned to our cars, humming "There's a Harp Waiting for Me in Heaven," played on tape during the service. Corb himself was the singer; his prophetic lyrics were:

I've got a harp waiting for me in heaven,
and I'm gonna play some jazz
at that big jam session in the sky.

Barney Bigard

Albany Leon "Barney" Bigard was one of the foremost exponents of the New Orleans–style clarinet. His delicate passages, though spoken very softly, shouted the clarion call of pure jazz. Undulating chromatic runs flowed smoothly from his Albert system horn, reshaping familiar melodies into thrilling new sounds. The warmth and vitality of Bigard's playing conjured vivid images of New Orleans. A longtime member of Duke Ellington's orchestra, he spent most of his life away from his hometown, yet the Crescent City's spirit always came through in Bigard's music and in the gentlemanly way he related to people.

He was born in a little house on Villere Street in New Orleans' French Quarter in March 3, 1906. His uncle, the jazz violinist Emile Bigard, encouraged him to study clarinet with Lorenzo Tio, Jr., the great teacher who also tutored such notables as Jimmie Noone, Johnny Dodds, Omer Simeon, and Albert Nicholas (see Chapter 4).

One of his first musical jobs was with bandleader Octave Gaspard, who asked Barney's grandmother for permission to employ the young clarinetist. This is how Bigard recalled that incident:

> She thought I was too young to play a job with him, but he volunteered to get me home safely, so she finally gave in. That night at the job we had a rough time. I couldn't get with those cats—the first thing they put me on was "Tiger Rag," and I was still trying to make the first part by the time they were already to the breaks. They were all holding their heads and moaning, but I didn't care, I wanted to learn, and I had what they called a "hard face" in those days. My desire to play made it impossible to insult me, and I guess it was a good thing. I played so badly they used to call me "the snake charmer."
>
> Then the sax came out. I got me a tenor and I discovered it was a lot easier to play than the clarinet. My reputation and my calls improved quite rapidly, and before long I got my revenge. If they wanted me, they had to pay double. That meant a dollar fifty a night instead of seventy-five cents.

Eventually Tio's tutelage became evident, and young Bigard played his clarinet in New Orleans bands led by Armand Piron and Buddy Petit. When he was eighteen years old and playing at Tom Anderson's Cafe on Basin Street, he received an offer to join Joe Oliver's band in Chicago. This group included some old friends from New Orleans, including Bud Scott, Paul Barbarin, and Albert Nicholas. Bigard reminisced:

> One day in 1924, I received a telegram from King Oliver in Chicago. Albert Nicholas and Luis Russell had gone on to Chicago before. When the King

asked them to recommend a tenor man, they mentioned me. We were to open Christmas Eve at the Royal Gardens, but we didn't get to because the place burned down that night.

Nicholas and I roomed together, scuffling 'til the King could get another job. We finally opened at the Plantation. Satchmo was across the street at a place called the Sunset Cafe. After a long run at the Plantation, we went on the road. The band got stranded in St. Louis and finally made it to New York—boxcar fashion, that is.

We worked on and off around New York, but it was rough, so when I got an offer from Charlie Elgar in Milwaukee, I was glad to take the job for the summer. I came back to New York and joined Luis Russell at a club called the Nest. It was here I met Duke Ellington. He used to come in and hear the band, and after talking things over I decided to join him and stayed fourteen years.

From 1928 to 1942, Barney Bigard added a New Orleans flavor to the Duke's rich orchestrations, carefully blending his horn with the eloquent phrasings of Johnny Hodges, Cootie Williams, Rex Stewart, Harry Carney, Joe Nanton, Lawrence Brown, and Juan Tizol. Under Ellington's guidance, this amalgamation of talent formed what many consider the greatest jazz orchestra of all time.

As a composer, Bigard made some monumental contributions to the Ellington songbook, including "Rockin' in Rhythm," "Saturday Night Function," "Clarinet Lament," "Clouds in My Heart," "Sophisticated Lady," and the dreamy 1930 tone poem "Mood Indigo." The Duke's expressive arrangements were greatly enhanced by Bigard's flowing improvisations. He left the Ellington band in 1942 when travel conditions became increasingly deplorable during World War II. Despite a succession of great players, no one has completely filled his chair.

During the next few years, Bigard accepted a few club jobs, worked with Freddy Slack, and played on several recording dates and studio sessions in the Los Angeles area. Few are aware that he was responsible for Kid Ory's emergence from retirement in the 1940s. Ory, inactive musically since 1933, raised chickens and turkeys during the Depression years. One night in 1942, Bigard urged him to bring his horn to the Capri Club, where the clarinetist was leading a small band that included nineteen-year-old Charlie Mingus on string bass. Ory soon joined the band and, with Bigard's help, recouped long-delinquent publisher's royalties on his old compositions "Muskrat Ramble," "Savoy Blues," and "Ory's Creole Trombone." He eventually reformed his Creole Jazz Band and resumed his career.

When Louis Armstrong assembled his All-Stars for a brief 1947 engagement at Billy Berg's Hollywood bistro, he selected Bigard to handle the clarinet chores. Although hastily assembled, the All-Star band was immediately successful. Bigard played with Satchmo for the next eight years, bringing traditional jazz to every corner of the world.

In September 1955, the clarinetist played his last job with Armstrong at Gene Norman's Crescendo on the Sunset Strip in Hollywood. His replacement, Edmond Hall, sat at our table, listening very carefully to the band's arrangements. Ironically, Hall had been selected to fill Bigard's chair once before, after Bigard left the Ellington band in 1942; he turned down that offer because of the rigorous wartime conditions. Now, thirteen years later, he again had the opportunity to succeed his New Orleans colleague. When Bigard joined us after each set, he and Hall reminisced about their early days back home, serving their apprenticeships together with bandleader Buddy Petit.

After leaving Armstrong, Bigard retired in Los Angeles, where he spent a quiet life with his beloved wife, Dorothe. Though still very much in demand for concert tours, jazz festivals, club dates, and television appearances, he accepted few offers, content to share his vast talent with Southern California Hot Jazz Society members during our monthly sessions at Larchmont Hall.

When he learned that the Louis Armstrong Statue Fund was established, Barney became the first Los Angeles contributor. He donated his services for the concert that officially launched the fund-raising activities, "Hello Louis!"

Barney and I became crawfishing partners. During the summer months we prowled the humid shores of the Los Angeles River, gathering "mud bugs" in nets made for us by Tudie Garland. After boiling them in Barney's torrid Creole broth, we would consume a mountain of the little red crustaceans with Lucille's potato salad and cold beer. During those jovial occasions he was most reflective. His tales were sometimes farcical, frequently apocryphal, but always intriguing. When he was in a jocular mood, he often spoke about the Pelican Trio, named after the state bird of Louisiana. The fabled group never actually existed until 1976, although Barney had been talking about it for years. Here's the story:

In 1945, a famous jazz critic insisted on interviewing the clarinetist after a long nightclub set. Exhausted, Barney suggested delaying the interview until the next day. When the writer persisted, Barney sent him off with some fabricated memories from the early days in New Orleans. "The guy kept bugging me all night long, and I wanted to rest," he told me. "To get him off my back, I invented the Pelican Trio." Barney told the critic that this fictional band and its mythical members played in the ornate parlor at Lulu White's Storyville brothel, Mahogany Hall, before World War I. Flush with this wealth of "new" material, the gullible writer published the complete story in a national magazine. The article created quite a furor, and the Pelican Trio took on a life of its own. Musicians told and retold the story, and rumors began to circulate that rare cylinder recordings by the long-lost trio were out there somewhere, waiting to be discovered.

This tale remained an inside joke until 1976, when Bigard put together a *real* Pelican Trio and recorded an album. Duke Burrell played piano and Barry Martyn played drums on this, the last of a very long chain of Bigard recordings that began in 1925. It is now available on CD (Jazzology JCD-228).

The Bigard tales about his jazz activities could fill a book—in fact, they do. In 1972, my friend Barry Martyn began recording Barney's reminiscences. After several years of taping and several more spent in transcribing and editing, Martyn had a very revealing manuscript. Macmillan Press finally published *With Louis and the Duke* in 1985.

Martyn and I had lured Bigard out of retirement three years before the Pelican Trio album. He was the star attraction in our first "A Night in New Orleans" show (1973), which also featured Trummy Young, the French clarinetist Maxim Saury, and Barry Martyn's Legends of Jazz. Invigorated by that activity, Bigard returned to his basic roots. His memories of Tio, Piron, Petit, Oliver, and Armstrong were still vivid, and his love for Crescent City music was evident in each production of "A Night in New Orleans."

In our 1975 edition, at Barney's suggestion, we included a special Duke Ellington segment when the tour reached Los Angeles. Billed as "Ellington Remembered," the act reunited Bigard with his old buddy Ray Nance, the ex-Ellington star, who flew out from New York for the event. The segment included pianist Duke Burrell, bassist Bobby Stone, and Louis Bellson on drums.

When Barney played his perennial feature, "Roseroom," I thought the applause would shatter the old Wilshire Ebell Theatre. Nance's beautifully muted trumpet on "Poor Butterfly" was a masterful expression of tone and substance. He switched to violin for a memorable version of "Come Sunday."

We did not know this would be Nance's final appearance. His flights from New York to Los Angeles and back were timed between scheduled kidney dialysis treatments. Ray Nance died within three months after his Los Angeles triumph.

With varying casts of about thirty people, "A Night in New Orleans" toured from 1973 through 1980 in the United States, Canada, and Europe. Barney was the featured artist every year except 1976, when a last-minute illness prevented his traveling; Benny Carter substituted for him. Carter enjoyed our European tour so much he joined us again in 1978, sharing top billing. We called them "The Reed Giants— Benny Carter and Barney Bigard."

The seriousness of Barney's illness became apparent during the 1979 tour. We learned he had been receiving treatment for lung cancer— but, determined to make the trip, he had kept the matter secret. We arranged to have wheelchairs waiting for him at airports and made every effort to ease the rigors of travel.

We decided to alter our concert program to make it easier for Barney, who usually closed the show. At each auditorium, during the intermission, the Bigard feature was set up on stage behind the closed curtain. The musicians were in place, and Barney was seated on a stool, before I made the introductory remarks in front of the curtain. As it slowly opened, the band began playing, and Barney, despite his weakened condition, sounded as good as ever. When the set concluded, the curtains closed, and we helped the great clarinetist off the stage. The audience was never aware of his frail condition.

Barney's deteriorating health prevented his appearance in the 1980 European tour of "A Night in New Orleans." We had an all-star cast that included Trummy Young, Carrie Smith, Cousin Joe, Freddy Kohlman, and the Legends of Jazz, but our star performer was still missed; fans and reviewers throughout Europe asked, "Where's Barney Bigard?"

When he died June 27, 1980, we decided to discontinue our series. Without him, there could never be "A Night in New Orleans." During his seventy-four years, spanning most of jazz's history, he brought the Crescent City spirit to millions of fans around the world. I am proud that our concert series gave this mature talent one more run in the spotlight.

My graveside eulogy, delivered on a knoll at Holy Cross Cemetery, was accompanied by a softly playing tape, "The Best of Barney," lovingly prepared by pianist Bruce McDonald.

Wild Bill Davison

He went after music as if leading a band into battle, often waving his hand in a circle above his head like John
Wayne leading a cavalry charge.

The Wildest One: The Life of
Wild Bill Davison, by Hal Willard

He was a very imposing figure seated on a high stool blowing his King
B-flat cornet with a wad of chewing gum bulging in his cheek—always
immaculately attired, a brilliant shine on his shoes, and never a hair
out of place. His sweet and often torrid tones, among the most recognized sounds in jazz, were also immaculate.

William Edward "Wild Bill" Davison was one of jazz's most charis-
matic figures. Sounding jaunty, crass, or lusty, depending upon the
number, he always played each note to accentuate the song's nuances.
He made every ballad his own, inevitably ending it with his trademark—a low, growling, insinuating coda that was "the musical equivalent of an innocent wicked wink," as Charles Champlin wrote in the
Los Angeles Times.

The famed jazz cornetist was born on January 5, 1906, in Defiance,
Ohio, a town whose name is synonymous with his lifestyle—and his
horn playing. His long career spanned seven decades; when he died in
1989, he left a wondrous trove of more than eight hundred recordings.

Davison was fifteen when he played in his first band, the Ohio
Lucky Seven (which he immodestly called "a damn good band").
Reared during the "rhythm and booze" years of the '20s, he played
with Bix Beiderbecke, survived the swing era of the '30s and '40s,
helped spark the New Orleans revival period of the '50s, and kept the
music alive long after most of his contemporaries had died.

Many of Davison's fans were introduced to his assertive, energetic
style by a wonderful 1943 Commodore 78 rpm recording: "Panama"/
"That's a Plenty." The cornetist punches his way through nine minutes
of compelling jazz, displaying the brash shouts, robust growls and
slurs, and strong harmonic embellishments that remained his trademark for another forty years. That sound, said Davison, was inspired
by the great Louis Armstrong: "I copied Louis' tone—and the feeling
in his heart—as much as possible. Just to be able to make one note
sound like Louis is an accomplishment." Armstrong and Davison became close friends, and in 1971, shortly before he died, Armstrong
told him: "If anything happens to me, I know you will keep on doing

what I'm doing." And so he did—Davison kept Satchmo's memory alive for eighteen years after the acclaimed musician died.

Those who knew Wild Bill were never sure if his nickname reflected his lifestyle or his cornet playing—probably both. He got the moniker years ago when a Chicago promoter hung a huge poster outside a Southside ballroom heralding the forthcoming appearance of "'WILD BILL' DAVISON—THE WHITE LOUIS ARMSTRONG." Davison was embarrassed, especially as the performance was in a black neighborhood, but the name stuck. Early in his career Davison earned a reputation for excess. Anne Davison, his "fifth and final" wife (they were married thirty-five years), earned the gratitude of jazz fans around the world by assiduously monitoring Wild Bill's drinking, smoking, and kleptomania. Her business card read: "ANNE DAVISON—SLAVE."

One of our last conversations was in his comfortable home in Santa Barbara, California. We were seated on a plush sofa, his cornet resting on a pillow between us. He was wearing pajamas—his usual attire when entertaining guests. Somehow it seemed appropriate. The pajamas were neatly pressed, the black leather slippers gleamed, and his white hair was meticulously combed. Although his manner seemed serious, a twinkle appeared in his eye when I asked if he had any hobbies. "Booze, broads, and fast cars," he replied. I inquired about their sequence, and he said: "It doesn't matter." He quickly added, "That, of course, was 'B.A.'—before Anne."

His on-stage humor was usually ribald. If Bill told a crude joke, Anne was always chagrined and severely admonished him. When he introduced a ballad with, "Here's an old piece—that's the only kind I get," Anne's angry reprimand was an incisive "Will-yiam!" Wild Bill frequently announced: "I am a deeply religious man; I have worn a heavy cross around my neck for many years." Pointing to Anne, he added, "There she is in the first row."

In later years, his between-tunes banter included: "I've just had some very serious surgery—they cut out my drinking!" If a heckler in the audience annoyed him, he would snarl, "Get your own damn band!"

By the 1960s Davison had become a bandleader in his own right; his fine Jazz Giants included Benny Morton on trombone, Herb Hall on clarinet, Johnny Giuffrida on bass, Buzzy Drootin on drums, and Nat Pierce on piano. He also had established a huge following in Japan, where a young cornet player named Akira Kohmo obtained a copy of Davison's album *Wild and Mild* in the mid-1960s. Kohmo, leader of a Dixieland band at Rikkyo University, used the LP as a teaching aid, transcribing every part note for note. The young musicians practiced these songs to perfection and finally performed the material in concert. Sadly, Akira Kohmo died soon after this performance.

Seventeen years later, the surviving band members staged a reunion concert to honor their departed friend. The Akira Kohmo Memorial Concert was presented in Rikkyo University's Tucker Hall on October 18, 1985. Davison himself sat proudly in Akira Kohmo's chair, leading a band that had used *Wild and Mild* as a textbook of traditional jazz. A recording was made of the concert, and it in the fall of 1994 it was finally issued in a special CD pressing. This beautifully packaged album captures the full emotional impact of an extraordinary concert. At seventy-nine, Davison played with verve and fiery passion. Reaching for low notes to underscore a ballad's tenderness or soaring with clear high tones, he retained the mastery that brought him to our attention four decades earlier. The Japanese musicians gracefully supported Davison's virtuoso playing. During an eventful lifetime, Davison played many concerts—but none was as deeply moving as the evening preserved on that CD.

Until his last days, Davison continued to reaffirm the mastery he displayed half a century before on those great Commodore recordings. In 1988, *Jazz Journal International* selected his album *Wild Bill Davison's All-Stars* as Jazz Record of the Year. During that year, he performed his distinctive music for listeners in the United States, England, Australia, New Zealand, Germany, Scandinavia, and Japan. He died on November 14, 1989, at the age of eighty-three.

The cornetist's fine band, now known as Tom Saunders and the Wild Bill Davison Legacy, has continued to tour the world and sustain his memory. His inspiration is apparent on the band's 1996 CD, *Call of the Wild* (Arbors Records ARCD 19146), which features some of Davison's favorite tunes. The group's lineup includes cornetist Tom Saunders, Bill Allred on trombone, Chuck Hedges and Rick Fay on the reeds, and a great rhythm section of pianist Johnny Varro, bassist Paul Keller, and drummer Warren Sauer.

Saunders, leader of the Legacy band, is the personification of Wild Bill and spent many years playing alongside him. His unabashed love and admiration for the man are apparent in his demeanor and his music. He blows the same model King cornet, reaches for the same dynamic tones, favors a navy blue blazer similar to Bill's, and has a tendency for an occasional bawdy remark.

Although he remains beloved by an international coterie of jazz fans, Wild Bill Davison never fully achieved the fame he deserved. He was continually on the threshold of stardom, but agents and record firms mishandled him. His modest financial rewards were never commensurate with his true worth. Davison's many recordings are still available, in formats ranging from 78s to CDs. They preserve his unbridled spirit and jaunty, husky tone. In these recordings, Davison's wild spirit will live forever.

On the first anniversary of his death, Anne hired a pilot to fly over Los Angeles towing a large banner that stated: "I Love You Wild Bill Davison!" At the exact hour of his passing, Anne watched from below as the flyer released a mass of rose petals she had picked from Davison's favorite bush. She is still his champion and continues to perpetuate her husband's image.

Rosy McHargue

I clearly recall the first time I saw Rosy McHargue. The year was 1947. Lucille and I ventured into a small Hollywood club, the Hangover, on Vine Street near Sunset Boulevard. Pete Daily's Chicagoans were on the stage, and Rosy was the band's clarinetist. I had never heard a live Dixieland jazz band before, and this event altered the course of my life. The passage of years has not dimmed the bright memory of our initial meeting; that fine little band created a deep and lasting impression.

Incredible as it might seem, Rosy McHargue performed professionally during each of the last *nine* decades — from the teens through most of the '90s. As a very young musician, he was inspired by Larry Shields, the clarinet player in the Original Dixieland Jazz Band. McHargue played his first professional engagement in 1917, shortly after hearing the initial ODJB recordings. He later became a proficient saxophonist; his rare C-Melody sax has not been manufactured since 1929.

James Eugene McHargue was born in Danville, Illinois, on April 6, 1902. His date of birth is often misstated in jazz publications, thanks mainly to McHargue himself. "When I started playing music," he told me, "I was supposed to be twenty-one because I was playing in nightclubs. I was only eighteen, but big for my age, so I told them I was twenty-one. Later, in the '30s, the big bands wanted young faces, so I

*Clarinetist Rosy McHargue (left) and the
author. Photo by Bill Wishner.*

went the other way and subtracted from my age. Those lies have
caused a lot of confusion over the years—but the truth is, I was really
born in 1902."

He picked up his nickname as a member of the Novelty Syncopators, the first band he played in, which he joined at the age of fifteen.
"I used to sing a novelty Hawaiian song, 'When Rosie Riccoola Do Da
Hoola Ma Boola,'" McHargue told me. "Since then, everyone has
called me Rosy." Eighty years later, he still crooned the song with enthusiasm and youthful glee.

As a young man, McHargue played with many of jazz's all-time legends, including Bix Beiderbecke, Frank Trumbauer, Eddie Lang, Jimmie Noone, King Oliver, and the Wolverines.

> I had been working in Chicago for about a year playing in Sig Meyers' or-
> chestra—that's where I met Muggsy Spanier. At the time, the Seattle Har-
> mony Kings were very popular. When they asked me to join the band, I left
> Sig Meyers and started with the Harmony Kings at the Million Dollar Pier
> in Atlantic City. Wild Bill Davison joined the band later. While we were at
> Atlantic City, we went to Camden, New Jersey, to record three sides at the
> Victor studios. I played about eight bars on the baritone sax—I think it was
> "Breezin' Along With the Breeze." I had to put my alto down and run

about ten feet to play the baritone, then run back. That's how they made records back in 1925.

Since that 1925 Victor date with the Seattle Harmony Kings, McHargue played his clarinet and saxophone in orchestras led by Roy Schoenbeck, Frankie Trumbauer, Ted Weems, Kay Kyser, and Benny Goodman. When small bands regained favor after World War II, Rosy's articulate horn sparked groups led by Pete Daily, Red Nichols, and Pee Wee Hunt. His intentionally hackneyed solo helped catapult Hunt's 1948 recording of "12th Street Rag" to sales of more than 12 million. Clarinetists throughout the world still struggle to emulate his burlesqued chorus.

McHargue played regular gigs well into his nineties. He charmed his audiences with his gracious attitude and relaxed air, singing songs popular long before his listeners—and, in many cases, their parents— were born. Those songs were an escapist relaxation of wartime tensions, youthful rebellious expressions against a conservative society, and tuneful images that brightened the dismal depression years.

He loved to sing the shocking second chorus of "Oh, What a Night for Love" and his perennial favorite, "When Rosie Riccoola Do Da Hoola Ma Boola." He dusted off once-beloved standards such as "Has Anybody Seen My Gal?" and "Indiana," as well as arcane melodies that no one else remembered, such as "Doin' the Raccoon," "My Canary Has Circles Under His Eyes," "She Looks Like Helen Brown," "I'll See You in C-U-B-A," and dozens more.

On April 6, 1997, more than five hundred people gathered at the Elks Club in Fullerton, California, to celebrate Rosy McHargue's ninety-fifth birthday. Recently recovered from a bout with cancer, he looked cheerful and spry. One of the highlights of the event, sponsored by the New Orleans Jazz Club of Southern California, occurred when the honoree re-created his first recording, "Wow Wow Blues" (originally produced with Roy Schoenbeck's Orchestra in 1924). After listening to the original scratchy record, the audience heard McHargue play the tune on his C-Melody sax with Mike Henebry's orchestra, using the exact arrangement from the old disc (as transcribed by clarinetist Dan Levinson). Sound engineer Bill Mintz taped the performance. This may well have marked the only time in history that a musician recorded a precise, note-for-note duplication of a tune he originally recorded seventy-three years earlier.

McHargue and an all-star combo provided the balance of the party's entertainment. The group included Mike Silverman on trumpet, trombonist Conrad Janis, Robbie Rhodes on piano, Jimmy Green on banjo, Ian Whitcomb on banjo-ukulele and accordion, and Don Beauchamp on the drums. Dan Levinson, a prodigy of McHargue's, came from New York to play alongside his mentor. The pair rocked the auditorium with a rousing saxophone duet on "China Boy." During an intermission, John Dieball, producer of the successful celebration, presented numerous tributes to Rosy, including a congratulatory letter from another famed saxophonist, President Bill Clinton.

The music continued long into the afternoon, and McHargue, showing no signs of fatigue, sang one song after another. Toward the end of the program he introduced a long-forgotten tune recorded by Frank Sinatra with Tommy Dorsey's orchestra in 1941. There were many tearful eyes in the room as McHargue sang the very appropriate lyrics to "Love Me as I Am." It was a touching finale to a remarkable party. McHargue was back at his regular Saturday afternoon gig, still charming audiences.

We saluted his ninety-seventh birthday on April 18, 1999, at Jazz Forum's monthly session at the Elks Hall in Santa Monica. That was one of Rosy's last appearances, other than his remaining few regular Saturday afternoon sessions a few miles away at the West End, a Santa Monica saloon.

We visited Rosy at his home two days before he passed away. He looked very pallid and fragile, watching birds fluttering outside his window. He asked me to sit on the edge of his bed and enjoyed reminiscing. He clearly recalled many of the jazz episodes we shared over the past fifty years. His voice was weak, but his laughter had its usual gusto—and he laughed a lot during our brief chat.

Before leaving, Lucille urged me to kiss him goodbye. I am glad she did. As I briefly held him in my arms, I knew this was the last time I would see him.

Rosy McHargue died on June 7, 1999. The lamentable news spread rapidly throughout the jazz world via telephone, fax, and the Internet. Those of us whose lives were inexplicably altered by his presence must now confront a world that will never be the same without him.

The week after he died, his little band gathered for the last time at that familiar watering hole. The Friends of Rosy McHargue occupied their usual places on the West End's small bandstand.

As the afternoon continued, the small band swelled when Rosy's friends eagerly mounted the bandstand to play for him. The room echoed with reverent versions of "Mandy," "Garden of Roses," "At the Storybook Ball," "My Blue Heaven," and Rosy's lovely composition "Arabian Rhapsody." When they all harmonized on the familiar songs, tears flowed freely on the stage, in the audience, and even behind the bar. (The usually stoic bartender was seen wiping a tear on his sleeve.)

There were no moments of silence. Rosy would not have liked that. He spent his life filling silence with his wonderful music. That music will continue being played by his bandmembers, who regard their tenure under his leadership as a wonderful educational experience.

As we all said goodbye to Rosy while the musicians played the happy tunes we heard him sing a hundred times, we were aware that this heartfelt tribute was an experience that would always linger in our memories.

Whenever I hear a small band swinging or a vocalist singing an obscure song from the Jazz Age, I am always reminded of Rosy McHargue. Like an old photograph, he is a link with the vision of yesterday. Old photographs can fade through the years. Thanks to Rosy, his old songs have not faded into obscurity. Sounds corny? Maybe it is. But his audiences always had beaming smiles that reflected his convivial radiance. They remind me of the happy night Lucille and I walked into the Hangover Club back in 1947.

Artie Shaw

"Jazz is an attitude," Artie Shaw said during an appearance in Southern California in the late 1980s. "I much prefer just calling it music— American informal music. The word 'jazz' makes no sense at all. No one has ever come up with a good definition for it. How can you talk about something you can't define?"

Shaw was appearing in a lecture series at California State University at Northridge. The hero of the swing era spoke for almost an hour— mostly about things that annoy him.

"The gap between what an artist does and what the audiences perceive is enormous," he said. "A vast ignorance surrounds this country's musical understanding. We are probably the most musically illiterate nation on earth. If I hadn't quit the business, I'd be a lunatic by now— many people will tell you I am one anyway. The audience gets in the way. They are not informed.

" 'Art' is a tough word," he continued. "Most people don't know what it means. I think art is something taking place when somebody with great skills loves what he is doing and works at the absolute top level of his ability. An artist does not do it to please an audience. An *entertainer* is trying to please audiences. Sometimes he can become so good he achieves an artistic position." To illustrate his point, Shaw recalled:

> The last big band I assembled was to conform to listeners' tastes. It was admittedly the worst band in the world. I found fourteen men willing to travel for the meager salary of $100 a week. They only had to read simple stock arrangements and own a suit. I bought the neckties.
>
> Our repertoire consisted of ten pop stocks, including "If I Knew You Were Comin' I'd've Baked a Cake." During the last engagement of the tour, the ballroom manager commented, "You've got a hell of a band, Mr. Shaw. This is the nicest night we've had since Blue Barron played here."

Some of Shaw's other remarks:

On music: "Music is sound on silence."

On jazz: "It was originally spelled 'jass.' I won't tell you what it meant in those days, but when they said 'Jass Me Blues,' they did not mean 'Kiss Me Blues!' "

On folk art: "That's an oxymoron. 'Folk' is not 'art,' and 'art' is not 'folk'—one word cancels the other."

During one segment of the program, clarinetist Abe Most and a rhythm section simulated Shaw's celebrated arrangement of the Hoagy Carmichael classic "Stardust." To help Abe, Shaw hastily sketched the famous clarinet chorus he improvised on the 1940 recording.

"My record of 'Stardust,' with Billy Butterfield, Jack Jenny, and one of the first string sections used by a jazz group, sold 16 million copies," Shaw noted. "It was recorded by Victor as a stunt to appear with Tommy Dorsey on the second side. When Dorsey heard our 'Stardust,' he declined to record the other side."

Shaw concluded with an anecdote about a much shorter lecture appearance:

> When Sinclair Lewis was hired to address literature students at Williams College in northern Massachusetts, his entire speech was limited to one or two sentences. He entered the stage and asked, "How many of you want to write?" A sea of hands was raised. Lewis said, "Then why the hell don't you go home and write?"—and left the stage.

During a reception after the lecture, Shaw obligingly chatted with the audience and graciously posed for pictures—but adamantly refused to sign any autographs. He grinned when Dorothe Bigard mentioned he was a favorite clarinetist of her late husband, Barney Bigard. Barney was also quite outspoken and rated Artie Shaw over Benny Goodman. During the swing years, Benny Goodman usually garnered recognition as the nation's top clarinetist, with Shaw and Bigard following in his wake. (In 1947 Goodman won the annual gold "Esky" awarded by *Esquire* magazine, and Barney received the silver statuette.)

Shaw seemed surprised when I told him he owed me fifty-five cents. That was the price I paid as a high school student to hear him at the old Palomar Ballroom in Los Angeles. Midway through the evening, I became aware that the clarinetist leading the band was not Artie Shaw but rather Tony Pastor, fronting in Shaw's absence. When I jokingly asked him for the refund, he smiled and reached into his pocket; but when I added that I felt entitled to full compound interest, dating back to 1939, he reneged.

Andy Razaf

Although he wrote the words to some of the world's best-known songs, Andy Razaf never enjoyed the fame and respect accorded his white contemporaries. His brilliant collaborations with Fats Waller endowed the world with such great standards as "Ain't Misbehavin'" (a tune written in less than an hour—and promptly sold to a publisher for $250), "Honeysuckle Rose," "Hand Full of Keys," "The Joint Is Jumpin'," "Blue Turning Gray Over You," and "Black and Blue"—all still vital parts of our nation's musical vocabulary. In collaboration with Waller and numerous other great composers, Razaf wrote his perceptive lyrics for more than a thousand songs, including "Memories of You," "On Revival Day," "Stompin' at the Savoy," "In the Mood," "12th Street Rag," "Christopher Columbus," "That's What I Like About the South," and many more.

"Black and Blue," which Razaf wrote with Waller for the 1929 musical *Hot Chocolates,* was probably the first song of racial protest ever sung on the Broadway stage. Razaf took great pride in his heritage, and he struggled against racial prejudice throughout his life. Even in old age, when he was confined to a wheelchair by a debilitating stroke and constantly in pain, Razaf burned with anger over the slights and insults he had endured over the years.

During my visits to his modest home on Country Club Drive in Los Angeles, the ailing songwriter and I would leaf through several large scrapbooks crammed with clippings, photos, and other mementos from his career. The books also evoked caustic memories, frustration, rage, and occasional tears.

He fumed bitterly about a publisher who cheated him on promised royalties, a trade magazine that ignored his success, and the mistreatment of black artists by corrupt managers. He complained that racism in the music business had curtailed his income; while Hollywood paid white lyricists such as Ira Gershwin, Oscar Hammerstein, and Larry Hart $100,000 per picture, he received an advance of just $150 and a guarantee of $25 per week during the run of his hit production *Hot Chocolates* at Connie's Inn. "They played my songs every night at Connie's Inn and the Cotton Club," he said, "but my people were not welcome there—it was whites only."

I often delved deeply into the scrapbooks and, with Razaf's permission, made notes about his life. He traced his lineage to Madagascar; his grandfather, a freed slave, eventually became the United States Consul, reportedly the first black member of the U.S. diplomatic corps. Razaf's mother married the Queen of Madagascar's nephew, but he was killed during the French invasion of the island. Fearing for the lives of his children and grandchildren, Razaf's grandfather left the country with his family, including Andy's mother, who was pregnant with him at the time. Razaf was born in Washington, D.C., soon after their arrival in 1895. He often said, jokingly, "If my family had stayed in Madagascar, I might have become king one day! My father was a successor to the throne."

Instead he went to work at a very early age. At seventeen, while employed as an elevator operator in a Broadway theater building, he wrote the words and music to his first published song, "Baltimo'." He gave a copy to a member of the Shubert organization, who added it to the score of the *Passing Show of 1913* at the Winter Garden Theater. The faded "Baltimo'" sheet music pasted in Razaf's scrapbook reads: "Words and Music by A. P. Razafkevifo." This was a shortened version of his Madagascaran name, Andreamenentania Paul Razafinkeriefo. He identified himself as "Andrea Razaf" on some songs in the '20s before trimming his name to Andy Razaf.

Scrounging for old records, I came across many tunes Razaf wrote under aliases in the '20s. He seemed pleased when I gave him 78 rpm pressings with labels crediting "Crooning Andy" or "Razaf, the Melody Man."

During one of my last visits with the ailing lyricist, Razaf loaned me a book entitled *Show Biz—From Vaude to Video,* by Abel Green and Joe Laurie, Jr. (Henry Holt and Company, 1951). The flyleaf was imprinted with his rubber stamp: "ANDY RAZAF—LYRICIST." He also gave me a copy of his August 1, 1953, review of the book for the *New York Age.* In it he made a blistering attack on the authors' failure to credit "the vital contributions of Negroes in show business." In two columns of caustic criticism, Razaf listed scores of neglected black artists, from Scott Joplin to Langston Hughes. The pages of the book itself were filled with angry marginal notations. He deplored the authors' description of the standard formula of colored acts—"chicken stealin', crap-shootin', gin-guzzlin, no-accounts." A question mark appeared next to the comment that Irving Berlin's "Alexander's Ragtime Band" gave ragtime "its biggest impetus in 1911." He favorably marked several mentions of entertainer Bert Williams and the black composing team of Cole and Johnson (which gave us "Under the Bamboo Tree"). In the book's lengthy index, Andy's bold pencil marks underscored a few references to black personalities. Razaf's review of the highly acclaimed best-seller concluded with: "Of its 565 pages, scant references are made to Negro showfolk—if placed together they would hardly fill six pages! As far as coverage to Negro showfolk—it's a 'bust.' "

Razaf died before I could return his *Show Biz.* Despite its affront to Razaf's intense racial pride, the book's extensive exploration of American theatrical life has been a valuable source of material for me.

I cannot remember the title of the book I loaned him in exchange back in 1973. I never saw it again!

The poet-lyricist sent annual Christmas greeting cards almost until his death. Each bore a three-stanza poem printed in green ink on a small white card with a wreath border. These messages reflected Razaf's indignation over wars and racial inequality. Bitter obsessions filled his later years. His chiding remarks in 1953 bristled against the "curse of war":

> This time each year, just for a few short days
> We lay aside our backward, ugly ways
> Replacing hate of color, race and creeds
> With friendly smiles and noble deeds.
>
> We, then, are as God meant us all to be
> Aglow with love and sweet humility
> Our mingled voices rise to Him in praise
> But is it only for a few short days?

The curse of war, disease and poverty
Of endless fear and insecurity
Will plague us 'til we keep our Yuletide ways
Throughout the year, not just a few short days.

In 1957, in a greeting titled "Lowtide at Yuletide," Razaf con-
tentiously addressed the emerging nuclear age:

Because of man's insanity
That may destroy humanity
The saddest words of tongue and pen
Are "Peace on Earth, good will t'ward men."

How merry can a Christmas be
In a world of increasing misery
Dictators, bigots and infamy
Godlessness and hypocrisy?

In this nuclear, astronomical age
When leaders and scientists engage
In talk of bomb shelters and World War Three
We can't fool God with a Christmas tree.

In 1962, Razaf commented on the Cuban Missile Crisis with this
Yuletide admonishment:

Another Christmas as we watch on high
For bombers that may someday dot the sky
And key cities of this earth will die
You say I'm wrong? Then make this poem a lie.

When Howard University in Washington D.C. asked Razaf for an
extended biography, he asked me to write it for him, which I considered a great honor. My manuscript was bound into each of several volumes of his compositions. The books still occupy a prominent position
in the university's library, commemorating Razaf's enormous contributions to American popular music.

The sensitive poet I knew was paradoxical—kind, gentle, and generous, but also racked with anger, resentment, and pain. His penetrating lyrics to the bridge of "Memories of You," written almost seventy
years ago, are almost biographical:

How I wish I could forget those happy yesterdays
That have left a rosary of tears

Andy Razaf died February 3, 1973.

Coot Grant and Sox Wilson in an early vaudeville publicity photo, ca. 1920.

Coot Grant and Sox Wilson*

My monthly "American Jazz Scene" column in the January 1953 issue of the English publication *Jazz Journal* included a plea urging assistance for Coot Grant and Sox Wilson. The veteran entertainers had recently moved from New York to Los Angeles, seeking a milder climate that might improve Wilson's failing health. Medical expenses had ruined the couple's finances, and they arrived in Los Angeles in very poor financial condition. Four of their trunks had been impounded during the move, and Wilson and Grant were unable to pay the freight charges of $139. This amount might seem insignificant in today's economy, but half a century ago it was a very formidable sum. The freight company threatened to auction their possessions to satisfy the unpaid bill.

The trunks contained complete original musical shows, photographs, letters, newspaper clippings, and other mementos. They also held original copies of more than four hundred of Wilson's compositions, including several unpublished songs he wrote for Bert Williams and three numbers Bessie Smith intended to record. If the couple couldn't come up with the money to pay back the freight company, the

*Honored by the International Association of Jazz Record Collectors—Best Article Awards for 1993.

material in their trunks would be auctioned off to retire the debt. My *Jazz Journal* column was a last-ditch plea to help the Wilsons retain a few remnants from their lifetime of achievement.

Wesley "Sox" Wilson and his wife, Leola "Coot" Grant Wilson, were seasoned vaudeville performers, dancers, comedians, songwriters, and early recording stars. The pair made a series of recordings in September 1925 with Louis Armstrong, then a relatively unknown sideman in Fletcher Henderson's Orchestra. For the first time, at the Wilsons' insistence, Armstrong's name appeared on a record label. In later years, Coot and Sox recorded for Mezz Mezzrow's King Jazz Records and appeared on Rudy Blesh's radio show, *This Is Jazz*.

The talented couple wrote hundreds of tunes that were recorded by various artists. Bessie Smith sang four of them on her last record date: "Do Your Duty," "Give Me a Pig Foot," "Take Me For a Buggy Ride," and "I'm Down in the Dumps." Wilson's 1940 hit, "Do You Call That a Buddy?," was recorded by Louis Armstrong, Louis Jordan, the Andrews Sisters, and Larry Clinton.

Grant appeared on early race recordings under various aliases, including her maiden name, Leola B. Pettigrew. She often spoke of a recording she made with King Oliver, the date of which has never been fully corroborated. Many collectors feel she was referring to "He's a Good Meat Cutter"/"Be on Your Merry Way" by Issie Ringgold (another of Leola's pseudonyms?). Both sides of the label identify Wilson as composer, and his distinctive piano playing is clearly recognizable. So, too, is the familiar timbre of Joe Oliver's muted cornet. Oliver receives no credit on the label, but he was under contract to Victor at the time, which may account for his anonymity.

Wilson's strange nickname came from an original tune he frequently sang, "Dem Sox That My Pappy Wore." He is heard on many Columbia 14000 series recordings, using the name "Pigmeat Pete" on some of them.

I met Coot and Sox when they attended a Southern California Hot Jazz Society meeting shortly after their move to Los Angeles in mid-1952. The members of our organization happily welcomed the legendary pair. The Wilsons, both in their mid-sixties, alternated between pride in their accomplishments and disconsolation about their financial woes. They eventually became very active in the SCHJS, performing at every meeting and becoming part of the local jazz scene. A large felt banner Coot made forty years ago is still in the SCHJS's archives.

Soft-spoken and matronly, Coot had a gentle disposition that contrasted sharply with her imposing stage presence, her robust voice, and her ribald songs. At the SCHJS's regular monthly meetings, she often sang one of Wilson's compositions, "Have Your Chill, I'll Be Here When Your Fever Rises," which she recorded with Fletcher Henderson's orchestra in 1925 (with young Louis Armstrong in the trumpet section).

Coot steadfastly maintained an ebullient facade. On stage, Sox's eyes would sparkle and his rotund face beamed brightly, but he was in poor health. Seated at the piano, his jovial demeanor masked a deep depression. In response to members' frequent requests, he often humorously sang his "Old Age Is Creepin' Up on You."

The freight auction was scheduled just ten days after *Jazz Journal* published my entreating story. One final blow from the auctioneer's hammer, and the documentation of the Wilsons' lifetime achievements would be in peril. That is when Andy Razaf's phone call offered a ray of hope.

"This is a terrible thing, Floyd," he said over the phone. "I am not a rich man, but my conscience would not allow me to stand by while they lose such valuable material. May I loan them the money necessary to save the trunks? Do you think there is still time?"

After frantic calls to the express company, I learned the trunks were in San Francisco to be included in an auction the following week. The firm agreed to return the Wilsons' treasures upon payment of the amount due—plus additional costs for shipment to and from San Francisco.

On the following day, Andy's check arrived with this letter:

Dear Floyd,

So glad I saw the item about Sox Wilson's problem in your *Jazz Journal* column.

I don't know either Wilson or his wife, but I know what illness and adversity means.

In sending this check, Dorothy and I are "casting bread on the water." Who knows? Perhaps we may need help some day.

As ever, Andy

I arrived with the check at the local freight office twenty minutes before closing. The clerk immediately wired San Francisco confirming payment had been received and promised the trunk would arrive at the Razaf address in a few days.

Another Razaf note in my files, dated eight months after the considerate loan, reads:

Hello Floyd,

Just to let you know I'm still punching away. Some days are quite painful, however I manage to continue my creative work and newspaper articles.

Mrs. Wilson got three of the four trunks but I never heard from her. Well, we don't regret having done a good deed.

Dot joins me in best regards to you and yours.

Cheerio, Andy

The Wilsons' overall financial condition did not improve during their stay in Los Angeles. Anticipating royalty performance payments from ASCAP, they made a small down payment on a tiny home in nearby Fontana. However, the royalties failed to arrive, and, unable to find work locally, they decided to return to the East. In one of Grant's letters to me, postmarked Whitesboro, New Jersey, she described their home as "a wooden shack on a back road two miles from postal service." My heart ached to think of them living in such conditions.

Sox died October 10, 1958, after suffering several strokes. When Coot died a few years later, no notice of her death appeared in the local press.

Presumably, the couple took their treasure-laden trunks back east with them, but their present whereabouts are unknown. Hopefully, their priceless memorabilia has been preserved and will eventually be found by jazz scholars. Maybe then Coot Grant and Sox Wilson will receive full recognition for their important contributions to American popular music.

Andy Razaf probably never received repayment for his loan to the Wilsons. The "bread cast on the water" will certainly remain in the "asset" column on his impressive character ledger.

The World's Greatest Jazz Band

The ten-piece band could roar with the impact of a large orchestra, but with such great players, they could also improvise freely like a small group. The varied material we played coalesced into a distinctive and unique sound, not like any other band before it.

Bob Wilber, *Music Was Not Enough*,
Oxford University Press, 1988

The 1968 lineup of the World's Greatest Jazz Band. Top row: Billy Butterfield, Carl Fontana, Ralph Sutton, Lou McGarity, Morey Feld. Center: Bob Wilber, Clancy Hayes. Bottom: Yank Lawson, Bob Haggart, Bud Freeman. Photo courtesy of Bob Haggart.

Although dream bands have always existed in jazz fans' minds, their fantasies rarely materialize. Financial disparities, temperamental differences, and booking and promotion problems have always been formidable deterrents. Top-caliber jazzmen lead extremely busy lives, and they often find it difficult to make long-range commitments. With the notable exception of Louis Armstrong's All-Stars, most star-studded groups have existed only briefly, playing together at benefit concerts, on special recordings, and occasionally on short tours. Seldom has an all-star aggregation worked together regularly.

That all changed in 1963, when a group of great players began an association destined to make jazz history. The concept gradually emerged at a series of annual jazz weekends produced by Colorado fan Dick Gibson. Each year, Gibson hired the best talent he could find to entertain friends, business associates, and fellow jazz lovers in Aspen, Vail, Colorado Springs, and other Rocky Mountain locales.

Yank Lawson and Bob Haggart, colleagues in the famed Bob Crosby Orchestra during the mid-'30s, continued their relationship as co-leaders of a popular recording group, the Lawson-Haggart Jazz Band. Each year, Gibson featured the pair at his party with a variety of fine musicians.

The band improved during successive sessions at Aspen, Vail, and Colorado Springs. As additional players were added, the group gradually took shape. By the time it went out into the world as an organized unit, the band had unusual instrumentation that included: Yank Lawson and Billy Butterfield on trumpets, Lou McGarity and Carl Fontana on trombones, Bud Freeman and Bob Wilber on the reeds, Ralph Sutton on piano, Haggart on bass, Clancy Hayes on banjo, and Morey Feld on drums. Lawson and Haggart were co-leaders.

This was no fantasy—it was a living, breathing band of the first order. Each member enjoyed worldwide recognition. With its expanded double front line and a book filled with Bob Haggart's first-rate arrangements of Dixieland standards and contemporary tunes (by Simon and Garfunkel, the Beatles, Burt Bacharach, etc.), the band was ready to go out and find its audience.

In 1965, billed as Ten Greats of Jazz, they were booked at Elitch Gardens in Denver—the same venue at which, three decades earlier, Benny Goodman had appeared en route to his momentous opening at the Los Angeles Palomar Ballroom, which launched the swing era. Encouraged by Dick Gibson, the band continued working together, and by November 1968, when they landed their first job in New York City (a five-week engagement at the Riverboat Room in the basement of the Empire State Building), they had the audacity to call themselves The World's Greatest Jazz Band. After an additional eight weeks at another Manhattan jazz club, the Down Beat, and a seven-month stint at the famed Roosevelt Grill, the band's future seemed secure.

Gibson arranged a worldwide booking agreement with Sol Hurok, an important promoter of classical music and ballet groups, and The World's Greatest Jazz Band was off and running with a series of extended dates, some one-nighters, and a successful tour of England. The musicians had a difficult name to live up to, but with each performance they proved themselves worthy of the title.

In 1971, Phoenix investor Barker Hickox succeeded Gibson as the WGJB's sponsor. Hickox, a prominent member of the Republican Party, arranged a prestigious booking at Richard Nixon's first inaugural ball in Washington, D.C., that provided wide exposure for the rapidly ascending jazz band. He also established the World Jazz Record Company and produced a series of albums showcasing the band's repertoire, including complete programs of songs by Cole Porter, George Gershwin, Duke Ellington, and Rodgers and Hart, plus a successful Christmas album.

Overcoming early skepticism, the dream band continued to gather momentum for a decade, with rave reviews following each engagement. An appearance by the World's Greatest Jazz Band usually meant a sold-out house. The group's musical trademark—rousing duels between Bud Freeman and Bob Wilber, Yank Lawson and Billy Butterfield, or Vic Dickenson and Benny Morton—brought audiences to their feet. Ralph Sutton's stirring stride piano numbers introduced the genius of Fats Waller, James P. Johnson, and Willie "The Lion" Smith to a broad range of listeners. Lawson and Haggart remained WGJB fixtures, but family commitments, illness, and other personal considerations forced changes within the ranks. Over the years, a few dozen celebrated musicians sported the familiar stylish blue blazers of the World's Greatest Jazz Band, including:

Trumpets: Billy Butterfield, Bobby Hackett, John Best, Ed Polcer, Zeke Zarchy, Randy Sandke, and Jon-Erik Kellso.

Trombones: Cutty Cutshall, Kai Winding, Eddie Hubble, Vic Dickenson, Benny Morton, Sonny Russo, Urbie Green, George Masso, Bob Havens, Rex Allen, and Ira Nepus.

Reeds: Peanuts Hucko, Tommy Newsom, Al Klink, Johnny Mince, Phil Bodner, Bill Stegmeyer, Eddie Miller, Dick Hafer, Kenny Davern, Abe Most, Dave Moody, and Ken Peplowski.

Guitar: Bucky Pizzarelli and Marty Grosz.

Piano: Lou Stein, John Bunch, Ray Sherman, and Roger Kellaway.

Drums: Bobby Rosengarden, Cliff Leeman, Nick Fatool, Jake Hanna, Gus Johnson, Jr., and Butch Miles.

Despite the inevitable personnel turnovers, Bob Haggart's brilliant arrangements enabled the band to retain its original style and thrust. With six horns and a sturdy rhythm section, he adapted vigorous up-to-date compositions to a traditional jazz format. Haggart also included original material composed by band members Wilber, Dickenson, Freeman, and Johnson while sustaining the classic Dixieland flavor he created for the Bob Crosby band many years earlier. As a result, the band earned a worldwide following and became a major influence on the jazz scene into the '80s.

By the 1990s the World's Greatest Jazz Band had ceased its full-time activity, but it still assembled for special events, including its first Japanese tour in 1995. Unfortunately, Yank Lawson's death early that year stilled his muted trumpet and ended a sixty-year partnership with Bob

Haggart. The bassist sadly fulfilled the scheduled Far East dates, with Ed Polcer valiantly substituting for Lawson. The band members were thrilled to be in Japan for the first time and appreciated the excitement of the knowledgeable Japanese fans. Promoter Yoshi Nishikage arranged a return visit the following year.

Bob Haggart remained at the helm—still tall and handsome at eighty-three, and still structuring clean linear bass figures. The resurrected WGJB included a pair of veterans: George Masso ('75-'76 and '80) on trombone and pianist John Bunch ('76). Haggart reprised the dual-instrument format with the best of New York's current brass players. Jon-Erik Kellso and Randy Sandke sustained the band's strong trumpet tradition. Trombone assignments were deftly handled by Masso, a veteran of the Jimmy Dorsey orchestra, and Ira Nepus, who as a youngster in Los Angeles had played with jazz greats Barney Bigard, Kid Ory, Teddy Buckner, Joe Darensbourg, and Ed Garland at Southern California Hot Jazz Society jam sessions. Ken Peplowski, a master of all the reeds, played tenor and clarinet, while Haggart staunchly anchored the rhythm section with Bunch at the piano and Butch Miles' facile percussion. Vocalist Banu Gibson was included as an added attraction. A recording of a July 1996 concert at Club Birdland in Tokyo will soon be available on compact disc.

The World's Greatest Jazz Band, a fantasy that materialized at Dick Gibson's Colorado jazz parties, sustained the swinging sounds that Yank Lawson and Bob Haggart conceived thirty-five years ago.

Bob Haggart died December 2, 1998.

4

THE INFLUENCE OF NEW ORLEANS MUSICIANS ON CLASSIC JAZZ

The city of New Orleans has long been recognized as the birthplace of jazz. Although some pundits would challenge that claim, it cannot be disputed that great numbers of jazz musicians have emerged from the Crescent City since the final decade of the nineteenth century. The Mississippi River was a two-way conduit, bringing the component elements to New Orleans and transporting the city's music to northern riverports. The city's deep musical roots remain vital today, partly because the music itself has such power but also because many people have worked to preserve that heritage. The articles in this chapter celebrate the lore of old New Orleans and the people who keep it alive.

The Jazz Journey—From Lulu White's Mahogany Hall to Carnegie Hall

A casual exploration back through jazz's fascinating history would lead us along a trail of colorful locales. Along the way, we might visit these important venues:

1944: Minton's Playhouse, New York City (the bop experiments of Dizzy Gillespie, Charlie Parker, etc.).

1941: The Dawn Club, San Francisco (Lu Watters, Turk Murphy, and friends launch the West Coast revival era).

Lulu White's Mahogany Hall, 353 Basin Street in New Orleans, 1948. Photo by Ken Kramer.

1935: The Palomar Ballroom, Los Angeles (Benny Goodman sets the pace for the swing era that followed).

1932: Chicago's Grand Terrace (where Earl Hines' nightly broadcasts excited nationwide listeners).

1927: The Cotton Club, Harlem (the tremendous impact of the Duke Ellington Orchestra).

1922: The Lincoln Gardens, Chicago's Southside (the King Oliver Creole Jazz Band with young Louis Armstrong).

1917: Reisenweber's Cafe, New York City (where the Original Dixieland Jazz Band introduced a new music to the world).

1899: Sedalia, Missouri (Scott Joplin's "Maple Leaf Rag" started a craze that has influenced popular music for almost a century).

Our retrospective trek would inevitably lead to the prime source: New Orleans; the infamous Storyville section; and Lulu White's Mahogany Hall.

Mahogany Hall was an imposing three-story structure built from rough-hewn granite blocks. It stood at 335 Basin Street near Iberville, just a block away from Tom Anderson's landmark saloon, the first bar-room illuminated by electricity in the country. Anderson's publication, the Blue Book, became the essential pleasure guide of the Storyville district. It listed each sporting house, with descriptions of the lavish interiors and lewd photos, addresses, and phone numbers of the individual whores. The yearly Blue Book was the most erotic public directory of prostitution ever printed in the United States.

According to the Blue Book, "Lulu White's Mahogany Hall, aside from the handsome women, possesses some of the most costly paintings in the South." The city's most famous bordello was housed beneath castle-like turrets. It faced the Mississippi River, approximately a half-mile from the Canal Street ferry landing. "Lulu White's parlor had mirrors that cost $30,000," Jelly Roll Morton recalled during his Library of Congress interview with curator Alan Lomax.

Historian Danny Barker told me, "The place was all colored lights and mirrors—lots of mirrors—some even on the floor where the girls danced. You talk about miniskirts—their dresses were up to *here*. They wore lace stockings and big garters and not much else. Each girl kept a bill inside her stocking way up by her thigh. The denomination of the bill was the girl's price. Some had $2 bills, some $5. Occasionally you'd spot a ten—not often."

The famed New Orleans composer Spencer Williams was born in Mahogany Hall, the most glittering of all the Basin Street mansions. His mother, Bessie Williams, was Lulu White's sister and one of the "entertainers" at the hall. His loving "aunts" helped raise him. Williams' classic compositions, "Mahogany Hall Stomp" and "Basin Street Blues," were musical tributes to his birthplace.

Early jazz musicians found Storyville a lucrative area. Most of the barrelhouses and gin mills employed piano players, known as "professors," to entertain their patrons. Tony Jackson and Jelly Roll Morton frequently played for sex dances in Lulu White's glittering, mirrored parlor on Basin Street. Proprietors of Storyville bordellos generally preferred using solo performers over bands, but Lulu White was one notable exception. The beautiful octaroon madam occasionally had bands playing for special occasions such as Mardi Gras and New Year's Eve. They performed in her adjacent corner saloon and in the hall's brilliantly decorated parlor. Kid Ory (who usually avoided revealing details of his early life in New Orleans) told me he played a band gig for Lulu White as a very young man. When he came to New Orleans from his birthplace, Woodland Plantation, this was one of his band's first jobs.

Mahogany Hall was just one of Storyville's many jazz venues. Around the corner, in a wooden structure on Bienville Street, Jimmie Noone and Buddy Petit entertained patrons at Frank Early's cabaret in the block behind Tom Anderson's Cafe. Lorenzo Tio, Jr., played clarinet with cornetists Freddie Keppard and King Oliver at the "Big 25" on Franklin Street. John the Greek's, across the street, was an early venue for Buddy Bolden's band. Papa Mutt Carey began his career nearby at the 101 Ranch. Oscar Celestin held forth from 8 P.M. until 4 A.M. the next morning at the popular Tuxedo, also on Franklin Street. Kid Ory's Brownskin Babies worked in the next block at Pete Lala's Cafe.

The action continued in the dance halls, saloons, and cafes where bands played nightly—the Primrose Orchestra, Jack Carey's band, and the Magnolia Sweets, to name just a few. In his book *I Remember Jazz* (Louisiana State University Press, 1987), historian Al Rose lists the names of more than two hundred musicians who worked in Storyville between 1898 and 1917.

The city of New Orleans scorned the presence of the "immoral" music. An editorial in a local paper, circa 1917, condemned jazz as "a musical vice." Decrying the fact that New Orleans was the birthplace of the "despicable style," the editorial urged: "We should suppress it! Its musical value is nil—its possibilities of harm are great! The music and the musicians are not acceptable!"

The tenderloin district flourished until 1917, when the navy closed it permanently in an overly protective gesture to "protect the health of the young servicemen in the area." The gilded palaces of sin were shuttered, and the ladies who worked there quickly transferred their activities to other parts of the city.

The city finally demolished Mahogany Hall in 1950, when the entire block was razed to create space for a department store warehouse. The New Orleans Jazz Club managed to save the huge marble cornerstone bearing the carved inscription, LULU WHITE; it is now exhibited at the Louisiana State Museum at the foot of Esplanade Avenue. During the demolition, Dr. Edmond Souchon salvaged some wallpaper from Lulu White's parlor and sent me a small piece.

Unfortunately, jazz has never completely lost the stigmatic image of its sinful past. While Storyville nurtured the developing music, it also branded it with an unholy connotation that endured for decades.

Jazz nearly died in the Crescent City until the 1940s, when the music was accorded worldwide acceptance as a respectable "art form." The musicians who remained there, then middle-aged, also became "acceptable." Although many were past their prime musically, they rapidly were revered as sources of pride rather than shame.

In the early 1960s, the same newspaper that years before urged the suppression of "despicable jazz" editorially praised the New Orleans Jazz Museum, referring to it as "a significant addition to the cultural heritage of the city."

The many healthy influences contributing to jazz's maturation have gradually diminished its stigmatic aura. The younger players are armed with educations at noted music conservatories. They have elevated jazz's image and extended their musicianship beyond the self-taught skills of the seminal heroes that preceded them.

Having survived the perilous journey from Lulu White's Mahogany Hall to Carnegie Hall, this American phenomenon has finally outlived its early blemishes and is universally recognized as our nation's true classical music.

Papa Celestin and the Voodoo Queen

Almost half a century ago, I pledged not to divulge this extraordinary story. Since none of the participants are still alive, the time has come to reveal it.

It happened around midnight one evening in March 1951. Lucille and I were seated at a front table in our usual Los Angeles haunt, the Beverly Cavern, enjoying Kid Ory's Creole Jazz Band. The Cavern's bandstand faced the entrance. During the last song of a late set, the musicians began making eye contact with one another and nodding excitedly toward the door. Someone very special apparently had entered the club. We turned around and watched a smiling black gentleman approach the stand. When the music stopped, Ory and his sidemen leaped off the stage to greet their visitor. We soon learned that the unannounced guest was none other than celebrated New Orleans trumpet star and bandleader Oscar "Papa" Celestin (pronounced "cell-is-stan").

His smile broadened as he climbed on the stage. "I did not come to play," he said. "I am on my way to Oakland to visit relatives. I just wanted to greet my old friend Kid Ory for the first time since he left

New Orleans trumpet great Oscar "Papa"
Celestin, 1950.

New Orleans in 1919. It's been thirty-five years since I last saw bassist Ed Garland. He played in my Tuxedo Jazz Band in Storyville. I remember Ram Hall; he was a young drummer boy when his folks moved to Chicago in 1917."

We watched the ecstatic bandstand reunion continue for the next ten minutes. Not realizing it was intermission time, Celestin picked up Andrew Blakeney's trumpet and declared, "How about playing something?" Turning to Ory, who looked surprised, he said, "Let's play 'Basin Street,'" and he tapped off the starting tempo. The band followed him, and Celestin took an extended solo. At sixty-seven, he still played with great vigor, blowing strong arched phrases tinged with vigorous emotional bursts. After singing the verse and two choruses, he played another long rousing solo and concluded the number. The Cavern shook with applause.

Ory looked disturbed. As he reached for the microphone, Celestin grabbed it and announced: "I'd like to play for you all night, but I'm gettin' kinda tired and I've got to get up in the morning and catch a train. I want to leave you with a number I play every night in New Orleans."

He began a lengthy unaccompanied solo on "Just a Closer Walk With Thee." The room fell silent as the audience fell under the tender hymn's spell. Gaining intensity after a few choruses, Celestin's muted tones gradually heated. With his eyes closed and his horn tilted toward the ceiling, he ended the third, thrilling chorus on a clear sustained note. Then, nodding to pianist Buster Wilson, who gracefully picked up the accompaniment, the aged trumpet king passionately sang the next twenty-four bars before signaling for the final chord. After a few moments of silence, the thrilled patrons roared their approval.

Beverly Cavern owner Rose Stanman, sensing a blockbuster booking, asked Celestin to return the following week as special guest star. He agreed, and she quickly hung a huge banner outside that read: "COMING NEXT WEEK—NEW ORLEANS GREAT—'PAPA' CELESTIN WITH KID ORY'S CREOLE JAZZ BAND—NO COVER—NO ADMISSION."

We were at our usual table the following week. Celestin strolled in ahead of the others and climbed onto the bandstand. We watched him remove his trumpet from a well-worn case, insert the mouthpiece, and carefully place the horn, a dented mute, and an equally dented metal derby on a small standard. He opened a carton, removed a stack of LPs, and piled them next to the trumpet stand. He was ready for business. Then, stepping off the stage, he sat in an empty chair at our table, extended a hand, he said, "It's nice to see you. My name is Celestin."

I shook his large, soft hand and praised his brief performance the week before. He cheerfully accepted an invitation to be a guest on my radio program, *Jazz on Parade,* and we chatted amiably until the rest of the band arrived.

Every seat was filled. The band sounded wonderful with the added horn; Andrew Blakeney gracefully blended a second trumpet part that greatly enhanced the ensemble strength. Celestin managed to maneuver every number into a feature spot and completely dominated each set. It soon became apparent that Kid Ory was not comfortable sharing the stage with the dynamic trumpet player, who was accustomed to being in charge.

The guest star attracted full houses throughout the week and delighted every audience. Few of the patrons had heard of the musician previously, but I am sure they never forgot him. However, Ory's displeasure increased as his fellow New Orleanian monopolized the spotlight with his vocal and instrumental mastery. He received requests every night to repeat "Just a Closer Walk With Thee." During the intermissions, he moved to our table to sell his LPs and happily autographed them for the fans. Between sales we planned the format of the forthcoming radio program, and I enjoyed several conversations with the legendary New Orleans jazzman.

Despite his visible annoyance with the situation, Kid Ory never sounded better. Stirred by a strong competitive spirit, he made his tailgate slurs into torrid slashing responses to Papa Celestin's impassioned muted horn. The crowd acknowledged each number with roaring applause while guitarist Bud Scott shouted approval, Celestin grinned—and Ory frowned. By the end of the week, conditions had deteriorated considerably. Listeners were aware they were hearing something very special; they also sensed Ory's hostility. His guest trumpeter blithely assumed the starring role, obviously with great enjoyment.

Kid Ory's anger reached a boiling point on the final night of Celestin's engagement. Throughout the evening the trumpet star was extremely ebullient. The closing number, his nightly reprise of "Closer Walk," became the highlight of the week. This time, he climbed off the stand to wander among the audience, blowing whispered notes into happy patrons' ears. On the stage, clarinetist Joe Darensbourg blew mellow low register harmony while the rhythm section churned softly. The applause did not abate until Celestin played two encore choruses—while Ory glowered.

The musicians left the stand and went into a small room next to the kitchen to pack their instruments. Lucille and I remained in the club with several fans, discussing the thrilling musical experience we had just shared. Some very disturbing sounds came from the kitchen area. We heard loud shouts, some cursing, and a clatter of breaking dishes. Soon a highly agitated Kid Ory stormed from the back room carrying his trombone case. He dashed through the club and out the front door.

Celestin appeared on my radio show the following night, and I asked him about the turmoil at the Cavern. "I'll tell you later," he said.

The old trumpet master was an ideal guest. Responsive and glib, he offered insightful fragments of jazz history. He was born January 1, 1884, on a plantation near Napoleonville, not far from New Orleans, and claimed to be the oldest New Orleans jazz musician still plying his trade. Other than a leg injury sustained in an automobile accident several years earlier and a slight hearing loss, he seemed in good health.

As the program evolved, I began to notice a striking similarity between Celestin and his contemporary, Jelly Roll Morton. His sharp memory, lack of modesty, and deep melodic voice tinged with a Southern drawl all called to mind the late piano legend. At one point I thought: this could be Jelly himself sharing the microphone with me.

The interview was generously sprinkled with anecdotes about Tuxedo Hall, Judge Fogarty, Storyville, Frankie Duson, Lake Pontchartrain, Manuel Perez, Mardi Gras, George Baquet, Basin Street, and Freddie Keppard—all pivotal chapters in the Crescent City saga. He had begun his career at historic Tuxedo Hall back in 1910, in a band that included trombonist George Filhe (who later joined King Oliver's Creole Jazz Band in Chicago), Alphonse Picou and Lorenzo Tio, Sr., on clarinets, and Peter Bocage and Celestin on trumpets. The band remained a fixture there until the manager, Harry Parker, was killed in a shooting brawl. Tuxedo Hall closed its doors permanently, but Celestin continued to call his band the Original Tuxedo Orchestra throughout his career, and he used the name for another group (the Tuxedo Brass Band) he founded in 1911. The collective personnel of the latter group reads like a who's who of New Orleans jazz.

Papa remembered old Judge Fogarty, the nemesis of New Orleans' lawbreakers. Fogarty, an imposing figure on the bench, applied a firm hand to those who strayed. A typical court exchange, Celestin said, might go like this:

"What have you got to say for yourself, prisoner?"
"Well, Judge, I ..."
"Thirty days! Take 'im away!"

"And off to the city jail he would go," Celestin laughed. "Incidentally, the condemned man had better not glance back. If he did, Fogarty would exclaim, 'Ten dollars additional!'"

Celestin also shared memories of trombonist Jack Carey, a brother of Mutt Carey. The pioneer jazzman won quite a following around the turn of the century for his spirited playing of "Tiger Rag." Carey was so closely associated with the controversial tune that fans called it "Jack Carey" and replaced the familiar "Hold that tiger" strain with the words: "Oh, Jack Carey!" Celestin had never heard Buddy Bolden, but he had certainly heard the legends regarding Bolden's powerful horn. "Folks said they could hear his horn for a distance of twelve city blocks," he said, adding: "Of course, Floyd, in New Orleans our blocks are much shorter than those you have here." Without waiting for a question, he continued:

I remember back in New Orleans around 1909 or 1910, when Kid Ory's band and my band would meet down on Sixth and Howard Streets, I think it was. We'd be in wagons, like they used to move furniture. Well, my band would play and his band would play—and we'd try to drown each other out in a fight to see which was best. We'd play maybe two or three hours, fightin' each other—and then we'd go to a saloon, have a few shots, and we'd all be friends.

When the program ended, I repeated my query about the previous night's fracas at the Beverly Cavern. Again, he evaded the question. Perhaps, aware of my close relationship with Kid Ory, he thought it best to avoid the subject. I wondered if I would ever hear details of the incident.

Less than a week after Papa returned to New Orleans, a long letter arrived from him. He wrote, in part

> I enjoyed being in your company and with Mrs. Floyd. I will never forget your friendliness, making me feel at home, and welcomed in your house.
>
> As for Kid Ory, I am disturbed and displeased with his actions the last night I was in the Beverly Cavern. He wanted to kill me! Such a man does not deserve the cooperation of you and your friends. He tried to get to me with—not one—but two long kitchen knives to stab me. That made me feel sick! That man should be shot!

When I showed the letter to bassist Ed Garland, he admitted to witnessing the episode Celestin described. The rest of the players had left, and Garland watched in horror while the two jazz patriarchs engaged in their horrible dispute. He asked me not to divulge the details of the affair. Until now, that request has been honored.

I visited Celestin later during a trip to New Orleans. He was playing at the Paddock Bar on Bourbon Street. Clarinetist Alphonse Picou, a veteran of the Original Tuxedo Orchestra, still played at his side. The two jazzmen had met shortly after the turn of the century while playing at Madame Lulu White's bordello on Basin Street.

Papa Celestin died December 15, 1954, a few hours before a sculpture of him was scheduled for presentation at a civil ceremony in his honor. His funeral, one of the largest in New Orleans history, was led by the Eureka Brass Band, followed by his own Tuxedo Brass Band. The procession included a dozen funeral limousines, thirty private cars, and thousands of walkers. The two bands played "Just a Closer Walk With Thee" repeatedly as the parade wound its way through the French Quarter. Newsreel footage of the drama was seen in theaters throughout the world.

The great trumpeter took many memories of jazz's birthplace with him. But he created at least as many memories for the fans who saw him play. I appreciate the opportunity to have known this great man. His priceless letters, photographs, and greeting cards are among the most prized mementos of my involvement with the musicians who created classic jazz.

Papa Celestin recited this interesting New Orleans voodoo tale on my radio program in 1951:

> There lived a conjure-lady, not long ago,
> In New Orleans, Louisiana—named Marie Laveau.
> She made a fortune selling voodoo and interpreting dreams.
> She was known throughout the nation as The Voodoo Queen.
>
> Folks came to her from miles and miles around,
> She showed them how to "put that voodoo down,"
> To the voodoo lady they would go—rich, educated, ignorant, and poor.
> She'd snap her fingers and shake her head,
> Then tell 'em 'bout their lovers—livin' or dead.
>
> An old, old lady named Widow Brown,
> She asked why her lover stopped comin' around.
> The Voodoo gazed at her and squalled,
> "I seen him kissin' a young girl up in Shakespeare's Hall,*
> Standin' near an oak tree in the dark."
>
> Poor Marie Laveau,
> Marie Laveau, The Voodoo Queen,
> Way down yonder in New Orleans.
>
> Old Widow Brown, she lost her speech,
> Tears start rollin' down her cheeks.
> She says, "Hush, my darlin' don't you cry,
> I'll make him come back by and by,
> Now sprinkle this snake dust on your floor,
> He'll be back Friday mornin', when the rooster crow."
>
> Poor Marie Laveau,
> Marie Laveau, The Voodoo Queen,
> Way down yonder in New Orleans.
>
> Marie Laveau helped them in her hand,†
> New Orleans was her promised land,
> Quality folks came from far and near,
> This wonder woman for to hear.

---

* "Shakespeare's Hall" was once a dance hall for the younger, more select Negro society in New Orleans. The hall was destroyed by fire before the Civil War.
† "In her hand" meant "right before their very eyes." She concocted the various colored powders, oils, or fetishes used to produce the voodoo spell while they watched.

They were 'fraid to be seen at her gate,
And would creep through the dark to hear their fate.
Holdin' dark veils over their head,
They would tremble to hear what Marie Laveau said.
Poor Marie Laveau, Marie Laveau,
The Voodoo Queen from New Orleans.

She made gris-gris†† with an old ram horn,
Stuffed with feathers and shucks from a corn.
A big black cat urn and catfish fin,§
Made a man get religion and give up his sin.

Poor Marie Laveau,
Marie Laveau, The Voodoo Queen,
She got rich on voodoo in New Orleans.
Sad news got out one mornin' at the dawn of day,

Marie Laveau had passed away.
In St. Louis' Cemetery she lays in her tomb,
She was buried at night on the waste of the moon.

Poor Marie Laveau, Oh, Marie Laveau.
The folks STILL believe in The Voodoo Queen,
'Way down yonder in New Orleans.'"

The mystic tale, laced with curious jargon, spurred my curiosity, and I decided to do some further investigation of the Marie Laveau story.

To clarify a few of the obscure references, I enlisted assistance from the late Dr. Edmond Souchon, a prominent New Orleans physician, who divided his time between medicine and the New Orleans Jazz Club. He gladly added many details to this story.

Catholicism was the principal religion of most seminal New Orleans jazzmen, but voodoo rituals and superstitions, inherited from slave ancestors, often played a secondary spiritual role in their lives. Jazz discographies list scores of early voodoo-themed tunes, including "Voodoo!," "Voo Doo Blues," "Witchcraft Blues," "Mojo Blues," and "Black Cat Blues." Jelly Roll Morton's 1928 Red Hot Peppers recording of "Boogaboo" expresses a sinister ritualistic theme. Morton, during his final years, believed a witch's curse from years before had caused his declining health.

Souchon and Celestin both told me the voodoo cult still flourished in New Orleans as practiced, perhaps, by ancestors of the infamous

---

†† "Gris-gris" (pronounced "gree-gree") is a fetish used to ward off evil spirits or produce harmful effects on an enemy.
§ "Catfish fin." Catfish are plentiful in New Orleans, and the fins are considered poisonous. Serious infection, even death, results from stepping on these long, sharp fins.

Marie Laveau. Yes, Marie was a real person. She lived and died before the turn of the century, dispensing voodoo lore until her death on June 16, 1881. Her mixed ancestry included black, white, and Indian blood, resulting in an exotic appearance that added to her allure and helped her attract followers.

The illegitimate daughter of Charles Laveau, she was born before the United States purchased the Louisiana Territory from France. She married Jacques Paris in New Orleans on August 4, 1819. Paris died shortly after the marriage, and, according to Southern tradition, Marie became known as "The Widow Paris"—even after her common law marriage to Captain Christophe Glapion, who served with Andrew Jackson in the War of 1812.

The mystical queen bore fifteen children by Glapion, and great-grandchildren of that union live in New Orleans today. Perhaps, as Doc Souchon suggested, some are still practicing Queen Marie's voodoo rites, using potent powders and gris-gris to protect them from "Papa La Bas"—the Devil.

Madame Laveau ruled a vast voodoo empire from her home in the Vieux Carré. The Paris cottage was situated close to famous Congo Square, where slaves danced every Sunday afternoon while their owners watched with avid amusement. Dressed in colorful robes, she told fortunes, sold gris-gris, and dispensed love powders to aid in *affaires d'amour*. Her restored cottage still stands on St. Ann Street between North Rampart and Burgundy Streets.

At nearby Milneburg, Marie Laveau's Maison Blanche was the setting for sordid activity. Here, for an appropriate charge, rich white merchants enjoyed the services of beautiful quadroon girls while Marie looked on. When whites were not present, the house became a weird stage on which orgiastic voodoo rites were performed, often accompanied by groups of New Orleans musicians. The Queen, wearing the ever-present "tignon" (a seven-cornered headpiece), led her followers in rites that included the drinking of warm blood from an animal sacrificed for the occasion. Boiling cauldrons, into which live black cats were tossed, added to the aberrant scene. Burning torches cast grotesque shadows that swayed to the maddening rhythm of tom-toms (usually oil cans covered with animal skin, beat with the leg bone of a large turkey). Naked bodies, dripping with perspiration, pulsated with undulating motion. Whiskey and rum in generous quantities added impetus to the shuffling feet and volume to the fetish songs. The rituals usually ended with the dawn, when the exhausted followers collapsed in pairs. Their sensual heap of writhing flesh, lost in the throes of voodoo abandon, reflected the dominance of the Voodoo Queen.

Similar ceremonial movements inspired dancer-choreographer Katherine Dunham, who conducted ethnic dance research in Haiti during the '60s. She very successfully incorporated voodoo imagery in her touring ballets with West Indian dancers and jazz musicians.

Fearful, dramatic voodoo rites are still enacted in New Orleans and other major American cities. Yes, the folks *still* believe in The Voodoo Queen, 'way down yonder in New Orleans.

Danny Barker — The Jazz Troubadour

At the 1969 New Orleans Jazz and Heritage Festival, in a corner of Beauregarde Square, a group of young black musicians crowded around a slight man wearing a striped blazer and a yellow straw hat. The kids clutched their battered and tarnished horns and listened attentively as their mentor readied them for their entrance into the square. "Let's get that beat goin'," he said. "We won't start playin' until we get their attention with that beat. Now, with the bass drum, let's go … boom, boom, boom, boom! That's right, start marchin'. … keep that beat goin'! Keep that beat goin'!"

With the thumping bass drum setting the cadence, the group of smiling youngsters strutted into the square preceded by the great Danny Barker. An expansive grin reflected his approval as the young musicians, marching under a banner marked "Fairview Baptist Church Christian Marching Band," moved through the crowd. On his signal they broke into a spirited "Bourbon Street Parade," leading a flock of teenage second-liners through the paths of the old commons, on the same ground that shook a hundred years earlier beneath the pounding feet of African slaves.

Then sixty-two years old, Barker had spent many illustrious years playing banjo in Cab Calloway's swing orchestra alongside Dizzy Gillespie, Tyree Glenn, Jonah Jones, Chu Berry, Keg Johnson, Milt Hinton, and other great sidemen. He had played on monumental recordings with some of the finest jazzmen of his time. His songwriting credits included "Save the Bones for Henry Jones ('Cause Henry Don't Eat No Meat)," made famous by Johnny Mercer and Nat "King" Cole, along with most of the fine blues tunes recorded by his talented wife, Blue Lu

*Danny Barker was a great performer,
composer, and historian.*

Barker. A gifted writer as well as a great musician, Barker authored two books of jazz history, *Bourbon Street Black* (1973) and *A Life in Jazz* (1986), both published by Oxford University Press. And *Hear Me Talkin' to You*, the highly acclaimed 1955 volume by Nat Shapiro and Nat Hentoff, included extensive quotations from him.

Barker loved his city and the music identified with it. The booming bass drum sounds that filled Beauregarde Square that afternoon in June 1969 were his pronouncement to the world that jazz was young again, and the youth of the Crescent City would keep it alive and swinging for future generations to enjoy.

Danny Barker was born into a family of fine musicians. His grandfather played with Bunk Johnson in the old Onward Brass Band, and his uncle, Paul Barbarin, was one of New Orleans' finest drummers. Barker could remember hearing Joe Oliver in Manuel Perez's Imperial Band and Sidney Bechet, then seventeen, playing clarinet with the Young Olympia Band. He also recalled hearing the Tuxedo Brass Band, Sam Morgan, Chris Kelly, and the legendary drummer Black

Benny. And he knew tidbits that brought the New Orleans jazz scene to life in vivid detail. Speaking of one local character, Barker said:

> He was called "Joe Never Smile," because he always had a grim expression on his face. Joe drove a team of horses that pulled the casket wagon at funerals. For an extra fee, he could arrange for the horses to cry during the procession—he squeezed onion juice in their eyes.
>
> When I was very young, I heard clarinet pioneer Alphonse Picou talking about a Negro symphony orchestra in New Orleans early in the 1890s. Historians have conveniently overlooked this cultural aspect of my heritage.
>
> It's a shame that the early jazz stars were never recorded. They were recording Enrico Caruso and John Philip Sousa at the time—but no one was interested in musicians like Buddy Bolden, Chris Kelly, Manuel Perez, and Buddy Petit. Some of the best early jazz players, like Kid Rena and "Big Eye" Louis Nelson, didn't record until long after their prime.
>
> The older people in New Orleans always talked about the great Buddy Bolden. They said his trumpet could be heard from Lincoln Park to downtown—over seven miles away. That legend, if true, can be attributed to the caliber of Bolden's blowing—and the area's swampy acoustics.

Barker also remembered the Boozan Kings, his childhood street band; one-nighters with Jelly Roll Morton; and a Broadway theater appearance with Mae West. He achieved fame and success, but he never forgot the arduous travel, the dingy hotels, or the heartless strictures of segregation.

Barker rose to prominence as rhythm guitarist and banjo player with famous bands led by Lucky Millinder, Cab Calloway, and Benny Carter. He played on innumerable recordings in every jazz style, from brass band to bebop. The list of musicians he has recorded with spans the whole history of the genre: Jelly Roll Morton, Louis Armstrong, James P. Johnson, Sidney Bechet, Wingy Manone, Papa Mutt Carey, Lionel Hampton, Lena Horne, Ethel Waters, Billie Holiday, Conrad Janis, and Wynton Marsalis.

In 1945 he recorded four songs with Sir Charles and His All-Stars, whose lineup included two young, unknown saxophonists. "They want a beat and big fat chords," pianist Charles Thompson told Barker. "You can do that." He did—and the recordings helped catapult Charlie Parker and Dexter Gordon to stardom.

A fine songwriter as well, Barker penned the suggestively titled "Don't You Feel My Leg" for his wife, Blue Lu Barker, and recorded it with her in 1938. Radio stations refused to play the record because they considered the lyrics too raunchy: "Don't you feel my leg, 'Cause if you feel my leg, You're gonna feel my thigh, And when you feel my thigh, You're gonna buy some rye, And if you buy some rye..." The song became a smash despite its lack of airplay; Decca Records even halted the pressing of Guy Lombardo records to meet the demand for Lu's big hit. "Don't You Feel My Leg" received a dramatic boost during a Harlem rally for President Franklin D. Roosevelt's third-term campaign, Barker recalled:

> About five hundred dignitaries were seated in a portable grandstand in front of a church at 137th Street and Seventh Avenue. I stood behind them, in a crowd of about a thousand, waiting for the president's arrival. We heard music in the distance. It grew louder. Soon a truck appeared. It slowly passed the church blasting Lu's record from a large speaker on its roof: "Don't you feel my leg. 'Cause if you feel my leg..." I was embarrassed. Someone shouted, "Danny Barker wrote that—I just saw him over there!" That's when I split—I ran down an alley.

Danny and Blue Lu Barker came to California in the early 1950s for a brief stay. His first job was with Albert Nicholas' quartet at the St. Francis Room on Eighth Street. Danny and Nick, both from New Orleans and veterans of the Fifty-Second Street New York scene, worked compatibly with pianist Gideon Honoré and bassist Leonard Bibbs.

Barker approached his playing with a casual assurance, deftly accentuating the music and giving a fresh interpretation to timeworn lyrics. His personal imprint on tunes such as "Bill Bailey" and "Hard-Hearted Hannah" brought new life to those old standards, and his humor verged on pathos. He was an exceptional entertainer; when he sang his saloon songs, you could almost smell the sawdust on the floor.

Barker's last LP, the 1988 release *Save the Bones* (Orleans Records No. OR1018), captures him at his best. Producer Carlo Ditta very astutely provided an ideal forum for Barker's glib conversation and music, showcasing him in an intimate setting rarely heard on record. The LP features him alone with his Gibson guitar, playing with the same warmth he displayed whether entertaining in the living room of his little New Orleans home on Sere Street or on stage before thousands of fans. Not since 1938, when the great Jelly Roll Morton left a rich legacy on a series of Library of Congress recordings, had a New Orleans jazzman so eloquently expressed himself.

Barker was a man of many interests and skills. In addition to his musical, compositional, vocal, and storytelling talents, he possessed a fine artistic sensibility. He painted beautiful landscapes and portraits exhibited in private art collections. Barker also was deeply concerned with the history of jazz; his two books included a trove of valuable material dredged from his seven decades as a musician.

Barker returned to his native New Orleans in 1965 and quickly assumed a role of leadership. With an eye toward the future of New Orleans jazz, he established the Fairview Baptist Church Christian Marching Band, a youth-oriented jazz workshop. Barker's energy and high ideals set a lofty example for his students. Under his loving guidance, scores of underprivileged black children received an opportunity to have fun and expand their experiences and skills. Using instruments collected from cellars and garages, Barker taught "his boys" to take pride in their heritage and to dare to succeed. Thanks to his encouragement and dedication, many youngsters eschewed street gangs for street parades. Many of today's successful New Orleans jazzmen are graduates of Barker's Fairview Baptist program.

With his abiding respect for the past and vast knowledge of jazz history, Barker was ideally qualified to serve as curator of the New Orleans Jazz Museum. Although he spent almost forty years away from his New Orleans roots, he always retained a firm grasp on the Crescent City idiom and was extremely proud of having had thirty-eight relatives who played jazz in New Orleans. During his tenure in the early 1970s, the museum attained a lofty position in the archival world.

In 1991 the National Endowment for the Arts presented Danny Barker with the American Jazz Masters Fellowship and Lifetime Achievement Award. A few months later, the U.S. Postal Service issued a jazz cachet in his honor. And the City of New Orleans declared January 29, 1994, "Blue Lu and Danny Barker Day." He was eighty-five years old when he died later that year.

I was unable to attend Danny's big, beautiful, noisy funeral. The procession included a band of more than forty musicians, six grand marshals, and a second line numbering in the hundreds. The parade was organized by Greg Stafford, trumpet player and graduate of Danny's Fairview Baptist Church band. Reading the reports in the New Orleans papers, I was reminded of Danny's unique version of "St. James Infirmary Blues," which captured the song's essence as only Danny could:

> When I die, I want you to dress me in straight laced shoes,
> (Put my shoes on because I might have to run from the devil.)
> I want a box-back coat and a Stetson hat
> (Put my hat on, because the cinders might be falling.)

Put a twenty-dollar gold piece on my watch chain
So all my (phoney, whiskey-head, reefer-head) friends
Will know I passed away standing pat.

I want sixteen snow white horses
(No ponies, no jackasses—all horses.)
Sixteen chorus girls from the Apollo
To sing and dance me a song.
Put a jazz band on top of my casket
To blow the "Memphis Blues" as they slowly stroll along.

At his last Los Angeles appearance, in the Hollywood Bowl in 1990, Danny Barker strode to the microphone and said: "I'm brave! I've gone through the Depression, six recessions, two World Wars, and forty years in New York's Harlem. I'm a genuine specimen of tragedy—but I'm brave. I'm gonna die standing up!" Actually, he died during his sleep on March 13, 1994. But, in the hearts of those who loved him, he still stands tall—as a jazz giant should.

Lorenzo Tio, Jr., and the Clarinetists of the Crescent City

THE DYNASTY OF LORENZO TIO, JR.

Johnny Dodds	(1892–1940)
Emile Barnes	(1892–1970)
Jimmie Noone	(1895–1944)
Wade Whaley	(1895–c1950)
Albert Nicholas	(1900–1973)
Omer Simeon	(1902–1959)
Albert Burbank	(1902–1979)
Darnell Howard	(1906–1966)
Barney Bigard	(1906–1980)
Louis Cottrell, Jr.	(1911–1978)

The record on the turntable, revolving at 78 rpm, cast a reddish glow in the stereo cabinet as the bright label reflected the beam of a small tensor lamp. The gold lettering on the old label seemed blurred, but with a slight rotation of my head I could read: "LOU'SIANA SWING. A.J. Piron, Piron's New Orleans Orchestra."

The music ended. I carefully lifted the fragile Okeh disc, holding a priceless link with the formative era of jazz. Consider the title,

"Lou'siana Swing." The tune was recorded in 1924—four years before Jelly Roll Morton first employed the verb-noun "swing" (on his 1928 recording, "Georgia Swing") and eight years before Duke Ellington firmly established the word in our musical vocabulary with his monumental "It Don't Mean a Thing, If It Ain't Got That Swing." Less than a decade after that profound pronouncement, we were deeply involved in the swing era—which, ironically, caused a temporary lull in New Orleans jazz's popularity.

The room was still ringing with sounds recorded three quarters of a century earlier. The spectral musicians included Peter Bocage on trumpet; John Lindsay on trombone; Louis Cottrell, Sr., on the drums; and the peerless New Orleans clarinetist Lorenzo Tio, Jr. This is one of the few recordings of Tio's classic French woodwind sound, which influenced scores of reed players. Tio was an active working musician, playing in the leading bands and orchestras of New Orleans, but he had his greatest impact as a clarinet teacher. His students are among the exalted heroes of jazz. They, in turn, influenced hundreds of younger musicians. As a result, the systemic influence of Lorenzo Tio, Jr., can be traced through much of jazz's history.

He was born in New Orleans in 1884. His father, Lorenzo Tio, Sr., and uncle, Luis "Papa" Tio, migrated from Mexico in 1881. They, too, were famous clarinetists, playing in the Excelsior Brass Band and in various Storyville saloons before the turn of the century. The earliest trace of Lorenzo Jr.'s activities dates to 1897, when, at the age of thirteen, his name appeared on the roster of musicians performing in the New Orleans Lyre Symphony. Later, he joined the Eagle Band, formed in 1911 by Frankie Dusen. That early group included three other promising youngsters—Sidney Bechet, "Big Eye" Louis Nelson, and the legendary Freddie Keppard.

Tio, Jr., followed his father and uncle into the Excelsior Band in 1914. He also played in New Orleans groups led by Oscar Celestin, Manuel Perez, Joe Oliver, and A. J. Piron, with whom he made his only recordings. Tio worked with Perez as early as 1915 in one of the first jazz bands to play a regular dance job in Chicago. A few years later, New York audiences heard him with the Piron orchestra at the Roseland Ballroom.

To a neophyte, the clarinet, seemingly of minor importance in a jazz combo, is subservient to the brassy sounds of trumpet and trombone. But seasoned fans recognize the small woodwind's significance in a traditional jazz band's front line. When skillfully blown, it can accentuate the true flavor of the music—like filé powder spices a gumbo. It can be low and mellow, or it can soar into high cascades of flowing brilliance and explode with a fusillade of spiraling sparks. In its middle register, the horn produces sensuous slurs and swooping dives. The clarinetist can weave a musical thread that merges with the brass instruments and binds them into a unified musical fabric.

The precursor of the clarinet was first used in orchestras three centuries ago. Its name, surprisingly, came from a trumpet. In the seventeenth century, brass sections in European orchestras usually had three different trumpets, each with a particular register. When the clarinet was introduced, it had the same tonal quality of the highest-pitched trumpet, the clarino. The new horn was called the "little clarino," or clarinette.

Over the years, the clarinet has appeared in a wider range of sizes and pitches than any other instrument. Most of those models have fallen into oblivion. We usually hear the B-flat horn today, but New Orleans brass bands favor the harsher E-flat clarinet, which is better suited for cutting through the heavy brass in the large street bands.

The Boehm system of fingering now in use was adapted from a flute method to facilitate faster playing, but many older New Orleans musicians preferred the earlier Albert system, which was easier to play and produced a mellower tone.

The clarinet is usually a hollow tube of ebony wood (metal horns are also used). The wooden horn has five separate close-fitting parts with thirteen keys and twenty side holes. Scores of tiny springs often malfunction; keypads become waterlogged; and a vibrating reed must be in perfect condition to produce a proper tone. Adding to the challenge, the clarinet requires different fingering in the upper register than its lower range. An agile player can fluidly span about three octaves on this demanding instrument.

The horn is deeply rooted in the history of jazz. Faded tintypes of the celebrated Buddy Bolden band, taken before 1895, show a pair of clarinetists—Frank Lewis and Willie Warner—proudly holding their Albert system horns.

The instrument figured prominently in the early popularity of jazz when the New Orleans bands moved north. They brought with them a wealth of talented reedmen that inspired generations of future clarinetists. Their young followers would eventually spawn the swing era and included such artists as Benny Goodman, Artie Shaw, Woody Herman, Buster Bailey, Joe Marsala, Clarence Hutchinrider, Peanuts Hucko, Matty Matlock, Irving Fazola, Jimmy Hamilton, and Sol Yaged.

In the mid-1940s, saxophones temporarily replaced clarinets as the preferred reed instrument among the bebop set. However, a few modern stylists still made effective use of the "blackstick," including Buddy DeFranco, Jimmy Giuffre, and Tony Scott. Although most modernists eschew the clarinet, its vintage sound permeates the classic jazz scene. Today the horn is played by such contemporary greats as Bob Wilber, Kenny Davern, Chuck Hedges, Bob Reitmeier, Antti Sarpila, Abe Most, Rick Fay, Ken Peplowski, Bob Draga, Evan Christopher, Mahlon Clark, Dan Levinson, Alan Vaché, Jacques Gauthé, Claude Luter, Brian White, Maxim Saury, Pete Fountain, and Bobby Gordon. Nearly all of these players have inherited, directly or indirectly, the wisdom of Lorenzo Tio, Jr.

During his long teaching career, Tio skillfully molded the talents of many of the great New Orleans players who brought jazz to the public's attention. His illustrious students carved out an important role for the clarinet in small jazz bands and larger orchestras. While all of Tio's pupils retained a semblance of their teacher's flowing, rhythmic staccato style, each developed a personal, readily identifiable sound. Each combined technical virtuosity with imaginative approaches to improvisation. An aural examination of the music created by these fine reedmen can be extremely rewarding.

Johnny Dodds was the prototype for all jazz clarinetists and, aside from Tio, the most influential. Chicagoans heard Dodds' rich, robust tone and powerful attack in King Oliver's Creole Jazz Band as far back as 1920 at the Lincoln Gardens. Among the nightly listeners was an impressionable young Benny Goodman, who frequently credited Dodds as his earliest inspiration. Goodman subsequently had his own following, continuing to pass down the gospel according to Tio and Dodds.

Emile Barnes was born in 1892, the same year as Dodds. His career, one of the longest in jazz, covered almost six decades. Unfortunately, he did not have an opportunity to record in his prime. Unlike most of Lorenzo Tio's pupils, Barnes spent his best years in New Orleans, playing in small clubs and dance halls where he received little exposure. Historian-producer Bill Russell did make some recordings of Barnes when the clarinetist was well into his sixties. Even at that age, Barnes demonstrated the deeply moving, emotional quality of his playing.

Jimmie Noone's tone was lighter, a bit more florid than Dodds' but typical of Tio's personal style. Noone's array of followers includes Buster Bailey, Joe Marsala, and fellow Tio trainees Barney Bigard and Albert Nicholas. The recordings he made during the late '20s with his Apex Club Orchestra in Chicago featured Earl Hines' piano and firmly established his reputation as one of jazzdom's all-time greats. The impassioned "I Know That You Know," his first Vocalion record, still exemplifies a perfect tone, solid control, and beautiful articulation.

When Noone died in 1944 on the day he was to appear on the weekly Orson Welles Mercury Theater radio broadcast in Los Angeles, Wade Whaley joined the Kid Ory band for a dramatic tribute. Whaley, who also studied with Tio in New Orleans in 1916, worked with the leading Crescent City bands before following Ory to California and became a regular member of his Creole Jazz Band. When Ory made his historic Sunshine recordings in 1921, Whaley was out of the city and missed the opportunity to participate in that epic event.

Albert Nicholas, who played beautifully on Jelly Roll Morton's recording of "Blue Blood Blues" in 1930, came into prominence on Morton's last record dates for Victor a decade later. His flowery yet extremely assertive style retained the familiar Tio flavor and pleased audiences in Europe and the United States.

Omer Simeon was probably Morton's favorite clarinetist; he appears on most of Jelly's Red Hot Peppers classics. Touches of Noone and Nicholas are evident in Simeon's tones, a further indication of the strong thread that links all the clarinetists Tio tutored. Simeon added a traditional voice to the reed section of Earl Hines' and Jimmy Lunceford's orchestras when swing was the thing. Later, that authentic touch sparked small bands led by Kid Ory, Zutty Singleton, and the De Paris Brothers.

Albert Burbank displayed a sharp stylistic contrast from the others. While the subliminal Tio aura flowed beneath the surface, his singing tone had an earthier quality, a distillation of jazz's basic elements. Burbank's individual style was based on this pure residue—the true essence of New Orleans music. He influenced George Lewis and his myriad of followers, including Dr. Michael White, the currently popular traditionalist in New Orleans.

Tio also tutored the Chicago musician Darnell Howard. Many years ago, Howard told me about his relationship with the great New Orleans teachers. To my knowledge, this segment of jazz history has not been previously documented.

One evening in a San Francisco hotel room, he explained how his path crossed Tio's:

> It was about 1924. I was hired to play tenor saxophone and violin in a band led by a New Orleans musician, Charlie Elgar, who was working at the Dreamland Cafe. When we moved to the Wisconsin Roof Gardens in Milwaukee, Elgar sent for Lorenzo, who played with him in New Orleans before World War I. After he joined the band, we became buddies. He liked my violin playing and offered to show me how to make the same runs on a clarinet. I bought a used horn in a pawn shop and, for a year, we spent hours together each night after the job. He was a wonderful teacher.

This story accounts for Howard's distinctive New Orleans feeling, which collectors have long been at a loss to explain.

Barney Bigard was undoubtedly the most successful of Lorenzo Tio Jr.'s disciples. While serving as an apprentice in a cigar factory, Bigard and a cousin, Don Albert (Albert Dominique), visited Tio's house daily for music lessons. Albert, who became a very successful trumpeter and bandleader in the '30s, spoke glowingly of Tio's skill teaching brass instruments in addition to reeds. Barney Bigard added, "Old man Tio would not let us blow our horns until we had mastered the rudiments of harmony. He insisted we learn to read music first."

Wellman Braud, the eminent New Orleans bassist, preceded Bigard in Duke Ellington's orchestra. When Ellington expanded the group for its debut at the Cotton Club in 1927, Braud suggested he hire Bigard. The clarinetist joined the band at the end of the year, and for the next fourteen years Bigard's Tio-tinged Creole horn provided the distinctive timbre that helped establish a worldwide reputation for the Ellington orchestra. His tenure with the Duke defined both of their careers; the productive liaison unleashed Ellington's inherent arranging skills and nurtured Bigard's astonishing style. The fantastic sweep and torrential majesty of those long glissandi on scores of the Duke's recordings remain quintessential definitions of jazz clarinet. Bigard's trademarks, the gliding flights up and down the chromatic scale, are reminders of his graceful agility. His firm imprint on the Ellington sound continued through the years, as each successor mirrored the patterns he developed.

Louis Cottrell, Jr., the last of Tio's students, led his own band until he died in 1978. (His father, Louis Cottrell, Sr., was the drummer on the A.J. Piron record that triggered this nostalgic flow.) I can still see his smiling face as he stood in the shadow of St. Louis Cathedral next to the towering statue of Andrew Jackson on July 4, 1976—Louis

Armstrong's birthday and the bicentennial of the nation. On that day we unveiled the long-awaited Louis Armstrong statue (see Chapter 8). Cottrell's soaring clarinet filled Jackson Square with a verve that would have pleased Professor Tio. As the television cameras recorded the unveiling of the new bronze figure of Satchmo, Cottrell's band and Danny Barker's Jazz Hounds played a joyous "Happy Birthday."

It is interesting to note that six of Tio's pupils—Dodds, Noone, Nicholas, Bigard, Howard, and Simeon—occupied the clarinet position in King Oliver's band. Similarly, during the early years of Kid Ory's Creole Jazz Band, the succession of Tio-tutored clarinetists included Noone, Whaley, Bigard, Simeon, and Howard.

Although none of Lorenzo Tio's protégés are alive today, their spectres haunt the sleazy bars on Bourbon Street, the old halls, and the posh hotels and restaurants in New Orleans. These establishments continue to reap a bountiful harvest from those fertile seeds planted years ago.

When Barney Bigard died in 1980, he was the last survivor of the regal Tio graduates. The influence of that dynasty has been sustained by several generations of succeeding clarinetists.

Surprisingly, New Orleans has produced few young players interested in perpetuating the artistry of their grandfathers. (But, after all, Florence has produced few Raphaels or Donatellos lately, either!) One brilliant exception is Michael White, a professor at Xavier University who plays at Preservation Hall and appears with his own group at various venues around New Orleans. He also plays in the Excelsior Band—the same band that featured Lorenzo Tio, Sr., and Luis Tio more than a hundred years ago. Tim Laughlin, another fine contemporary clarinetist with a stellar reputation in the Crescent City, is a protégé of Pete Fountain. Laughlin was born in New Orleans, leads his own band, and has recorded several CDs.

The Holiday Inn Downtown Superdome recently commemorated the clarinet with a 150-foot-high mural on the side of the hotel. Undoubtedly the world's largest painting of the horn, it advertises the hotel's popular Clarinet Club, where Brian O'Connell appears five nights a week playing first-rate clarinet inspired by his mentor, Willie Humphrey.

Talented young clarinetists have come from Europe, bringing back to New Orleans the original music that swept the world. Chris Burke, an Albert Nicholas–Barney Bigard admirer, moved to town from England several years ago, keeping the buoyant spirit of New Orleans music alive with his youthful enthusiasm and talent. Another jazz émigré, French clarinetist Jacques Gauthé (a Sidney Bechet student), has forsaken his career as a leading chef to devote himself full-time to playing and promoting the music he loves. Besides making regular appearances with his Creole Rice Jazz Band, Gauthé has produced a nightly series of traditional jazz performances at the Meridien Hotel on Canal Street, just across from the French Quarter. Clarinetists Brian White and Sammy Rimington make frequent visits from London; Claude Luter, Pierre Atlan, and Maxim Saury drop in regularly from France; and Orange Kellin travels routinely from Sweden. These European musicians, with their deep appreciation of jazz, are preparing for the future while remembering the past.

It would be unfair to suggest that Lorenzo Tio, Jr., and his students were the only important New Orleans clarinetists. Many others contributed greatly to the rich heritage we are still enjoying. This long list of important musicians includes Leon Roppolo, Yellow Nunez, Joseph "Brother Cornbread" Thomas, Sidney Arodin, Tony Parenti, Edmond Hall, Herb Hall, Clarence Hall, Joseph Cordilla, Lester Bouchon, Paul Barnes, Theo Purnell, Dink Johnson, Charles McCurdy, Harry Shields, Larry Shields, Alphonse Picou, Achille Bacquet, George Bacquet, Sidney Bechet, Bujie Centobie, Raymond Burke, Lawrence Duhé, Israel Gorman, John Casmir, John Handy, Andrew Morgan, Gussie Mueller, Wooden Joe Nicholas, George Lewis, and Big Boy Goudie.

Similar lists could be assembled for each band instrument. No city in the world has, or ever will, produce such a wealth of musical talent.

The resonant sounds of the clarinet will always add luster to jazz. They remain as living tributes to the brilliant dynasty launched by Lorenzo Tio, Jr., almost a century ago.

Willie James Humphrey, Jr.

Until his death in 1994, Willie Humphrey was the undisputed dean of New Orleans clarinetists. He traveled the world with the Preservation Hall Jazz Band, gathering fans and friends along the way. Despite the fame, he always retained a gentle affability that reflected the warmth of his New Orleans heritage. Thousands of admirers shared a great affection for the great clarinetist. It was impossible not to love Willie Humphrey.

The Humphrey name has been highly respected in New Orleans for generations. Willie's grandfather, "Professor" Jim Humphrey, was a great teacher, and his father, Willie, Sr., also a teacher, played clarinet in the Eclipse Brass Band from 1901 to 1910. Willie's brother Earl, a fine trombonist, died in 1971. His youngest brother, Percy, one of jazz's most underrated trumpeters, played a beautiful melodic lead. His relaxed phrasing seemed nonchalant, but, blowing into his dented metal derby, he generated an intense heat in Preservation Hall that almost charred the walls of the hundred-year-old structure. Willie and Percy played side by side in the Preservation Hall Jazz Band for more than seven decades, but they seldom spoke. The younger brother's subdued, almost stoic, attitude contrasted with Willie's demonstrative verve. Percy was ninety when he died on July 22, 1995.

Born in 1900, Humphrey first learned to play the violin. As a teenager, he sat in with Kid Ory at Pete Lala's Big 25 in Storyville. Willie began playing E-flat clarinet in the Excelsior Brass Band in 1919, staying with this group for years. He played at Tom Anderson's restaurant on Rampart Street, on Mississippi riverboats with Fate Marable, and with Freddie Keppard and King Oliver in Chicago. Willie appears in newspaper photos with Oliver's band playing between innings at the 1919 World Series—when the Black Sox bribery incident rocked the sports world.

I have an enduring image of the great jazzman sitting on an antique wooden chair in Preservation Hall in front of pianist Sing Miller and between Percy and banjoist Narvin Kimball. He had occupied that same chair since 1961, when the hall opened. The audience, just a few feet away, seated on the floor in front of the bandstand, was oblivious to the dusty atmosphere, the humid air, and the cramped seating arrangement. From my favorite position, near the door to the carriageway, I had a good view of Willie charming the tourists, many of whom were hearing New Orleans jazz for the first time.

Humphrey also led his own Crescent City Joy Makers and was a regular with the Eureka Brass Band, led by Percy. Following the Humphrey family tradition, Willie also found the time to teach aspiring young musicians.

I became a fan and friend in 1954 during his appearance with Paul Barbarin's New Orleans Band in Los Angeles. Barbarin's nephews, trumpeter John Brunious and acclaimed New Orleans guitarist Danny Barker, were also in the group. The evening wasn't complete until Willie sang and did a little jig to "Liza Jane." The routine continued pleasing crowds for the next forty years.

During one of his many visits to Los Angeles with the Preservation Hall Jazz Band, Humphrey consented to a brief interview backstage at

*Willie Humphrey, longtime clarinetist with the Preservation Hall Jazz Band,
1968.*

UCLA's Royce Hall. I asked him about Storyville, New Orleans' famous red light district, and he laughed, saying: "I'm too young to remember those days. I started playing professionally after World War I.
The district had already been shut down. I did play at the saloon on
Rampart Street that Tom Anderson ran just a block toward Canal
Street from Lulu White's Mahogany Hall—which was closed." Willie
expressed pride in having raised and educated four children on a musician's income. "I'm not a millionaire, but I feel like one. I enjoy when
fans tell me, 'You're the best!' I always tell them, 'You haven't heard
them all yet!'"

The famed French clarinetist Claude Luter, an admirer of
Humphrey's, often traveled to the Crescent City, and he heard his
American counterpart play during every visit. Luter grew concerned
over the condition of Humphrey's timeworn clarinet, which he carried
in a scarred old case patched with tape. The bell of the ancient Albert
system horn was cracked, and rubber bands supplanted broken springs
on several keys. Luter finally commissioned the Selmer Company in
Paris to manufacture a custom horn for his friend. This was a formidable and very expensive task: Albert system tooling was no longer in
use, so many parts had to be made by hand.

The following year, Claude Luter returned to New Orleans, proudly carrying a new instrument made from special aged ebony with shiny silver keys. Willie's name was carved in the bell. The engraved gold nameplate on the handsome leather case said: WILLIE HUMPHREY, NEW ORLEANS, U.S.A.

On Claude Luter's opening night at the Meridien Hotel with Jacques Gauthé's Creole Rice Jazz Band, Willie appeared as guest artist. A large crowd filled the lobby bar and overflowed onto an adjacent stairway to the balcony. Luter and the band played the first set, and the surprise presentation took place during the intermission. Claude spoke very little English, so he asked me to introduce Willie and make the presentation for him. After an ornate fanfare, I called Humphrey to the bandstand and, flanked by Luter and Gauthé, handed him the beautiful case. When he opened it and viewed the contents, he embraced Claude, Jacques, and me and tearfully expressed his appreciation.

But when the second set began, he left the new instrument with his wife, Ora, and climbed onto the bandstand holding the old horn. Assisting him up the steps, I asked him why he did not bring the Selmer. "I'm gonna have to get used to it first," he said. "It will take a while before can I play it in public." We were all disappointed, but an instrument is a highly personal thing; after playing one clarinet for so many years, Willie needed some time to become acquainted with the gift.

Several years later, when I asked him about the new horn, Willie confided: "Floyd, I've never played it. It was wonderful of Claude to get it for me. I've never seen such a beautiful thing. I know it cost a lotta money. But I just could not get used to it. The action is different—the keys respond differently. I guess I'm just too old to re-learn."

Willie Humphrey died on June 7, 1994, at the age of ninety-four. When my wife and I visited Ora at the Humphreys' Cadiz Street home a few years later, I recognized the leather Selmer case standing in a corner. The instrument had never been played. It was next to the battered old horn Willie continued playing until the end.

The day after Willie Humphrey died, a full-color photograph of him spread across three columns of the *New Orleans Times-Picayune*'s front page. A cartoon on the editorial page depicted a winged angel holding a clarinet and asking a winged harpist, "Can I sit in?"

I am sure she said yes.

Willie Humphrey exemplified an adored patriarchal New Orleans figure, a consummate showman, a great musician, a historian of New Orleans jazz—and a dear friend.

George Lewis

One of history's most unusual recording sessions took place in clarinetist George Lewis' New Orleans home on St. Philip Street one day in 1944.

Lewis was confined to bed, slowly recovering from a severe injury received while working as a laborer on the Mississippi docks. He had not played his horn for several weeks. Two of his friends, banjoist Lawrence Marrero and bass player Alcide "Slow Drag" Pavageau, accompanied him on a somber hymn and an untitled blues. Eventually issued on Bill Russell's new American Music label, the two recordings did much to advance the reemergence of classic jazz.

"Just a Closer Walk With Thee" reintroduced gospel music to jazz's vocabulary, and "Burgundy Street Blues" (pronounced "Bur-GUN-dy") became one of the most famous and most imitated clarinet solos in the history of classic jazz. Lewis had never played the tune before; the wistful blues theme, unmatched in feeling and tone, was improvised during the recording. Wherever George Lewis played for the next two dozen years, "Burgundy Street Blues" was his most requested number. He recorded many subsequent versions of the tune, always under better conditions, but he never surpassed the emotional impact of the initial effort.

Those important 78 rpm American Music discs delighted fans of traditional jazz, who were clamoring for authentic New Orleans recordings. Russell subsequently produced historic recordings by Bunk Johnson's band, with Lewis on clarinet. Both men played vital roles in launching the revival era.

Lewis was born in 1900. The self-taught clarinetist played with the Black Eagle Band at age eighteen and worked with Buddy Petit and Joe Rena in the early 1920s. He formed his own band (the New Orleans Stompers) and played with the Eureka Brass Band, Olympia Orchestra, and Bunk Johnson.

After his seminal 1944 recordings, the clarinetist founded his own group. George Lewis' New Orleans Jazz Band swept to national prominence, spearheading the revival movement in the 1950s. The great little band had many brilliant facets. They displayed a versatile approach to rags, blues, stomps, and pop tunes. Each of the influential jazzmen became an icon to generations of musicians.

Lewis' low-register clarinet produced an unusual amalgam of mellow tones and boiling ardor. Trombonist Jim Robinson vitalized the

*George Lewis' 1944 recording of
"Burgundy Street Blues" became one
of the most famous clarinet solos in
the history of classic jazz.*

music with up-from-the-ground slurs and slides; his gold tooth glistened brightly in the spotlight whenever he smiled. Avery "Kid"
Howard's Armstrong-influenced horn punched out powerful leads,
and his sensitive muted choruses revealed an intuitive feeling for the
blues. Drummer Joe Watkins, a nephew of the great banjoist Johnny
St. Cyr, was an extremely nimble drummer with a lusty parade beat.
His effective use of tom toms buoyantly spurred the surging ride-out
choruses, and he sang with gusto. He was also an impressive emcee
(Lewis, eloquent on his clarinet, was too shy to speak on the microphone). Lawrence Marrero's subtle banjo, Slow Drag Pavageau's articulate slap bass, and Alton Purnell's exuberant piano playing kept the
beat churning.

  True to the Crescent City tradition, these performers worked hard
to entertain. Purnell, Watkins, and Howard shared humor and distinctive vocals; Robinson, when moved by the music, often waved a white

handkerchief and danced a sprightly jig, while diminutive Slow Drag, dwarfed by his huge string bass, flirted jovially with nearby female patrons.

In 1952, they came to Los Angeles to appear in the giant Dixieland Jubilee at the Shrine Auditorium and were the hit attraction, with Lewis' impressive solo on "Burgundy Street Blues" highlighting the long program. Based on their initial success, Lewis and his band returned for the next four Dixieland Jubilees. After their second appearance, they were booked into the Beverly Cavern, temporarily replacing Kid Ory's Creole Jazz Band.

This was the band's first club date away from New Orleans, and the musicians spent their intermissions in the kitchen, as was the custom in segregated New Orleans. Though Lucille and I urged them to join us at our table, they timidly remained in the back room. Finally they yielded to our invitations and mingled amiably with fans during their breaks. Before the engagement ended, their demeanor had changed drastically, and they relaxed between sets with their new friends.

Robinson enjoyed imbibing, and one evening he accepted too many drinks from generous patrons. During the coda of "Muskrat Ramble," he moved his slide to its most extended position, leaned too far forward, and toppled off the high bandstand. The sixty-year-old trombonist bounced against the table beneath him, causing glasses and ice cubes to fly through the air, but he landed on his feet and completed the coda without missing a note! The band played Kid Ory's "Muskrat Ramble" every night, but that was Jim's only flight.

To save the band costly hotel bills, members of the Southern California Hot Jazz Society arranged inexpensive housing for them. Our friend Monette Moore, a prominent blues singer in the '20s, volunteered her large home, and the Jazz Society provided nightly transportation to the Cavern. Several parties at Monette's house warmed our relationship with the Crescent City jazzmen. We hated to see them leave when their Cavern engagement ended, and they were just as sorry to go. For the first time, they had received open, welcoming hospitality from white people, something they had never enjoyed under the racial conditions that still existed in New Orleans.

When we took them to the train station, Alton Purnell, who had been drinking, was most upset. He sat on his suitcase, tightly holding Lucille's hand, and insisted he would stay in Los Angeles. I had to physically assist him onto the train. Eventually, Alton did move West and became a vital part of the local jazz scene.

I renewed my friendship with George Lewis whenever he came to Los Angeles; when we visited New Orleans, we always heard him playing at Preservation Hall. He died in 1968.

Thirty years after his death, those wonderful bedside recordings from 1944 remain among jazz's most important landmarks. Clarinetists throughout the world, most of them born after that historic session, are still striving for Lewis' plaintive lucidity. The sweet, simple sounds of his "Burgundy Street Blues" still reverberate at jazz clubs throughout the world. The individual styles of Lewis and his sidemen have been perpetuated by generations of musicians. As a result, each is assured of immortal status.

Alton Purnell

He never will brag, but you and I know
Of his worldwide career on the keys
He's played for presidents—royalty, too
And plays with the greatest of ease!

> From "Alton," a poem by
> Alicia "Judy" Wood, 1987

Some unfathomable destiny must have been at work the day New Orleans piano giant Alton Purnell was born. He came into the world in 1911 in the small house on St. Peter Street now known as Preservation Hall. A small "honky tonk" barroom sat adjacent to the house, providing the infant Purnell with his first exposure to jazz piano. Perhaps he absorbed some of his future keyboard prowess from the three legendary "professors" who played next door—Manuel Manetta, Fats Pichon, and Walter Decou. As he matured, Purnell received additional inspiration from an underrated local pianist named Burnell Santiago, whose rolling, percussive style meshed perfectly with the surging New Orleans beat for which Alton became famous.

"When I started playing the piano, it was considered a rhythm instrument," Purnell often told me. "Those bands didn't want you to play all over the keyboard. You play just chords and back up the man who is soloing. That's how I play. Maybe the other fellows sound good to the public. I try to sound good to the musicians I'm playing with. I'm a band piano player."

He benefited from excellent on-the-job training playing in New Orleans bands led by "Big Eye" Louis Nelson, Avery "Kid" Howard, Oscar "Papa" Celestin, Isaiah Morgan, and Sidney Desvigne. Working regularly as a singer and pianist at the Famous Door on Bourbon Street, he soon had a reputation as one of the city's most popular entertainers.

Equally skilled as a vocalist, Alton always probed deeply into the meaning of lyrics and expressed them beautifully. He attributed much of his singing skill to the innovative New Orleans entertainer Pleasant Joseph, also known as "Cousin Joe" and "Smilin' Joe."

"'Cousin Joe' often said, 'You gotta tell a story. Those words are as important as the music. Tell the folks what they mean!'" When Alton crooned "I love you," distaff hearts fluttered.

He left New Orleans in 1945 to join Bunk Johnson's band at the Stuyvesant Casino in New York City. Working with Johnson and, later with George Lewis, he gained a solid following among traditional jazz fans. Those two bands, with almost identical personnel, epitomized the elusive New Orleans sound postwar listeners avidly sought. Both paved the way for the tremendous revival of classic jazz that occurred in the '50s and '60s. Young musicians, especially European traditionalists, emulated the style of the Johnson and Lewis bands, and Purnell became a role model for aspiring trad pianists. The last surviving member of the Johnson-Lewis period, he continued to have a strong influence on emerging generations of musicians.

I met Purnell backstage at the Shrine Auditorium in 1952. The George Lewis band was in Los Angeles for the Dixieland Jubilee, making its first appearance west of Louisiana. During the next few years, the band returned several times, playing at the Beverly Cavern in Los Angeles and the Club Hangover in San Francisco. With each trip, Purnell's love for California grew. In 1956 he decided to leave Lewis' band and move to Los Angeles permanently. For more than three decades, his brand of music and humor brightened the local jazz scene.

His first L.A. job was with the Roaring '20s Creole Jazz Band at Ben Pollack's Pick-A-Rib on the Sunset Strip. The group included Minor Hall, Johnny St. Cyr, Buddy Burns, Keg Johnson, George Orendorf, and Barney Bigard. (Pollack repeatedly promised he would produce an album by this wonderful band, but the recording date never took place.) Purnell also regularly attended the monthly Southern California Hot Jazz Society sessions, often bringing a group of New Orleans expatriates that included Mike Delay, Ed Garland, Sammy Lee, Paul Barnes, and Teddy Edwards. Those Sunday afternoons at Larchmont Hall were memorable events.

As word of the pianist's musical skills spread, he began receiving offers from abroad. In 1964 he starred on the BBC television program *Jazz 625* with Keith Smith's Climax Jazz Band, sparking a love affair with British audiences that flourished for decades. The following year he was featured at the 20th Australian Jazz Convention, becoming the first New Orleans pianist to perform at the Sydney Town Hall. Geoff Bull wrote in the convention program, "I feel sure that Alton Purnell will be a source of lasting inspiration for many in this country." That prophecy was correct; Purnell won the hearts of Australian fans thousands of miles removed from his St. Peter Street roots. In 1966 he toured Europe with the New Orleans All-Stars under the aegis of Keith Smith. On St. Patrick's Day 1970, Sid Bailey's Fair City Jazz Band featured him at Kelly's Pub in Dublin, making Alton Purnell the first New Orleans musician to appear with an Irish band.

The pianist's status abroad soared in the 1970s. He toured Europe with Barry Martyn's English band in 1967, 1970, 1971, and 1972. In December 1971 he was a special guest at a mammoth Louis Armstrong tribute concert in San Remo, Italy, appearing with American jazz stars Roy Eldridge, Bobby Hackett, Earl Hines, and Albert Nicholas. A year later, he charmed Italian audiences as headline artist with Luciano Invernizzi's Bovisa New Orleans Jazz Band in Milan. Recordings made in Denmark, Germany, France, and Belgium added to his international popularity. The greatest overseas triumph occurred a few years later in Japan. A double album with the New Orleans Rascals in Osaka demonstrated the extent of George Lewis' inspiration. Each member of that enduring band, which is still active after forty years, retains the influence of Lewis and his colleagues.

In 1970 Purnell became president of the Southern California Hot Jazz Society, and the organization benefited greatly from his judgment and guidance. Under his leadership, the SCHJS energetically supported the Louis Armstrong Statue Fund, and he acted as the fund's unofficial spokesman as he toured the world.

When Barry Martyn moved to Los Angeles to form the Legends of Jazz in 1973, Alton Purnell was the logical choice as pianist. The recordings he made with the Legends and special guest Barney Bigard vividly testified to the artistry of the self-proclaimed "band piano player." Under Martyn's direction, the Legends of Jazz became the foremost traditional jazz band of the 1970s, showcasing such stellar musicians as Joe Darensbourg, Andrew Blakeney, Louis Nelson, Ed Garland, and Purnell on numerous domestic and international tours.

For several years, the Legends of Jazz starred in the "A Night in New Orleans" concert series that I co-produced with Martyn. It was my privilege to introduce Purnell to audiences throughout the United States, Canada, and Europe. I watched the warm response each evening as he strode to the piano, beaming broadly, and softly played a blues background while I introduced the rest of the band. I remember Alton proudly leading the Eagle Brass Band in a street parade down West Berlin's broad Kufurstendamm advertising our "Night in New Orleans" concert at the giant Philharmonie Halle in May 1976.

Purnell's health began to fail during the mid-'80s, forcing an end to his touring days, but he continued to work in the Los Angeles area. He frequently played with George Marois' New Bull Moose Party Band and Chris Kelly's Black and White Jazz Band. He made his final local appearance at the 1986 Los Angeles Classic Jazz Festival, playing with the latter group, led by Bob Allen on trumpet.

When Purnell died on January 14, 1987, he left behind thousands of adoring fans, dozens of outstanding recordings, and untold numbers of pianists who emulated his smooth, sensible keyboard style. And he left knowing that the house in which he was born still swelled every evening—as it had in his childhood—with the sounds of the music he loved, the music he was born to play.

More than a decade has passed since we followed the Resurrection Brass Band escorting Alton's bier to its gravesite at Inglewood Park Cemetery. Lucille tearfully plucked a small sprig of daisies from the flower-draped casket. They beamed brightly for several days in a small vase on our window sill.

Those little yellow blooms eventually withered; but our fond memories of the band piano player remain very strong.

Bill Russell

Bill Russell was probably the world's foremost authority on New Orleans jazz. As a journalist, scholar, historian, record producer, composer, and performer, he devoted most of his eighty-seven years to exploring the music and its deeply shrouded history, and he played a vital role in passing traditional jazz down to a new generation of listeners. As a direct or indirect result of his efforts, serious jazz clubs today exist throughout the nation; a major jazz festival takes place somewhere in

*Bill Russell, record producer and
gentleman scholar of New Orleans jazz,
1970.*

the world almost every day; hundreds, maybe thousands, of popular jazz bands perform in clubs, concerts, festivals, parties, and cruises; and the genre supports a thriving recording industry.

A gentle and selfless man, he lived very simply in a tiny French Quarter apartment without telephone or air conditioning. The doorbell had not worked for decades. His crowded main room, illuminated by a single hanging bulb, was cluttered with piles of papers, records, letters, and files. The walls were covered with pictures of his beloved jazz musicians and autographed photos of three famed classical violinists: Fritz Kreisler, Jascha Heifitz, and Eugene Ysaye.

He was born Russell William Wagner in Canton, Missouri, in 1905. He first heard jazz as a boy, listening to the music wafting in from riverboats on the Mississippi River. After studying classical music with Arnold Schoenberg at Columbia University in New York City, he set his sights on becoming a composer, changing his name to William Russell so that people wouldn't confuse him with the famed German composer Richard Wagner. Russell eventually abandoned those ambitions and joined an itinerant Chinese shadow puppet show, accompanying the drama on dozens of Eastern percussion instruments. In a 1970 interview, he told me:

> I traveled back and forth across the country with the Red Gate Shadow Players for six years. The performances were at night, so I spent every day searching for old jazz records in barns and attics. I could never eat lunch because my hands were so dirty from handling the dusty records. I always carried bananas with me. A banana could be peeled and eaten without taking the time to wash.
>
> Around 1929, I found a record by Jelly Roll Morton's Red Hot Peppers. It was "Shoe Shiner's Drag." I liked it so much, I never stopped collecting. I remembered my childhood music teacher, who always said, "Don't listen to jazz. It'll corrupt your taste!" I realized he was wrong. This was in the Depression, and you could buy records for a few cents each. After finding that first Morton record, I could not stop. Eventually I owned every Morton recording.

Russell came to New Orleans for the first time in 1937. "It was an exciting experience just being there," he recalled. "I roamed the streets all day and all night, absorbing the sounds and the smells of the city." During his six years on the road with the Shadow Players, Russell began interviewing musicians and writing articles for small publications. Serious jazz criticism was virtually nonexistent at that time, but Russell's perceptive writings helped get it started. One of his essays, published in France by Hughes Panassie in *Le Jazz Hot,* was the first important article about boogie-woogie piano. In 1939, Russell collaborated on *Jazzmen,* the first anthology of jazz. *The Jazz Record Book* soon followed. Each of these landmark publications helped reestablish New Orleans music as a viable genre worthy of serious attention.

Russell began writing during the heart of the big-band era, at a time when the major record firms had no interest in recording early jazzmen or reissuing any of the treasures held in their vaults. But Russell's articles and books demonstrated that New Orleans jazz still enjoyed a devoted following. Eventually he would help prove that it commanded a record-buying audience—and the power to attract new listeners.

During Russell's interviews for *Jazzmen,* Louis Armstrong and Clarence Williams told him about a long-forgotten New Orleans trumpet player named William Geary "Bunk" Johnson. He was then sixty-two years old and working as a field hand in New Iberia, Louisiana. In 1942, Russell produced recordings of the legendary musician, a contemporary of Buddy Bolden and reputedly Louis Armstrong's teacher. On the strength of those records for Russell's American Music label,

Johnson and his band were booked in New York City. They were a huge success. Soon the entire world was aware of New Orleans' vital role in musical history.

Russell's American Music label eventually popularized many other overlooked New Orleans musicians, including George Lewis, Jim Robinson, Wooden Joe Nicholas, Dink Johnson, and Baby Dodds. Without those valuable recordings, we might never have learned of these surviving pioneers, and we certainly would never have heard them playing New Orleans jazz as it sounded around the end of the nineteenth century. (The very influential American Music recordings have recently been reissued on CD by the George H. Buck Jazz Foundation in New Orleans.)

In 1958, Russell was named curator of the newly established William Hogan Archive of New Orleans Jazz. He began a series of oral history interviews with assistance from Richard Allen. This vital program continues today under the aegis of Tulane University. He also amassed an enormous personal archive, which he stored in cardboard boxes stacked from floor to ceiling in his apartment. Russell boldly labeled each box with the subject's name: "MORTON," "ARMSTRONG," "PICOU," "DODDS," "OLIVER," "NOONE." He knew where each priceless document belonged and could easily locate any item.

Russell's hoard included the most important Jelly Roll Morton collection in the country. The two met in 1938 while the pianist was appearing in a run-down nightclub in Washington, D.C. Russell's interviews with Morton launched a lifelong project that culminated only a few months before the writer's death in 1992. After years of research, he finally completed his long-awaited definitive biography, *Oh! Mister Jelly* (recently published in Denmark). The information in those boxes and the knowledge imprinted on his brain were raw material for three other books on jazz. Two of them (*Bill Russell's American Music* and *New Orleans Style*) were compiled and edited by Barry Martyn and Mike Hazeldine and published after his death by Jazzology Press in New Orleans.

When I visited Bill, he always pointed out the box bearing my name. It contained every item I ever sent him—letters, clippings, our Christmas and birthday greetings—over a thirty-year period. Also stored there was an old manuscript, a chapter he had asked me to write for his Morton book. He had received a grant to support the project and insisted on paying for the chapter, sending me a check in 1970 for $35 over my objections. I decided to keep the check as a souvenir.

Bill Russell's archives included perhaps the greatest collection of New Orleans jazz memorabilia ever assembled, including a box labeled with the author's name (at right). Copyright Historic New Orleans Collection. Photo by Jan White Brantley.

A few months later he sent me an irate letter: "My check has not cleared. You are screwing up my bookkeeping and the grant is in jeopardy. Please deposit at once." I made a photostat copy and complied with his demand.

The last time I saw him—many, many years later—he opened the carton labeled with my name and took out some cash. "Here's the $35 I owe you for the Anita Gonzales story. You never cashed my check!" Again I refused, saying, "Bill, I cashed your check twenty years ago."

I thought that was the end of the matter, but Russell apparently had not given up. After he died on August 9, 1992, I received a letter from the Historic New Orleans Collection, the willed repository of his priceless data. Attached to the letter was a four-page inventory listing the contents of his "Floyd Levin" carton, now preserved in acid-free folders. The list included seventy-nine items, including photos, clippings, manuscripts, magazines, letters, cancelled checks ... and $35 in cash.

Here is a typical example of Bill Russell's unassuming demeanor:

In 1988, Lucille and I were invited to attend the unveiling of a bronze head of Eubie Blake, our gift to the William Ranson Hogan Jazz Archive at Tulane University. I knew Bill Russell was also invited, and since he lived just a few blocks from our hotel, I offered to drive him to the university. He said, "Thanks, Floyd, but that would be an imposition. I'll take the streetcar." I insisted and said we would pick him up at 9 A.M.

He was waiting in front when we arrived, holding a paper sack and a folding canvas chair. He told me the sack contained a sandwich and some notes he promised to Curt Jerde, the curator of the Tulane Jazz Archive. When I asked about the chair, he said, "I don't want to occupy a seat; there will be a lot of important people there." He scoffed when I said, "Bill, you will be the most important person in the room."

A large crowd attended the reception. The room overflowed with dignitaries—writers, politicians, academicians, and fans. After the speeches and the unveiling, a caterer served cocktails and appetizers. Looking around for Bill, I found him at the back of the room. He was seated on the little folding chair, nibbling his sandwich. When I asked why he did not have the delicious barbecued shrimp, he said, "I wanted to make sure there was enough for all the prominent guests."

5

THE GREAT
LOUIS ARMSTRONG

I met Louis Armstrong on his forty-eighth birthday—July 4, 1948. At least, that was the day he *celebrated* his forty-eighth birthday. As a waif in New Orleans, Armstrong probably did not know his exact date of birth, and Independence Day 1900 was likely an arbitrary choice. Drummer Zutty Singleton, his boyhood friend, told me: "Louis and I were the same age, and I was born in 1898." In *Louis Armstrong, An American Genius* (Oxford University Press, 1983), James Lincoln Collier also concluded that July 4, 1900, was an incorrect birth date. Various sources have indicated that Armstrong was born August 4, 1901. But the national holiday has always seemed an appropriate day to commemorate the life of a man who became a national treasure—and so July 4 remains his "official" birthday.

On the day I met him, Armstrong had just returned from a successful European tour with his recently formed All-Stars and was appearing at the Bal Tabarin, a questionable venue in southwest Los Angeles. With a borrowed tape recorder, I meekly ventured backstage and asked if I might be allowed to tape an interview for my radio program, which was heard only by those few who had discovered that recent innovation, FM radio.

I was ushered into an adjacent room and greeted by a smiling Louis Armstrong, who sat nibbling a piece of birthday cake—stark naked! He was changing clothes between sets and agreed to talk to me as he dressed. After our brief conversation, he invited me to remain and interview the members of his band. Before the evening was over, I had recorded conversations with Barney Bigard, Jack Teagarden, Earl Hines, Arvell Shaw, and Cozy Cole—enough material for six broadcasts.

Over the years, scores of books have carefully depicted Armstrong's illustrious accomplishments. His instrumental and vocal innovations influenced generations of artists, and he remains one of jazz's most beloved and most respected heroes many years after his death. It was my privilege to know him personally, and I admired him not only as a musician but also as a man. His status as jazz's most visible personality—its first and greatest celebrity—often overshadowed his accomplishments as a musician. But each phase in his long career is a vitally important part of the music's history.

Louis Armstrong's Underrated Recordings during the Big-Band Era

During his first six years as a professional musician, Louis Armstrong played in small groups—King Oliver's eight-piece Creole Jazz Band and Armstrong's own Hot Five and Hot Seven. He spent the last twenty-five years of his career leading a small All-Star band at worldwide concerts and club dates. But for almost two decades between those important periods, Louis Armstrong led big bands. This segment of Armstrong's career, approximately 40 percent of his professional life, has been overlooked or discounted by most jazz critics. Many thought he sold out to commercial interests during this period, abandoning his jazz roots to become an entertainer. These same detractors felt Armstrong played only a minor role in the swing era of the late '30s and early '40s. Such opinions ignore the fact that swing came as a direct outgrowth of Armstrong's musical innovations in the '20s and early '30s. They also fail to recognize the quality and significance of the trumpeter's big-band work. A careful reassessment of Armstrong's recordings reveal that his influence on the music scene—and on American culture as a whole—expanded greatly during those twenty productive years.

From 1928 through 1947, the trumpeter fronted various orchestras bearing his name. However, he never was the true business leader of those groups. Armstrong disliked the administrative duties and mundane responsibilities that leadership required. Leaving those chores to

Chick Webb, Les Hite, Luis Russell, and others, he was free to let his adventurous musical instincts roam. The result: a succession of recorded masterpieces that will always be studied and admired.

Incredibly, most of those recordings were made after or in the midst of an exhausting road trip. Armstrong and his sidemen would rush into a studio in New York or Chicago and record unfamiliar tunes, often using only sketchy lead sheets as "arrangements" for mediocre numbers selected by the record companies. Under these deplorable conditions, Armstrong transformed dozens of songs into definitive jazz standards. His highly inventive phrasings and imaginative improvisations—both instrumentally and vocally—still delight fans and inspire singers and musicians.

Armstrong made his first big-band recording with Carroll Dickerson's orchestra, which he joined during a 1929 engagement in Harlem at Connie's Inn. There he was reunited with his hometown buddy, drummer Zutty Singleton, with whom he had played in Fate Marable's riverboat band several years before. His first record with Dickerson's group featured "Black and Blue" and "Ain't Misbehavin'," two hit songs from *Hot Chocolates,* in which he starred both on Broadway and in Harlem. This landmark record, the first of many featuring Andy Razaf–Fats Waller gems, marked a turning point in Armstrong's career. Until then his records (most of them recorded for the Okeh label) had appeared on the "race" list and were marketed only to black customers. With the Dickerson recording, Armstrong began a transition to more commercial material, opening new vistas that expanded with his warmth, inventiveness, and individuality. Armstrong's exemplary versions of these two great compositions still rank among his most unforgettable efforts.

Armstrong originated a format that soon became standard—an orchestra fronted by a brilliant instrumentalist, singer, or public personality. Louis was all three—and a great showman, too. That familiar gravel-toned voice, previously heard in a semi-comic fashion, evolved into a vocal extension of his imaginative trumpet playing. Poignancy and emotion shaped ordinary lyrics beyond their intrinsic meaning and created hit after hit. Satchmo established guidelines that still govern the way pop tunes are played and sung.

In 1930, Armstrong began appearing with the house band at Frank Sebastian's Cotton Club in Los Angeles. He made a dozen 78 rpm recordings for Okeh with this band, billed as Louis Armstrong & His Sebastian New Cotton Club Orchestra. Led by Leon Elkins and, later,

Les Hite, the group featured Lawrence Brown's trombone and a young Lionel Hampton on drums. Among the most memorable tunes Armstrong recorded with this group were "Body and Soul," "Shine," "Confessin'," "Memories of You," and "Sweethearts on Parade."

After Armstrong's California triumphs, he returned to Chicago to lead a group assembled for him by Zilner Randolph, Al Washington, or Mike McKendrick (depending on whom you believe). He was very comfortable with this lineup, which included New Orleanians Preston Jackson on trombone, John Lindsay on bass, and Tubby Hall on drums. During 1931 and 1932 they accompanied Armstrong on twenty-four of his greatest recorded hits—including "Chinatown," "Stardust," "Lazy River," and the song that would become his theme, Leon and Otis Rene's "When It's Sleepy Time Down South."

A short tour fronting Chick Webb's orchestra in a revival of *Hot Chocolates* resulted in a few records for the Victor label. The 1932 session introduced another Leon and Otis René composition, the sentimental ballad "That's My Home," which Armstrong converted into another masterpiece. His Victor relationship also produced twenty-three recordings with the Randolph-McKendrick orchestra, which Armstrong led through the South on an extended tour of theaters and dance halls. This band's roster of young musicians included pianist Teddy Wilson, Keg Johnson on trombone, and Keg's brother Budd, then a promising young reedman. Though suffering from severe lip problems, Armstrong made some fine recordings with this band. "Some Sweet Day," written by Storyville "professor" Tony Jackson, provides a direct link with music heard in New Orleans before the turn of the century. "Laughin' Louis" and "I Gotta Right to Sing the Blues" also remain favorites.

After the Victor sessions, Armstrong took a two-and-a-half-year break from recording, except for a single session for French Polydor Company in 1934. Produced in Paris after the culmination of a lengthy European tour, the recordings featured a group of multinational players organized by clarinetist Peter Du Congé, a New Orleans expatriate and student of Lorenzo Tio, Jr. Du Congé, Ada "Bricktop" Smith's husband, put together a band that included the famed American pianist Herman Chittison. The session yielded six sides; however, the recording of "Song of the Vipers" was completely withdrawn a few weeks after its release when French authorities detected a forbidden title reference to marijuana. Branded as inferior by many critics, those six sides were rare collector's items until their reissue in the United

States thirteen years later. Louis often referred to the two-sided "Sunny Side of the Street," issued on the French Brunswick label, as his best recorded effort.

After concluding another European tour in 1935, Armstrong began his longest tenure as a big-band leader, a very successful eight-year association with Luis Russell's orchestra. "Jubilee," recorded with Russell, is an exhilarating parade number Louis sang in his second motion picture, *Every Day's a Holiday,* starring Mae West. Hoagy Carmichael's rousing melody receives an authentic New Orleans treatment from the band's Crescent City musicians: Henry "Red" Allen, Albert Nicholas, Luis Russell, Pops Foster, and Paul Barbarin.

Three years later Armstrong achieved one of his greatest musical triumphs. "When the Saints Go Marching in," a Baptist hymn recorded in 1924 by the Elkins-Payne Jubilee Singers, was just another gospel number until Louis Armstrong recorded it in 1938. A sterling moment in his recording career occurred when "Reverend Satchmo," "preaching" against Paul Barbarin's New Orleans street beat, led "Brother Higgenbotham down the aisle with his 'trambone.'" Ever since, "Saints" has been one of the most frequently requested tunes for Dixieland combos around the world. Ironically, *Down Beat* magazine severely lambasted "Saints" in its May 1939 issue. The unnamed reviewer dismissed the Decca record as "a novelty with fair Higgenbotham trombone and Armstrong trumpet work … neither what we expect from Louis." Perhaps the writer was simply having a bad day; in the same issue, he branded Benny Goodman's enormous hit "And the Angels Sing" as "very average stuff."

In retrospect, Louis Armstrong's big-band recordings stand out as some of the finest of his long career. During the years he fronted big bands, all his talents came into balance; he became the world's most recognizable jazz musician, the first jazz soloist to gain a following among non-jazz fans—the first to become a star. Satchmo's brilliant aura, almost three decades after his death, shows no indication of fading—his timeless influence continues.

"Ambassador Satch" on the World Stage

In 1947 Armstrong returned to the small-group format with his All-Stars. The inaugural edition included Jack Teagarden, Barney Bigard,

Dick Cary, Sid Catlett, Morty Corb, and Velma Middleton. Over the years, the band's shifting personnel included Earl Hines and many other extraordinary musicians. Thanks mainly to the marquee value of their ebullient leader, the All-Stars gained a huge following not only in the United States but overseas as well.

In late 1955 the All-Stars made a successful concert tour of Europe, creating excitement wherever they played. Satchmo's ardent admirers filled concert halls that still bore wartime scars. The band's appearance in Geneva, Switzerland, merited front-page coverage in the *New York Times*. Noting the huge crowds at every stop on the triumphant tour, the article asked: "Why does the United States, with all the money it spends for propaganda to promote democracy, overlook subsidizing the continental travels of jazz bands? American jazz has now become an international language. America's secret weapon is a blue note in a minor key. Right now, its most effective ambassador is Louis (Satchmo) Armstrong."

It was sheer coincidence that the All-Stars got started just as the cold war was settling in. But it was no accident that Iron Curtain barriers often came down when Ambassador Satch appeared. Returning from a European tour in the late 1950s, Louis told television commentator Edward R. Murrow: "When we played in West Berlin, people from the East Zone risked sneaking across the twelve-foot wall to attend our concerts. They dodged machine gun emplacements in the eastern area designed to stop them. They would not take that risk for food or clothing. Even the Russians came. Few spoke English—the music did the talking." (The footage originally appeared in an hour-long TV broadcast called "Salute to Satch" and later in the film *Satchmo the Great*.) Barney Bigard, clarinetist with the All-Stars, told me that, despite the language barriers, musicians from the Communist bloc were anxious to talk to American musicians. When Barney shared a box of reeds with a Russian clarinet player, the young man, gleaming with joy, warmly kissed him.

During the '50s, Louis Armstrong was one of the world's most famous Americans. In one *New Yorker* cartoon from that period, a U.S. State Department official muses: "This is a mission of utmost delicacy. The question is: Who is the best man for it—John Foster Dulles or Satchmo?" The State Department actually arranged for him to tour the Soviet Union in 1957; however, Armstrong canceled the tour to protest the government's weak enforcement of integration measures in the Arkansas public schools. He missed his chance to become the first American jazz musician to perform behind the Iron Curtain.

Eastern Bloc fans still managed to get access to Armstrong recordings, as I learned in the mid-1970s while traveling with our production
"A Night in New Orleans." A menacing East German soldier had
boarded our tour bus to check our passports as we were reentering the
West German zone on the outskirts of Munich. He stalked the aisle
belligerently until he saw Lucille's button, which bore Armstrong's picture and the phrase: "I contributed to the Louis Armstrong Statue
Fund." The guard's stony face suddenly broke into a broad grin.
"Satchmo!" he hollered. I pointed to our illustrious passengers—
Benny Carter, Barney Bigard, Ralph Sutton, Art Hodes, Red Callender,
Cozy Cole, Clyde Bernhardt, Sammy Rimington, etc.—and tried to explain that these were all famous American musicians. He and another
soldier vigorously shook hands with each musician, kissed Lucille on
the cheek, and left with buttons, posters, and a stack of records and
autographed photos we gave them.

In 1960, three years after his aborted trip to the Soviet Union, Armstrong completed a series of African concerts arranged by the State Department. Co-sponsored by Pepsi-Cola, the tour included performances in the Congo, Uganda, Kenya, Rhodesia, Liberia, Guinea,
Mali, Tanganyika, and Zanzibar. The All-Stars attracted overflow audiences in stadiums that held more than fifty thousand people. The
itinerary included several dates in South Africa, but the apartheid
regime banned the group at the last minute because Armstrong refused
to play to segregated audiences. The South Africans also objected to
the group's racial mixture—the All-Stars included black, white, and
Hawaiian members.

The African tour included some of Armstrong's most inspiring performances and his most poignant interactions with fans. When the All-
Stars returned to the United States, Barney Bigard gave me a carton
full of mementos. "When we got off the plane in the Belgian Congo,
thousands were waiting for us," he said. "They lifted Louis on a large
canvas throne and carried him through the streets to the stadium
shouting, 'Satchmo!' 'Satchmo!' It was hotter'n hell, and all the concerts were outdoors—but they were always jam-packed."

"Louis actually stopped a war," he added. "At one place, we arrived
during a civil uprising. Opposing factions halted their fighting to meet
us at the ferry landing. They all had rifles over their shoulders but sat
together listening to the concert. After we left, the shooting resumed."
By any measure, Louis Armstrong's tour of Africa was a huge diplomatic success. More than two million Africans enjoyed the great trum-

peter's music and homespun charm. Photos of him surrounded by throngs of smiling Africans appeared in newspapers around the world.

Because of his prominence and his travel abroad, the FBI kept a file on Louis Armstrong. Recently unsealed under a Freedom of Information Act request, it includes two dozen pages of material. None contain derogatory matter. One document says, cogently: "His decades of touring in the United States, Europe, Africa and Australia, have ensured his position as one of America's foremost unofficial ambassadors of good will."

Thousands of African fans and two gruff East German soldiers were aware of that long before it was officially recognized in the United States.

A Sentimental Journey—Louis' Funeral

You lost a gold mine
When you lost me!

> Louis Armstrong and His Hot Five, "That's When I'll
> Come Back to You," Okeh Record 8519, 1927

I made the cross-country trip from Los Angeles International Airport to say a final "good-bye" to Satchmo. Boarding the jet, I realized it was exactly a year since we had met Louis' plane when he arrived in Los Angeles to star in "Hello Louis!"

Entering the arrival terminal, he brightened the entire airport with his beaming smile as the Southern California Hot Jazz Society's Marching Band saluted him with "Hello, Dolly!" I will never forget the emotional impact a few days later when 6,000 fans cheered while Louis climbed the stairs on the Shrine Auditorium stage to cut the world's largest birthday cake.

Settling into my seat for the trip to New York, I thought about the thousands of flights Armstrong had made, taking his music to every corner of the world. Enthusiastic audiences came to see the man whose exciting career charted much of jazz's development.

As my flight streaked eastward, our vast country spread beneath the billowing white clouds far below. He had visited most communities down there during grueling one-night stands over the years. Louis was a familiar figure to all Americans who were touched by his charm.

The plane's in-flight stereo program listed the 1931 classic "I Got Rhythm." Forty years after Satchmo recorded those stratospheric choruses, sophisticated jet travelers were enjoying them 37,000 feet in the air! (The program also listed Miles Davis' "Paraphernalia," a vivid certification of the long thread of influences Louis wove into the fabric of jazz for half a century.)

Soon, a view of glittering Las Vegas appeared under the left wing. It brought to mind my last visit with him. It was Christmas 1970 when Louis' All-Stars were making their final appearance in the Nevada city.

The shocking news of Louis' sudden death Tuesday morning, July 6, 1971, came only two days after our last phone conversation. I called to wish him a happy seventy-first birthday. His voice was cheerful. He had recently been released from the hospital and was looking forward to "getting back on the mound." (The plane's copy of *Time* magazine carried a brief story about Louis' "recovery." It mentioned his plans to return to work and quoted him as saying, "That's what life is all about, man!")

When the plane landed, I immediately took a taxi to the large Seventh Regiment Armory at Sixty-sixth Street and Park Avenue in Manhattan, where Satchmo's body had been on public display since early that morning. Mourners began lining up at 4:00 A.M., six hours before the announced opening.

Louis' widow, Lucille, and his second wife, the great jazz pianist Lil Hardin, viewed the body privately before the doors opened. They walked together through the cavernous, quiet building in the most fashionable part of Park Avenue.

Louis was dressed in a navy blue suit, pink shirt, and a gray and silver tie. Pausing at the casket, Lucille put a white handkerchief in her husband's left hand. "He didn't look right without it," she said. When I arrived, approximately 25,000 people had slowly passed the open bronze and copper casket. When my turn came, I tried, unsuccessfully, to visualize the world without him. As the years pass, I realize his presence remains. That familiar voice and image are heard and seen almost daily on TV, radio, and film.

The mourners in the silent procession paused momentarily as they passed the body—some wept openly. When I left at 10:00 P.M., several thousand were still outside, waiting four abreast in a line circling the entire block. These were the people who for years enjoyed Louis Armstrong's music in concerts, movies, television, and jukeboxes. They waited patiently to pay a last sad tribute. The Armory remained open until 9:00 A.M. the next day.

On Friday morning, July 9, a group of Louis' closest friends assembled at his home in Corona, Long Island, where he had died just three days earlier. Most of the modest homes in the black neighborhood were still decorated with American flags honoring the nation's Independence Day and Louis' birthday a few days earlier.

Automobiles jammed the streets in a six-block radius. They were slowly moving in the direction of the two-story house on 107th Street where Armstrong had lived for more than twenty years. Many teary-eyed fans threw kisses and tossed flowers as they drove past the house.

The Associated Booking Corporation, the firm that handled Louis' business affairs for decades, was in charge of the funeral details. After exchanging anecdotes, and a final toast to the great man, we received an ABC ticket authorizing admission to the services. Limousines were waiting to drive us to the church.

When we arrived, the streets around the Congregational Church of Corona were crowded with throngs of fans and curiosity seekers. They had been standing in the broiling sun several hours awaiting the scheduled 1:00 P.M. funeral. The sidewalks were banked with mountains of flowers. Neighbors stood on rooftops and leaned out windows, watching the guests arrive.

Hundreds of news cameramen flanked the entrance to the church, photographing the arrival of jazz luminaries: Gene Krupa, Dizzy Gillespie, Zutty Singleton, Ella Fitzgerald, Tyree Glenn, Noble Sissle, Lil Armstrong, Benny Goodman, Jonah Jones, and many more. They all loved Louis and were influenced in some way by his music and style of life.

Among the five hundred invited to the funeral services were: Governor and Mrs. Nelson A. Rockefeller, New York Mayor John V. Lindsay, and Moon Landrieu, mayor of New Orleans. Voice of America's jazz expert, Willis Conover, represented President Nixon.

Inside the small church, which was not air-conditioned, we tried to cool ourselves with paper fans distributed by the ushers. From my seat, I could see such notables as Duke Ellington, Harold Arlen, Dick Cavett, Johnny Carson, David Frost, Guy Lombardo, Tyree Glenn, Arvell Shaw, "Wild Bill" and Anne Davison, George Wein, and Milt Hinton. I sat next to Benny Goodman and his wife, Alice. Mike Douglas was in front of me and Billy Taylor was in the row behind.

Peggy Lee, accompanied by Cy Coleman, opened the brief services with the Lord's Prayer. Her unamplified voice could barely be heard above the fluttering of paper fans. We sweltered as the humid temperature exceeded 100 degrees. Several banks of television lights added to our discomfort.

Al Hibbler's robust voice filled the room with "Nobody Knows the Trouble I've Seen" and "When the Saints Go Marching in," the New Orleans funeral song converted to a jazz standard by Louis' 1938 recording.

Lucille Armstrong, Louis' devoted wife for thirty years, tearfully gazed at the closed casket. It was blanketed with bright red roses and a small red sash imprinted with "My Darling." A silver cornet, its bell filled with additional roses, was on a nearby table. More than a thousand mourners stood behind police barricades in front of the red brick building. They heard the forty-minute service over a public address system. The funeral was broadcast to sixteen nations via TV satellite.

The crowd outside listened to Fred Robbins' heartfelt eulogy. He compared Armstrong with such twentieth-century geniuses as Picasso, Stravinsky, and Casals. Robbins said, "No one spread more joy to the world, and all of us are so much better for his having been here. Move over, Gabriel! Here comes Satchmo!"

Despite the intense heat outside, they listened attentively and sadly awaited the emergence of the casket. When it was slowly carried into view, the large crowd surged forward and completely engulfed us as we left the church. Pressing through the hot, churning mass, we returned to our cars to begin the ten-mile trip to Flushing Cemetery.

The cemetery route was lined with admirers tossing flowers at Lucille Armstrong's limousine that led the procession of about one hundred cars. The entire trip was filmed by a television camera crew atop a station wagon in front of the long caravan.

Our slow motorcade through the Borough of Queens was solemnly watched by fans lining both sides of the road. Several held signs. One, scrawled on a large sheet of kraft paper, said, "WE LOVED YOU, SATCHMO!"

The graveside services took only a few minutes but were delayed by throngs of unruly young people in a holiday mood who gathered there ahead of the official funeral party. They crowded close to the enclosed private area, trampling adjacent tombs in their zeal to witness the proceedings. After a brief prayer, we watched the casket being slowly lowered into the grave. The bronze vault cover had only the embossed name LOUIS ARMSTRONG and, beneath that, the word SATCHMO.

At the conclusion of the services, most of the viewers slowly departed, clutching flowers they snatched from the gravesite. Some of us remained. We were reluctant to conclude that last moment with our friend. For an hour, we exchanged additional Armstrong anecdotes. Trombonist Tyree Glenn, musical director of the All-Stars, was most vocal. "He was so generous," he said, "the most generous man I ever met. If you needed or wanted something, he got it for you!"

Shortly after Louis' death, I reread his six-page handwritten letter to me in which he expressed an eloquent homespun philosophy that probably capsulized the great man's life. Reviewing his recent illness, he wrote: "A person dies only when his time has come. There are a thousand ways for a man to die, but only one way to live—the right way!"

During his closing performance in New York's Waldorf Astoria a few months before he died, Louis sang Bob Thiele's new lyrics to "When the Saints Go Marching in." With twinkling eyes and flashing white teeth, he sang:

> Now I know why I was born,
> To play jazz on this old horn.
> I wanted the neighbors to be proud of Louis,
> A Boy from New Orleans!

Until July 6, 1971, the twentieth century was brightened by the presence of that "Boy from New Orleans." The brilliant glow has not been dimmed by his death. He will continue to live in the minds and hearts of those whose lives he enriched by his dynamic talent and personality.

God Bless You, Satchmo!

$$\left(6\right)$$

JAZZ ON THE
WEST COAST

Among the various periods of jazz history, none was more successful than the wave of nostalgia half a century ago that brought back the Jazz Age's sounds.

As the following chapter reveals, efforts to resurrect the spirited music that lost favor during the swing era occurred in various parts of the United States, Europe, and Australia. It was, however, on the West Coast where the most vigorous revival activity took place. Several independent record firms led the way. Most were undercapitalized and poorly distributed.

When an ambitious young company acquired many of the independent labels, it reissued the material and also released a barrage of new traditional jazz recordings. That's when the revival period achieved its full momentum.

That momentum continues thanks to the pioneering efforts of many fine jazz bands and the Good Time Jazz Record Company, founded by Lester Koenig in 1949.

Los Angeles in the Swing Era

When I was in high school, back in the late 1930s, radio was in its golden age. The wonderful sounds emerging from the fabric-covered speaker of my old Packard Bell radio profoundly influenced my life.

And the greatest influence by far came from Al Jarvis, the dean of American disc jockeys, who dispensed a daily flow of magic on his *Make-Believe Ballroom*.

As he passed the "mythical baton" from leader to leader (complete with fake applause and recorded crowd noise), I pictured the splendor of that imaginary ballroom and the immaculately attired musicians seated before their handsome music stands. Jarvis exposed me to the exciting sounds of Jimmy Lunceford, Benny Goodman, Erskine Hawkins, Glen Gray, Artie Shaw, Larry Clinton, and the Dorsey brothers.

I can now confess that I cut classes each morning to enjoy those great records. I carefully arranged my high school schedule to include second period study hall, third period gym, and fourth period lunch. Every morning, after attending my first class, I'd dash home to listen to Jarvis until fifth period. I do not recall how this crime was justified to my teachers and parents, but somehow it worked. I have rationalized my truancy with the belief that the acquired musical knowledge compensated for whatever academic information might have been missed. (In gym class?)

The *Make-Believe Ballroom* devoted its entire Saturday schedule to a roundtable session in which visiting bandleaders discussed current recordings with Jarvis. Duke Ellington, a frequent guest, refused to criticize any of the records. Unlike his fellow reviewers, who eagerly expressed their pedantic opinions, the Duke praised every record; he always found something favorable to say about a Blue Barron release or a new Jan Garber recording.

The evening radio hours were filled with great jazz presented by the ebullient Jack the Bell Boy. Throughout the night, between records, Jack expounded the merits of his sponsor, "Leo Sunshine Fontlerow, at the Victor Clothing Co., the genial-generous-gentleman of clothing!" He recited this advertising message from memory, but as the evening wore on and the Bell Boy's imbibing mounted, he invariably began to stumble through the familiar pitch. Every artist had a special Jack the Bell Boy name. He joyously introduced records by Benny "The Good Man," "Artie, the Shaw Kid," and "Glenn 'Killer-Diller' Miller."

Nat Cole and Lionel Hampton collaborated on Jack's recorded theme, "Jack the Bell Boy," on a Victor recording. During the holiday season, when Hampton's "Gin for Christmas" was on the turntable, you could hear Jack's ice cubes tinkle behind Ziggy Elman's trumpet chorus.

Jack the Bell Boy's was an all-request program. He would frequently sputter, "Call us at Drexel 2391—ring it and let it ring!" It was almost impossible to get through to him, though, as every teenager in Los Angeles was trying to dial Drexel 2391. Most of the callers were not interested in talking to Jack; they were using the number as a huge party line. Scores of voices could be heard over the busy signal, each one shouting a phone number. When the boys heard an attractive female voice, they carefully noted the number and quickly phoned her. Often those clandestine conversations culminated in blind dates or parties. Many romances began because of Jack the Bell Boy.

The band remotes were the most exciting radio segments during the mid-'30s. These were live broadcasts from the ballrooms and nightclubs featuring leading dance orchestras of the day. I can clearly hear the announcer's resonant voice proclaiming, "From the dining, dancing, and entertainment center of the West, the beautiful Palomar Ballroom at Third Street and Vermont Avenue in Los Angeles, California, we bring you the music of Artie Shaw, his clarinet and his orchestra!" Or, "From far out in the blue Pacific, overlooking the harbor lights on the romantic island of Catalina, the world famous Casino Ballroom brings you the Dixieland stylings of Bob Crosby and his Orchestra, featuring the Bob Cats!" Tommy Dorsey's Casino Gardens in Ocean Park was the Dorsey band's Southern California home. When Dorsey was on the road, the house orchestra was led by trombonist Jimmy Walsh, whose theme, "Mama's Gone, Goodbye," introduced the nightly radio broadcast.

I discovered the most thrilling music on a nightly KMTR broadcast from the Club Alabam' on Central Avenue featuring Lorenzo Flennoy's orchestra. I realized black bands offered an exciting brand of music and soon found the wonderful sounds of Jimmy Lunceford broadcasting from the Casa Manana in nearby Culver City.

The ultimate thrill was to visit these glamorous spots and become a part of the crowd, whose thunderous applause created the illusion of a large assemblage (with the urging of the announcer to respond loudly after each tune). The old Palomar Ballroom became my Friday evening headquarters.

I saw some outstanding orchestras in that cavernous ballroom on Vermont Avenue. When Glen Gray brought the Casa Loma Orchestra to the Palomar, I stood next to the bandstand during the broadcast and watched the radio announcer introducing "the music of Glen Gray and the Casa Loma Orchestra, featuring the vocal interpretations of handsome Kenny Sargent and the instrumental stylings of Pee Wee Hunt and Sonny Dunham." The theme "Smoke Rings" faded, and the program began.

It is quite easy to trace my earliest jazz interest back to that old Packard Bell radio. My most monumental acquisition was the used $10 phonograph attachment I wired to the set's hot tube. This paved the way for my introduction to the joyous cornucopia of record collecting—but that is another tale.

The Palomar Ballroom Fire*

Though the crisp clarity of hindsight often dims as years pass, my memories of October 2, 1939, remain vivid. On that momentous date more than half a century ago, the famed Palomar Ballroom in Los Angeles was destroyed by a blazing fire at 12:45 A.M.—and I was there.

I was among the two thousand fans at the beautiful dance palace that evening enjoying the music of Charlie Barnet and his orchestra, who were playing the penultimate night of a six-week engagement. A large electric sign on the building's roof line announced the next attraction: "Coming, Count Basie—October 4."

The headlines in the *Los Angeles Times* blared: PALOMAR BALLROOM RAZED BY FIRE. MORE THAN 2000 FLEE; ESTIMATED LOSS PLACED AT $500,000 BY OFFICIALS. In a follow-up story, the *Times* reported: PALOMAR FIRE LAID TO IGNITING OF RESINED RAG. ACCORDING TO ACTING FIRE CAPTAIN E. R. WHELAN OF THE ARSON SQUAD, "THE RESIN-COVERED RAG WAS DROPPED BY THE BASS VIOL PLAYER ON A 150 WATT FOOTLIGHT BULB." A few days later, the front-page story in *Down Beat* magazine announced, "The blaze came suddenly. Dancers were forced to flee. Musicians scrambled from the stand with their horns in their hands. Barnet and his boys returned to New York immediately." A Hollywood nightlife publication, *Out With the Stars,* added: "The fire started during the intermission when a cloth lying on the equipment of a radio engineer burst into flames and sent dancers scrambling for the exits." The day after the fire, the *Times* offered a new report: "One of the musicians in the orchestra told police he saw a flash in a switch box on the stage a few moments before the drapes began to burn."

*Honored by the International Association of Jazz Record Collectors—Best Article Awards for 1997.

Fire destroyed Los Angeles's famous Palomar Ballroom in 1939.

According to my research, only the last report was accurate. All of the details in the other stories were incorrect. Nationwide press reports of the disaster also distorted facts, and subsequent references have sustained those errors. Now, after sixty years, the true sequence of events that caused that sensational fire will finally be revealed.

The beautiful Palomar Ballroom, on Vermont Avenue between Second and Third Streets, was built in 1925. Originally named the El Patio Ballroom, it billed itself as "the largest and most famous dance hall on the West Coast." The building featured a large mezzanine, a balcony, and a 7,500-square-foot patio. The dance floor could accommodate four thousand couples. Admission was forty cents for gentlemen and twenty-five cents for ladies. Opening night brought out twenty thousand onlookers and attendees, including many of Hollywood's silent screen stars. The bright klieg lights illuminated the minaret structures on the roof and formed dramatic silhouettes against the sky.

Raymond Lewis purchased the property, added an indoor miniature golf course, and changed its name to Rainbow Gardens and, later, the Palomar Ballroom. It soon became a prime venue for the big bands that were rapidly gaining popularity. On August 21, 1935, Benny Goodman began his first Palomar engagement, marking the start of the swing era. During the last two weeks in 1937, box office sales exceeded fifty thousand tickets.

The ballroom hosted the nation's most popular orchestras, including those led by Clyde McCoy, Tommy Dorsey, Glenn Miller, Artie Shaw, Ted Fio Rito, Dick Jurgens, Glen Gray, Isham Jones, Will Osborne, Jimmy Dorsey, Kay Kyser, and Buddy Rogers. Nightly radio broadcasts on local station KHJ enabled millions of listeners to join the large crowds at the "Dining, Dancing, and Entertainment Center of the West." An aircheck from a Charlie Barnet broadcast is included on the LP *Radio Rhythm* (IAJRC 14). The famed structure provided the backdrop for several major Hollywood films, including *The Big Broadcast of 1937*, made during Benny Goodman's return engagement, and *Dancing Coed*, which starred Lana Turner and Artie Shaw's band.

By 1939 the Palomar had been remodeled. A modern cooling system was installed, cocktail lounges and soda fountains were added, and the dance floor was enlarged; the exotic Moorish decor, however, was not changed. An advertisement announcing the gala reopening predicted "a premier audience of more than 20,000 persons—the expected attendance to be on hand for the gayest of all openings!" Admission cost seventy-five cents for gentlemen and forty cents for ladies. On Sunday nights, a special dinner-dance ticket cost $1.25. It included a reserved table in the posh palm-lined Palomar Terrace for the entire evening, a seven-course dinner, a floor show, and dancing until 2 A.M. Valet parking was fifteen cents extra.

Charlie Barnet's booking occurred during the peak of the swing craze. It was shortly after he recorded Billy May's arrangement of "Cherokee," which became a big hit and firmly established Barnet as a star. Radio personality Al Jarvis, heralding the Palomar date, played Barnet's popular Bluebird recordings daily on his program, *Make-Believe Ballroom*. The band, making its first West Coast appearance, attracted six thousand people when it opened on August 23, 1939. The attendance topped all previous figures except the record established by Artie Shaw a few months before.

An opening-night review in the September issue of *Tempo* said: "With its seven brass and six saxes (with Barnet), this band is loud and lusty, but it swings. The band can tone down when they try; but the Palomar is no place to tone down, and Barnet keeps the throttle wide

Bandleader Charlie Barnet and his orchestra on the bandstand of the Palomar Ballroom. Bassist Phil Stevens is at right. Photo courtesy of Gordon Salyer.

open practically all night. Barnet, whose alto work is nearly as good as his tenor (and that's about as good as any), is the leading solo highlight with close competitors in Bill Miller (piano) and Bob Burnet (trumpet), a youngster from Chicago playing his first job with a name band."

On October 2, 1939, I was seventeen years old and had recently graduated from high school. I considered myself an expert on big-band music. My large collection of 78 rpm recordings included several by Charlie Barnet. On previous visits to the Palomar, I had heard Benny Goodman, Glen Gray, Clyde McCoy, and Gene Krupa.

During most of the evening, I stood against the bandstand enjoying the thrill of listening to live renditions of the very familiar recordings Al Jarvis played daily on his radio program. The fire occurred during intermission before the last set. The master of ceremonies, comedian Lionel Kaye, was entertaining on the stage in front of the curtain that covered the empty bandstand; I was seated on the dance floor in front of him. During his "daffy auction" he "sold" souvenir matches, napkins, and candles from the Palomar Terrace tables.

As Kaye continued through his routine, a quiver of smoke emerged from beneath the curtain on the left side of the stage. A fan called it to his attention, and he quipped about the Palomar being "the hottest joint in town!" But as the smoke increased, he realized that a serious problem existed. Remaining calm, he suggested that we slowly leave the building through the Third Street exit "until this situation is corrected."

As we moved toward the doors, Kaye stayed at the microphone, casually instructing us not to rush. He continued his witticisms and calm assurance that we were not in danger. As we neared the exit, a few wisps of flame flickered beneath the curtain at his back. When I reached the door, Kaye was still on the stage. The curtain behind him was beginning to blaze, and a cloud of smoke was filling the ballroom. He continued to say, "Walk slowly! You can all return soon when this little fire is under control." Lionel Kaye continued his banter until the last patron was safely outside. He was later observed seated on a fire truck's fender, bleakly watching the flames consume the building.

Contrary to the published reports, we were not "forced to flee." There was no rushing, no panic. No one was injured. The heroic Lionel Kaye prevented potential chaos and kept two thousand frightened patrons from trampling each other while dashing for the exits. Few newspaper accounts gave Kaye proper credit for his courageous conduct.

After exiting the building, we stood in the parking lot watching the fire redden the sky and waited for the fire engines to arrive. By the time sirens announced their approach, the flames were leaping high into the air, threatening several adjacent apartment houses. Shortly after the firemen arrived, the roof of the Palomar collapsed. A quivering shower of brilliant sparks splashed down on us and ignited the roof of a convertible in the parking lot. In less than an hour, the Palomar was little more than a box of embers. Beneath the rooftop minarets, the darkened marquee announcing the forthcoming opening of Count Basie remained clearly visible in the amber haze.

Might that sign have provided a clue to the fire's cause? Some would later say so. The management of the Palomar followed a strict racial policy; to my knowledge, the Basie orchestra would be the first black band booked there as a regular attraction. On one occasion, a prominent Los Angeles disc jockey had arranged for a special afternoon appearance by Floyd Ray, a black bandleader whose fine group had appeared at several Central Avenue clubs. Unfortunately, a group

of teenage hoodlums created an ugly incident, which was later described as a "race riot." That was the last time a black band appeared
at the Palomar. There has always been conjecture that Basie's impend-
ing appearance (he was to open two days hence) provoked a racist reaction—that someone burned the ballroom to the ground to keep the
Count from performing there. The theory has never been proven.

Racists might also have wished ill fortune upon Charlie Barnet, who
had helped break down the policy of segregation then prevalent in the
music business. As early as 1934 he included Benny Carter in his reed
section, and in 1938 he added Dizzy Gillespie and Charlie Shavers to
the band. "They called Charlie the 'White Ellington,'" bassist Phil
Stevens told me in 1996. "He played many of Duke's tunes—he was
one of the Duke's best friends." Recalling the fire, he said:

> On that night, during our last intermission, many of us went out the side
> door and had a couple drinks at Smitty's Bar across the street. I ran into the
> arranger Phil Moore and I was talking to him. I looked out and saw people
> running from the Palomar. I said, "What the hell's going on?" So I ran back
> in—I was quite athletic then. The bandstand was full of flames. I jumped
> up on the bandstand and grabbed my old Italian bass—it was burning—
> and I grabbed Johnny Owens' trumpet and Charlie's mouthpiece, and I ran
> out. There was a gas station right across the street on the corner, and I used
> the hose to put out the fire [on the bass].
>
> I carried the smoking instrument back to the Palomar parking lot and
> played "Throw Another Log on the Fire." Everyone got a kick out of that.
> Soon, we watched the roof collapse. The Palomar was burning furiously—
> and finally the fire engines came. They had gone to Third and Fremont in-
> stead of Third and Vermont. All the firemen did was run in and grab the
> booze from the bar—we watched them loading up the fire truck with all
> that liquor. Later the fire got worse, and they tried using the ballroom's fire
> extinguishers. Not one of them would work. They didn't give a damn about
> the place. They let it burn.

While there was no way of confirming these incredible assertions,
Stevens assured me they were accurate in every detail.

> As far as the fire is concerned, they tried to blame it on me. They said, "The
> bass player threw a resin rag in the floodlights." I never owned a resin rag!
> Here is the truth about how that fire started. We heard that a potential fire
> was averted during the engagement of a band that preceded us. Their vocal-
> ist was seated on the left side of the bandstand next to an electrical outlet. It
> began throwing sparks that scorched the coat draped on her chair. Fortu-
> nately, the sparks subsided.
>
> One night, about two weeks after we opened, the sparks started again.
> Charlie ran over and threw a pitcher of water on the source. We asked the

management to repair the faulty outlet, but they didn't do a damn thing about it. And that's where the fire started the night the place burned down—in that same electrical outlet.

If we had been on the bandstand instead of taking a break, we'd have been able to put it out again. They said I threw a rag in the footlights—but the fire started on the other side of the stage, and I was across the street at the bar when it started. The newspapers said, "Hot bull fiddle player causes fire." That was a lotta crap! I was on the other side of the stand on a riser in the curve of the piano. Later, a police officer came to see me and wanted to know who paid me to start the fire.

Sound engineer Cecil Charles, who was employed at Kelly Music, across the street from the Palomar, confirmed Stevens' recollection about the ballroom's electrical problems. He recalls servicing the venue's sound system and advising the management that the circuit was dangerously overloaded. Apparently, as Stevens said, the problem was not corrected.

Despite press accounts indicating that the band's instruments were all destroyed, according to Phil Stevens, most of the horns were recovered.

Charlie's sax was slightly damaged, but we were able to do a Bluebird recording session just a week later. Our library of three hundred tunes was lost, but 80 percent of them were "head" arrangements. We knew most of our numbers by memory—so the recordings were made without too much trouble. [Ironically, "Are We Burnt Up?" was one of the numbers recorded that day. It was never issued.] After we recorded eight tunes, we got some arrangements from Count Basie and Benny Goodman and worked our way back to Boston.

Shortly after the band returned to New York, Stevens left Barnet to join Tommy Dorsey. He returned to Los Angeles in 1941 and became a very successful studio musician. The bassist worked with Bing Crosby for seventeen years and accompanied Fred Astaire on many RKO soundtracks. His Capitol recordings with Pete Daily have become sought-after collectors items. He retired a dozen years before my interview with him. At the time of his retirement, Stevens was still using the fire-scarred nineteenth-century Tyrolian-Lombardian bass saved from the Palomar, which he had bought for $400 in 1930 while he was in Benny Meroff's band. He later sold it to a dealer for $18,000. "It had a wonderful sound. That instrument is probably still being played today."

Billy May, another member of the Barnet band, also had clear memories of the incident. Like Stevens, he remembered hearing of the bandstand's electrical problem about a week before the big fire. Barnet's pianist, Bill Miller (who later served as Frank Sinatra's accompanist for many years), also substantiated many of Phil Stevens' comments. He, too, was at Smitty's when the conflagration broke out and said that most of the band members had no knowledge of the drama that was unfolding across the street until it was too late.

The October 15, 1939, issue of *Down Beat* reported: "The Palomar was uninsured, companies having refused to risk it because they lacked proper safety devices." Conflicting reports indicated that there had been an insurance settlement of $400,000. No attempt was made to rebuild the great ballroom. The elongated sign reading "Coming, Count Basie—October 4" remained on the building's charred exterior wall. There were frequently publicized announcements that reconstruction would soon be underway, but the remaining walls were eventually razed, and a large supermarket was constructed on the site.

The Firehouse Five and the Good Time Jazz Record Company

In 1995, the Good Time Jazz Record Company released a boxed set of four CDs titled *The Good Time Jazz Story*. The five hours of music documented three decades of classic jazz, highlighted by the GTJ recordings that helped spearhead the revival era in the '40s. When producer Ralph Kaffel asked me to write the historical background of the Good Time Jazz Record Company for the CD booklet, he was not aware of my personal involvement in the genesis of the influential record label. I happily accepted the assignment, which provided an opportunity to reveal the true origin of the heroic little firm that helped reestablish worldwide interest in authentic New Orleans jazz.

On New Year's Eve 1948, Lucille and I were invited to a jazz party in a large rehearsal room above Roy Hart's Drum City, a percussion store on Santa Monica Boulevard near Vine Street in Hollywood. We invited our friend Bob Kirstein to join us. Kirstein had an elaborate collection of early jazz records and conducted a weekly radio program, "Doctor Jazz," on a tiny Hollywood FM station. The musicians were setting up their instruments when we arrived at Drum City. To our astonishment, they were attired in bright red shirts, black pants, white suspenders—and firemen's helmets! The trombonist, Ward Kimball,

The Firehouse Five Plus Two: from left, banjoist Harper Goff, clarinetist Clarke Mallery, drummer Jim MacDonald, bassist Ed Penner, trumpeter Johnny Lucas, and trombonist Ward Kimball. Pianist Frank Thomas is not pictured. Photo courtesy of Ward Kimball.

wore a tin badge that identified him as the "Fire Chief." This unusual garb contrasted vividly with the accepted 1948 band dress code— tuxedos or dark suits. We learned that this was the group's initial outing, little suspecting that they would quickly become internationally famous as the Firehouse Five Plus Two.

A capacity crowd enjoyed a succession of high-energy stomps, authentic blues, and spirited re-creations of early jazz classics we had heard only on rare recordings by King Oliver, Jelly Roll Morton, and Louis Armstrong. When we sipped champagne at midnight and the band played "Auld Lang Syne," the venerable Scottish melody was embellished with a clanging fire alarm bell and a shrieking siren. The Firehouse Five Plus Two and the year 1949 were launched simultaneously, emphatically—and unforgettably.

The New Year's party was their first public appearance, but from the tight, well-rehearsed arrangements, it was obvious that the little band had been playing together for some time. In an interview with

Bob Greene published in *Record Changer* magazine (September 1949), leader Ward Kimball recalled that the musicians first played together at noontime jam sessions at Walt Disney studios.

"It happened that we had a New Orleans band working here without our knowing about it," he said. "Frank Thomas, our pianist, is an animation director; Ed Penner, our bass sax man, is a writer; Jim McDonald, the drummer, is in charge of sound effects; and Clarke Mallery, the clarinetist, is also an animator." Kimball was a cartoonist, and Johnny Lucas, a Pasadena writer, also played at the sessions, wrote arrangements for the band, and blew some fiery trumpet on the band's initial recordings.

The jam sessions continued at Disney and expanded to Kimball's house every Friday evening. "We were hired for a dance and didn't have a name, so we dreamed up the 'San Gabriel Valley Blue Blowers,' named after San Gabriel, the little town near Pasadena, where I live." For their formal debut at Drum City, Kimball drew inspiration from his interest in antique fire engines and trains; he had an 1875 railroad station, a full-size Baldwin railroad locomotive (with tender and car attached) sitting on 650 feet of track, and a fully restored 1914 American LaFrance fire engine in his back yard.

After the New Year's party, Bob Kirstein was very enthusiastic about the band. He told me that his close friend, Lester Koenig, who shared his interest in jazz, might be interested in recording them. Koenig, whom Kirstein met when they both attended Dartmouth University, had written a jazz column for the school paper and later became a successful assistant producer at Paramount Pictures. During the 1947 hearings of the House Un-American Activities Committee, several prominent Hollywood film personages, including Koenig, were defamed and given no opportunity to defend themselves. They were carelessly implicated and, shamefully, blacklisted. As a result, he was looking for a suitable investment opportunity and considered reverting to his earlier role as a record producer.

As Kirstein predicted, Les Koenig was very interested. The Firehouse Five was scheduled to play at a forthcoming dance at the Valley Country Club, and Koenig attended the event with Kirstein and was instantly enamored. Recalling the episode in his liner notes on the first GTJ LP release, Koenig wrote:

> While the firemen were packing their leather helmets, fire bells, and sirens, I was introduced to Ward Kimball. "Will you record for me?" I asked po-

litely. "What company are you with?" asked Kimball. "None," I told him. "But if you record for me, I'll have one."

A few weeks later (on May 13, 1949), at Radio Engineers' famous Studio B in Hollywood, with engineer Lowell Frank at the controls, the first Firehouse Five session began with their theme, "Firehouse Stomp"—the auspicious start of a great recording career.

In addition to "Firehouse Stomp" and "Blues My Naughty Sweetie Gives to Me" (GTJ No. 1), they also recorded "Fireman's Lament" and "San" (GTJ No. 2). Koenig promptly rented a small vacant store near Paramount Studios. Kirstein, employed as an "administrative assistant," helped Koenig fill orders for the two new ten-inch vinyl 78 rpm records (retail price: seventy-nine cents).

I feel justified in claiming the role of catalyst in the formation of the Good Time Jazz Record Company. I was responsible for Bob Kirstein's introduction to the Firehouse Five, which led directly to Les Koenig's interest in recording the band. (I acknowledge an assist from Senator Joseph McCarthy.)

Since facts force me to cast all modesty aside, I must also admit to providing Good Time Jazz with its first international publicity. The initial public announcement of their recordings appeared in my monthly "American Jazz Scene" column in the July 1949 issue of *Jazz Journal*. I wrote, "The Firehouse Five Plus 2 has at last been recorded. Four fine sides have been cut for the Good Time Jazz label, to be distributed by Jack Lewerke." (Lewerke subsequently became GTJ's general manager.)

The following month, I authored the first published review of a Good Time Jazz recording. It said, in part: "'Firehouse Stomp,' complete with whistles, bells, and sirens, captures the true spirit of the band. Adapted from the popular march, 'Under the Double Eagle,' and featuring Harper Goff's exciting banjo, it is the best of the four sides. On 'Fireman's Lament,' Johnny Lucas' trumpet work is outstanding."

In September 1949, when the young company had been in existence only four months, *Record Changer* magazine featured a color caricature of the Firehouse Five on its front cover, and a humorous ad for Good Time Jazz, highlighted by Ward Kimball's offbeat artwork, filled the back cover. The issue was dominated by Bob Greene's five-page article about the Firehouse Five and George Avakian's review of their first recordings. Avakian, who had produced the pioneering documentary jazz album *Chicago Jazz* for Decca Records and later compiled a series of great jazz albums for Columbia, said, "The music fits the

Les Koenig founded the
Good Time Jazz label.

beautifully scrolled label. There's a cocky beat and carefree sound on
every groove, and if you don't feel like laughing just out of happiness
when you hear these sides, then you've never enjoyed a silent movie—
or W.C. Fields. ... Ward Kimball is the daring young man on the slid-
ing trombone, and Johnny Lucas plays a rare batch of trumpet."

His description of the "beautifully scrolled label" was quite accurate. Koenig always paid fastidious attention to the graphic design of
his labels, carefully selecting antique typefaces and creating a custom
design for each artist. A few years later, "Firehouse Stomp" became the
leadoff number on Good Time Jazz's first ten-inch LP (GTJ-33-1), one
of the first independently produced albums in the new 33⅓ rpm format. It included the tunes from the first two Firehouse Five Plus Two
sessions.

Many of the GTJ album covers were very attractively decorated
with Lom LeGoullon's zany artwork. The sleeves were illustrated with
fine jazz photography by noted cameramen Ray Avery, William Clax-
ton, Bob Best, and Cecil Charles. When Kid Ory joined the Good Time
Jazz roster, the albums were decorated with his authentic Creole
recipes for crawfish bisque, gumbo filé, etc. The superior sleeve notes
probed deeply into jazz history, providing valuable information that
contributed greatly to listeners' knowledge and appreciation of the mu-

sic. These interesting essays were usually serialized—"continued on the next volume"—a very shrewd marketing device.

Like the locomotive in Ward Kimball's back yard, Good Time Jazz rapidly gathered a full head of steam. Over the next twenty years, the Firehouse Five recorded 150 tunes during thirty sessions for the increasingly successful label. The band released LPs with such diverse titles as *The Firehouse Five Goes to Sea, The Firehouse Five Crashes a Party,* and *The Firehouse Five at Disneyland.* (Incidentally, George Probert, who later played soprano sax with the Firehouse Five, has recently resurrected the famed Firehouse Five trademarks. The penetrating siren and the fire alarm bell are now regularly featured with his popular Monrovia Olde Style Jazz Band. The Firehouse Five format has also been adopted by a few bands in Europe.)

To appreciate the heroism of Les Koenig's venture, one must recall how dismal the traditional jazz scene was in 1949. Very little of this music was accessible—live performances were sporadic, and very few records were available. There had never been a jazz festival; there were no organized jazz societies. And the three major record firms (there were only three!), flush with the success of their big-band recordings, steadfastly refused to reissue the many cherished gems gathering dust in their vaults. GTJ dared to challenge an industry that turned its back on the "old-fashioned" music. Koenig overcame the challenges posed not only by the established swing bands but also by the emerging bebop artists. Dave Dexter, Jr., in his carefully researched *The Jazz Story From the 1890s to the 1960s* (Prentice Hall, 1964), said of the Firehouse Five Plus Two: "Their records and albums, on Lester Koenig's Good Time Jazz label, reportedly outsold [Dizzy] Gillespie's at the height of the bop craze."

From those initial 1949 releases, Koenig's little firm grew into one of the most important traditional jazz record companies. The label, documenting a wide variety of legendary classic jazz musicians in their prime, also released recordings by Jelly Roll Morton, Willie "The Lion" Smith, Bunk Johnson, Turk Murphy, George Lewis, Pete Daily, Bob Scobey, and Lu Watters' Yerba Buena Jazz Band.

Koenig died November 21, 1977. His son, John, operated the firm until 1983. Today, GTJ is a subsidiary of Fantasy Records. Despite the passage of years and the introduction of increasingly progressive jazz styles, Fantasy has sustained the founder's vision by keeping much of his valuable material in its catalog.

The Yerba Buena Jazz Band
and the Jazz Man Label

In 1939, at the peak of the big-band era, the late Lu Watters formed his Yerba Buena Jazz Band. They began at the Big Bear Tavern, a hillside roadhouse above Oakland, California, launching a twelve-year journey that profoundly altered the traditional jazz scene. In *Jazz West—1945 to 1985* (Cypress Press), K.O. Eckland writes: "Despite its relatively short active life span, the Yerba Buena Jazz Band had as much influence on jazz, in particular the sound of jazz, as any band in history. Less this be constructed as a reckless statement—taking into consideration the Original Dixieland Jazz Band, Armstrong, Morton, and other early groups, when size of audience is considered, the reach and effect of the YBJB can only be described as enormous."

In 1941, Les Koenig and David Stuart, who operated the Jazz Man Record Shop in Hollywood, produced the first recordings by the Yerba Buena Jazz Band. These eight titles launched the important Jazz Man label and firmly established Lu Watters' band as a musical force. The tunes included "Black and White Rag," "Maple Leaf Rag," "Irish Black Bottom," and "Memphis Blues." Priced at $1 apiece, those Jazz Man 78s seemed quite a luxury at the time (issues on the competing Bluebird and Decca labels were only thirty-five cents). But time has revealed them to be more than worth the extra cost. These recordings are now viewed as historic milestones that changed the course of jazz history.

The original Yerba Buena Jazz Band lineup included Lu Watters and Bob Scobey on trumpets, Turk Murphy on trombone, Bob Helm on clarinet, Wally Rose on piano, Dick Lammi on tuba, Harry Mordecai on banjo, and Bill Dart on drums. Through their Jazz Man releases and a heavy schedule of live performances, this group unleashed a torrent of interest in the authentic New Orleans music that had been dormant since the onset of swing. Helm introduced a new generation to the low-register clarinet solos popularized by Johnny Dodds two decades earlier, while Murphy reinvigorated Kid Ory's celebrated coda on "Muskrat Ramble." (Murphy, incidentally, is credited with coining the term "traditional jazz.") As the YBJB's audience grew, Jazz Man added additional recordings by Kid Ory, Turk Murphy, Pete Daily, and Darnell Howard to its catalog. Later, under the management of Marili and Nesuhi Ertegun, the label issued historic 1938 acetates by Jelly

Serigraph of the Yerba Buena Jazz Band by Clark Wright.

Roll Morton, obtained from a private collection. The valuable documentary items, major contributions to jazz's history, were recorded toward the end of Morton's career, shortly after he made his epic Library of Congress records.

Les Koenig purchased all of the Jazz Man masters in 1952 and promptly reissued the pioneering YBJB recordings in ten-inch LP format on his Good Time Jazz label (GTJ LP-8). In his liner notes, Nesuhi Ertegun said, "The eight sides on this LP constitute one of the most significant recording sessions in jazz history, for they marked the start of the great New Orleans Revival and affected the development of jazz throughout the Nineteen Forties in America and abroad." Acknowledging the fiftieth anniversary of these recordings, Doug Parker, writing in *Rag Times* (November 1991), said: "These first Watters recordings of 1941 and '42 may have been the most historically important jazz records since the first Original Dixieland Jazz Band issues of 1917–18."

In 1993, Good Time Jazz issued an elaborate set of four CDs entitled *Lu Watters' Yerba Buena Jazz Band—The Complete Good Time*

Jazz Recordings (4GTJCD-4409–2). The ninety-six selections constituted everything the band recorded for the Jazz Man and West Coast
labels, plus recordings of broadcasts previously released on Riverside
and Fairmont—all "processed in the latest digital technology."

More than a half a century after Watters' first recordings, the YBJB
material is still a permanent part of the GTJ catalog; and the pioneer
band continues to be a major influence on successive generations of
jazzmen.

Benny Strickler

During World War II, the San Francisco–based Lu Watters band was
torn apart. Many of its members were in the service; others were engaged in activities restricting their musical efforts. An ad hoc version of
the band played at the Dawn Club, their early Bay Area jazz venue.
Burt Bales played piano; Bob Helm and Ellis Horne shared the clarinet
role; Russ Bennett was featured on banjo; Bob Bardin played trombone; and Clancy Hayes handled the drums. Watters' regular sidemen
occasionally sat in with this group, and they inevitably came away
with exciting descriptions of the little trumpet player who sparked the
band. Sickly and thin, he played in a lyrical style similar to that of the
early New Orleans cornetists. Those who were fortunate to hear his
soulful horn firmly believe his name should be included with the im-
mortals of jazz.

His tenure with the wartime Yerba Buena Band was very short; a series of tragic events ended a promising career too soon. One evening he
collapsed on the stand with a crimson hemorrhage flowing from his
stilled lips—and the soulful horn of Benny Stickler was heard no
more.

Strickler had left his Arkansas home in the early 1930s at the age of
eighteen, hitchhiking to Los Angeles to search for musicians with
whom he could express himself. Those were the famine years for classic jazz; organized jazz bands were rare. Strickler and a good friend,
trombonist Bob Logan, jobbed around town together for many years,
playing dance music at the Rustic Inn on Vermont Avenue and later
working in the pit band at the Burbank Burlesque Theater. But
whether he was playing society schmaltz in local hotels or accompanying aging strip queens at the Burbank, Strickler's longing for jazz never
subsided.

He and Logan were inseparable. They played together in bands fronted by Rube Wolf, Larry Kent, and Segar Ellis; I recall hearing the Ellis group at the Casino Gardens in Ocean Park while I was still in high school. The unique structure of Ellis' band was all brass with rhythm, plus Irving Fazola's New Orleans clarinet. In Larry Kent's hotel orchestra, Strickler welcomed his sets in the "band-within-a-band"—an opportunity to play in the relaxed style he enjoyed. During the Kent orchestra's appearance in Salt Lake City, Strickler and Logan found diversion during their jam sessions far out on the salt flats with a local guitarist. After the evening's work, in the quiet hours before dawn, the quiet salt flats reverberated with strains of "Dippermouth Blues," "Muskrat Ramble," and "Tin Roof Blues." Their heartfelt music melted away all thoughts of the stilted commercial arrangements used in the hotel job. Bob Logan recalled, "We wore out every guitar player in Salt Lake City."

A succession of band jobs followed. Months on the road, endless one-nighters, not much sleep, perhaps too much liquor—they all took their toll, doing irreparable damage to Strickler's already slight frame. After a short tour with Wingy Manone, he joined the Bob Wills band in 1941. Contrary to popular perception, this cowboy group played with a tremendous beat and included many jazz tunes in its repertoire. For eleven months, Benny enjoyed the freedom of the Wills outfit, playing alongside cornetist Danny Alguire, later a member of the Firehouse Five Plus Two.

Unlike most horn men, Benny never had an off night, according to Alguire. His cordial attitude, coupled with the lofty quality of his musicianship, won Strickler the admiration of almost every musician who heard him. He is spotlighted as trumpet soloist on Wills' Okeh recording, "10 Years," and his strong section lead is evident on "Whose Heart Are You Breaking Now?" During rehearsals, Benny's favorite expression was, "Let's just make the tune sound good."

Alguire recalled many incidents when Benny thrilled the band. Once, working an entire evening with a split lip, he played with his usual vigor despite the blood flowing past his chin. Between songs, he leaned toward Alguire and said, "The pressure of the mouthpiece against my lip seems to relieve the pain … it only hurts when I stop playing."

Motivated by a strong determination to find the right place for himself in the music profession, Benny left the Wills band in 1942. While briefly filling Lu Watters' chair at the Dawn Club in San Francisco, he rapidly endeared himself to musicians and jazz fans in the Bay Area. He began feeling ill but steadfastly refused to see a physician. As his condition deteriorated, he was forced to sit while playing, but his clear tone still cut through the dense atmosphere at the Dawn Club. When the band expressed concern, Benny smiled and said, "I'll be okay; I'm just a little tired."

One night he collapsed on the stand; his small body was twisted with pain, and he was bleeding internally. Emergency medical attention confirmed the condition as tuberculosis. The band helped pay his way back to his home in Arkansas, where he entered the state sanatorium for treatment. On December 8, 1946, Benny Strickler died; he was only twenty-nine years old. His wife, Francis, and daughters, Diane and Janet, were not alone in their loss. The world lost a great musician that sad day.

Fortunately, there is a happy coda to this grim tale. One evening in 1942, the Yerba Buena Jazz Band did a radio broadcast from the Dawn Club over a local station. This was the band's only airing, and a jazz fan, Hal McIntyre, made acetate recordings of the program. Strickler, although very ill at the time, played beautifully, as always. Some time later, Bunk Johnson heard the acetates during a visit to San Francisco. Without hesitation, the venerable New Orleans jazzman said, "That could be no one but Joe Oliver!" He could not believe it was a young white musician too sick to stand on his feet.

When Les Koenig, president of Good Time Jazz Records, heard the recordings, he immediately secured the rights to release them. Four wonderful sides appeared in 1950: "Jazzin' Babies Blues," "Kansas City Stomps," "Fidgety Feet," and "Dippermouth Blues," all great jazz standards.

George Avakian wrote a glowing record review in the September 1950 issue of *Record Changer* magazine: "This is one of the best broadcast transcriptions ever issued commercially ... the best trumpet playing issued on a record this year! 'Kansas City Stomps' has not been played so marvelously since the original Jelly Roll Morton Red Hot Peppers version with Ward Pinkett in 1928."

Those four Good Time Jazz 78s are all that remain of Benny Strickler's music. But the memory of Benny the man remains strong in the hearts of those who knew him. Several years after the release of the records, Strickler's Bob Wills colleague, Danny Alguire, told me: "Even if he never had played a note, I would have loved Benny for his gentlemanly manner—his inherent decency. He was a real guy."

Turk Murphy, Dick Lammi, Bob Helm, Bob Short, Wally Rose, and Claire Austin, 1952, Italian Village, San Francisco.

Turk Murphy's Final Triumph

In 1997, commemorating the tenth anniversary of his death, the Sweet and Hot Music Festival in Los Angeles saluted the memory of esteemed San Francisco leader-trombonist-arranger-composer Melvin E. "Turk" Murphy. Pat Yankee, who achieved fame singing with him at Earthquake McGoon's in San Francisco, presented her expressive "Turk Murphy Story," a loving tribute featuring musicians associated with him.

The full extent of Turk's importance cannot be overly emphasized. His steadfast leadership, spanning more than four decades, was greatly responsible for an international phenomenon—the ongoing explosion of interest in traditional jazz.

For those of us who learned our jazz history via phonograph records, Murphy played a vital role when he participated in the organization of the Lu Watters Yerba Buena Jazz Band in 1940. The YBJB's first recordings, on the Jazz Man label, fostered a worldwide revival that continues to smolder. Their recordings of early compositions by Scott Joplin, Joe Oliver, Clarence Williams, and Jelly Roll Morton introduced these giants to a new audience of young listeners that began listening more than half a century ago. Some of us are still listening, and learning—and writing books like this.

Turk Murphy's hundreds of recordings have been a vital inspiration to several generations of musicians. Today, scores of bands in Europe and the United States are still trying to achieve that identifiable Murphy sound. The familiar bravado of Turk's trombone that rippled on the shores of San Francisco's Bay for years is currently echoing against the banks of the Thames, the Seine, the Arno, the Rhine, and, yes, even the Mississippi.

His particular affinity for tunes recorded by legendary Joe "King" Oliver's Creole Jazz Band in the early 1920s was evident throughout Murphy's career. It was initially vitalized with the Yerba Buena Jazz Band's imitative dual trumpet format. The group of traditionally minded players continually strived for that Armstrong-Oliver ensemble effect that makes those early Gennett, Okeh, Paramount, and Columbia recordings so alluring to jazz historians.

Turk's final appearance in Los Angeles was during the 1986 L.A. Classic Jazz Festival. At the time, some of us were aware of his debilitating illness. Weeks before the festival, it was suggested to the event's management that they recognize Turk's achievements with a special citation. Unfortunately, dissension at a board of directors meeting negated any action.

During that festival weekend, his horn sounded a bit less robust, and his voice was unsteady; but, although he was painfully facing death, Turk's compelling spirit propelled each performance.

Despite the affront in Los Angeles, Turk Murphy received international honors and admiration for more than fifty years. The trombonist's most important recognition occurred the following year, just a few months before he died.

On January 10, 1987, more than three thousand fans crowded into New York's prestigious Carnegie Hall to hear a very important concert brilliantly produced by bandleader Jim Cullum. Fortunately, Stomp Off Records' engineers fully captured the excitement and drama of that sentimental tribute to one of jazz's key figures. The resulting album is titled *Turk at Carnegie* (SOS 1155).

I proudly sat in the fourteenth row at the newly refurbished Carnegie Hall witnessing an impressive Murphy tribute. A sellout crowd filled every seat. Several rows of chairs, added on stage, accommodated additional enthusiasts anxious to be a part of this historic event.

We were still reeling from a gala party the previous night in the Grand Hyatt Hotel's ballroom. The huge room glittered with sequined gowns and elegant tuxedos. Two thousand of Turk's friends watched him modestly accept gifts and citations from civic groups, jazz organizations, trade unions, California's governor, and the president.

Dance music was provided by Vince Giordano's Nighthawks, the Hot Antics Jazz Band, and Turk Murphy's Jazz Band of San Francisco. The entire evening was a celebration of love and appreciation for Turk and his music. Present Past Productions videotaped the activity for later release.

The following evening, Jim Cullum opened the Carnegie Hall program, leading his fine jazz band from San Antonio, Texas, on the tune "Fireworks" by Spencer Williams. Cullum's steaming program also included a memorable expanded concert version of "Washboard Blues."

Befitting the occasion's importance, France's Hot Antic Jazz Band appeared in full dress. This remarkable six-piece group, led by Michel Bastide on cornet and valve trombone, offered a touch of Gallicism as they authentically reached to the core of American jazz. Many Hot Antics numbers were inspired by early Jabbo Smith recordings. The eighty-year-old trumpet star, a contemporary of Louis Armstrong's in the 1920s, was beaming from a box at stage left. Jabbo's pleasure was reflected in the appreciative audience's rousing applause.

During intermission, an expectant crowd eagerly awaited Turk Murphy's first New York appearance in more than twenty-five years. They came to salute the man who kindled a flame that kept the music warm and alive for half a century.

When the seventy-two-year-old jazzman entered the stage, an affectionate wave of applause spread through the hall. His usually vigorous trombone, although considerably weakened, still punctuated ensembles with the brittle verve that continues to influence a third generation of revivalists.

Turk's carefully selected program included five original tunes, one by Watters, three by Joe "King" Oliver, and a pair of Jelly Roll Morton classics. "The Pearls," reverently soloed by pianist Jim Maihack, followed Jelly Roll's mighty "King Porter Stomp." The multi-strained "Red Flannel Rag" was most impressive of Turk's compositions.

"Minstrels of Annie Street," introduced by Murphy as "my chop buster," recalled an alley behind San Francisco's Palace Hotel where the old Dawn Club hosted initial efforts by the Lu Watters Yerba

Buena Jazz Band in 1940. The era Watters and Murphy launched on Annie Street reached its zenith that night on Carnegie Hall's stage.

"Mack the Knife" dramatically brought to full circle a series of events started in the 1920s. In Germany, Kurt Weill, greatly influenced by Louis Armstrong's Hot Five recordings, began an adaptation of *The Beggar's Opera* that eventually became *The Three Penny Opera*. When it was revived off-Broadway in the 1950s, Turk heard "Mack the Knife" and wrote a great arrangement later recorded by Louis Armstrong. It became a huge hit for Satchmo; he sang that arrangement at every performance the rest of his career. Turk's Carnegie Hall vocal completed the circle.

For the combined band finale, pianist John Sheridan, heard earlier with Jim Cullum's band, arranged Turk Murphy's theme, "Bay City." Cullum's muted cornet floated majestically against the resonance of the twenty-piece group.

There were few dry eyes in Carnegie Hall during ailing Turk Murphy's closing bow. A vast outpouring of love filled the auditorium. A bright glow of thousands of faces rivaled the gilt trim on the lovely ninety-six-year-old hall's newly painted walls. We knew the tremendous significance of the event; it was apparent that we had witnessed his final major performance.

Sadly, it dropped a curtain on the musical drama that premiered almost half a century before in that little alley in San Francisco.

Happily, it also beamed a bright spotlight toward the future by underscoring Turk's most important achievement—an enduring influence. He left monumental guidelines for generations of jazzmen that will continually follow in his large footprints. Look around and listen. They are probably playing at concerts, festivals and jazz cruises at this very moment.

Turk died May 30, 1987, just four months after his Carnegie Hall triumph.

I Remember Bob Scobey

Scores of great musicians have left their indelible marks on jazz during our music's brief history. Most respected members of this distinguished group were veterans who helped shape the genre.

The Original Dixieland Jazz Band commercially established the style when Bob Scobey was only one year old. Bix Beiderbecke left a strong

Bob Scobey's Frisco Jazz Band, 1952. From left: Jack Buck, Ellis Horne, Bob Scobey, Burt Bales, Clancy Hayes. Front: Fred Higuera. Photo by Ed O'Shaughnessy. Courtesy of Ray Avery.

imprint on our music before Bob picked up his first horn. Louis Armstrong was born almost half a century before Scobey appeared on jazz's horizon.

Bob Scobey, a founding member of the Lu Watters Yerba Buena Jazz Band, became prominent after three generations of jazzmen had already honed their craft into a seasoned artform.

He was unlike most instrumentalists of his age, who, understandably, imitated rather than originated. His unique contribution, tinged with an esteem for Bunny Berigan and Louis Armstrong, merits a lofty position in the annals of his beloved music.

Considering classic jazz's current popularity, it is difficult to imagine the music situation when Scobey's saga began. The swing era was in full sway, and the music that fueled the Jazz Age just a decade earlier was long forgotten. Suddenly, new 78 rpm records by Lu Watters' Yerba Buena Jazz Band appeared on the independent West Coast label, Jazz Man.

Collectors were thrilled by sounds of Watters' and Scobey's unison trumpets, emulating the 1922 format of King Oliver's Creole Jazz Band. Eight titles, produced by David Stuart and Les Koenig, launched the heroic Jazz Man Record Company and stimulated an international response.

Groups influenced by the Yerba Buena Jazz Band soon formed in the United States, France, England, and Australia. Those early efforts unleashed a torrent of interest in authentic New Orleans music. Classic jazz's prominence, as we know it today, can be traced back to those first Lu Watters records and Bob Scobey's major role in their success.

Later, with his own band, he continued to revitalize a sleeping artistic phenomenon, classic jazz, and soon became a highly respected and influential member of the jazz fraternity.

I met Bob Scobey in 1949 during a trip to northern California. He recently left Lu Watters and was working at Victor and Roxie's, a small Oakland club. Jack Buck played trombone, and the pianist was Burt Bales. Banjoist Clancy Hayes shared vocals with Bob. Twenty-two-year-old clarinetist George Probert was playing one of his first steady jobs. They were billed as "Alexander's Jazz Band" (Bob's middle name was Alexander).

While retaining Watters' driving flair, Scobey veered toward a lilting Chicago style. By continuously expanding his visions, he eventually established a polished, free-swinging approach still admired by musicians throughout the world.

A year later, during Bob's thirty-fourth birthday party at his home in Fremont, California, he excitedly told me about the first recordings by his Victor and Roxie band. Flying home from San Francisco in a rattling DC-3 airliner, I carefully cradled a pair of 78 rpm Jazzman Records purchased from Vivian Borneman's Yerba Buena Jazz Record Shop in Oakland. They still occupy a cherished place on my record shelves.

For fifteen years, I diligently followed the Frisco band's rapidly flourishing popularity. Bob's name appeared on records issued on the Good Time Jazz, Verve, and RCA Victor labels. He recorded with Sidney Bechet, Bing Crosby, Matty Matlock, and Art Hodes. Riding the crest of popular acclaim, he appeared in the nation's most prestigious venues. Scobey's 1960 engagement schedule listed consecutive dates from January 1 to December 31, with days off only for travel.

The following year, he acquired an interest in a Chicago club called Bourbon Street. When visiting the Windy City, I always spent a won-

derful evening at his bistro on Rush Street, enjoying intermission inter-
ludes by pianist Art Hodes and listening to Bob's relaxed, swinging
style, which ignited his band's blazing ensembles.

I will never forget my last visit with him. He had completed a successful tour of Europe with the Harlem Globetrotters, and I wanted to
hear about his adventures.

It was a humid evening in spring 1962. The bright Midwest twilight
contrasted with Bourbon Street's darkened interior. Before becoming
accustomed to the shadowy setting, I was escorted to a ringside table.
The beautiful hostess that seated me was Jan Scobey; she and Bob were
married a few months before his European trip.

I immediately noticed a different trumpet player was on the stand. I
asked "Where's Bob?" She pointed to a rear booth. My eyes were then
adjusted to the darkness, but when I approached the booth, I did not
recognize its occupant until he smiled, extended a hand, and offered a
cheery "Hello, Floyd!"

It had been several months since I last saw him. His fragile appearance was a severe shock. He looked gaunt and pallid. His hair was thin
and gray. Noticing my concern, he explained, "I guess that European
tour was too much. We traveled through nine countries in three
months—one-nighters. The constant pace and the rich food caused my
ulcer to act up. I'm okay now, but I've been told to take it easy. I'm not
supposed to play for a while. I hired Bob Ballard to take my place. I'm
just singing a few numbers in each set."

The new Mrs. Scobey told me that, immediately upon his return to
Chicago, he entered Caldwell Hospital for emergency surgery on a perforated ulcer. I did not know until later that, after surgery, a pathology
report revealed the presence of cancer.

When I returned to Chicago the following summer, I learned Bob
had just died. He was only forty-six years old, but during those brief
years he made a vivid imprint on jazz history.

In 1991, to celebrate the seventy-fifth anniversary of Bob's birth,
Jan Scobey and her supportive husband, Gene Paleno, courageously
produced a mammoth festival in Santa Rosa, California. A stellar roster of West Coast, Midwest, and New Orleans colleagues of Scobey's
appeared, including Wally Rose, Bob Helm, Bill Napier, George Probert, Bob Mielke, Pete Clute, and Jim Beebe.

I eagerly accepted Jan's invitation to be master of ceremonies, but
the festival was a great disappointment. Despite a wonderful roster of
musicians and elaborate promotional activity, local jazz fans did not

support the event. The attendance was very poor. A distraught Jan Scobey suffered a tremendous financial loss.

A team of engineers videotaped the three-day festival. She hoped to recover her losses with sales of a videocassette. For the benefit of the cameras, I dutifully introduced each segment to just a few dozen fans. The musicians, playing to a near empty auditorium, spared no effort as they magnificently paid homage to Scobey's music.

The cameras also recorded an interesting interview I conducted with clarinetist Bob Helm and ragtime pianist Wally Rose. They were the only survivors of Lu Watters' Yerba Buena Jazz Band. Their recollections filled many gaps in the historical documentation of West Coast jazz's critical period.

To add to Jan Scobey's woe, a review of the videotapes later revealed faulty recording of the soundtrack's public address segments. To attain a commercially viable product, costly re-recording would be necessary. Sadly, a very notable project will probably never be completed.

Scobey's memory was posthumously honored very successfully during the 1993 London Bridge Dixieland Festival in Lake Havasu, Arizona. Jan Scobey was the special guest. Except for her unsuccessful Santa Rosa event, the Arizona festival was the first to recognize Bob's achievements—thirty years after his death.

There are hundreds of bands playing at classic jazz festivals now occurring regularly around the world. These groups include fine younger players who never heard Bob Scobey in person, but they have listened carefully to his records. Without that bountiful influence, festivals like these would not exist today.

Recordings by festival artists are abundantly available. Often, the number of titles on each band's CDs surpasses the total recorded output of some important early groups. In contrast to the dismal period preceding jazz's revival, record firms are now actively reissuing practically every note recorded during the Jazz Era. Several of Scobey's albums have reappeared on the Good Time Jazz label. His last recordings (from 1956–1960) are available on Jazzology.

The present state of the art is, indeed, very healthy. This thriving activity reflects initial efforts by Lu Watters and the offshoot thrusts of sidemen Turk Murphy, Wally Rose, Clancy Hayes, Bob Helm, and my friend Bob Scobey.

The beautifully illustrated book, *He Rambled! 'Til Cancer Cut Him Down,* painstakingly documented by Jan Scobey, tells her late husband's story from beginning to end. (Available from Jan Scobey Hot Jazz, Box 6, Upper Lake CA 94585—price available upon request; also autographed on request.)

Although the paths along which the music trod were already deeply worn when Bob entered the scene, he helped expand those paths into broad thoroughfares along which a mighty throng of jazzmen now traverse.

Bob Scobey died on June 12, 1963. The passage of years has not dimmed memories of this dedicated jazzman. I remember the crisp sound of his horn, his abiding commitment to jazz's history, and that strong determination to achieve a respectful status for the music he loved.

He attained his goal.

Dave Dexter, Jr.

In 1945, producer Dave Dexter, Jr., supervised a historic recording date in Los Angeles for Eddy Laguna's Sunset label. It was unusual then for a group of Dixieland musicians to gather in a Hollywood recording studio; such bands simply did not exist during that swing-crazed era.

Dexter gathered several studio and dance-band musicians and let them record the spirited jazz they loved. These were the first recordings by Pete Daily and his Chicagoans—and they were a huge success. Here, at last, was a small band playing the traditional New Orleans–style music long overlooked by the record firms. The appearance of "Redlight Rag" and "Sugarfoot Strut" made it apparent that the faded sounds of the pre-swing era were poised to make a comeback.

"In these days of phoney re-bop [*sic*] music," wrote Peter Tanner, reviewing the disc for the English monthly *Jazz Music*, "it is a pleasure to welcome the reappearance of Pete Daily and the others he gathered around him for this session. Music such as this will live on long after most of today's so-called jazz has been forgotten, and long after swing has reaped its last bop."

A few years later, after becoming an executive director at Capitol Records, Dexter reminisced about that first Pete Daily recording date. "We were very lucky," he said. "There was an old mandolin-style piano in the studio's hallway. Freddy Slack used it a few weeks before for some barrelhouse effects he wanted on a record date. It was slightly out of tune, but we brought it into the studio, and Don Owens played it during the session. I think that sound had something to do with the success of those records."

Dexter, a former editor of *Down Beat* and *Music & Rhythm* magazines, covered the music scenes in Kansas City, Chicago, New York, and Hollywood as an editor, writer, and radio commentator. He was born in Kansas City in 1915 and served his apprenticeship writing about jazz in the local press. His pioneer reporting documented the early careers of Bennie Moten, Count Basie, Joe Turner, Mary Lou Williams, Pete Johnson, Jay McShan, and Andy Kirk's Clouds of Joy.

In the early 1940s, while working for *Down Beat,* he became an early champion of what was probably the big-band era's most revolutionary group—the Stan Kenton Orchestra. Dexter lauded the "Artistry in Rhythm" band in his regular column and had such confidence in Kenton that, he once told me, he loaned the bandleader money to meet his payroll during a slow period.

In 1942, disc jockey Al Jarvis began praising the band daily. His frequent airing of the band's few daring radio transcriptions resulted in several local one-night stands for the new orchestra.

I was among a small cult of loyal supporters who followed the dedicated young musicians to their first major booking at the Rendezvous Ballroom in Balboa, California. Nightly radio broadcasts hosted by Jimmy Lyons lured an enthusiastic college crowd.

After joining newly organized Capitol Records, Dexter urged the company to sign the pioneer of progressive jazz to a long contract and produced a succession of records that firmly established the orchestra's reputation.

Dexter worked the same wonders for Pete Daily's career. After the memorable 1945 recording session that launched the Chicagoans, Daily's little band began a lengthy tenure at the Hangover Club in Hollywood. Live Dixieland jazz gradually emerged from a decade of hibernation. Daily continued to lead the two-beat revival with a series of recordings released on the Jump and Jazz Man labels. In June 1949, Capitol Records quietly issued Pete's version of Bennie Moten's "South," dressed in a jaunty Rosy McHargue arrangement. Within a few months, without any fanfare, the record sold more than a hundred thousand copies, and sales continued soaring through the balance of the year. For the first time, a Dixieland band headed the *Billboard* record charts.

Encouraged by this success, Dave Dexter produced a string of recordings that helped establish Pete Daily as a permanent fixture in the world of traditional jazz. During the '50s, Daily was so important to Capitol Records' sales figures that the company issued his albums simultaneously in all three formats—78, 45, and 33⅓ rpm.

Dave Dexter's crowning achievement was *The History of Jazz,* a series of four 78 rpm albums he produced for Capitol Records in 1944. He conceived the idea, assembled the impressive array of musicians, and personally supervised the entire project. To this day, those great recordings remain among the most ambitious anthologies of jazz history. Twenty years later Dexter wrote *The Jazz Story—From the '90s to the '60s* (Prentice Hall, 1964). It remains among the most valuable jazz reference books available.

In 1955 a European conglomerate bought a controlling interest in Capitol Records. Eventually this label released the Beatles' huge-selling albums in the United States. Based on the success of this phenomenal group, Capitol reduced its emphasis on jazz, and Dexter was relegated to lesser roles and eventually fired. The respected writer-producer spent his last years depressed and frustrated. His personal life deteriorated, a young son died, and his health failed. Unable to obtain employment in the record industry, he acquired a menial job in *Daily Variety*'s shipping room.

When I called the last time, Dave was no longer there. His home phone had been disconnected. He became a bitter recluse, and I never saw him again. When he died, no news organization reported this information. In an attempt to confirm the exact date of his death, I checked the personnel files of Capitol Records, *Down Beat* magazine, and *Daily Variety*. His name did not appear in their files, and no one in those organizations had ever heard of Dave Dexter, Jr. When I posted a query on the Internet, Jeff Atterton of Riverdale, New York, advised me that Dexter died in Sherman Oaks, California, on April 19, 1990, at the age of seventy-four.

Dexter, an unsung hero of the revival era, deserved better. At a time when big-band jazz dominated the record business, Dexter played a hunch that traditional jazz still had an audience. His gamble paid off—and jazz fans the world over shared in the jackpot.

Unfortunately, until now, his great contribution to jazz has never been properly acknowledged. Among the many books written about jazz history, Dexter is mentioned briefly in only a few. Hopefully these words will partially correct that serious oversight.

The Poor Angel Hot Jazz Society

The Poor Angel Hot Jazz Society was one of Southern California's best-kept secrets. It was not a society in the true sense; there were no officers, no board of directors, no charter. Rather, it was the personal domain of a dedicated man determined to showcase the tremendous jazz talent in the Los Angeles area.

For almost two decades, Bob Taber charted the course of the PAHJS with a series of jazz dinner-concerts. The fee was modest, the food was tolerable—and the music was always exemplary. This was strictly a no-frills operation. There was very little promotion—only a brief announcement mailed to Taber's regulars. The letterhead was a line drawing by his granddaughter of a threadbare trumpet-blowing angel in flight.

Beginning in 1973, Taber produced eighty-two programs. In his words, "Some were great, some were not quite great, some showed a profit, and some were in the red." The bimonthly events created work for fine musicians and provided wonderful evenings of jazz entertainment for a small but loyal coterie of patrons. Taber's motto was: "Take a young person out to hear some real live jazz."

The initial Poor Angel concert, held on June 16, 1973, starred clarinetist Barney Bigard with Dick Cary, Bob Havens, Ray Leatherwood, Marvin Ash, Nick Fatool, and vocalist Marge Murphy. The $10 admission charge included a chicken dinner. Over the years, the Poor Angel Hot Jazz Society sessions featured a total of 130 different musicians, including many of the best in the nation. Matty Matlock, Eddie Miller, Abe Lincoln, Peanuts Hucko, Joe Darensbourg, Red Callender, Dan Barrett, Babe Russin, and Johnny Guarnieri were among the participants. In an interview just before the final Poor Angel concert, I asked Taber to name the most prominent musicians he had had over the years.

> I guess I used Eddie Miller and Nick Fatool more than any others. Except Barney Bigard, the biggest name I've had is Bud Freeman, which was about eight years ago. Bud was visiting in town. I contacted him, and he said yes. He said he would come as a guest artist and play a couple of numbers or, perhaps, a set.
>
> Dick Cathcart was the leader that night. When the band started, Bud was in the hall standing back at the bar. By the time they were sixteen bars into the tune, he was opening his sax case. He ran up on the stand and joined the last half of the first number—and remained on the stand throughout the evening. Although Dick was supposedly the leader, believe me, when Bud Freeman is within a couple of miles of you, Bud Freeman is the leader! It was a wonderful session, and I really enjoyed having him.

Bud Freeman created the musical vocabulary for several generations of sax players. During the '30s, his rolling tenor sax style added impetus to Tommy Dorsey's Clambake Seven, Benny Goodman's orchestra, and Freeman's own Summa Cum Laude Orchestra. In recent years, he had been touring with the World's Greatest Jazz Band, sharing saxophone duties with Bob Wilber.

The Freeman session, held on January 9, 1982, at the Skytrails Restaurant in Van Nuys, California, was the thirty-eighth of the long series. A tape of the session, titled *Bud Freeman—California Session,* was eventually released on the Jazzology label (JCD277). Betty O'Hara played her valve trombone and double-bell euphonium during that memorable evening. On "'S Wonderful," blowing through her euphonium's alternate bells, she traded profound statements with herself. After her soaring solo on "Struttin' With Some Barbecue," Bud Freeman kissed Betty on the cheek. On the CD, you can hear him say, "That's the first time I've ever kissed a trombone player."

The eighty-second and final Poor Angel event took place on December 1, 1990. The double-barreled program, titled "A Farewell Bash," spotlighted a pair of bands led by Abe Most and Dick Cathcart. At the conclusion of his final concert, with a tear in his eye, Taber cut a large cake depicting a tattered angel wearing a halo and blowing a tenor saxophone. He introduced each of the participating musicians, and Betty O'Hara sang parody lyrics to "And the Angels Weep," which I had written for the occasion. Bob Taber's tenure as an unsung jazz impresario reached a momentous finale.

Record producer Dan Grant assumed the reins of the PAHJC and tried valiantly to sustain its momentum during the next few years. He reluctantly closed the curtain when continually rising costs excessively elevated the price of the dinner concerts.

The Poor Angel Hot Jazz Society created some choice moments of jazz virtuosity—all of them taped by Bob Taber. The 1982 Bud Freeman recording was the first PAHJS session to appear on a commercial label—and a hint of the valuable material remaining in Taber's collection.

Dick Cary's Tuesday Night Band

On Tuesday, April 12, 1994, a group of outstanding musicians gathered in a cluttered rehearsal room in Dick Cary's modest home in the

San Fernando Valley. Arriving individually through the rear entrance, they were warmly greeted by Linus, Cary's gentle German shepherd. The room, as usual, was a jumble of musical scores, microphone cables, and music stands. One of Cary's half-smoked cigars lay in an ashtray, and the scent of stale tobacco lingered from the previous session. The dusty piano was illuminated by a single bulb suspended on a frayed cord. A yellowing sign, probably used on a stage easel years before, hung askew on the wall behind the piano. It read: "DICK CARY AND HIS TUESDAY NIGHT FRIENDS."

As they did every Tuesday evening for the last twenty years, the "friends" chatted amicably while setting up their instruments, adjusting reeds, plugging in amplifiers, and tuning up. For the first time, though, Dick Cary was not there.

News of his death a week earlier shook the local jazz community. As press service bulletins distributed the information, the world soon learned a great jazzman had died. Undaunted by their grief, his colleagues, drawn to their familiar Tuesday evening haunt, came to rehearse as usual. I also succumbed to an inexplicable urge to be there.

These were Los Angeles' most esteemed professional musicians, several of them leaders of their own groups. Some came after completing a day's work at film or television studios. Gene Estes took several trips to carry his drums in from his van, then assembled his kit near the rehearsal room door. Putter Smith stood next to Gene, adjusting the bridge of his string bass. Tommy Newsom, famous as Doc Severinsen's first lieutenant in the *Tonight Show* orchestra, set up a clarinet, a tenor sax, and a soprano sax on the rack next to his music stand. He was flanked by another former *Tonight Show* bandsman, sax and clarinet player John Bambridge, and baritone sax specialist David Angel.

Clarinetist Abe Most, acclaimed for sterling performances on the renowned Time-Life re-creation series, sat next to the drums. Roger Newman, on tenor sax, was across the room, facing the rest of the million-dollar reed section. Betty O'Hara unpacked her trumpet and sat between Newman and the piano. Trombonist Ernie Tack, another *Tonight Show* veteran, was seated against the wall opposite guitarist David Koonse. Dick Hamilton, termed "the genius" by Cary, formerly played one of the trombone parts. This time he sat in the leader's piano chair and placed his trumpet on the adjacent stand.

On several previous visits, I watched Cary gracefully shifting from the piano keyboard to the trumpet he held in his lap. He played an important part in the band's rhythmic conception and bolstered the ro-

Dick Cary.

bust quality of the brass section. Hamilton, also a multitalented musician, was the ideal successor for the important role Cary played in the orchestra.

The musicians located their folios from among the sixteen hundred tunes Cary composed and/or arranged for the group. They welcomed the opportunity to play Dick's intricate arrangements that challenged their reading and technical skills. Everything was ready. Linus settled beside Abe Most, and I found a stool next to Putter Smith. Dick Hamilton counted off the beat. The first tune filled the room.

Fittingly, it was "Ring Dem Bells," written in 1930 by Duke Ellington, one of Cary's favorite composers. Later in the evening, Cary's old friends played his arrangements of Duke's "Jumpin' Pumpkins" and "Raincheck." Except for one Horace Silver tune, the lovely "Summer in Central Park," the balance of the rehearsal featured Dick's original compositions. "Caprice," apparently receiving its first run-through, was intricately dressed in a Latin beat. "Back Door" featured the rich sounds of the powerful reeds. "Play-off" was scored for ensemble all the way. "Acorn Street" (later renamed "Bud") was dedicated to famed saxophonist Bud Freeman, with whom Cary wrote the tune years before.

Although their erstwhile leader was missing, his presence dominated every moment. Each note, every chord, was faithful to Cary's elaborate score. Hamilton carefully counted off every beat in the exact tempo Dick would have preferred. The tones floated through the open window and warmed the neighborhood with happy music.

They were still playing when I departed.

Dick Cary was born to create music. At the age of eleven he was already playing violin with the Hartford Symphony Orchestra. He spent three years in prep school, attended Wesleyan University in Middletown, Connecticut, and was soon brightening the New York Jazz scene as a solo pianist at Nick's in 1942.

His many compositions have been performed by jazz combos, big bands, and symphony orchestras throughout the world. He wrote for Jean Goldkette and Benny Goodman and played with the famed Casa Loma Orchestra. If the band was short in the brass department, Cary hauled out his large F-trumpet or the battered GI-issue alto horn he had picked up during World War II.

A prolific recording artist, he played with Joe Marsala, Muggsy Spanier, Wild Bill Davison, Billy Butterfield, Eddie Condon, Bud Freeman, Bobby Hackett, Pee Wee Russell, and other leading jazz musicians. In 1947 he served briefly as the original pianist with the Louis Armstrong All-Stars.

Cary moved to Southern California in 1959 and recorded extensively in Hollywood. Producers of popular, classical, Latin, country-western, and Dixieland records eagerly sought his talents. He wrote orchestral libraries for five different rehearsal bands, each with several hundred arrangements. His annual bill for manuscript paper exceeded his budget for the numerous cigars he smoked. An avid sports enthusiast, Cary used to sit in a deep, well-worn chair and write harmonies for a twelve-piece band while watching a baseball game on television. There was no piano in the room, but he occasionally reached for his trumpet (which he kept on the floor beside him) to confirm a note or phrase.

"Writing is a very therapeutic experience for me," he said when I interviewed him in 1991. "I don't drink any more or do lots of things I used to. What else is there? It's very fulfilling—and it seems to satisfy the musicians I have a great respect for."

Cary possessed an encyclopedic memory and savored the controversial or shocking exploits of famous jazzmen—stories that could never appear in print. Asked what he considered his greatest accomplishment, he replied: "I think it was to have known all those wonderful people as well as I did. Eddie Condon, for instance, and Louis Armstrong, and Jack Teagarden, and Barney [Bigard], and Rex [Stewart], and ... oh, all those people who played that kind of music."

Although he never achieved tremendous fame, Dick was not resentful of those who did. "I am very lucky," he said. "I think I might not have the type of mentality to stand being a star—whatever that is. But I don't envy anybody who's always in the limelight wherever he goes. I think that must be a pain in the ass."

When not appearing at worldwide jazz events, Cary played regularly with Bob Ringwald's Great Pacific Jazz Band, often wearing one of the loud Hawaiian shirts he favored. If the ensembles sounded particularly hardy, it was because Cary was usually blowing one of his horns from the piano bench.

The Tuesday night rehearsal band was his greatest pride. Each week, the all-star orchestra played Cary's original tunes and his arrangements of lesser-known songs by Duke Ellington and Bix Beiderbecke, his two favorite composers. During each rehearsal, the band brought to life four or more charts Cary had created during the previous week. The music was seldom heard by an audience; those attending the 1990 Los Angeles Classic Jazz Festival had the rare opportunity to hear this great orchestra. Fortunately, Cary recorded some of the Tuesday-night sessions on the huge console that filled one end of the rehearsal room. Arbors Records issued those recordings on a CD. Titled *Dick Cary and His Tuesday Night Friends Playing Dick Cary Originals* (ARCD 19132), it vividly captures some magic moments.

Jim Turner, Cary's long-time student, friend, and confidant, has become a dedicated curator of the mountain of scores and manuscripts Dick Cary left behind. The various documents, totaling three thousand arrangements, have been carefully sorted, collated, and preserved in special indexed cartons. The handsomely refurbished rehearsal room now serves as a modern recording studio; Turner produced a CD featuring the current Tuesday Night Band that has been released on the Klavier label.

When I toured the rejuvenated site with Turner, he said: "At the time of his death, Dick Cary led the best rehearsal band in Los Angeles—perhaps anywhere. It was, and still is, an institution."

The weekly rehearsals continue under Dick Hamilton's leadership. Cary's library contains sufficient material to occupy those sessions for years to come.

UNSUNG HEROES

In every art form, there are many contributors who, regardless of their skills, never achieve proper recognition. This unfortunate disparity between talent and reward is especially prevalent in the music business. For every big-name player who enjoys popular acclaim and lofty financial gain, there are hundreds of musicians working in the trenches who are just as dedicated to their art—and often are just as proficient. Indeed, top-ranking stars often gain favor despite being less talented than hundreds of unheralded contemporaries.

Stories about the unsung heroes of jazz could easily fill a large book. Here are just a few whose uncompromising dedication and creativity has brought infinite enjoyment to me and many others.

Pete Daily

In the 1951 film *Pete Kelly's Blues,* Jack Webb portrays a jazz bandleader and cornetist in Prohibition-era Chicago. While watching Webb's character on the screen, some in the audience might have noted striking similarities with a real-life figure: bandleader Pete Daily. Webb and his writers spent many evenings in the old Hangover Club studying the horn player's style and mannerisms, and the film's storyline was based on segments of Daily's career.

Trumpeter Pete Daily served as the model for the title character in the film Pete Kelly's Blues.

Webb was seen in the picture, but young Dick Cathcart recorded the brilliant cornet soundtrack. The band also included Matty Matlock on clarinet, Moe Schneider on trombone, Ray Sherman on piano, George Van Eps on guitar, Jud DeNaut on bass, and Nick Fatool on drums. Pete Kelly's Big Seven, as featured in the film, landed a Capitol recording contract and appeared at the 1951 Dixieland Jubilee just ahead of Pete Daily's Chicagoans. Few in the large audience realized the film character, Pete Kelly, was inspired by the cornetist that followed the Big Seven on the program.

In 1948, when Los Angeles disc jockeys Gene Norman and Frank Bull launched their successful "Dixieland Jubilee" at the Pan Pacific Auditorium, Pete played before the largest audience of his career. The initial event featured such giants as Louis Armstrong's All-Stars, Kid Ory's Creole Jazz Band, Wingy Manone's band, and a Condon group with Wild Bill Davison. Amid such stellar attractions, The Chicagoans received the longest standing ovation.

At the following year's Dixieland Jubilee, held in the sprawling Shrine Auditorium, six thousand fans watched as seventy-five players filled the huge stage for the finale, a spirited rendition of "Muskrat Ramble." Daily, playing a tiny slide trumpet, stood in the trombone section alongside Kid Ory, King Jackson, Irving Varette, Warren Smith, Ward Kimball, Lou McGarity, Joe Yukl, and George Phillips. Daily's was the only band that appeared in all thirteen Dixieland Jubilees.

Thaman Pierce Daily was born in Portland, Indiana, on May 5, 1911. His family moved to Muncie, Indiana, and then to nearby Gary. When Pete was nine years old, he had a single cornet lesson in grade school. He switched to baritone horn when he entered high school.

His first professional job was with Jack Davies' Kentuckians at the College Inn in Calumet City, Illinois. During the 1930s he worked with bands led by Art Van Damme, Bud Freeman, Boyce Brown, and Wild Bill Davison. He made his first records with the Kentuckians on December 8, 1930.

After working in small bands in Chicago for several years, Daily came to California in 1942, played with trombonist Mike Riley at the Radio Room on Vine Street, and soon joined Ozzie Nelson's orchestra. After World War II he assembled a group of Chicago colleagues, and Pete Daily and His Chicagoans were born. The band opened at the Brass Rail in Glendale before launching an extended engagement at the Hangover in Hollywood.

An interesting event occurred during Pete's 1951 engagement at the Royal Room in Hollywood. Harry Hermalin, a local sign painter and devoted patron of the establishment, offered to paint an oil portrait of Pete for the club. In exchange, the owner was asked to pay the cost of materials and provide him with free drinks.

The proprietor, Abe Bush, sensed the publicity value of the project and agreed to Hermalin's terms. Advanced news regarding the official unveiling of the finished portrait appeared in the club's advertisements. During a regular Sunday afternoon jam session, the participating musicians formed a jazz parade down Hollywood Boulevard to ballyhoo the unveiling. They returned, leading scores of patrons back into the club.

A ceremonious removal of the velvet drape exposed the large painting. The perspective was somewhat amiss, and the central figure bore only a slight resemblance to the cornetist. But the appreciative crowd applauded briskly and Harry Hermalin rose from his bar stool to graciously accept their plaudits. The jam session resumed and continued into the night.

The story of the portrait and the parade appeared in Monday's editions of the Los Angeles papers. Their photographers captured many of the parade musicians playing in front of the Royal Room—as Abe Bush had anticipated.

There have been various stories about Pete Daily's rusty old Holton cornet. Before World War II, he paid $15 for the used horn and carried it with him around the world during his service years. By 1975, the battered relic leaked air and would not stay in tune. At a Southern California Hot Jazz Society board meeting, we decided to raise the money to purchase another instrument for him.

As president, I wrote a letter to the Holton Company mentioning the poor condition of Daily's cornet (Serial No. 23434) and requested a price for a new horn. I received a prompt response from Vito Pascucci, head of The Holton Company, then a division of G. Leblanc Corporation, in Kenosha, Wisconsin. He expressed amazement that the 1913 model was still in service, and added some wonderful news. A new cornet, with Pete's name engraved on the bell, would be shipped in a few days—with his compliments!

During a dramatic segment of the Jazz Society's monthly session in December 1975, I had the privilege of presenting Pete with the shiny new horn we received from Mr. Pascucci. In a later conversation, Pascucci said that the Holton Company expected absolutely no publicity and they were proud Pete Daily played their instrument for so many years. After more than two decades, this gesture of corporate generosity is finally being disclosed.

In my files, a handwritten letter from Pete thanking me for obtaining the horn concludes: "It means more to me than I can say! I hope the horn and I will be able to return to all of you a small part of the pleasure you have given to me."

Pete's music brought joy to thousands throughout his career. Ironically, pain and misfortune played a prominent role in his own life. It seemed that fate always dealt him a bad hand. The final blow occurred in July 1979. After playing a benefit for the Valley Presbyterian Hospital, he suffered a massive stroke and remained partially paralyzed and almost speechless for the rest of his life. Despite confinement to a wheelchair, he had an indomitable spirit. Daily continued listening to music and enjoyed being with friends and fans. He always acknowledged a greeting with a big smile, a thumb pointed skyward, a sly wink, and the only words he could say: "I O.K.!"

Pete Daily died on Saturday, August 23, 1986. The memory of his boyish smile and the robust, biting tones emerging from the bell of his cornet will always linger in the hearts and minds of fans and musicians who admired his style.

Writer-musician K. O. Eckland, in his tender eulogy published in the August 1986 issue of *And All That Jazz,* said: "Pete Daily's gone—but is he forgotten? No man is ever really forgotten until the last person who remembers him dies. In Pete's case, that will be a long, long time."

Stew Pletcher

During World War II, I worked at a Douglas Aircraft production plant in Santa Monica, California. Each day, when weather permitted, factory personnel entertained during lunch period in the outdoor "Punch Bowl." About once a week a jazz band performed, and one member of the group, the trumpet player, stood head and shoulders above the rest. I found myself looking forward to hearing his distinctive horn—a sound I have never forgotten.

One day the trumpeter casually mentioned that he had worked with several famous bands, including ones led by Smith Ballew, Irving Aaronson, and Red Norvo. Frankly, I was skeptical. I owned an early edition of Charles Delaunay's *Hot Discography,* and I decided to see whether there was any truth to my co-worker's boast. Sure enough, there, in a book that documented the work of America's best-known musicians, was the name of Douglas Aircraft's lunch-hour horn man: Stew Pletcher. The book credited him with recordings on the QRS, Okeh, and Columbia labels; some were made while he was still a student at Yale University.

Pletcher used to carry his instrument to work in a brown paper sack with his lunch. He would quickly gulp down his sandwich, then climb on the bandstand to play a few numbers before the factory whistle summoned us back to the assembly line. His warm tone was ideally suited to the sentimental ballads so popular at the time. When muted, his horn projected a crisp metallic beauty that accented the purity of his improvisations. He often repeated a phrase several times but always altered a note or injected a subtle inflection. The effect was delightful. The Punch Bowl band usually finished with a rousing uptempo tune such as "Panama" or "Royal Garden Blues." For the rest of the afternoon, as a "production control expeditor," while searching for an elusive hydraulic fitting or sheet-metal screw, I could still hear Stew's tender and torrid sounds reverberating in my mind.

Whenever the opportunity arose, I would ask him about his background. He always seemed anxious to talk about "the old days."

> I replaced Bunny Berigan when he left Red Norvo's band back in 1935. Red soon took us into the Famous Door on Fifty-Second Street in New York. It was a small combo—Red on xylophone, Herbie Haymer on sax, Eddie Sauter played mellophone, and Dave Barbour was the guitarist. Red occasionally doubled on piano. People don't realize that he was a fine pianist; he made some very good piano solo recordings during that period.
>
> Eddie Sauter, who later wrote for Benny Goodman, made some wonderful arrangements for Red's band. Eddie played second trumpet and wrote very advanced scores—we recorded many of them. They were harmonized riffs for trumpet, clarinet, and sax, an unusual voicing in those days. I think Eddie's best arrangement was "Remember," an old Irving Berlin ballad. He also arranged "Rockin' Chair" for Mildred Bailey [Norvo's wife]—one of her greatest recordings. I'm sure you've heard it.
>
> The band could swing, but it never was loud. I used a felt fedora to get a softer sound. Hank D'Amico played clarinet with us—a fine musician. I think he's overseas now. He played with Bob Crosby before the war. I'll always remember the wonderful work he did on "Smoke Rings"—sort of noodling behind Mildred's vocal. I enjoyed hearing that every night.

Probably because of a contractual arrangement Norvo had with the Decca Company, Stew Pletcher was designated leader on several recordings the Famous Door band made for the Bluebird label. Among those 1936 releases was an Armstrong-inspired "I Hope Gabriel Likes My Music." Pletcher's strong admiration for Armstrong's genius literally floats from the grooves of those old 78 rpm disks.

Later in 1936, Red Norvo was offered an engagement with a full band at the Hotel Commodore. He took Pletcher, Berigan, Haymer, and Sauter with him. "Herbie Haymer played tenor sax and wrote some harmony for the reeds," Pletcher recalled. "The last I heard, he was playing with a Navy band some place in the Pacific."

With Stew Pletcher leading the way on trumpet, the Red Norvo Orchestra made a series of innovative recordings on Brunswick Records. Norvo's smooth approach to swing provided a welcomed contrast to the ebullient sounds of his contemporaries. Booked as "Mr. and Mrs. Swing," Norvo and Bailey contributed greatly to the big-band era.

I lost contact with Pletcher after the war; we did not meet again for about seven years. Then, during the 1952 Dixieland Jubilee at Los Angeles' huge Shrine Auditorium, I immediately recognized him playing in Nappy Lamare's Straw Hatters Jazz Band. Stew was playing a stronger lead than I remembered from the Punch Bowl days. The band received a rousing ovation.

We renewed our friendship backstage after the concert, and Pletcher invited Lucille and me to Sardi's, where the band was opening the following week. This very posh club on Hollywood Boulevard, just a few feet west of Vine Street, was the site of the popular daily radio program, *Breakfast at Sardi's*. We spent many memorable evenings there sipping our fifty-cent beers and listening to this wonderful band. Lamare happily strummed his guitar with a group of fine musicians resplendent in red-striped blazers, white trousers, bow ties, and straw hats. By today's standards this might sound hackneyed, but in the days just after World War II we welcomed any sign of frivolity that would help brighten the dark memories of the previous years.

My collection includes some old records by the Lamare band on Gene Norman's Dixieland Jubilee label. The session included most of the musicians who had entertained us at Sardi's: Stew Pletcher on trumpet, Pud Brown on tenor sax, and Brad Gowans blowing his unorthodox valve trombone, with a slide he activated when glissandi were needed. Clarinetist Johnny Costello, who recorded in the '20s with Bailey's Lucky Seven and the Original Indiana Five, completed the front line. New Orleans drummer Zutty Singleton added an authentic flavor to the rhythm section, which included Bud Hatch on tuba, Harry Gillingham on piano, and Nappy Lamare playing banjo and guitar and singing the vocals.

The tunes recorded by this tight little band for Dixieland Jubilee were: "After You've Gone," "Palestina," "Black and White Rag," and "Johnson Rag." The records are probably very difficult to locate today; to my knowledge, they have never been issued on LP or CD.

Sardi's, like most jazz spots of the 1950s, closed after a few years. A moviehouse soon occupied the site; today it features porno films. Stew Pletcher also faded from view. Very few remember him today; his name appears only briefly in a few reference books, and his old records are hard to find. Those fortunate enough to own his recordings can still enjoy Pletcher's brisk, straight-ahead trumpet style and the solos he played with such sincerity and taste.

It is not generally known, but Stew Pletcher was also a poet. My files include some of his articulate verses, given to me by his son, Tom Pletcher, an exemplary cornetist devoted to the mellow style of Bix Beiderbecke. Tom's authentic horn graces the wonderful soundtrack of the 1990 film *Bix: An Interpretation of a Legend.*

Years ago, when a new seafood restaurant, the Oasis, opened in Los Angeles, it offered a prize for the best limerick submitted. Stew penned these words of poetic wisdom (which did not win the prize):

> The slob who's never been to the Oasis
> Just doesn't know the end on which his face is!
> For piscatorial pleasure
> And luscious seafood treasure
> No other joint compares with how this place is!

He also wrote his own epitaph:

> When you think of me, please think of laughter
> This I would like in my hereafter
> To those who, since my folks begat me
> Chose to laugh *with,* and not *at* me,
> Happy giggles to you all
> Thus—let the final curtain fall.

Stew was seventy-one when he died on November 29, 1978. Those of us fortunate enough to have known Stew Pletcher remember an amiable, warm-hearted individual.

Sammy Lee

Saxophonist Sammy Lee appeared in every edition of "A Night in New Orleans," the jazz concert series I produced with Barry Martyn during the 1970s. His performances never failed to excite the crowd, but it was his exuberant personality as much as his playing that produced this response. He could enter a room filled with strangers, roar an unintelligible greeting—"Ya!-Wa!-Wow!-Wow!"—and within minutes have everyone relaxed and laughing. He had the unique ability to exude warmth and love to a group of any size. I have seen him enchant a handful of friends in my home during private parties—and watched two thousand fans wildly cheering him in Berlin's staid Philharmonie Halle.

His affable spirit could quickly transcend any language barrier. One night, after a long bus ride over the Alps during one of our "Night in New Orleans" tours, I found Sammy in the hotel lounge long after the rest of the musicians had retired. He was having an animated conver-

Sammy Lee's trademark song "Hi! Ho! Silver!" was a perennial favorite among "A Night in New Orleans" audiences.

sation with a dozen Italian tourists, who were completely captivated. None of them spoke English, and Lee could not speak or understand Italian, yet the room bristled with laughter. The next morning, when he climbed on the bus with us, his new friends were waiting to wish him a fond farewell, complete with tears and enthusiastic embraces.

Sammy always wore two wristwatches during our European tours. His explanation: "One is on Los Angeles time, so I knew when to go to the bathroom." Typically, he had a simple solution to a familiar tourist dilemma.

On stage, his trademark tune was the boisterous "Hi! Ho! Silver!" adapted from an old Joe Turner blues. Waving a white handkerchief wildly and thrusting his saxophone between his legs to simulate a jockey in the final stretch, he joyously sang the inane lyrics ("Yak! Yak! Yak-ity Yak!"), then leaped from the stage and surged through the audience, playing chorus after chorus. He encouraged listeners to press his octave key, causing a squealing sound that provoked roars of laughter. His fans never tired of witnessing this unforgettable performance—and he never tired of giving it.

Lee was at his best during an ill-fated New York concert. Our local agent had failed to advertise the event properly, and when the show started the RFK Theater was almost empty. We were without air conditioning, box-office attendants, ushers, a curtain, or a sound system. It was a disaster. But Sammy ignored the negative situation and did his usual thing—and he was brilliant. John Wilson's *New York Times* review overlooked the problems and praised Lee's "hard, grainy tone—like Coleman Hawkins."

Sammy Lee was born on February 15, 1911, in Napoleonville, Louisiana, about seventy miles from New Orleans. His family moved to the Crescent City when he was a young boy, and he began his musical career at the age of nine playing the violin to accompany his uncle, guitarist Dave Ross, a blind street musician. The only formal musical training he received was from Emanuel Sayles and David Jones, who ran a music school in New Orleans.

When he was fifteen years old, Lee's teachers bought him a saxophone to play in the Cloverland Dairy Band. He was hired by Andrew Morgan and joined the popular orchestra at a jitney dance hall on Iberville Street. Soon he was appearing with bands led by Bebe Ridgley, Oscar "Papa" Celestin, Sidney Desvigne, and Henry Allen, Sr. He became a member of Cap'n John Handy's Louisiana Shakers in the early '30s. Later, with his own trio, the Sammy Lee Footwarmers, he entertained Bourbon Street revelers with a circular breathing technique and acquired the nickname "Hold-That-Note Lee."

I met Lee shortly after he moved to Los Angeles in 1952. He attended several Southern California Hot Jazz Society monthly sessions and quickly assumed a vital role in the local jazz scene. During frequent performances with fellow New Orleanians Barney Bigard, Joe Darensbourg. Mike Delay, Al Morgan, Johnny St. Cyr, Alton Purnell, Ed Garland, and Teddy Edwards, Lee inevitably got requests for "Hi! Ho! Silver!" His illustrious colleagues happily played the elongated vamp while Sammy spread joy through Larchmont Hall.

Few fans were aware of Sammy's serious side. He was devoted to the children in his neighborhood and made every effort to interest them in music and church activities instead of drugs and gangs. Often, when I visited, I would find him with several youngsters sitting on his front porch of his small house. Drawing from his own childhood experiences on the streets of New Orleans, he beguiled them with his wisdom and whimsy. A very religious man, he was the deacon of the

Greater Cornerstone Baptist Church in Los Angeles. He did not drink or swear. Despite his carefree facade, he felt deeply about music and friends.

When Barney Bigard died, it was my sad chore to deliver the eulogy at the funeral. With pianist Bruce MacDonald's tape of Barney's beautiful clarinet solos playing softly in the background, I looked over the podium and saw tears streaming down Sammy's face. When pianist Alton Purnell's health was failing, Sammy rallied to his support and participated in the campaign to raise money for his friend.

Although he spent the last forty years in Los Angeles, he never relinquished his ties with New Orleans. He and Lady, his beloved wife for six decades, went home for Mardi Gras each year, returning to Los Angeles with colorful parade beads. For several years, Sammy was a featured artist at the annual Festa New Orleans Music in Ascona, Switzerland. Frequent tours as a guest artist with leading European jazz bands created a multitude of dedicated fans in England, Belgium, Switzerland, Italy, and Holland.

My last meeting with Sammy was on May 19, 1990, when I conducted an oral history interview for Tulane University's Hogan Jazz Archive. It was only a few weeks before he died. He was very weak, and his voice lacked the vigor of the past. His mind was agile, and he recounted events that took place seventy years earlier. As I left, he smiled, held my hand, and said: "Floyd, you don't know how bad you can feel until you're sick."

When he died in July 1990, it took a while before I stopped watching the door expecting him to burst in with his joyous "Ya!-Wa!-Wow!-Wow!" My memories of him provide a warm glow that continues to brighten my life.

Pud Brown

Albert "Pud" Brown was just thirty-two years old when he came to Los Angeles, but by then he'd already spent more than a quarter-century in the music business. Born in Wilmington, Delaware, in 1917, he came from a musical family; his mother, father, and four siblings were all talented musicians. They traveled together throughout the country in a large truck with built-in living quarters and a portable stage at the rear. Pud joined the Brown Family Band at the age of five, publicized as "The World's Youngest Saxophone Virtuoso." Over a period of ten years the band eventually played in every state in the nation and portions of Canada and Mexico. "That old bus racked up more than six hundred thousand miles before the cable on the mileage indicator broke!" he remembered many years later.

The Brown Family Band finally gave up touring in 1933 and settled in Shreveport, Louisiana. Pud, still a teenager, continued traveling, playing the vaudeville circuit with small groups. He also worked with territory bands and pit orchestras, becoming a seasoned professional musician at an age when most jazzmen were just starting out.

Brown was a fine mechanic, which made it easier for him to find band work. Musicians usually traveled by car in the '30s, and a broken-down vehicle could keep a band from its next job—and its next paycheck. Brown, who traveled with a complete set of tools, could fix any ailing jalopy in time to make the next gig. He also claimed that, when his colleagues had dental problems, he could pull teeth.

Brown eventually moved to Chicago, where he played with Phil Lavant's band (a local favorite), Lou Breeze, Jimmy Dorsey, and Lawrence Welk. He rejoined his family in Shreveport in 1945 and spent five years operating a motorcycle shop.

In 1949 he moved to Los Angeles and resumed his musical career, becoming a familiar figure on bandstands at the Royal Room, Sardi's, the Roaring '20s, and the 400 Club. For twenty-seven years we enjoyed hearing his saxophone and clarinet (and, occasionally, cornet) in groups led by Nappy Lamare, Pete Daily, Rosy McHargue, Jack Teagarden, Teddy Buckner, and Kid Ory.

Brown's romping interpretation of the 1917 tune "Johnson Rag" became his personal musical signature. He played chorus after chorus of blues-tinged phrases, building to a dramatic tenor sax climax. His 1949 recording of the song launched Gene Norman and Frank Bull's Dixieland Jubilee label, and his 1950 version with Pete Daily became one of Capitol Records' best-selling hits.

In 1973, Brown relocated in New Orleans, blending perfectly into the city's musical landscape. Concentrating on the clarinet, he played with numerous local bands in Bourbon Street clubs. He opened with his own band at the Famous Door and soon had a permanent role in the successful play *One Mo' Time*. His recording career burgeoned when he signed with George Buck's New Orleans–based GHB label. When the new Palm Court opened on Decatur Street, Brown was featured several times a week, and fans from many parts of the world came to hear him play.

Brown lived in an apartment overlooking St. Peter Street—the same one Tennessee Williams lived in when he wrote *A Streetcar Named Desire*. An addictive collector, Brown filled the small apartment with an array of treasures—or rubble, depending upon your viewpoint. A vintage oil-dripping motorcycle, leaning against an ancient gasoline pump, dominated the main room. All horizontal surfaces were covered with instruments in need of repair, spare parts for the bicycle he used for transportation around the French Quarter, magazines, paintings, photos, used clarinet reeds, etc. There was no place to sit—every chair was heaped with Brown's "stuff." Later, when he moved to larger quarters across the river, he kept the apartment—it was impossible to move the vast volume of material.

When I learned that Pud never had a business card, I designed one for him and sent a box of one thousand as a gift. It had a handsome design of crossed clarinet and saxophone embossed on silver card stock. About a year later, he casually asked me why the card said "Alfred" instead of "Albert." Chagrined with the information about the printer's error, I promised to have them remade immediately.

"Don't bother, Floyd," Pud said. "I'll just continue crossing out the 'Alfred' and writing 'Albert' on the card."

I did send another box with the correct name. The last time I saw him, he was still using the original cards— with his handwritten correction!

Pud Brown was seventy-nine years old when he died of a sudden heart attack on May 27, 1996. I will always remember him—and I will always wonder what happened to all his "stuff."

Bob McCracken

On July 3, 1970, the Association of Southern California Jazz Clubs presented "Hello Louis!," a special concert to honor Louis Armstrong on his seventieth birthday. Every jazz musician in the country clamored for an opportunity to be a part of this historic performance—including Bob McCracken.

Tall and lean with very broad shoulders and a square jaw, McCracken didn't look like a musician. His massive hands seemed capable of destroying the delicate clarinet he played so nimbly. Audience members used to remark that he looked like a ranch hand or a small-town lawman—hence McCracken's nickname, "The Sheriff." But he was a gentle man despite his robust appearance, and he handled his horn with great tenderness.

By the time McCracken inquired about the "Hello Louis!" concert, several other clarinetists had already signed on, including Joe Darensbourg, Matty Matlock, Caughey Roberts, Max Murray, Barney Bigard, Joe Marsala and, from Paris, Maxim Saury and Claude Luter. Bill Grosvenor, our overworked director, was unable to find another spot. As the show's producer, I had the unpleasant chore of informing Bob he could not participate.

"Whatta ya mean, ya can't use me?" he drawled in response. "I spent several years traveling around the world with Pops—I've gotta be a part of that show!"

We were aware of McCracken's illustrious background and knew he emerged from the same Texas roots as his boyhood friend, Jack Teagarden. They recorded together as early as 1927. Born in Dallas in 1904, McCracken performed in Chicago and New York in a band led by Willard Robison. Over the years, he worked with Joe Venuti, Wingy Manone, Frankie Trumbauer, Bud Freeman, Jimmy McPartland and Benny Goodman. Before briefly replacing Barney Bigard in Louis Armstrong's All-Stars, he toured Europe with Kid Ory's Creole Jazz Band.

Regardless of these achievements, I could not envision a place for Bob in the crowded cast of "Hello Louis!"

Attempting to quell his ire, I explained, "Bob, you are undoubtedly one of the finest musicians in the country, but, dammit, hundreds of musicians have worked with Louis over the years—and we cannot possibly accommodate all of them in our concert!"

He persisted. Hardly a day passed without a phone call renewing his determination to be in the show. I told him we already engaged nine clarinetists to appear with five bands. How could we possibly use him? Nothing would appease McCracken who continued insisting we add his name to our long list.

Finally, Bill Grosvenor made the monumental decision that ultimately created a most memorable portion in the entire show. He decided to feature Bob in a solo spot during the Teddy Buckner sequence.

Frankly, I thought this was a mistake. Buckner and his band were re-creating the Louis Armstrong Hot Five, and a clarinet feature would greatly disturb the continuity of the show. Grosvenor prevailed, and McCracken was finally added to the roster. I was not happy with the arrangement, and Teddy Buckner also had a dim view of the situation.

The events on that exciting evening proved Bill Grosvenor's decision to be, as usual, correct—especially his compromise to spotlight the persistent clarinetist during Buckner's segment of the program. McCracken's introduction evoked only mild applause, but before he completed the first chorus of "After You've Gone," six thousand fans in the Shrine Auditorium knew something truly special was happening.

Probably inspired by the presence of "Satchmo" beaming in the wings, the Sheriff sailed through chorus after chorus, gaining momentum with each flowing phrase. The bright spotlights reflecting on his silver keys decorated the huge auditorium with lightning flashes that added to the excitement. After reaching the apogee of his solo, he burst into a final, searing chorus.

Calmly acknowledging the audience's roaring approval, McCracken slowly strode from the stage with casual nonchalance. As he passed me in the wings, he flashed an expansive grin—and thanked me.

That warm evening in Los Angeles three decades ago included some dramatic moments, but none surpassed the thrill of hearing the lanky Texan fulfilling his determined wish to say, "Hello Louis!"

He died exactly two years after the concert. Thanks to Bob's persistence and Bill Grosvenor's perception, the clarinetist's brief appearance added immeasurably to the event's success.

Pat Gogerty

Pianist Pat Gogerty never received full recognition for his astute keyboard interpretations of classical ragtime and jazz. A careful student and researcher, he scrutinized Jelly Roll Morton's fine material and enjoyed playing that master's timeless piano solos. Gogerty was particularly intrigued by the work of Joseph Lamb, an underrated ragtime pianist and one of the few white composers to achieve greatness in this predominantly African American genre.

In a series of meticulous recordings produced in 1992, Gogerty deftly interpreted Lamb's entire body of work, beginning with his first published composition in 1906. Regretfully, this privately released set of tapes did not achieve broad distribution, but it was warmly welcomed by the ragtime fraternity.

Gogerty's crowning achievement was his 1994 CD re-creation of *In Dahomey*. Like a skilled artist carefully restoring a faded Renaissance fresco, Gogerty accurately replicated the texture, color, and beauty of a

pivotal Broadway show from the ragtime era. *In Dahomey* opened in
1903 at the New York Theater, becoming the first black musical to appear in a major Manhattan site. It was staged by Bert Williams and
George Walker, the popular minstrel duo immortalized on the original
cover of Scott Joplin's "Maple Leaf Rag." The show eventually toured
Europe, popularized the cakewalk, and helped establish an international awareness of ragtime.

On the CD, the Ocotillo Orchestra, "under the baton of Patrick K.
Gogerty," is actually his resourceful work with a pair of Roland key-
boards recapturing the sound and spirit of the original theater orchestra directed by Will Marion Cook. He simulates brass, woodwinds,
strings, marimba, xylophone, tuba, percussion, and sixteen different
piano voices. The numbers credited to "chorus" are assembled from
multiple vocal tracks by Gogerty. His solo voice is expressive on several tunes. He also handled the engineering and recording on eight-
track DAT in his Palm Springs studio.

Almost a century ago, sophisticated Broadway audiences were humming those songs long after they left the theater. Gogerty revitalized
that important music on his cogent recording of *In Dahomey,* an intriguing glimpse at a significant period in American music—and an accomplishment of monumental proportions. (In his album notes,
Gogerty credits ragtime historians Ian Whitcomb and Richard Zimmerman with the discovery of the show's original music in a London
warehouse scheduled for demolition.)

Pat Gogerty died of a respiratory ailment at 2:30 A.M. on Friday,
April 5, 1997. He was sixty-one years old.

Rick Fay

Rick Fay's fans agree that he was a Jack-of-all-reeds—and a master of
them all. His tenor sax was rich and sonorous. He was lyrically expressive on the soprano sax, and his mellow clarinet was soul warming.
Fay was also a romantic crooner, a poet, a skilled comedian, and a virtuoso on the "teenie weenie whistle."

"I can trace my interest in jazz clarinet back to my high school days
in Chicago when I heard a great Duke Ellington record," he told me in
an interview. "It was 'I Don't Know What Kind of Blues I've Got.' Barney Bigard played an elegant clarinet solo before and after Herb Jeffries' vocal. First there were mellow low tones, and later he was soar-

ing beautifully in the upper register. A few weeks later, a friend loaned me an old metal clarinet, and I began working on that lovely solo. I guess I had a knack for it, because after a few days I could play the whole thing."

That was Rick Fay's response to my first question during an interview on March 22, 1998, after the International March of Jazz Party in Clearwater Beach, Florida. He was seventy-one years old, and, with his supportive wife, Becky, applauding in the front row, he played magnificently during the four-day event despite the severe illness he discussed candidly during our interview.

He told me that, after mastering the Bigard solo, he took a few lessons, practiced with fellow students, and was soon getting calls to play in local social clubs and barrooms. At nineteen he joined the Musicians Union and embarked on a lifelong career as a professional jazzman.

Richard Melvin Fay was born in Evanston, Illinois, on Christmas Day 1926. His mother, Romelle, was a veteran pianist and organist accompanying network radio soap operas that originated in Chicago. She was from Davenport, Iowa, and had attended Davenport High School a few grades behind Bix Beiderbecke. Romelle recognized Beiderbecke's early skills and accompanied him on his first local jobs. They often relieved pianists at silent film theaters and improvised music to match the action on the screen.

When Rick's mother followed the radio industry to Los Angeles, he soon became part of the local jazz scene. In 1966, while playing in Nick Pelico's band with Matty Matlock and Jackie Coon at the Gaslight Club, Fay met a patron, Mat Domber, a New York attorney who frequently came to Los Angeles on business. "Mat had a fondness for reed players," Fay later recalled. "Although he was a lawyer, he had the ear of a musician. We shared an admiration for Sidney Bechet, Pee Wee Russell, Muggsy Spanier, and the Eddie Condon players. We were two peas in a musical pod. He was like a brother I never had. When the Gaslight Club closed, Mat and I kept in touch, exchanging letters, tapes, and holiday greetings."

In 1976, after spending a decade as a musician at Disneyland, Rick was transferred to Disney's new facility in Orlando, Florida. It so happened that Domber also moved his operation to Florida, and he found Fay playing at Disney's Grand Floridian Hotel and leading his own band at a nearby tavern.

"Mat and his wife Rachel liked the group and asked if we had made any records," Fay remembered. "When I said no, he offered to sponsor the project. So, on September 25, 1989, at the age of sixty-three, I took my band into Lone Pine Studios in Orlando and made my first record as a leader."

The release, *Rick Fay's Hot Five Live at Lone Pine,* appeared on Domber's newly created Arbors label. (The name is a phonetic combination of the first three letters of Rachel's maiden name, Arbuthnot, with the last three letters of Domber.) The album includes Fay's now famous "Teeny Weeny Blues," played on a two-inch toy whistle. The tiny "instrument" was offered as a promotional premium by Oscar-Mayer back in the 1960s. A playful Arbors ad in *West Coast Rag* termed the CD "The 'Wurst' in Jazz."

A second Rick Fay CD soon followed, and then a third. Mat Domber was now thoroughly entrenched in the record business. In its first decade, Arbors produced almost a hundred CDs featuring the nation's finest classic jazz artists. Fay continued to rank among the label's main attractions, recording a dozen CDs as leader and several others as a sideman. Laughing, he said, "I showed him how to make a shoe-string out of a fortune!"

Fay also became a prominent member of the Statesmen of Jazz, a dream band of senior jazzmen created by Domber and his associate Maurice Lawrence. This stellar group has appeared in festivals and youth seminars under the sponsorship of the American Federation of Jazz Societies.

Rick Fay's Sax-O-Poem, Poetry and Jazz became the first album to combine the works of a jazzman-poet-composer-performer. Each number is a brilliant merger of his insightful words with original and standard melodies. Cut number ten is a heartfelt tribute to his hero, Barney Bigard. It concludes with:

> Although you passed in near obscurity
> You left a song the world will long recall
> A melody that haunts a listener's ear
> "Mood Indigo"—the bluest blues of them all.

Fay retired from his Disney job in October 1997 when he became aware of his illness. "I have liver cancer aggravated by cirrhosis. It's pretty deadly! I got it from hepatitis C. I've never been a needle user, but the doctors suspect the virus was the result of an emergency blood transfusion after an auto accident years ago. I don't want this to impede my playing. I am booked at several festivals and jazz events for the next few months, so I'm taking one day at a time."

He was very optimistic about his treatments with an advanced chemotherapy technique at the Florida Mayo Hospital. Fay's closing words in our interview were:

"I've been very lucky, Floyd. I've been able to make a living playing music, doing what I love. That's the real secret of happiness—doing the things you love. I'm going to continue playing as long as possible!"

Jazz fans around the world are also lucky to have Rick's music so readily available on the record label he inspired. The kind words he wrote about his idol, Barney Bigard, now, appropriately, define our memories of Rick Fay:

> You left a song the world will long recall
> A melody that haunts a listener's ear

Rick Fay died March 22, 1999. The Central Florida Jazz Society has established the "Rick Fay Scholarship Fund." Tax deductible donations can be sent to: Central Florida Jazz Society, Box 40133, Orlando FL 32854-0133.

THE SEVEN-YEAR
CHALLENGE TO COMPLETE
THE LOUIS ARMSTRONG STATUE

A Fund Is Created in Old New Orleans

My last conversation with Louis Armstrong, like my first, took place on his birthday: in this case, July 4, 1971. Lucille and I phoned him at his home in New York to extend our usual birthday greeting. He was very cheerful; his health was improving, he said, and the doctor had allowed him to blow his horn again after a long hiatus. Louis was looking forward to getting back on stage; he already had several jobs booked in the New York area.

Two days after that happy conversation, Louis was dead, and I was en route to New York to attend his funeral. I was sad for myself, for his wife, for his many friends, and for music lovers around the world. My only consoling thought was that, before he died, Louis was able to see how much his fans and many friends loved him. On his seventieth birthday, a year and two days before his death, we had staged a tribute concert in Los Angeles titled "Hello Louis!" This special event had a dual purpose: to honor and thank a man who had given us so much joy through his music; and to launch a campaign to raise money for a permanent statue of the great man.

This chapter has been adapted from various articles written during the Armstrong statue fund-raising campaign. One, entitled "A Fund Is Created in Old New Orleans," originally appeared in the December 1969 issue of *Second Line* and was widely reprinted; another, titled "For the Love of Louis," was written by Ned Brundage in 1972.

The tall bronze statue that now stands proudly in New Orleans' Louis Armstrong Park is a loving gift from jazz fans throughout the world. The arduous fund-raising effort constitutes an extraordinary saga that has never before been disclosed.

The idea for the statue originated in the summer of 1969, during the New Orleans Jazz and Heritage Festival. We were relaxing with musicians and members of the press at Pete Fountain's plush club, Storyville, being feted by local jazz enthusiast and businessman Joe Gemelli. A very distinguished group had been invited to this informal luncheon. I recognized such stalwarts as Clark Terry, Danny Barker, James Stuber, Blue Lu Barker, Don Albert, Benny Carter, Sharkey Bonano, Roland Kirk, Stanley Dance, Dan Morganstern, Helen and Don Perry, and Ira Gitler. After lunch, we boarded an air-conditioned bus for a tour of the Crescent City. Our guides, Danny Barker and Scoop Kennedy, pointed out many landmarks that evoked memories of the colorful era that spawned the music we call jazz.

With his remarkable memory and thorough knowledge of New Orleans history and lore, Barker took us back half a century, to his early teens. He showed us Back O'Town and vividly recalled The Battlefield, where toughs like drummer Black Benny reigned. From his articulate description, we visualized the brawling saloons with blood-splattered walls, the pimps and prostitutes.

When we passed Jane Alley, the site of Louis Armstrong's birth, Danny Barker lamented that important historic buildings were being razed to make room for modern municipal structures. He said, "Politicians have never been interested in jazz history." As we drove along Robert E. Lee Boulevard, Barker, looking up at a large statue of Lee, commented, "This is the only city that builds monuments to generals who lost a war! Someday, perhaps, there will be a collection to create a tribute here to a real hero, Louis Armstrong."

From a few rows forward, Clark Terry leaped to his feet and shouted, "Let's start that collection now—here's the first dollar." I handed him the second. As the bus continued to roll through the fashionable residential district of the city, Terry gathered money from everyone on the bus. Each vowed to return to his community and spread the word about our idea to create an enduring tribute to jazzdom's greatest artist. A few weak protestations about the awkwardness of building a monument to a living person were quickly brushed aside. This tribute was too important to be made posthumously.

Benny Carter, leading much of the discussion, suggested that funds be solicited from Louis' fans around the world. It seemed like such a simple undertaking to us as we rode around New Orleans on that air-conditioned bus. Had we known what we were getting into, we might never have attempted the project.

When the Jazz Festival ended and we were all back in our respective homes, I rapidly laid the groundwork for a very ambitious campaign. By my estimate, it would take $30,000 to commission a statue and pay other expenses associated with the venture. We began looking for historians, art experts, architects, landscape designers, and others to help us in our cause.

Benny Carter agreed to serve as nominal head of the fundraising committee. His busy schedule, which included worldwide tours, recording dates, and film scoring, prohibited day-to-day administrative responsibilities, but the use of his name as titular chairman added credence to the venture and opened many media doors. We asked jazz fans and clubs in every part of the world to donate funds. At the end of 1969, I called for donations in an article published in *Second Line* and reprinted in music publications across the globe. Each donor was promised an acknowledgment from Carter and a souvenir Armstrong button. We hoped to complete the fundraising process on Armstrong's next birthday, his seventieth, with a huge concert in the Hollywood Bowl.

Slowly we began to receive many expressions of love for Louis Armstrong, usually accompanied by donations that, however modest, helped our morale immensely. A fifteen-year-old boy in Kartuska, Poland, sent twenty *zlotychs* and wrote, "I love Louis Armstrong's music and would like the monument to have a piece of Poland." One hundred *deutchmarks* accompanied a letter from South Africa that read, "Good old Satchmo will always be my favorite jazzman!" An anonymous contribution included this note: "Saints have always been recognized with statues. Churches over the world have them. Parks have them. Bedrooms have them. Now, his birthplace in New Orleans needs another statue honoring a Saint. Here is my offering." A $5 contribution from Flushing, New York, came with this remarkable message: "I am deaf, but I can feel his music in my veins, his tremendous personality, and his sincere glowing smile."

The heartfelt messages continued.:

> I can't express how much Louis has given to me. Bless those of you organizing the Fund and letting us show at least a token of the gratitude we feel.

Forty-five years ago my late husband and I celebrated our wedding at Frank Sebastian's Cotton Club in Culver City. Louis came to our table and sang "Always" to us—unforgettable.

From his heart—through his horn—a message was blown. God bless this man.

Few things have ever touched me so deeply as the moment when I first heard Louis Armstrong.

Satchmo is a true American hero in every sense of the word. I am proud to contribute to his remembrance.

Please accept this humble donation. I am a schoolboy in Australia and hope the statue is as majestic as the gentleman himself.

Every century produces a few very great men whose presence on this earth makes it a better place to live. Louis Armstrong is one of those few.

Our naive optimism to complete the project promptly ran into multiple snags. A decade would pass before our dreams finally became a reality.

The following article, "For the Love of Louis," is the work of Ned Brundage, a hard-working member of the jazz society consortium that launched the Statue Fund with our production "Hello Louis!" Ned wrote this articulate analysis in 1972. He accurately expresses the joys and anguish connected with the concert production, and our efforts to complete the Statue Fund.

"FOR THE LOVE OF LOUIS," BY NED BRUNDAGE

This is a love story. A story about a group of dedicated people who envisioned a statue of Satchmo in New Orleans. The Louis Armstrong Statue Fund is approaching adulthood. How did it grow so big? What's in the future?

Most of you are familiar with the beginning—it was June 1969. A bus was passing the site of Louis Armstrong's birthplace in New Orleans, and Danny Barker said, "Someday, perhaps, a collection will be made to erect a tribute to Louis Armstrong here in New Orleans."

Floyd Levin, then president of the Southern California Hot Jazz Society, promptly wrote an article announcing the establishment of the Statue Fund. He returned to Southern California to administer the twelve long months of labor which culminated in the really meaningful birth of the Fund—the "Hello Louis!" birthday concert in Los Angeles.

Floyd told Bill Grosvenor and Ray Fehring, members of the New Orleans Jazz Club of Southern California, he'd found what they'd been looking for—a theme for a special jazz event. At that moment, the good ship

"Hello Louis!" was launched. This ship was to spring a thousand financial leaks, run into dozens of legal storms, face towering waves of apathy, and battle an apparent jinx. It came perilously close to sinking.

First, realizing the NOJCSC couldn't handle such an undertaking alone, all local jazz clubs were invited to participate. Only four other clubs showed interest. Procrastination prevailed until December 12, 1969, when the Association of Southern California Jazz Clubs came into being. (The five clubs: Southern California Hot Jazz Society, New Orleans Jazz Club of Southern California, Society for the Preservation of Dixieland Jazz, Jazz Incorporated, and Valley Dixieland Jazz Club.)

Their first consideration was—Where? They agreed the Hollywood Bowl would be just dandy. It was checked out—they needed a $500.00 deposit, $1,500.00 to handle tickets, $375.00 to print tickets, $175.00 for insurance, plus security patrols, etc., etc., etc. Almost $3,000! Back to the meeting house.

They decided to find out how much money the newly formed Association could raise. There was a possibility of $500.00 (if each jazz club could come up with $100.00). Using such tactics as raffles, threats, and dipping into personal bank accounts, they raised the $500.00, and each club promised to pay an additional $200.00 by April 15.

Meanwhile, Floyd Levin talked up a storm of blues and convinced the management of the Shrine Auditorium to hold the night of July 3 open without any deposit until the association could make a token payment of $375.00.

Now the amateur entrepreneurs had (besides their love of Louis) the *when*, the *where*, and a minute quantity of the *wherewithal*. It was time to try for the *who*—especially Louis Armstrong—and the other *whos*, musicians to perform for minimum scale and celebrities who loved Satch and were willing to donate their talent.

Floyd tried to line up some "names" for Master of Ceremonies. Bing Crosby, Sammy Davis, Jr., Steve Allen, and others didn't reply. Della Reese's manager said she would appear for her usual $12,000 fee. Underlings said "no" for Frank Sinatra, Danny Kaye, and Danny Thomas—they would not be available. Ethel Waters' manager suggested someone should create a statue for her!

Then Floyd Levin found his groove. Hoagy Carmichael, the Association's first choice as Master of Ceremonies, agreed to participate when promised a co-master of ceremonies would announce the historical portion of the program. Benson Curtis, *the* jazz disc jockey of Southern California radio, accepted immediately and said he would be glad to do the bits Hoagy felt uncomfortable about.

Al Hirt told Floyd he would be on stage for sure. Sarah Vaughan volunteered her voluptuous voice and sensuous self. Best of all, Louis Armstrong's personal handwritten letter to Floyd promised he would be present as guest of honor!

The Association of Southern California Jazz Clubs won the first pot in a poker game where every other card was to be wild. Some believe winning the first hand in poker is the worst kind of luck. Much of what happened to "Hello Louis!" seemed to confirm that superstition.

When he got the "names," Publicity Director George Anderson took his first steps along the publicity trail. George, who admitted his vast ignorance of such matters, wisely recruited jazz club members who might "just possibly" know a little about the complicated world of commercialism.

Jim Herron, a newspaper editor, soon found himself writing news releases before there was any news to release. Then Anderson called me.

"Ned," he said, "will you write some 10, 20, 30, 45 and 60-second radio spots? When I get a Community Service Number from the Southern California Broadcaster's Association, I'll need them to send to all the radio stations. With the number they'll advertise 'Hello Louis!' free as a public service."

I had written advertising, news releases, magazine articles, a book, short stories, poetry, and graffiti on restroom walls, but I never wrote radio announcements. I soon learned it was an art—the art of saying volumes while ticking seconds held you to sentences.

Meanwhile, Gene Smith and his lovely little wife, Jean, were banging their heads against a wall of total noncooperation surrounding the TV shows. Gene was also producing 8 x 10 glossy photos for the cost of supplies, and Jean's boss, a printer, furnished copies of our propaganda for the cost of the paper.

Bud Bjoralt covered retirement communities and mobile home parks with a mass of enticing literature emphasizing the joys of taking a busload to the concert.

Floyd reserved a deluxe suite for Louis and Lucille Armstrong at Century Plaza Hotel and arranged housing for the out-of-town participants. He talked Air France into providing round trip transportation for Claude Luter and Maxim Saury from Paris in exchange for an ad in the program book.

Chet Jaeger, a schoolteacher with access to the school's press, produced a few thousand crude hand-done brochures placed in laundromats, supermarkets, and elsewhere, with or without permission of the management. It was rumored that some were illegally stuck under windshield wipers but, since nobody got caught, we deny the allegation. Al Robertson was shaking up the Ventura area. My brother Frank was making publicity waves around Monterey Bay.

It was crazy! The Publicity Committee was working like mad to sell tickets not yet printed, while Walt Greenawald's Ticket Sale Committee took orders and collected money to pay for the nonexistent tickets. (The printer insisted on C.O.D.)

While George Anderson tried to untangle the web of requirements regarding that precious Radio Community Service number, two radio jazz jockeys were love-casting without the number and making the cause sound like a new religion. Chuck Cecil boosted "Hello Louis!" during his "Swinging Years" show on KFI-AM and Benson Curtis was blowing all out on his KRHM-FM "Strictly From Dixie."

Benson, a small, serious man, was born with a long and kindly face that shows a smile when the jazz is good; but, when things get bad, Benson's face becomes longer than the space between paydays. It soon became very long indeed; just a month before the scheduled concert, things began falling apart.

First, the Southern California Broadcaster's Association refused our request for their Community Service Number authorizing radio stations to provide free air time. They did not consider a memorial to Louis Armstrong and scholarships from the fund to be "philanthropic or cultural and of interest or benefit to the citizens of Los Angeles as a whole" (their wording).

Second, Al Hirt's manager said Al would not be available. (He had told Floyd Levin at least four times he would make the scene, saying "Man, I'll be there! ... I gotta do this for POPS! I owe that man a lot," and other affirmative exclamations.)

Treasurer Ray Fehring announced that the bank account was near zero and suspected checks might be bouncing if there were not "Louis Lovers" among the bank personnel.

The Musician's Union ruled that Barry "Kid" Martyn's band from England "cannot appear on the stage with our union members." They also refused to sanction a tape of the concert by KBCA-FM, even if the tape would only be used as a public service to promote the Statue Fund.

Finally, Floyd learned that a television producer who had offered $250,000 for the filming rights couldn't get any prime network time, while a producer who had arranged network time couldn't find a sponsor.

Shining through the gloom, barely discernable, were TV guest spots Jean Smith had finally arranged. Satch was on the David Frost show with

Orson Welles and they talked about the concert. Since then, there had been little TV coverage.

Now, suddenly, there were TV spots three days in a row! On June 24, Billy Daniels, who appeared on "Tempo," spent a few minutes discussing "Hello Louis!," but he talked mostly about himself. But it was exposure. Next day Hoagy Carmichael used an entire fifteen-minute segment of the "Boutique" show talking about Louis. One week before the concert, actor Richard Deacon, a dedicated jazz buff, went on "Tempo" with more good plugs.

Still, we were not selling very many tickets. And the jinx refused to go away. Just a week before the concert, Sarah Vaughan announced she couldn't appear because she had accepted an engagement in the east the following day. The entire cue and lighting schedules had to be rewritten to move her to the opening spot, so she could catch a plane at 11:00 P.M., the night of the concert.

Next, an unhappy ticket agency started a rumor that Satchmo would not appear. Meanwhile, Roy Brewer, in charge of printed programs, could only sell enough advertising to pay for the cost of printing. There went a big chunk of sorely needed and expected income.

When these reverses slammed producer Floyd Levin in the face, he didn't get shook; he started to do some shaking. He shook up the entire Southern California entertainment industry and tried to turn its facilities loose on the "Hello Louis!" problem.

Frantic telephone calls to Floyd's many friends sold several hundred tickets. One record distributor bought a hundred—but neglected to pay for them until we threatened legal action! Benson Curtis contacted every local radio personality with a plea for help, and they did.

The Publicity Committee went back to the windshield wiper caper. They forced bumper stickers on strangers, put out a news release every other day, and told everybody the tickets were going fast! In a letter to Jim Herron, George Anderson pleaded, "Let's all kill ourselves for Louis!"

As a last gasp, the Association hired a professional publicity man who did PR work for Armstrong. He did almost nothing for us, but was at least there to take part of the blame.

It became so critical, the committee seriously considered giving away the remaining tickets so Satchmo would not have a sparse audience! Five jazz clubs were about to go under. All that remained was love ... so we planned to give out tons and tons of it when Louis' plane arrived June 30th. Would a public display of affection sweeten some of the sour notes?

Maybe the mayor would help. Floyd received a note: "Mayor Yorty, who is now in Japan, will be pleased to go to the airport to greet Louis; he will proclaim July 4 Louis Armstrong Day, but can't be at the concert, as he'll be in South America."

Alton Purnell, a New Orleans piano man who is almost as well known as Satch in many parts of the world, headed the Hospitality Committee. Alton asked everyone to be at the airport at 7:30 P.M. I spotted Benson Curtis there, walking slowly toward the entrance. His face was even longer than usual. Ticket sales must still be bad, I thought.

I wish I could mention all those wonderful people, because everyone who worked so hard to create this apparently unsuccessful event was there in front of the United Air Lines building to greet Louis.

The music of the Southern California Hot Jazz Society Marching Band reached out to all parts of the huge airport complex, saying "Follow me, children." And strangers followed—and when they found the sound, they saw a beautiful sight. Sylvester Rice banged a roll-off on the snare drum and the band marched into the building with a hand-clapping congregation behind it. The strangers, like children following the Pied Piper, were hypnotized by the tremendous vibrations of love and joined the throng.

Leading the parade was Alton Purnell wearing a bright, multi-colored "parade basket" and waving a matching fan. This traditional New Orleans costume, handmade of thread, fur, and feathers, is said to come from the Cajun Indians. After the parade, the basket is customarily destroyed in honor of the success its spirit brought to the festivities. If Benson Curtis' face was any indication, Alton would have no reason to destroy that parade basket.

Behind Alton, Gordon Mitchell led the fourteen-piece band followed by a twelve-foot banner announcing "Hello Louis!" Behind them—were people, people, people!

We all waited at ramp No. 82, impatient, restless and noisy. Then we saw the man—Louis himself—grinning that famous grin, and shaking hands with all who reached toward him. Lucille Armstrong smiled and accepted an armful of roses. Louis' doctor worried in the background. The band played, people cheered, people cried ... it was bedlam! Ticket-selling bedlam! And TV cameras were recording everything!

Throngs followed Louis into a nearby press room where a cake was waiting and they sang "Hello Louis!" to the tune of "Hello Dolly." Everyone was soon perspiring from the heat from the TV lights and Satch was using those famous white handkerchiefs by the dozen. He was obviously enjoying himself—signing autographs and laughing and joking with reporters.

After the formalities, the crowd, the band, the reporters, the cameramen, and the banner bearers followed Louis to his limousine (rented in exchange for a large ad in the concert program book). Satchmo was still grinning, his wife was still smiling, and his doctor was still worrying.

As the car pulled away, I noted Benson Curtis. Despite all the joy and music and excitement, his face was still long and sad. Ticket sales must really be horrible!

Horrible wasn't the word. When Louis Armstrong arrived three days before the concert, we had sold only 1,700 of the 6,000 seats in Shrine Auditorium.

Where was Mayor Yorty? Nobody knew. One of Sam's "underlings" had given Louis the symbolic key to the city outside the building where the gesture wasn't seen or recorded. No, His Honor didn't help sell any tickets, but he tried to help in another way.

The night of the concert, Louis was scheduled to complete a TV film at NBC Studios in Burbank at 8:00 P.M. Producer Floyd Levin wondered how he could get Satch across town to the Shrine Auditorium in half an hour? The answer came. He requested the use of the mayor's helicopter.

But the TV bit was rescheduled and the copter was not needed. Fifteen minutes before the concert started, a phone call came in back stage. "Where the hell's Louis?" the pilot wanted to know. (I wonder who forgot to tell the mayor his air service would not be necessary?)

Television coverage of Satchmo's arrival was very disappointing. Three major networks shot thousands of feet of film at the airport, but each showed only about a few minutes of the excitement on the 11:00 P.M. newscasts. Why? Because the show's jinx caused Pat Nixon to choose that day to return from an earthquake disaster in South America. The networks gave priority to her coverage.

The following evening Alton Purnell and his Hospitality Committee returned to the airport. It was carefully planned—musicians from all over the world would arrive at about the same time.

The French jazzmen Maxim Saury and Claude Luter came in ninety minutes late. Clark Terry arrived thirty minutes early. Tyree Glenn was on time but couldn't be found. Doc Evans did not show up until the next day's rehearsal. Barry Martyn's British Band decided to travel by car from someplace. (London?)

So Alton's welcoming committee—Dick Rice, Ellie O'Brien, Barney Bigard, Dorothe Bigard, Al Rieman, and myself—kept the bartender very busy.

Alton somehow got all the visiting musicians in the right place despite the "wrong times." But when I phoned him the next day, he sounded like Benson Curtis looked. He couldn't remember what hotel he'd put them in or where it was. He had to read directions to me from his notes.

On July 3, the day of the concert, the jinx persisted. A ticket agency had announced they would return only 300 tickets. At 6:30, two hours before kickoff, they turned in 1,100!

That night, I delayed going into the auditorium until the last possible moment because I didn't want to look at all those empty spaces. I walked directly to my seat, sat down, and reluctantly turned around. Except for a few seats in the balcony ... the house was full! About the third time I twisted my neck, Lucille Levin said, "Don't worry, Ned, they won't go away."

The Shrine Auditorium box office sold over 1,800 tickets that day! Ticket agencies were overwhelmed with last minute sales!

But the jinx was still hanging around. Sarah Vaughan, who had been rescheduled to open, forgot her gown. While everybody helped her wait for it to arrive, Barry Martyn's band entertained us. They played in the pit, thus "complying" with the Musicians' Union edict prohibiting their appearance on the stage.

Backstage, Director Bill Grosvenor was busily jousting with the jinx as a new crisis arose every moment. Bill handled it like an old pro, demonstrating courage and conviction. The behind-the-scenes team-like performance caused Floyd Levin to remark, "Now I know how it must feel to a trumpet player when the trombone slides in at the exact place and the clarinet weaves between them."

Bill and Floyd tried to convince Sarah she should do her act in street attire. She refused. Barry Martyn's band continued playing in the pit. The band sounded great and the audience was not aware of the starting delay.

It was decided to start the show without Sarah Vaughan's scheduled opening. Leonard Feather introduced Floyd's historical format, a musical chronology with six all-star groups. Forty-six famed musicians would re-create the important eras of Louis' career—the Riverboat Band, King Oliver's Creole Jazz Band, the Hot Five, the All Stars and a stellar group, the Ambassador Satch Band. To start the proceedings, Leonard brought out Hoagy Carmichael who immediately introduced Louis Armstrong.

It was unbelievable—the sound of over 6,000 people expressing love! It was "Love for Louis," a small man who became a giant, one of the biggest and most revered persons in the world. He was hailed by presi-

Advertisement for "Hello Louis!" The concert raised several thousand dollars for the Louis Armstrong Statue Fund.

From left: Trummy Young, Louis Armstrong, and Bob McCracken. From the Collection of Duncan Schiedt.

dents of the United States as "our best foreign ambassador." Ambassador Satch! King Louis the First—and the only King of Jazz!

Later, when Sarah Vaughan and her silvery-shimmering slack suit came on to interrupt the continuity, she couldn't believe the response. The audience had so much love left over that the parking lot attendant could have tied his shoelaces on stage and received a standing ovation.

Benson Curtis, who probably has more jazz history in his head than anyone in the world, honored Producer Levin by memorizing his script verbatim. Benson's beautiful!

The cake was eleven feet tall and weighed 800 pounds but, as far as those present were concerned, Louis stood taller and his contributions to jazz weighed tons more than that "world's largest birthday cake."

There were no candles. None were needed. Satchmo's smile spread more light than a thousand candles, and the hot notes of forty-six great jazz musicians expressing their "love" created more heat than a million candles. But even the cake was jinxed. The trumpet on it had four valves.

Just before midnight, Louis climbed to the top of seven steps and Hoagy handed him a knife. Satchmo stood on his toes, reached up, cut a slice of cake and quipped, "This is for Tyree [Glenn]. He always likes to get the first piece."

Louis Armstrong and his 70th birthday cake during the "Hello Louis!"
concert.

A few minutes later it was July 4. The crowd sang "Happy Birthday" as
Louis and our nation celebrated their birthdays together. Then Benson
Curtis peeked out from the wings. He was wearing a big smile … a smile
for the Love of Louis.

Within a few days reviews acclaiming the event appeared in U.S. and
European papers. Leonard Feather, in the *Los Angeles Times,* reported
Louis Armstrong's reaction: "'I've had a lot of wonderful honors in my life,
but tonight has been the biggest thrill of all.' And then, in a rare display of
off-stage emotion, he kissed producer Floyd Levin on the cheek."

In his column in London's *Melody Maker,* Feather praised the efforts of
24-year-old Barry Martyn and his English band that saved the day, filling
the period when Sarah Vaughan delayed the show's opening.

The author and Louis Armstrong after the "Hello Louis!" concert. Photo by Ed Lawless. Courtesy of Dottie Lawless.

Harvey Siders in *Down Beat Magazine* devoted two full pages extolling the concert. *Daily Variety*'s rave concert review said, "The production 'Hello Louis!' contributed to showbiz history." Dick Winslow, in Musicians Union Local 47's *Overture,* wrote, "No celebration shall ever top the memorable 'Hello Louis!' presented at the Shrine Auditorium by the Association of Southern California Jazz Clubs." Not bad for a bunch of amateur entrepreneurs!

Bing Crosby to the Rescue

Despite the success of "Hello Louis!" we still had a long way to go before realizing our dream. The concert had brought in much-needed funds, but we were still far short of our goal. We hadn't even begun to look for an artist or select a site, and a whole range of other tasks remained.

David Stuart, an internationally known art authority and founder of the Jazz Man Record Company, was chosen to head the Artist Selection Committee. The other members were Gerald Nordland, director of the San Francisco Museum of Art; Walter Hopps, director of the Corcoran Gallery in Washington, D.C.; James B. Byrnes, director of the Isaac Delgado Museum of Art in New Orleans; and Ward Kimball, producer/cartoonist for Disney Productions (and leader of the Firehouse Five Plus Two). New Orleans art dealer Lorenz Borenstein and I were ex officio members. After many months of careful research, the committee recommended Elizabeth Catlett, a noted black sculptor then teaching in Mexico City. She knew Louis Armstrong, and her illustrious background included art degrees from Howard University and Iowa State University (where she studied under Grant Wood), plus two grants from the Julius Rosenwalk Foundation. She had taught at several colleges and universities, including Dillard University in New Orleans. At that time Catlett headed the sculpture department at the University of Mexico's National School of Fine Arts.

These efforts were interrupted by the untimely death of Louis Armstrong in July 1971. We were heartbroken that he would never see the statue; but his passing made us that much more determined to complete our project.

By June 1973 the fundraising total had reached $13,612.98. This amount represented almost a thousand individual contributions from twenty-six nations. Several groups had made large donations, including the Potomac River Jazz Club, the Detroit Jazz Society, the Society for the Preservation of Dixieland Jazz, the New Orleans Jazz Club, the Southern California Hot Jazz Society, the Dick Gibson Jazz Party, the Australian Jazz Convention, the New Jersey Jazz Society, the Australian Broadcasting Commission, Atlantic Records, the American Broadcasting Corporation, the Appleton Wisconsin High School Band, the Dublin (Ireland) Jazz Society, and the British Institute of Jazz Studies. Without these large contributions, the remaining gifts averaged about $3.50 each.

We took great pride in our progress, yet we were still less than halfway to our goal. Despite worldwide publicity, no major contributor had stepped forward to underwrite the remainder of the costly project. We were offered no support from any of the film studios or

This Los Angeles Times *cartoon three days after Louis Armstrong's death expressed the world's sentiments. Copyright 1971 by Paul Conrad. Distributed by the Los Angeles Times Syndicate. Reprinted by permission.*

major recording firms that reaped millions from Satchmo's efforts. Nor did we hear from the musical instrument manufacturers, airlines, nightclubs, hotels, booking firms, or public relations agencies that were swept along in the wake of Armstrong's meteoric career.

Myra Menville, editor of the New Orleans Jazz Club's *Second Line*, tried hard to overcome the meager support from Crescent City fans. She wrote entreating letters to several local publications in May and June 1976 urging them to promote the project. There is no indication that any of the letters were fruitful. The *New Orleans Times-Picayune* responded with a cryptic preprinted note: "The *Times-Picayune* is unable to make use of the material, which is herewith returned." Myra sent me a copy of her memo to *Louisiana Weekly* with her notation: "No reply or story."

We applied to thirty major philanthropic funds and charitable foundations for grants. All thirty turned down our request. Various reasons were given: "Committed to other more worthy causes" ... "Our budget precludes participation" ... "Other projects have higher priority" ... "Not within the scope of our program" ... "Funds are limited—appeals are not" ... "All funds have been committed for the current year." It was very, very discouraging. The lowest ebb was an unidentified envelope from Mason City, Iowa. It contained a strip of pink toilet tissue bearing the racist message: "White Power."

By the spring of 1976, we had exhausted every means of attracting a major contributor and were still $10,000 short of our estimated goal. Elizabeth Catlett indicated the work was almost completed. In a few weeks I would fly to Mexico City to approve the clay form and arrange for the casting. Her fee would then be due; the foundry would require advance payment; and we also faced the cost of transporting the casting to New Orleans for the scheduled July 4 presentation to the city.

My contemplation of this dismal predicament was interrupted by a phone call. The voice said, "I would like to speak to Floyd Levin. This is Bing Crosby."

There was no mistaking that familiar voice. I gulped, and replied, "This is Floyd."

"I am doing a few benefit concerts around the country," he said, "and I noticed in the *LA Times* an article about the problem you are having raising funds for the Louis Armstrong statue. I might do a concert in San Francisco, and if I do, I would be willing to allocate part of the funds toward your very worthy goal. But I have to be very careful with concerts done for charity. I find a lot of the proceeds are dissipated in administration charges and operational expenses. I'd appreciate if you would drop me a line letting me know the status of your project, the costs you have incurred against the total receipts, etc. I'd like this information as soon as possible."

That cheery conversation was like a bright beacon illuminating the end of a long, dark tunnel. In the six-year history of the Louis Armstrong Statue Fund, this was the first offer of support we had had from any major artist. I wrote Crosby a letter the following day explaining that our only expenses were for postage and printing costs and offered to send him a copy of our complete balance sheet. I quoted John Fanning, writing in the Monterey Jazz Society's *Hot Notes* shortly after Louis' death: "This statue is coming from the people—with no participation from politicians—no overhead for paying some 'fat cat' to administer the Fund. The people are going to look at it with a lump in their throats and a tear in their eyes, thinking of the notes he's no longer going to play again."

A few days later, during another phone conversation, Bing said, "Floyd, the San Francisco concert is set for June 2 at the Masonic Auditorium. We'll have Rosemary Clooney, Flip Wilson, the Joe Bushkin Quartet with Herb Ellis, Nelson Riddle's Orchestra, plus my wife Kathryn and our children." And then he uttered these wonderful words: "The net proceeds will go to the Louis Armstrong Statue Fund." My sigh of relief was of gale proportions.

The concert was tremendously successful. The *San Francisco Chronicle* reported that Bing, then seventy-two, sang an extended medley of thirty-three songs in nonstop succession. Myra Menville sent a copy of the San Francisco review to columnist Thomas Griffin, who wrote about the statue effort in his New Orleans column "Lagniappe." He quoted from the review and from a letter Bing Crosby sent to Archbishop Hannan in New Orleans, which read in part: "I was pleased that I was able in a very small way to contribute something toward the completion of the Armstrong statue. I think it was something that had to be done for probably one of the greatest music men to ever come out of the South—or anywhere for that matter." Griffin's column concluded with Myra Menville's sardonic comment: "The City of New Orleans will soon have the statue. But the city deserves no credit. Very little money was postmarked from here."

Encouraged by Crosby's contributions, but still apprehensive about the fund's precarious financial status, I flew with Lucille to Mexico City to give the final approval of the work. The tension mounted as we drove through bustling Mexico City en route to Elizabeth Catlett's studio, located on an obscure street in an industrial area. Awaiting us was the tall clay version of the Louis Armstrong figure, ready to enter the foundry. We were the first to view the figure, completed just a few days earlier. This was the culmination of seven years of intensive activity.

As we approached the studio, we could hear the happy sounds of children at play. Across the street, clusters of tiny shacks bristling with television antennas rimmed a dusty vacant lot. Rows of freshly laundered clothes drying in the warm air added a splash of brilliant color to an otherwise barren scene. An ice cream vendor pushed a white cart toward us. His battery-operated amplifier filled the area with his cry, "Gelato! Gelato!"

We parked in front of the studio. A tall cement wall topped with shards of broken glass separated the studio from the street. Elizabeth Catlett unlocked the heavy wooden door and welcomed us into a small courtyard. We saw piles of plaster, empty drums, paint cans, molds, and a rusting Datsun. Through a plaster-spattered window in the adjacent building, we had our first glimpse of the completed piece. The huge figure, shrouded in heavy plastic sheets, almost filled the room. A pair of large clay shoes was visible beneath the flowing polyethylene covers. Partially exposed at one side, a massive clay hand clutched a perfectly sculpted three-foot trumpet. At Catlett's softly spoken request, two young assistants carefully lifted the plastic covers. We held our breath as the figure was slowly undraped. There, standing more than ten feet high, was her majestic tribute. It was finally completed.

A table in front of the scaffold was strewn with scores of photographs of the trumpet star. To the left stood a small-scale model from which the larger figure had been adapted. As our gaze moved upward, we saw the finely contoured lines of Satchmo's trousers. His legs rose like strong tree trunks supporting a massive torso. A raised hand held the always-present handkerchief. The other hand, holding the horn, seemed poised to move the instrument toward his clay lips. The sculptor's helpers walked along scaffolds, spraying water on the tan clay to prevent cracks that would occur if the material dried. When a small crack was noticed on Louis' knee, Elizabeth went aloft with a ball of clay and tools to make the necessary repair.

I climbed a ladder to the highest riser and stood on the shaky wooden planks for a better view of Louis' head. It was almost double life-size, with a calm yet powerful expression—just a hint of the famous Armstrong grin. The lips were almost six inches wide, and the cheeks were plump and full. Although he was a musical giant, Louis was a small man. It seemed quite strange to see that familiar figure expanded to such proportions.

I suggested one minor correction for the statue: It needed the scar Louis had developed on his upper lip, caused by mouthpiece pressure over the years. Catlett joined me on the high scaffold and, with my guidance, carved an inverted arc in the clay. She then descended to the base and slowly scratched a modest "E.C." next to Louis' right heel. "I didn't want to sign it until I was sure it was correct," she said.

I asked her why she did not depict Armstrong blowing his horn. She explained, "If the instrument was in a playing position, it would form a horizontal line and continually attract birds; their droppings would

Sculptor Elizabeth Catlett with the Louis Armstrong statue.

permanently stain the bronze. Wherever possible, we avoid creating such roosting surfaces. Even though Louis was famous for his expansive smile," she continued, "that is not an appropriate statuary expression. A smile, forever frozen in bronze, loses its realism. I have given him a serene visage as he gazes toward the city.

"I have always admired Mr. Armstrong. I wanted to capture his dignity and dynamism. My aim was to create a good portrait and a good sculpture at the same time, so those who knew a lot about Louis and little about sculpture—or vice versa—will be able to appreciate both."

Before leaving the studio, we paused in the doorway for one final look at the powerful form. We could feel the strength and courage of the man from New Orleans who brought his warmth and talent to the world. Elizabeth blushed when I kissed her and thanked her for creating a work of art destined to become a landmark in the Crescent City.

The work was now finished, and the casting would begin the following day. We drove a few miles to the foundry to check the schedule to be certain the one-ton bronze monument would be completed in time for the New Orleans unveiling on July 4, 1976—the seventy-sixth anniversary of Louis Armstrong's birth, and exactly twenty-eight years after the great jazzman, sitting naked in his dressing room and eating birthday cake, first smiled and said hello to me.

During the return flight from Mexico, I relived those thrilling moments when I viewed the work and witnessed the artist carving her initials in the soft clay. When I arrived home, I learned that a check for $10,000 was waiting for me at Bing Crosby's Los Angeles office.

July 4, 1976

We unveiled the Louis Armstrong statue on the nation's bicentennial. Hundreds of fans, perspiring in the humid air around Jackson Square in New Orleans, sang "Happy Birthday" to their hero. Louis, who had died five years before, was there in spirit only—but each person witnessing the climax of the statue project could feel his spectral presence.

A steam engine towed a flat railroad car to the front of the old square. The car carried a huge wooden crate, the precious cargo from Mexico City that had arrived during the night. Elizabeth Catlett and I proudly climbed onto the end of the car. With the Mississippi River at our backs, we faced the old statue of Andrew Jackson astride his rearing horse. We watched as a crew, using heavy crowbars, carefully pried

*The Louis Armstrong statue
after its April 1980 dedication.*

Vol. XXXII　　　　　New Orleans Jazz Club　　　　　Summer, 1980

EDITOR'S COMMENT

Louis Armstrong Park, which is border-ed by North Rampart, North Villere, St. Peter and St. Philip streets was officially dedicated on the afternoon of April 15, 1980. About 12,000 people were in attendance, including Louis' widow, Mrs. Lucille Armstrong, who is an efferves-cent extension of Louis' own unique per-sonality.

It is a grand memorial to a man who was a prime mover in making "New Orleans" and "jazz" synonymous in every part of the world.

Mrs. Armstrong declared it was, "The most important day of my life, with the exception of one. And that was the day I married Louis "Satchmo" Armstrong." (October 12, 1942).

There were numerous speeches by politi-cians, some of whom even had a hand in planning and developing the park. When the 20-foot, two ton bronze statue of Louis (see cover) was dedicated, there was more oratory and more plaudits thrown around. Somehow, in all of this V.I.P. ceremony, the several thousand "little people" who contributed almost all of the $30,000 for the statue were overlooked. Also noticeably overlooked were the major fund-raising efforts of Floyd Levin and the New Orleans Jazz Club of South-ern California and our own New Orleans Jazz Club. Although Louis Armstrong knew kings, presidents, millionaires and other V.I.P.s, he was most comfortable with the people who truly loved his music — the real jazz fans of the world. It is un-fortunate that they were not acknowl-edged.

It should be stated that belated arrange-ments were made to present Floyd Levin with an "Honorary New Orleans Citi-zen" certificate (the keys to the city). This presentation was to be made at 5:30 at a location far from the mainstream of events. Floyd could not be present, and it is probably just as well, because the rep-resentative from City Hall never showed up, and the envelope was very informally given to me, as Floyd's stand-in, by one of the stage managers.

In behalf of the "little people" and the New Orleans Jazz Club, we would like to extend our sincere appreciation to Floyd Levin for all of his untiring efforts in see-ing the Armstrong statue through to reality.

Lest this sound like a criticism of Arm-strong Park in general, it is not. The park is laid out with walk-ways and unique bridges over the large lagoon area. It is a delightful place to take a walk or have a picnic during the day time. The dedica-tion ceremony was highlighted with per-formances by Count Basie, Lionel Hamp-ton, Dave Brubeck, the Olympia Brass Band and numerous other New Orleans musicians. It was a festive occasion com-plete with beer and food, including Louis' favorite red beans and rice.

The park will suffer for a while due to lack of sufficient funding for proper mainte-nance and security. A recent walk-through indicated a need to cut weeds which were knee high. And, sadly, the mouthpiece from the statue's trumpet has already been ripped off.

On a more optimistic note, The North Rampart Street Association, headed by Martin Shambra of Marti's Restaurant, is getting involved in revitalizing the en-tire area and making Armstrong Park a living, growing and musically active part of the city.

Donald Marquis
Editor

Donald Marquis' account of the dedication of Louis Armstrong Park, in The Second Line.

the lid from the crate. Inside, beneath several heavy pads, was the statue of Louis Armstrong. An adjacent crane slowly lowered a heavy chain toward the opened crate. The square fell silent as workers attached the chain's large hook to a bracket on the casting. The heavy piece was slowly lifted. As it gradually appeared, the bronze head glittered in the morning sun. Danny Barker's Jazz Hounds burst into a brisk chorus of "Happy Birthday to You," and cheers echoed against the levee behind us. I held Elizabeth Catlett's quivering hand.

The cheers became a roar when the huge figure eventually stood erect next to us on the rail car. Louis Armstrong, standing tall and proud, looked down upon the scene. Teams of network video cameramen captured the activity, which was being broadcast as part of the nation's bicentennial celebration. Viewers throughout the world witnessed the dramatic event.

When Mayor Moon Landrieu joined us on the flatcar, I made the presentation to the city on behalf of the one thousand fans who contributed to the Louis Armstrong Statue Fund, with special thanks to Bing Crosby, who came to our rescue at the last minute. As my voice reverberated throughout the square, I saw Myra Menville, who had tried very hard to garner local support for the project. She was standing quietly nearby—with a tear running down her cheek.

At last, after seven years, a dream became a reality. The Armstrong statue finally stood in New Orleans.

Despite our elation, we learned that the statue was to be stored in a warehouse awaiting completion of Louis Armstrong Park. It remained in storage for four long years. On April 15, 1980, the $12 million Louis Armstrong Park was officially opened.

Lucille underwent serious surgery the week before park's the dedication, so I was unable to attend the culmination of this eleven-year struggle. I deputized Don Marquis, the editor of *Second Line,* to represent me at the opening ceremonies, which he did in a candid editorial in the magazine's next issue.

For almost two decades, the huge bronze giant has gazed across the park toward ancient Congo Square, where Louis Armstrong's slave ancestors pounded the dust dancing to African rhythms centuries ago. This sculpted monument, glistening with almost blinding iridescence in the New Orleans sun, stands in lasting tribute to the great man.

The GHB Foundation in New Orleans has undertaken the costly production of a three-CD set from a recently discovered tape of the

"Hello Louis!" concert. It will feature all forty-six of the musicians involved in the historical event. All participants have granted their authorization. The CD will preserve the sounds of that evening in 1970, and the proceeds will go into a permanent fund to guarantee perpetual care of the statue and its surroundings.

EPILOGUE

Somewhere in a stack of treasured material there is a round tin containing fifty feet of 8mm movie film I shot while on a Mississippi riverboat cruise about thirty years ago.

On the third day of the trip, midway between Cincinnati and New Orleans, the steamer tied up on the shore shortly after sunset, as it did every evening—the old *Delta Queen* was not permitted to travel after dark. The next morning, while Eddie Bayard was playing his cornet up on the deck, and Vic Tooker was accompanying him on the ancient steam calliope, I walked down the gangplank to the soggy riverbank and scratched "Mississippi Mud" in the moist shoal. While I was photographing my "artwork" with my new Eastman movie camera, a passing barge created a gentle wake that rippled toward the riverbank. In the camera's viewfinder, I watched my muddy etching gradually dissolve in the mild wave.

Although my waterlogged message quickly disappeared, that memory is still strongly etched in my mind. One day, I hope, I will locate the old reel of film and enjoy watching the incident again—if my rusting projector still operates.

This book is filled with similar vivid memories, recalling episodes that greatly enriched my life. I welcome the opportunity to have shared these personal views of the music and the musicians.

F. L.

INDEX

jazz *(continued)*
first recordings of, 40; historical venues of, 177–78; Jelly Roll Morton's contribution to, 111, 120, 123. *See also* classic jazz; *specific forms of jazz*
Jazz Age, 4; dancing in, 67; first recorded hit of, 68–72; Kid Ory's contributions to, 11–12
"Jazz Baby," 66
Jazz Band of San Francisco, Turk Murphy's, 253
Jazz Forum, 46, 162
Jazz Giants, 157
Jazz Hounds, 201, 311
"Jazzin' Babies Blues," 250
Jazz Incorporated, 291
Jazz Journal, 1, 2, 15, 20, 22, 85, 108, 129, 169, 170, 171, 243
Jazz Journal International, 158
Jazz Man label, 251, 255–56
Jazz Man Record Company, 302
Jazz Man Record Shop (Hollywood), 12, 117, 246
Jazzmen, 5, 214
Jazz Monthly, 20
Jazz Music magazine, 259
Jazz Odyssey: The Autobiography of Joe Darensbourg (ed. Vacher), 45
Jazzology label, 258
Jazz on Parade (radio program), 2, 135, 183
Jazz Photographers Association, Milt Hinton Award, 141
The Jazz Record Book, 214
Jazz Records 1887–1942 (Rust), 22, 67
The Jazz Singer (film), 132
Jazz 625 (TV program), 211
The Jazz Story From the 1890s to the 1960s (Dexter), 245, 261
Jazz West—1945 to 1985 (Eckland), 246
Jean Goldkette Orchestra, 142, 144–45
Jefferson City Buzzards brass band, 49
Jeffersonians, 26, 36
Jeffries, Herb, 283
"Jelly Roll Blues," 37
Jenny, Jack, 83, 164
Jerde, Curt, 217
Jess Stacy, the Quiet Man of Jazz (Coller), 139
Jitterbug House (Los Angeles), 6
Joe Bushkin Quartet, 305
Joe, Cousin, 155
Johnny Fischer's Brass Band, 49
Johnson, Bill, 36, 41, 50
Johnson, Budd, 221
Johnson, Charley, 106
Johnson, Gus, Jr., 175

Johnson, James P., xx, 99–104, 100, 108, 127, 175, 192
Johnson, Keg, 190, 210, 221
Johnson, Keith, 95
Johnson, Lillie Mae, 101
Johnson, Oliver "Dink," 6, 17, 19, 30, 36–38, 99, 114, 119, 202, 215
Johnson, Pete, 107, 260
Johnson, William Geary "Bunk," 12, 14, 24, 48, 55, 58, 191, 206, 210, 214–15, 245, 250
"Johnson Rag," 274, 279
John the Greek's (New Orleans), 180
"The Joint Is Jumpin'," 165
Jolson, Al, 132
Jones, David, 277
Jones, Isham, 83, 235
Jones, Jonah, 190, 227
Jones, Quincy, 140
Jones, Rufus, 90
Jones, Snag, 32
Joplin, Scott, 24, 66, 104, 106–8, 109, 131, 167, 178, 251, 283
Jordan, Louis, 170
Joseph, Pleasant, 210
Joseph, Willie ("One-Leg" Willie), 133
Joy, Jimmy, 83
"Jubilee," 222
"Jubilee Stomp," 94, 96
"The Judge Meets the Section," 141
"Jumbo" (New York Hippodrome), 76
"Jumpin' Pumpkins," 265
"Jump for Joy" (Ellington production), 117
Jump Record Company, 7, 85–89, 148
Jurgens, Dick, 235
"Just a Closer Walk With Thee," 183, 186, 206
"Just Before Daybreak," 102
"Just Before the Beginning," 90

Kaffel, Ralph, 240
Kahn, Catherine C., 81
"Kansas City Stomps," xix, 37, 250
Kaye, Danny, 291
Kaye, Lionel, 236–37
Keepnews, Orrin, 5, 34
"Keep Off Katie's Head," 69
"Keep Off the Grass," 101
Kellard, Carl, 87
Kellaway, Roger, 175
Keller, Keith, 139
Keller, Paul, 158
Kellin, Orange, 202
Kellso, Jon-Erik, 175, 176
Kelly, Chris, 191, 192, 212
Kelly, Peck, 149

Designer:	Nicole Hayward
Compositor:	Impressions Book and Journal Services, Inc.
Text:	10/13 Sabon
Display:	OCRB and Scala Sans
Printer:	Edwards Brothers, Inc.
Binder:	Edwards Brothers, Inc.